BILINGUAL HEALTH COMMUNICATION

This book examines interpreter-mediated medical encounters and focuses primarily on the phenomenon of bilingual health care. It highlights the interactive and coordinated nature of interpreter-mediated interactions. Elaine Hsieh has put together over 15 hours of interpreter-mediated medical encounters, interview data with 26 interpreters from 17 different cultures/languages, 39 healthcare providers from 5 clinical specialties, and surveys of 293 providers from 5 clinical specialties. The depth and richness of the data allows for the presentation of a theoretical framework that is not restricted by language combination or clinical contexts. This will be the first book of its kind that includes not only interpreters' perspectives but also the needs and perspectives of providers from various clinical specialties.

Bilingual Health Communication presents an opportunity to lay out a new theoretical framework related to bilingual health care and connects the latest findings from multiple disciplines. This volume presents future research directions that promise development for both theory and practice in the field.

Elaine Hsieh is the 2015–2016 Core Fulbright US Scholar and an Associate Professor and Director of Graduate Studies in Communication at the University of Oklahoma. She has served as the Associate Editor of the *Journal of Immigrant and Minority Health* since 2010.

BILINGUAL HEALTH COMMUNICATION

Working with Interpreters in Cross-cultural Care

Elaine Hsieh

NEW YORK AND LONDON

First published 2016
by Routledge
711 Third Avenue, New York, NY 10017

and by Routledge
2 Park Square, Milton Park, Abingdon, Oxon, OX14 4RN

Routledge is an imprint of the Taylor & Francis Group, an informa business

© 2016 Taylor & Francis

Library of Congress Cataloging in Publication Data
Hsieh, Elaine, author.
  Provider-patient communication in bilingual health care : working with interpreters
in cross-cultural care / Elaine Hsieh.
     p. ; cm.
  Includes bibliographical references and index.
  I. Title. [DNLM: 1. Professional-Patient Relations. 2. Translating. 3. Cultural
Competency. 4. Multilingualism. W 21.5]
  RA418.5.T73
  362.1089–dc23   2015030079

ISBN: 978-1-138-99944-2 (hbk)
ISBN: 978-1-138-99945-9 (pbk)
ISBN: 978-1-315-65830-8 (ebk)

Typeset in Bembo
by Out of House Publishing

CONTENTS

INTRODUCTION

In this book, bilingual health care[1] is defined as provider–patient interactions in which providers and patients do not share the same language.[2] Bilingual health care is a highly complex phenomenon involving not just interpreters' behaviors. By definition, bilingual health care involves healthcare services provided in intercultural contexts,[3] in which providers and patients need to communicate with each other through differences in languages, cultures, illness ideologies, socioeconomic statuses, and educational backgrounds, to name a few. Despite the interdisciplinary nature of bilingual health care, most work on interpreter-mediated health care is limited to linguistics or interpreting studies, focusing on interpreters' discursive strategies.[4] By not incorporating perspectives from medical sociology, health communication, interpersonal communication, and medicine, researchers have overlooked interpreters' functions in and impacts on interpersonal relationships, health literacy, provider–patient communication, and healthcare delivery.

Although this book centers on interpreter-mediated medical encounters, my primary focus is not on interpreters' linguistic performance. Instead, my goal is to examine the phenomenon of bilingual health care, highlighting the interactive and coordinated nature of interpreter-mediated medical encounters. This is an area of study to which I have dedicated my career for over 15 years, with more than 40 publications in top journals, including *Social Science & Medicine*, *Journal of General Internal Medicine*, *Qualitative Health Research*, *Patient Education and Counseling*, *Journal of Applied Communication*, and *Health Communication*.

Few professional interpreters become researchers of this field. After graduating with an MA in translation and interpretation from the Monterey Institute of International Studies and working as a professional medical interpreter at UCSF Stanford Health Care, I went on to pursue my Ph.D. in health communication at the University of Illinois at Urbana-Champaign. In 2006, I obtained a three-year NIH grant as the principal investigator to examine providers' needs in interpreter-mediated encounters. The American Medical Association's *Office Guide to Communicating with Limited English Proficient Patients* has adopted my work as the primary theoretical framework in conceptualizing different types of interpreters and their corresponding impacts (American Medical Association, 2007).

Over the years, I have collected a wide variety of data, including ethnographic data, participant observation, in-depth interviews, focus groups, and surveys, to examine interpreter-mediated medical encounters. By adopting a mixed-method approach and synthesizing my previous work, I propose my Model of Bilingual Health Communication, an interdisciplinary communication model for bilingual health care. This book represents my effort to lay out a new theoretical framework, connect the latest findings from multiple disciplines, and examine future research directions to advance the theories and practices of the field.

This book is influenced by many important scholars, including Wadensjö (1998), Metzger (1999), Roy (2000), and Angelelli (2004), who have paved the way in conceptualizing healthcare interpreters' active roles and functions in the discursive process. At the same time, I aim to extend the understanding of healthcare interpreting to provider–patient interactions in intercultural contexts, highlighting the challenges all participants face as they manage the blurred boundaries of culture, language, and medicine. Some of the arguments are innovative and original, while others may be controversial. Nevertheless, by recognizing that Quality and Equality of Care is central to the process of bilingual health care, the Model of Bilingual Health Communication can provide insights into and solutions for many undertheorized and overlooked interactional dilemmas in interpreter-mediated medical encounters.

Chapter Organization

Chapter 1 presents a comprehensive review of the latest findings on interpreters in healthcare settings. In particular, I will examine how different disciplines have examined interpreters' roles and functions in healthcare settings. Building on earlier studies on interpreter visibility and roles in healthcare settings, I will examine how institutions develop policies and strategies to limit interpreters' influences over provider–patient relationships/interactions. Finally, I will challenge findings from recent reviews that suggest a preference for professional interpreters by highlighting a problematic understanding of interpreting errors and an oversimplified view of bilingual health care.

Chapter 2 provides a review of the important and emerging trends in conceptualizing bilingual health communication. I begin the chapter by challenging the interpreter-as-conduit model that is prevalent in interpreter training and codes of ethics. The trends that are highlighted here represent important shifts in conceptualizing bilingual health communication, providing insights into research questions and directions that have been largely ignored in the past literature. While these trends may be interconnected, each promises exciting potential for theorists and practitioners of bilingual health communication. The four trends identified are: (a) acknowledging the complexity of clinical demands in healthcare settings, (b) exploring contextual factors in bilingual health care, (c) examining medical interpreting as a coordinated accomplishment, and (d) recognizing interpreters as active participants in medical encounters.

Chapter 3 provides background information about the different types of data and analysis that will be reported in this book. The data will include one-year ethnographic data, participant observation, in-depth interviews, focus groups, and survey data that I have collected over the last 15 years. This book will adopt a mixed-method approach, involving both qualitative and quantitative data and analyses.

Chapter 4 presents a revision of my earlier typology of healthcare interpreters. In 2006, I proposed a typology of healthcare interpreters (Hsieh, 2006), which was later adapted by the American Medical Association (American Medical Association, 2007). However, recent studies have suggested the need to recognize differences between family interpreters and other types of nonprofessional interpreter. In addition, because healthcare providers have developed different strategies to incorporate their medical Spanish (or other limited second languages) in their healthcare delivery, it may be useful to reconsider how to best conceptualize bilingual medical professionals when providing care to language-discordant patients. This chapter critically and systematically reexamines the wide range of professionals and nonprofessionals who work to reduce language barriers for language-discordant patients through their interpreting/language skills.

By recognizing the diversity of interpreters in healthcare settings and shifting the traditional focus on interpreters' roles and performances to the multi-party coordination of communicative tasks, identities, and relationships, Chapter 5 presents the Model of Bilingual Health Communication. I conceptualize interpreter-mediated medical encounters as a goal-oriented communicative activity that involves active participation from the provider, the patient, the interpreter, and any other participants (e.g., the patient's family members). The normative approach to interpreter-mediated medical encounters forms the basis of my Model of Bilingual Health Communication (the BHC Model). In this chapter, I will explore (a) the individual-level constructs, (b) the interpersonal-level constructs, and (c) the propositions of the BHC Model. In this model, I will delineate how participants' diversity, agenda, and agency in the medical encounter help shape their role performances and expectations (for self and others) during the communicative process. In addition, I will situate interpreter-mediated provider–patient interaction in interpersonal contexts and examine how institutional structures and cultures, as well as medical ethics and values, orient and influence all participants' behaviors, social norms, and communicative strategies.

By examining the blurred boundaries of language, culture, and medicine in bilingual health care, Chapter 6 explores the distinctive challenges faced by interpreters as they navigate the barriers in cross-cultural healthcare delivery and the tensions in provider–patient–interpreter relationships. In particular, I will identify the inherent tensions both within a participant's multiple goals and between participants' competing, if not conflicting, goals, and explore the various strategies interpreters use to manage these tensions. I will end the chapter by examining the challenges that arise when individuals in interpreter-mediated medical encounters do not share the normative framework in their speech conventions and explore the corresponding clinical and ethical implications.

Despite state legislations and a blind preference for professional interpreters, multiple studies have demonstrated that healthcare providers use professional interpreters less than 20 percent of the time. Chapter 7 examines this phenomenon by exploring the various factors that shape providers' choice of interpreters. Rather than simply noting such behaviors as inappropriate, I will situate providers' choices in clinical contexts, exploring how their clinical specialties and clinical demands may shape how they choose and collaborate with interpreters. I will demonstrate that providers (a) are unaware of their competing expectations of interpreters that often require interpreters to adopt non-neutral behaviors, (b) view interpreters as tools that are available to execute their agenda, and (c) have a complicated understanding about their clinical demands (e.g., clinical complexity, clinical urgency, and the role of language in the treatment process) that require interpreters to assume multiple roles depending on the context. I will examine specific contextual variables (e.g., time and trust) and demonstrate how recognizing providers' complicated understanding of these variables is essential to the development of practice guidelines for interpreter-mediated medical encounters. Finally, I will provide some guidelines and principles for providers to consider as they contemplate the necessity of and strategies for working with a particular type of interpreter (e.g., on-site, telephone, bilingual staff, ad hoc, and family interpreter).

Healthcare interpreting is a unique form of interpreting (see also Chapter 2.C) because it is ancillary to a larger communicative event, cross-cultural care, which often entails specific goals (e.g., achieving optimal care). Chapter 8 critically examines how the meaning of Quality and Equality of Care (QEC) is understood and enacted through individuals' management of communicative goals in interpreter-mediated encounters. In particular, I will examine how patient empowerment and patient autonomy are constructed and understood by interpreters and providers. I will then use examples of (a) interpreters as co-diagnosticians and (b) interpreters' emotion work to explore the tensions in individuals' normative attitudes. I will demonstrate how a normative approach can help explain and predict interpreters' behaviors and others' evaluations. By recognizing providers' and interpreters' tensions in managing and coordinating control in interpreter-mediated interactions, I will explore whether and how interpreters' strategies can improve or hinder patients' health literacy, autonomy, and quality of care in their illness events.

Chapter 9 serves as the concluding chapter as I examine how normative attitudes may create tensions and challenges to the theories and practices of cross-cultural care. By revisiting system-level constructs (e.g., cultural norms and QEC) and the temporal dimension of the BHC Model, I critically discuss how these issues can be applied in cross-cultural contexts. By focusing on the goal-oriented nature of interpreter-mediated interactions and adopting a normative approach to interpreter-mediated medical encounters, I will demonstrate how the BHC Model can advance theory development and practice implications for cross-cultural care when providers and patients do not share the same language.

In summary, the Model of Bilingual Health Communication (i.e., the BHC Model; Chapter 5) serves as an anchor for this book. The reviews and critiques of the literature (Chapters 1 and 2) lead up to my understanding and conceptualization of the Model. After providing the details of my data and research design (Chapter 3) and presenting a modified typology of interpreters (Chapter 4), I present the BHC Model, a normative model that asks: (a) how should individuals behave if they wish to achieve desired outcomes and why, and (b) when people behave in a particular way, how will they be evaluated? By adopting a heuristic, normative approach, the BHC Model views interpreter-mediated medical encounters as an interactive, goal-oriented communicative activity that is situated in the larger communicative event of provider–patient interactions. In addition, the Model presumes that QEC is a transcending value that guides all participants' interpretation of and practices in interpreter-mediated medical encounters. By examining the specific theoretical components relevant to bilingual health care (Chapters 6–8), I will demonstrate the versatility and cross-cultural applicability of the BHC Model. More importantly, because the BHC Model is applied, I present guidelines and solutions to common problems individuals face in interpreter-mediated medical encounters.

Acknowledgments

Early in my career, a friend asked me how I feel about being recognized for my scholarship. She was puzzled and almost disappointed when I said, "I feel very lucky." She felt that I had failed to take ownership of all my hard work and trivialized what I have accomplished. Of course, I was proud of what I have accomplished. Nevertheless, to say that I did not feel lucky would have been a lie.

The literature on cross-cultural communication has found that self-serving bias (e.g., attributing success to an individual's internal traits and effort) tends to be prevalent in Western cultures; in contrast, people from Asian cultures tend to exhibit modesty bias (e.g., attributing success to external factors; Mezulis,

Abramson, Hyde, & Hankin, 2004). Despite knowing my potential bias, I cannot imagine completing this book without my good fortune.

We often under-recognize the influences of sociocultural and sociopolitical environments in shaping individual scholarship; however, my research program can only flourish in a place where individual well-being is not defined by or reduced to biomedical status. For that, I am grateful that I live in a society that embraces individuals' right to communicate as a critical prerequisite to their quality and equality of care. In addition, I am blessed that my institutions and mentors, including John Caughlin, Michael Pfau, and Michael Kramer, always recognize that a constructive, supportive environment is a necessary condition to nurture productive scholarship. Even though they may not know much about bilingual health care, their commitment to high quality publications provided me the freedom and courage to chart my own course.

Without my parents' support, I would not have dreamed of pursuing an academic career in the United States. I am also thankful for the encouragement of my advisor, Dale E. Brashers, and the support of NIH funding, both of which provided me with the much-needed momentum at the beginning of my career as I contemplated a way to integrate interdisciplinary research interests on interpreter-mediated medical encounters. My research assistants, Haiying Kong, Hyejung Ju, and R. E. Davis have worked tirelessly and provided important feedback throughout all phases of my studies. Many of the arguments presented in this book first appeared as conference papers and journal articles, with my research assistants and my graduate advisees, including Soojung Hong, Dyah Pitaloka, Sachiko Terui, and Guoyu Emma Wang, as my co-authors. They have been tremendously valuable in helping me to generate the larger theoretical framework that I'm putting forth in this book.

In Fall 2013, I was surprised by two undergraduate students' requests to serve as editorial assistants when I started preparing for this book. Valerie Kastens (University of Oklahoma) and Sonya Dave (University of Illinois), both planning a career in medicine, provided meticulous editorial notes as they reviewed the manuscript with great patience. I cannot thank them enough for their dedication to this project.

My husband, Dr Eric M. Kramer, has always been my biggest cheerleader. During the two years that I worked on this book, he published four of his own. Yet he always showed me much more enthusiasm and excitement when talking about my book than his. Without any reservation, he supported me by providing critical feedback and challenging me to push my theoretical framework further. Our constant debate allowed me to find the delicate balance between theoretical perspectives and applied practice. Thank you for believing in me. I love you, always.

Notes

1   There has been some inconsistency in English about the spelling of healthcare versus health care. In this book, I use *health care* as a noun (e.g., "bilingual health care is

important") and *healthcare* as an adjective (e.g., "healthcare interpreting is a complex communicative activity").

2 Although it is possible that more than two languages may be involved when providers and patients face language barriers (e.g., an English-speaking provider needing to communicate with a Spanish-speaking parent about his/her deaf child's illness symptoms), I decided to use the term bilingual health care (as opposed to multilingual health care) to simplify the discussion.

3 Traditionally, in the field of medicine, the term cross-cultural care is used when providers and patients do not share the same cultures. However, in the field of communication, intercultural communication and cross-cultural communication differ in their research focuses. According to Gudykunst (2003, p. vii), "Intercultural communication generally involves face-to-face communication between people from different cultures, but the term is also used to frequently to include all aspects of the study of culture and communication. One area of the research within the broad rubric intercultural communication is cross-cultural communication (i.e., the comparison of face-to-face communication across cultures; for example, comparing speech convergence in initial interactions in Japan and the United States)." From this perspective, communication in interpreter-mediated medical encounters should be considered intercultural communication rather than cross-cultural communication. To maintain consistency throughout this book, I have decided to use the term *cross-cultural care* as it best reflects how interpreter-mediated medical encounters are understood in the field of medicine. However, in other situations, I use the term *intercultural* to refer to situations in which individuals from different cultures interact with one another and the term *cross-cultural* to refer to (a) situations in which individuals in different cultures may act in similar or different ways or (b) applications of variables across different populations or cultural groups.

4 In recent years, an increasing number of physician researchers have conducted research on bilingual health care (e.g., Bischoff, Hudelson, & Bovier, 2008; Diamond et al., 2014; Hadziabdic, Albin, Heikkilä, & Hjelm, 2010, 2014; Kosny, MacEachen, Lifshen, & Smith, 2014; Rosenberg, Leanza, & Seller, 2007). By incorporating perspectives from healthcare providers and patients and investigating health outcomes as variables (e.g., patient satisfaction), these scholars have demonstrated the tremendous value in looking beyond interpreters' discursive practices.

References

American Medical Association. (2007). Official guide to communicating with limited English proficient patients (2nd ed.). Retrieved March 30, 2008, from www.ama-assn.org/ama1/pub/upload/mm/433/lep_booklet.pdf.

Angelelli, C. V. (2004). *Medical interpreting and cross-cultural communication.* Cambridge, UK: Cambridge University Press.

Bischoff, A., Hudelson, P., & Bovier, P. A. (2008). Doctor–patient gender concordance and patient satisfaction in interpreter-mediated consultations: An exploratory study. *Journal of Travel Medicine*, 15, 1–5.

Diamond, L. C., Chung, S., Ferguson, W., Gonzalez, J., Jacobs, E. A., & Gany, F. (2014). Relationship between self-assessed and tested non–English-language proficiency among primary care providers. *Medical Care*, 52, 435–438.

Gudykunst, W. B. (2003). Foreword. In W. B. Gudykunst (Ed.), *Cross-cultural and intercultural communication* (pp. vii–ix). Thousand Oaks, CA: Sage.

Hadziabdic, E., Albin, B., Heikkilä, K., & Hjelm, K. (2010). Healthcare staffs perceptions of using interpreters: A qualitative study. *Primary Health Care Research and Development*, 11, 260–270.

Hadziabdic, E., Albin, B., Heikkilä, K., & Hjelm, K. (2014). Family members' experiences of the use of interpreters in healthcare. *Primary Health Care Research and Development*, 15, 156–169.

Hsieh, E. (2006). Understanding medical interpreters: Reconceptualizing bilingual health communication. *Health Communication*, 20, 177–186.

Kosny, A., MacEachen, E., Lifshen, M., & Smith, P. (2014). Another person in the room: Using interpreters during interviews with immigrant workers. *Qualitative Health Research*, 24(6), 837–845.

Metzger, M. (1999). *Sign language interpreting: Deconstructing the myth of neutrality.* Washington, DC: Gallaudet University Press.

Mezulis, A. H., Abramson, L. Y., Hyde, J. S., & Hankin, B. L. (2004). Is there a universal positivity bias in attributions? A meta-analytic review of individual, developmental, and cultural differences in the self-serving attributional bias. *Psychological Bulletin*, 130, 711–747.

Rosenberg, E., Leanza, Y., & Seller, R. (2007). Doctor-patient communication in primary care with an interpreter: Physician perceptions of professional and family interpreters. *Patient Education and Counseling*, 67, 286–292.

Roy, C. B. (2000). *Interpreting as a discourse process.* New York: Oxford University Press.

Wadensjö, C. (1998). *Interpreting as interaction.* London: Longman.

1

INTERPRETER-MEDIATED MEDICAL ENCOUNTERS AS A FIELD OF RESEARCH

Interpreter-mediated medical encounters represent an interdisciplinary area of research as it highlights the intersection of languages, cultures, and medicine, all of which entail distinct values and norms. Since 2000, there has been a significant increase in related research (Brisset, Leanza, & Laforest, 2013), with the United States being the country with the most publications in this area. In countries that are considered multi-ethnic societies (e.g., Australia and Canada) or that represent a destination of intensive immigration (e.g., Denmark, Germany, The Netherlands, Spain, Switzerland, the United States, and the United Kingdom), there have been strong collaborations between the government, the healthcare industry, and the research community to ensure quality care for patients who experience language barriers in healthcare settings. In this book, I use the term *language-discordant patients* rather than patients with limited English proficiency (LEP) or hearing impairment to include the broader category of patients who do not share the same language with their providers, including all signed and spoken languages.

The recent increase in research publications signals an important confluence and paradigm shift in the conceptualization of interpreter-mediated medical encounters. In particular, researchers from a wide variety of traditions and disciplines, including translation and interpreting studies, linguistics, communication, and medicine have provided unique perspectives to the conceptualization and investigation of this area. Rather than situating healthcare interpreting in a particular disciplinary tradition, my goal is to put the phenomenon of interpreter-mediated medical encounters front and center. In particular, in this chapter, I will:

- situate interpreter-mediated medical encounters in multiple disciplines
- explore the theoretical contributions of interpreter visibility and roles
- investigate institutional control over interpreter performances
- examine the assumptions of and preferences for professional healthcare interpreters.

A. What Is an Interpreter-Mediated Medical Encounter?

Depending on the disciplinary tradition, interpreter-mediated medical encounters have been called and/or conceptualized differently. Compared to the long traditions of translation studies, which are rooted in comparative literature and religious studies (Kelly, 1979), interpreting studies[1] is a fledgling discipline that first gained its professional identity through simultaneous interpreters (now often called conference interpreters) during the Nuremberg Trials after World War II (Gaiba, 1998; Pöchhacker & Shlesinger, 2002). Interpreter-mediated medical encounters did not become a topic of interest in interpreting studies until the 1990s, when healthcare interpreters begin to demand a professional identity through accreditation and training (Harris, 1997). Within the field of interpreting studies, it's often called *medical interpreting* or *healthcare interpreting*, referring to interpreting activities (i.e., relaying information from one language to another) that take place in healthcare settings. A search of the literature suggests that the first use of the term medical interpreting appears in *The Multilingual Manual for Medical Interpreting*, a reference tool that allows providers to communicate through phonetic transliteration to diagnose and examine patients who do not speak English (Guercio, 1960). The first use of the term healthcare interpreting appears much later (i.e., in the late 1990s) in journal articles (Morgan, 1998; Pöchhacker & Kadric, 1999). In recent years, there have been proponents for each term. Some argue that healthcare interpreting encompasses a broader definition of health-related interpreting activities than medical interpreting, much like legal interpreting is a richer category than court interpreting. Others argue that medical interpreting lends more weight to the importance of interpreters' work (A. Clifford, personal communication, August 14, 2013).

In this book, I choose the term healthcare interpreting/interpreter (rather than medical interpreting/interpreter) to avoid confusion with health professionals who often need to interpret medical records for diagnostic and treatment purposes. Healthcare interpreters include any individual who provides interpreting services to patients who do not share the same language as their providers. Healthcare interpreters therefore include both signed and spoken language interpreters, working in different modalities with varying degrees of professionalism (see Chapter 4).

In the field of interpreting studies, healthcare interpreting is also understood as part of the larger category of *community interpreting* (Hale, 2007). Community interpreting is at times used interchangeably with public service interpreting, ad hoc interpreting, cultural interpreting, escort interpreting, liaison interpreting, contact interpreting, three-cornered interpreting, or dialogue interpreting. It's important to note that because interpreting studies is a young discipline, the specific terms for its subfields are still changing. Each term highlights a slightly different aspect of the interpreting activity. For example, community interpreting and public services interpreting involve interpreters who provide services to assist individuals to access resources (e.g., court services, social welfare, public services, and healthcare services) within a specific social system or community (Pöchhacker, 1999). Ad hoc interpreting suggests that the interpreters are typically untrained and provide makeshift services (Roberts, 1997). Liaison interpreting, along with escort interpreting, contact interpreting, and three-cornered interpreting, highlights interpreting activities involving interpreters who interact *directly* with at least two parties (Gentile, Ozolins, & Vsilakakos, 1996). Dialogue interpreting highlights the interactive and dynamic nature of the communicative activity. All these terms are contrasted with simultaneous conference interpreting,[2] in which interpreters are highly trained professionals who provide simultaneous interpreting (i.e., interpreting while the speaker is talking) in a remote booth (often located at the back of a conference room) while their clients use headphones to listen to the interpreting.

In the fields of medicine and public health, interpreter-mediated medical encounters are generally situated in the larger subfields of *minority health* and *cross-cultural care*, which often are concerned about (a) health disparities (i.e., differences in the access to care as well as the processes, quality, and outcomes of care) experienced by minority and marginalized populations (e.g., patients with limited English proficiency (LEP) or hearing impairment) and (b) the unique social determinants (e.g., sociocultural norms, illness ideologies, cultural beliefs, education, insurance status, among other social constructs) that shape these individuals' illness experiences (Hogue, Hargraves, Collins, & Fund, 2000). Within the field of minority health, interpreter-mediated medical encounters are often conceptualized under the umbrella topic of *language barriers* or *language access* to care. Researchers of this topic area are concerned about how language-discordant patients can have equal access to and the same quality of care as their language-concordant counterparts.

The literature has provided conclusive evidence that when patients do not share the same language as their providers, they experience significant health disparities. They often receive fewer preventive services, fewer public health services, fewer referrals/follow-ups, and poorer quality of pain treatment, but utilize more resources (e.g., more diagnostic tests and longer hospital stays) when they do visit healthcare institutions (David & Rhee, 1998; Flynn et al., 2013; Jimenez,

Moreno, Leng, Buchwald, & Morales, 2012; Lindholm, Hargraves, Ferguson, & Reed, 2012; Woloshin, Schwartz, Katz, & Welch, 1997). At an interpersonal level, they and their family members also receive lower quality of care, including but not limited to reduced interpersonal support, less patient-centered communication, and less patient satisfaction even in areas unrelated to language (Baker & Hayes, 1997; Karliner, Hwang, Nickleach, & Kaplan, 2011; Thornton, Pham, Engelberg, Jackson, & Curtis, 2009).

Parents' LEP status is also a major predictor of their children's health disparities. Children of parents with LEP (compared to those with English-proficient parents) have delayed illness care, reduced routine care, higher resource utilization for diagnostic testing, longer hospital stays after an adverse event, and longer visits in the emergency department (Flores, Abreu, & Tomany-Korman, 2005; Lion et al., 2013). Parents with LEP have a higher risk of problematic medication dosing (Flores et al., 2005). They are also associated with triple the odds of a child having fair/poor health status, double the odds of a child spending at least one day in bed for illness in the past year, and significantly greater odds of a child not being brought in for needed medical care for six of nine access barriers to care (Flores et al., 2005). Compared to child patients whose families do not have language barriers, those whose families have language barriers have a significantly increased risk for serious medical events during pediatric hospitalization (Cohen, Rivara, Marcuse, McPhillips, & Davis, 2005). Although researchers are uncertain about the exact processes and pathways in which language barriers create health disparities (Jacobs, Chen, Karliner, Agger-Gupta, & Mutha, 2006), interpreters have been viewed as the standard solution to improve language-discordant patients' access to and quality of care.

Following the traditions of medical sociology, applied linguistics, and communication, researchers have examined the content and processes of interpreter-mediated provider–patient interactions to explore (a) individuals' discursive practices in performing and negotiating specific roles, functions, and identities, and (b) participants' attitudes, expectations, and evaluations of effective and appropriate behaviors in interpreter-mediated interactions. In these fields, interpreter-mediated medical encounters often are categorized under *provider–patient communication*, a subfield of health communication. The early breakthroughs and momentum in the theoretical developments in interpreter-mediated medical encounters are from researchers who adopted these approaches. In particular, researchers were influenced by Goffman (1959, 1979) and Bakhtin (1981), exploring interpreters' management of the discursive process (e.g., Wadensjö, 1998) and role performances (e.g., Kaufert & Koolage, 1984). They conceptualized interpreters as active participants in mediating other participants' diverse goals and objectives in healthcare settings.

It is important to note that interpreter-mediated medical encounters were investigated in the fields of medicine and social sciences for decades before researchers in interpreting studies recognized their significance (Pöchhacker &

Shlesinger, 2005). In particular, early publications largely emerged in the field of mental health as healthcare practitioners pondered about the roles, functions, and professional boundaries of interpreters in mental health care, an area in which language (performance) is both the site of a patient's symptom and the tool of the provider's diagnosis and treatment (Alderete, 1967; Bloom, Hanson, Frires, & South, 1966). To these scholars, a successful interpreter-mediated medical encounter is not just about interpreters' linguistic performances in relaying information from one language to another. Rather, researchers and practitioners conceptualized interpreters' functions and performances as an element of the therapeutic processes of healthcare delivery.

It is from this perspective that I extend my support for a paradigm shift in conceptualizing interpreter-mediated medical encounters. Rather than simply scrutinizing interpreters' "accurate" transfer of information from one language to another, we need to recognize that the success of healthcare interpreting cannot be evaluated through equivalences between the source texts and target texts alone. Healthcare interpreting is situated in a larger communicative event (i.e., provider–patient interaction) that entails specific goals (e.g., improving patients' health), which are accomplished through healthcare delivery. While these arguments may have been proposed by other researchers, few have proposed a theoretical model for the corresponding changes in conceptualizing interpreter-mediated medical encounters. What does it mean when such a paradigm shift is applied to bilingual health care?

Patients' health outcomes, including the quality of care and quality of life, cannot be overlooked as one considers the quality and success of interpreter-mediated medical encounters. In addition, the communicative event is situated in organizational settings/contexts, which may impose obligations and limitations of individual behaviors (for providers, patients, and interpreters alike). Interpreters are not simply there to relay information. They are part of the healthcare delivery team, shouldering the shared responsibilities and objectives with other health professionals.

Interpreter-mediated medical encounters, thus, represent a unique form of interpreting activity. The interpreter, as part of the healthcare team, is obligated to honor the organizational objectives in providing quality care that enhances the patients' health outcomes. These objectives can be operationalized and their success can be measured (e.g., patient-centered communication, resource utilization, biomedical markers, and patient satisfaction). The criteria for evaluating the success of provider–patient interaction should be no different than those for assessing the quality of interpreter-mediated medical encounters. From this perspective, language-concordant provider–patient interactions can serve as the control group for interpreter-mediated interactions, a unique condition for studies of interpreter-mediated interactions. In other words, the interpreter performances are optimal when patients in interpreter-mediated interactions experience the same or better quality of care than their language-concordant counterparts, resulting in their improved health outcomes.

It is important to note that I do not argue that interpreter-mediated encounters should have the *same* quality of care as their language-concordant counterparts. The literature suggests that low health literacy (e.g., not having adequate skills to seek, process, and utilize health information to make informed health decisions) is a common problem in the United States, with only 12 percent of the population having proficient health literacy (National Network of Libraries of Medicine, 2013). We can assume that most people, including English-speaking individuals, do not have adequate communicative competence in provider–patient interactions. Low health literacy is linked to poorer health outcomes and knowledge, problematic health behaviors, and disparities in resource utilization (e.g., increased hospitalization and emergency care and decreased preventive care; Berkman et al., 2011). There may be situations in which an interpreter can enable a language-discordant patient to enjoy a quality of care that is *better* than that of his/her counterpart. In later chapters, I will explore how such possibilities may exist and how they can be accomplished. For now, I want to emphasize that having language-discordant patients outperforming language-concordant patients is not a problem or a failure of interpreter performances.

Even when providers and patients share the same language, they can still experience problematic communication due to low communicative competence (Cegala, Street, & Clinch, 2007). While this is an important problem, challenges in language-concordant provider–patient interactions are beyond the scope of this book. Although language barriers are a major contributor to low health literacy, language-discordant patients often experience many other barriers to care that are not limited to language (Gregg & Saha, 2007; McKee & Paasche-Orlow, 2012). By conceptualizing healthcare interpreters as part of the healthcare team, researchers and practitioners can investigate areas, including but not limited to language, in which interpreters can facilitate the process and quality of care. Because interpreters are communication experts in cross-cultural care and can be knowledgeable about the various available resources in healthcare settings, it is entirely within reason to expect that language-discordant patients may benefit in areas that are not limited to language as well.

B. Interpreters' Visibility and Roles

B.1. Interpreter Visibility as a Valuable but Limited Concept

The challenge faced by healthcare providers is that although interpreters are present because of a lack of a common language shared by the provider and the patient, the impacts of interpreters are not limited to language and language barriers. The physical presence of an interpreter inevitably changes the interpersonal dynamics of provider–patient interactions (Bruce & Anderson, 1976).

The turn-taking spaces that interpreters occupy in provider–patient interactions make their presence unmistakable. Even when interpreters operate in simultaneous interpreting mode (i.e., interpreting as the speaker is talking) to minimize their presence, the overlapping of voices contradicts our social norms and can be intrusive or distracting at close quarters. In fact, interpreters' visibility in provider–patient interactions has been a salient topic since some of the first publications on healthcare interpreting.

For example, Bloom and colleagues proposed three interactional positions that an interviewer (i.e., a speaker) can instruct an interpreter to adopt in the communicative process (Bloom et al., 1966): (a) interpreter as the interviewer, (b) interpreter as a tool, and (c) interpreter as a partner-specialist. These interactional positions not only project different interpersonal relationships between the interpreter and the clients but also imply specific limitations on interpreter visibility in the communicative activities. For example, the interpreter as a tool suggests a hierarchical relationship between the interviewer and the interpreter, removes an interpreter's subjectivity, and requires the provider to "use" the interpreter with "as great precision as possible" (p. 215). As Bloom and colleagues elaborated on the strengths and weaknesses of these interactional positions, they also considered how an interpreter's existing identity and relationships may pose limitations on the types of interactional positions available to the interviewer. For example, a patient's family member may not willingly give up their agency and be used as a tool. They concluded, "The use of an interpreter varies with the purpose of the relationship one wants to establish" (Bloom et al., 1966, p. 217).

Several early researchers were mindful about how interpreters' existing identities and relationships may influence their performances. Richie (1964) discussed the strengths and weaknesses when using school-aged children, bilingual neighbors, bilingual school teachers, or clergymen as interpreters. Lang (1976) noted that although physicians often treated orderlies who provide interpreting services as colleagues, physicians should provide explicit instructions to orderlies about when to adopt a strict interpreter role and "to abandon his role as colleague" (p. 176). For these early scholars, interpreter visibility is part of the realities that providers have to work with because interpreters generally are untrained and assume other social roles (e.g., patients' family members or hospital orderlies). Providers were cautioned about how interpreters' visibility may pose challenges to provider–patient interactions (e.g., Bloom et al., 1966; Richie, 1964). Interpreter visibility in provider–patient interactions was conceptualized as something to be managed *by the provider* to meet the therapeutic objectives, rather than as something to be eliminated or ignored. This valuable insight was later lost in the literature, partially due to the professionalization[3] of healthcare interpreting.

Translator (in)visibility has been a major research topic in translation studies (Venuti, 2008). Translators adopt specific strategies to assume an invisible voice/presence in their translated work, despite the fact that their interpretation of the source texts is inevitable (and essential) as they identify the proper rendition in the target texts. The illusion of transparency is necessary to claim credibility for their work and thus uphold the authentic voice of the source texts (Hsieh, 2002; Venuti, 2008). The rise of professional interpreting after World War II was predominately in international politics and the justice system (e.g., the Nuremberg Trials), which shaped the theoretical development of interpreting by highlighting the importance of neutrality, detachment, and faithfulness to the source narratives (Gaiba, 1998; Wadensjö, 1998). In these professional settings, interpreters often work for one specific client, interpreting unidirectionally in isolated booths. In short, interpreter visibility is not only hidden from the physical environment but also becomes a taboo topic in interpreting practice. After all, suggesting interpreters' subjective interpretations were involved in speaker narratives in international courts is unthinkable. For these professional interpreters, claiming invisibility is necessary to maintain credibility and trustworthiness in contemporary British-American culture (Venuti, 2008). The development of codes of ethics has been heavily influenced by these historical backgrounds. Professional interpreters are *trained* to claim invisibility by adopting various strategies that allow them to create the illusion of transparency (for more discussion, see Chapter 6).

The professionalization of healthcare interpreting has shaped our expectations for interpreting in a fundamental way. Because untrained, ad hoc interpreters often assume other social roles (e.g., patients' family members or bilingual nurses), they generally do not need to be preoccupied with their credibility or trustworthiness as there is minimal expectation of impartiality or neutrality. In addition, their credibility and trustworthiness may already be established through their other social roles. In contrast, professional interpreters are the unfamiliar others (to both the patient and the provider) and need to gain their legitimacy through their "professional" conduct, which often entails converting their identities into a fixed set of expert skills in an increasingly dehumanizing, specializing, and impersonal system (e.g., healthcare settings; Todres, Galvin, & Dahlberg, 2007). This attitude is further reinforced through healthcare interpreters' codes of ethics and training, emphasizing "a mode of interpretation that calls for an objective, neutral role for interpreters that is similar to the interpreter's role that evolved in American Sign Language (ASL) programs and in court interpreting programs, where training and codes of conduct for interpreters have been legislated" (Kaufert & Putsch, 1997, p. 75). Professional interpreters, thus, were removed from the interpretive process of communication.

However, perception always involves interpretation (Schmidt, 1984). Researchers of hermeneutics have long recognized that interpretation is inevitable in all human communication (Ricoeur, 1981). By claiming invisibility in the communicative process, professional interpreters deny the very nature of human communication. Nevertheless, if they acknowledge their subjective interpretation of the messages and meanings conveyed, interpreters may not only risk their credibility but also compromise the integrity of their work (Hsieh, 2002). This dilemma delayed the theoretical development on interpreter practice as any discussion about interpreter agency, subjectivity, and visibility can challenge the legitimacy of their work and their identities. It was not until the late 1980s and early 1990s that researchers systematically questioned the appropriateness, necessity, and practicality of constructing interpreter visibility, particularly in healthcare settings.

A major momentum in rejecting the notion of an invisible interpreter comes from two camps: physician researchers and scholars who are also practicing interpreters. Kaufert was one of the first physician researchers to challenge the ideology of a passive, invisible interpreter (Kaufert & Koolage, 1984). By examining Canadian aboriginal interpreters' practices, Kaufert and colleagues noted that healthcare interpreters are "both witnesses and participants" in provider–patient interactions (Kaufert & Putsch, 1997, p. 84). By using case studies to examine interpreters' mediation of conflicting values (e.g., truth-telling and informed consent) between the provider, the patient, and the patient's family members in end-of-life decision-making, they raised concerns that the codes of ethics for healthcare interpreters' specialized functions and obligations were being developed prematurely (Kaufert & Putsch, 1997; Kaufert, Putsch, & Lavallée, 1999). Without a proper understanding of the complexity of healthcare interpreters' practices, health interpreters' codes of ethics do not necessarily improve the quality of care, facilitate provider–patient communication, or honor values of healthcare contexts (e.g., patient empowerment and autonomy). Instead, the codes of ethics are ideologically driven and fail to provide meaningful prescription to interpreter practices.

Wadensjö, a Swedish–Russian interpreter-scholar, was among the first to highlight interpreters' active management of provider–patient interactions. Following Hatim and Mason's (1990) notion of translators' central role in the communicative process, Wadensjö (1998) demonstrated interpreters' complex verbal and nonverbal strategies to mark the discourse, acting as a co-participant in shaping the meanings of provider–patient interactions. Metzger, a signed language interpreter-scholar, challenged the illusion of neutrality in interpreter-mediated interactions by arguing that interpreters inevitably shape the process and content of communication due to the footings (i.e., conversational frames that construct interpersonal relationships) and communicative contexts they generate in the discursive process (Metzger, 1999). Metzger concluded that there are significant discrepancies between interpreter practices and the codes of ethics. Angelelli, a Spanish–English interpreter-scholar, further argued that professional interpreters in various contexts perceive their roles to be visible and enact their visibility through their role performances (Angelelli, 2004). Although visibility suggests a dualistic condition, in which one is either visible or invisible, Angelelli proposed that there is a continuum of visibility. In particular, Angelelli found that interpreters enact two forms of visibility: minor visibility (i.e., interpreters' occasional involvement as co-owners of texts) and major visibility (i.e., interpreters as owners of texts). For example, for minor visibility, an interpreter may introduce their roles to the patient without informing the provider that they have done so. In contrast, for major visibility, an interpreter may replace the monolingual interlocutor by taking control over the process and content of communication. Angelelli (2003, p. 24) explained:

> [i]nterpreters become visible when they do the following: explore answers, expand and summarize statements, broker comprehension and explain technical terms, bridge cultural gaps, express affect and replace interlocutors. As the interpreter determines the text, visibility increases. As visibility increases, the interpreter's role is more consequential.

It is from this perspective that visibility as a theoretical concept that has provided major momentum in recent theoretical development faces its limitations. By noting a continuum of interpreter visibility in the discursive process, researchers highlight the various shades of presence and influence that an interpreter can exert in provider–patient interactions. While Angelelli's dichotomous categorization demonstrated the variations of visibility, it (a) focused on interpreters' management of texts and (b) failed to account for the subtle variations and performances of visibility. This is where the term visibility fails us. Visibility, as a theoretical concept borrowed from translation studies, relies heavily on texts. Researchers compared source texts and target texts to determine whether and how a translator was visible in the final product. However, interpreters' management of the discursive process can be much more intricate and nuanced.

With a subtle change of tone, an interpreter can imply disagreement even when a "complete, accurate" source text was provided. Imagine an interpreter relaying a physician's sincere comment, "I think this procedure is good for you," in an unenthusiastic, cynical tone. How about in a caring, concerned voice? Would that change the patient's perception or even decision? What if the provider said the comment in a matter-of-fact voice but the interpreter used an empathetic, encouraging tone? Would that be appropriate? Why do we feel strongly about the interpreters' manipulation of providers' tone yet do not reach the same conclusion about these two different manipulations?

Whereas most people may be concerned when interpreters use an impersonal tone to relay a provider's compassionate voice, I suspect few would raise eyebrows when an interpreter uses a caring tone to relay an absent-minded provider's comment. In both cases, the interpreter exerts influence in provider–patient interactions and shapes the meanings of the discourse. However, our evaluations about the appropriateness of interpreters' behaviors diverge significantly. This is because in these scenarios, interpreters not only relay the texts but also shape the identities and attitudes of the providers. Interpreter visibility is not only reflected in their target texts but also in their management of others' identities and communicative contexts. More importantly, we expect an interpreter to behave in a certain way. Maybe it is to make the provider look good as a professional. Maybe it is to improve the quality of care for the patient. Later in this book, I will explain how a normative approach to interpreter-mediated medical encounters can explain and predict interpreters' communicative strategies as well as our attitudes/assessment about the appropriateness of interpreters' behaviors. This is a topic we will explore more throughout this book. However, for now, my argument is that this example exposes our normative belief: When it comes to healthcare interpreting, we are not simply concerned about whether an interpreter is (in)visible but also how such (in)visibility is performed.

B.2. Interpreter Roles and Interactional Contexts

This normative belief is reflected in researchers' investigations on interpreter roles. In contrast to (in)visibility, which implies a dualistic condition (i.e., invisible versus visible), roles provide a wider range of performances that accommodate the continuum of visibility. One of the earliest publications on interpreter roles was by Bruce and Anderson (1976). By noting the interpersonal dynamics in interpreter-mediated interactions, they argued that interpreter roles are (a) ambiguous and/or undefined during the discursive process, (b) overloaded with unrealistic expectations from others, and (c) vulnerable to interactional pressures from other speakers. These conditions can lead to interpreters experiencing role conflicts, such as dilemmas in deciding what types of role performance (e.g., conduit, ally, or advisor) to assume.

The Cross Cultural Health Care Program (CCHCP), one of the first and leading training programs for healthcare interpreters, proposed four roles of healthcare interpreters (Institute for Innovation in Health and Human Services, 2014; Roat, 1996). A *conduit* is the default role and involves rendering in one language literally what has been said in the other without any additions, omissions, editing, or polishing. A *clarifier* is a role interpreters assume when they adjust speakers' register, interject their explanations, describe terms that have no linguistic equivalent, or check for understanding when necessary. A *cultural broker* provides a necessary cultural framework for understanding the message being interpreted. An *advocate* works on behalf of the patient outside the bounds of an interpreted interview, ensuring the patient's quality of care in addition to quality of communication. The CCHCP training program suggests "the 'appropriate' role for the interpreter is the least invasive role that will assure effective communication and care" (Roat, Putsch, & Lucero, 1997, p. 18). In other words, all roles are legitimate depending on the situation. Although these roles serve as a prescription to interpreter performances during interpreter training, they are proposed from a top-down approach and do not necessarily reflect interpreter practices. In reality, interpreters do not always actively move between these roles due to various concerns and institutional constraints (Hsieh, 2008). We will revisit this issue in the next section.

Rather than proposing a set of ideological roles for interpreters to perform, many researchers have investigated interpreter roles based on empirical data.

Kaufert (1984/1999)	Language interpreter		Informant			
			Culture broker			
				Advocate		
Drennan & Swartz (2002)	Language specialist		Institutional therapist			
			Culture specialist			
				Patient advocate		
Hatton & Webb (1993)	Voice box		Callaborator			
				Excluder		
Davidson (2001)			Convert co-diagnosticien			
			Institutional gatekeeper			
Miller (2005)	Black box		Therapy conduit			
Leanza (2005)	Linguistic agent	System agent		Lifeworld agent		Integration agent
Hsieh (2008)	Conduit	Professional	Manager		Advocate	

$$\longleftarrow \hspace{5cm} \longrightarrow$$

System   *Lifeworld*

FIGURE 1.1 Summary table of interpreter roles (adapted from Brisset et al., 2013)

Some researchers focused on elaboration of a specific role (Davidson, 2000, 2001; Hsieh, 2007; Kaufert & Koolage, 1984; Miller, Martell, Pazdirek, Caruth, & Lopez, 2005), while others aimed to present comprehensive typologies of interpreter roles (Hatton & Webb, 1993; Hsieh, 2008; Leanza, 2005). Using Habermas' concepts of the Lifeworld (contextually grounded experiences) and the System (decontextualized rules), Brisset and colleagues argued that all interpreter roles fit into a continuum in which "interpreters oscillate between the Lifeworld and the System" (see Figure 1.1; Brisset et al., 2013, p. 136).

Looking at Figure 1.1, readers may question the need for the various typologies. Although there are some overlapping areas for some roles (e.g., voice box, black box, linguistic agent, and conduit), each typology represents a distinct perspective in conceptualizing interpreters' roles and functions in interpreter-mediated medical encounters. By investigating how specific roles are enacted, the researchers demonstrate interpreters' management and coordination of the interpersonal dynamics of medical encounters. For example, Leanza (2005) created the typology by examining *interpreters' management of cultural differences* between the patient and the provider. An interpreter who adopts the system agent role is likely to ignore cultural differences between the provider and the patient by actively overlooking the patients' cultural needs and working in favor of providers' cultural expectations. An interpreter who acts as an integration agent would actively locate resources to facilitate migrants in making sense of and negotiating meanings as well as showing an "in-between" way of behaving. On the other hand, Hsieh's (2008) typology was based on interpreters' self-perceived roles by identifying *the communicative goals and strategies* that are associated with specific role performances. For example, when adopting the role of conduit, an interpreter's goals include transferring complete information and reinforcing the provider–patient relationship. When assuming the role of manager, an interpreter's goals are to conserve medical resources, regulate appropriate and ethical performances (of others), and manage optimal exchange of information. In short, the seemingly overlapping roles and/or typologies highlight distinct perspectives and approaches to the understanding of interpreter roles and their management of interactional dynamics (see Chapter 8).

The investigation of interpreter roles has provided valuable momentum to the theoretical development of interpreting studies. Based on Goffman's (1959) work, role as a theoretical concept allows researchers to examine how, by assuming certain roles, individuals can define and control the contexts and thus define the frame as well as the performances of others. In other words, by conceptualizing interpreter performances as role performances, researchers can expand the scope of analysis to "the dynamics of interpreter-mediated interactions" (Wadensjö, 1998, p. 15) and the "different interrelated relational issues" associated with roles (Brisset et al., 2013, p. 136). As we consider the appropriateness and effectiveness of different interpreter roles, we inevitably make judgments about the appropriate roles and relationships for other participants in healthcare settings.

For example, if an interpreter is expected to assume a conduit role, the implicit expectation is that other speakers will be responsible for noticing and addressing any communicative problems. For instance, if a patient feels that a provider is expressing a discriminatory attitude, the patient (as opposed to the interpreter) should be responsible for initiating a complaint. If an interpreter (but not the patient) senses discrimination, then it is not the interpreter's place to voice concerns. A provider is expected to understand cultural differences and to communicate to a patient in a way that is culturally appropriate. In contrast, if an interpreter is expected to assume a cultural broker role, we assume that providers and patients may misunderstand each other even when they do not perceive any problems. For example, a provider may ask a Chinese patient "Do you take any other medication?", without realizing most Chinese patients do not consider the traditional Chinese medicine they take through food therapy as medication. However, ginkgo, a common traditional Chinese medicine ingredient in Chinese dishes, may increase the risk of bleeding during and after surgery (Andersen, Sweet, Zhou, & Standish, 2015; Jiang & Quave, 2013; Wong, Gabriel, Maxwell, & Gupta, 2012).

Interpreter roles highlight the issues of *contexts* and *others*. With role, there are specific expectations, perceptions, and actions that are implied (in the normative model), and this is what allows the participants (i.e., speakers and audiences) to perform in the frame. This is why Goffman's initial interest in roles eventually led him to the investigation of frame, footing, and interaction order (Goffman, 1974, 1979, 1983). Understanding interpreter performances through role allows researchers to discuss these aspects of frame (including the coordination of identities, relationships, and tasks), and to examine how interpreters use their roles to define contexts and thus impose control on others' performances.

More importantly, role allows researchers to examine not just interpreters' performance, but *other participants'* performance. This is essential to Goffman's understanding of social interactions (Rawls, 1987). No single individual has full control of the frame. After all, when one assumes the role of a teacher, the individual automatically altercasts and imposes the conversational other in the role of a student; similarly, when one assumes the role of an expert authority, the conversational other is altercasted as an inexperienced subordinate (Tracy, 2013). In other words, by claiming certain roles, the speaker can then force others into specific roles, creating a frame that puts pressure on all participants involved to behave accordingly (Goffman, 1959, 1974). Because all participants in medical encounters are involved in the negotiation of role performance and interactional frame, an interpreter may face specific pressure due to the roles altercasted and frames constructed by other speakers (see Chapter 6). In addition, role is not static. As such, individuals often challenge each other's role performances and negotiate to achieve a mutually agreeable frame (Goffman, 1959). By conceptualizing interpreter performances as roles, interpreters are viewed as performers, and roles are dynamically, emergently co-constructed between the participants of the frame/event. This new perspective allows researchers to move their investigation beyond texts and interpreters and begin to examine how conversational others may shape interpreters' performances and the interpreter-mediated medical encounters.

This marks a critical point in the theoretical development in interpreting studies that sets it apart from translation studies, because audiences for translations are often invisible and silent recipients of the texts. In contrast, in interpreting studies, particularly in dialogue (or liaison/community) interpreting, all participants are visible, active, and participating members of the discursive process. Granted, not all interpreting activities are the same (Gavioli & Baraldi, 2011). In simultaneous conference interpreting, an interpreter remains invisible as s/he is often located in an isolated booth. In court interpreting, an interpreter is under significant pressure to minimize his/her presence and interference in the court proceedings. In contrast, a healthcare interpreter is part of the healthcare team that aims to ensure the quality of care. The success of healthcare delivery is dependent on all participants' ability to identify and negotiate their goals and expectations. Healthcare interpreting, thus, represents an exceptional setting for researchers. By observing the dynamic, emergent co-construction of meanings between multiple parties in medical encounters, researchers are able to observe (a) interpreters' management of their roles and functions, (b) how individuals negotiate, challenge, and collaborate on the meanings they co-construct in these conversational frames, and (c) how interpreters and other speakers identify/generate the shared goals of medical encounters. (I will explore the limitation of role as a theoretical concept later in Chapter 6.)

In summary, as researchers have shifted their analytical focus from interpreter visibility to role performances, the scope of analysis has expanded significantly as communicative contexts and other speakers' performances come into play. Rather than viewing the interpreter as the central *and* only person who is responsible for the quality of interpreter-mediated interactions, this new theoretical expansion recognizes that all participants can actively influence the content and process of communication. A successful interpreter-mediated medical encounter is a collaborative achievement among all participants.

C. Institutional Responses to Interpreters' Power and Control

Traditionally, to ensure the quality of interpreter-mediated medical encounters, researchers have focused on interpreters' performances. Several issues have contributed to this approach. From the perspective of clinical medicine, one could argue that if a provider is competent in communicating, diagnosing, and treating a patient when they share the same language, there are few reasons to suspect that the provider would not be competent when an interpreter is involved. In other words, interpreter-mediated medical encounters may fail due to an incompetent or unqualified interpreter but not due to an incompetent provider (or patient).

On the other hand, translation and interpreting studies traditionally have focused on the examination of the translator/interpreter performance and texts (as opposed to authors/speakers or readers/audiences). As a result, when considering how to improve the quality of translation and interpreting, few researchers consider the possibility of changing the authors'/speakers' communicative styles or behaviors or improving readers'/audiences' communicative competence. These disciplines converged with a consensus that a healthcare interpreter is *the* person who is responsible for the quality of interpreter-mediated medical encounters.

The interpreter, being the only person who can understand and communicate in both the provider's and the patient's languages, can easily manipulate information without others' knowledge, interfering with the content and process of provider–patient communication. As such, researchers and practitioners were quick to recognize interpreters' influence and power in medical encounters. Prior to the 1990s, there were few professional interpreters in healthcare settings. Providers' concerns about the appropriate choice for interpreters include topic-appropriateness for school-aged bilingual children, confidentiality concerns for bilingual friends, or communicative competence concerns for hospital orderlies (Lang, 1976; Richie, 1964). However, a range of expected performances for qualified interpreters has emerged. For example, in addition to cautioning providers to watch out for interpreters' language proficiency and cultural competence, Richie (1964, p. 28) noted "the interpreter may use his position for malicious purposes." Richie recounted an incident in which a daughter-in-law who served as an interpreter for an elderly patient informed the patient that her condition was worsening when a nurse told the patient that she was making satisfactory progress. After examining interpreting errors in a psychiatric clinic, Price (1975) concluded that interpreters' "apparent competence can be mistaken for true competence." When examining orderlies' practices as interpreters, Lang (1976, p. 173) argued that "the interpreter should not be initiating any utterances of his own" but recognized that "this ideal standard of interpreting behavior cannot be maintained in a study with the orderly-as-interpreter." When providing guidelines for providers who work with interpreters, Launer (1978, p. 935) suggested, "Greet the patient to establish direct contact. Be seen to be in charge of the interpreter. ... Finally, use the interpreter to tell the patient everything you would tell him if he could speak your language."

These early publications on healthcare interpreting have thus laid the foundations for institutional control through specific assumptions: (a) the provider–patient relationship is the primary relationship in interpreter-mediated interactions, (b) provider–patient communication should remain the same with language-concordant and language-discordant patients, (c) ideal interpreters provide passive, supplementary services without interfering with the content and process of provider–patient communication, and (d) an interpreter may "go bad" if left unmonitored. These assumptions are reflected in the professionalization of interpreters.

By professionalization, I mean that they develop formal training and an official certification process, uphold standards of practice through codes of ethics and specific qualifications, and form professional organizations that make exclusive claims on expertise (Tang, 2008). Signed language interpreters in the United States were pioneers in claiming a professional status through establishing a professional organization in 1964 and developing a certification process in the early 1970s (The Registry of Interpreters for the Deaf, 2013). Its codes of ethics, including principles such as confidentiality and fidelity, were influential in the later drafting of codes of ethics for spoken languages in other settings (Pöchhacker, 1999). Legal interpreting was one of the early areas for the professionalization of spoken language interpreters (Pöchhacker, 2007). In tracing the professionalization of interpreters, Pöchhacker (2007, p. 13) noted:

> [It] is even more striking to read what Governor Antonio de Mendoza, the Viceroy and Governor of "New Spain" had stipulated in the early sixteenth century for the interpreters' standards of performance: Interpreters had to be duly sworn to perform their task "well and faithfully," expressing the matter before them "clearly and frankly," "without hiding or adding anything," "without acting in favor of any of the parties," and "without deriving any profit from their task other than the pay due to them". (cf. Mendoza, 1548)

In the area of court interpreting, with its historical roots in the Nuremberg Trials, the ideology of interpreter-as-conduit is rigorously reinforced. By distinguishing the activities between *translation* (i.e., an objective, mechanistic, transparent process in which the interpreter acts a mere conduit of words) and *interpreting* (i.e., activities in which an interpreter decodes the message and attempt to convey their understanding of speaker meaning and intention), court interpreters are instructed that they are "not to *interpret* – this being an activity which only lawyers are to perform, but to *translate* – a term which is defined, sometimes expressly and sometimes by implication, as rendering the speaker's words verbatim" (Morris, 1995, p. 26). The expectations for a neutral, non-interpretive role are so intense that many court interpreters argued that their clients are not people (e.g., the language-discordant person or the service provider who paid them) but language. "Language as client" allows a court interpreter to claim neutrality and impartiality (Hale, 2004). This ideology is not only defined by legislation (Fenton, 1997), but any deviation from the conduit role is sanctioned with "a citation for contempt, disciplinary action or any other sanction that may be imposed by law" (Washington Courts, 1989, p. 1). The codes of ethics, thus, serve as implicit contractual obligations for interpreters to monitor and control their performance to ensure what is perceived to be an appropriate and/or good practice.

The codes of ethics for healthcare interpreting were heavily influenced by the codes of ethics for signed language interpreters and court interpreters (National Council on Interpreting in Health Care, 2004). In an analysis of codes of ethics developed for interpreters from more than 20 healthcare institutions, Kaufert and Putsch (1997) concluded that many of the codes emphasize a mode of interpreting that calls for an objective and neutral role for interpreters. In another review, Bancroft (2005) concluded that interpreter competence, accuracy and/or completeness, and impartiality are the core values that exist in virtually all standards of practice and codes of ethics for interpreters around the world. All three core values are embedded in the interpreter-as-conduit model. An ideal, competent interpreter acts as a conduit, transmitting information accurately and faithfully without distortion between provider and the patient (Dysart-Gale, 2005). In short, interpreters-as-conduits is a prevailing ideology in interpreting models, which often reflects the public's attitude and expectations for interpreters and encourages the pursuit of matching a source text with a target text (i.e., finding exact equivalence between two languages).

The development and enforcement of codes of ethics highlight healthcare interpreters' desire to claim a professional status in healthcare settings. Parsons (1951) conceptualizes professionals as instrumental action actors as their individuality and individual perspectives are minimized. Instead, they function as instruments in the larger social system to accomplish specific goals through defined, formal processes that are highly regulated and controlled (Parsons, 1951; Treviño, 2001). In healthcare settings, professional competence often entails the norms of *universalism* and *affective neutrality* (Agich, 1980), two of the pattern variables (i.e., particularism vs. universalism; affectivity vs. affective neutrality) proposed by Parsons for instrumental action (Treviño, 2001). Universalism means that health professionals need to apply the same attitudes when interacting with all patients. Affective neutrality means that health professionals' actions need to be disciplined and calculative, adopting an impersonal orientation that avoids expressions of emotions. For healthcare interpreters, their professionalism also involves *specificity*, another pattern variable (i.e., diffuseness vs. specificity) for instrumental action.

Specificity means that the interpreter functions within restricted expectations and interests to narrow and limited aspects of services. Based on the codes of ethics for healthcare interpreters, specificity entails limiting interpreters' involvement to transferring information from one language to another. Other forms of involvement or interference would violate the expectation of specificity and thus would make the interpreter's behavior "unprofessional" or inappropriate.

These norms of professional roles project a healthcare interpreter as a technical professional who serves a restricted and limited role in providing linguistic services in an objective, neutral, and impersonal manner. The process of professionalization is a process of generating institutional control to facilitate or encourage individuals of the particular profession to perform in a standardized manner that meets the expectations of the larger social system.

Healthcare interpreting is not only well organized but is also extensively studied in various multi-ethnic societies (e.g., Australia and Canada) and in countries that represent a destination of intensive immigration (e.g., Sweden, Denmark, Germany, The Netherlands, Spain, Switzerland, the United States, and the United Kingdom). The rise of professional healthcare interpreting requires strong sociopolitical support for language access in healthcare settings. The Department of Immigration in Australia established the Telephone Interpreter Services in 1973 and supported several state-level initiatives later that decade, including a mobile unit of healthcare interpreters in New South Wales (Pöchhacker, 1999). In the 1970s, the Swedish government established a system for the training and accreditation of interpreters and published the first codes of ethics for interpreters (Niska, 2007). The code's main principle is that the interpreter is neutral and impartial (Niska, 2007). In the United Kingdom, the professionalization of interpreters was accomplished through collaboration between government agencies and interpreters (Pöchhacker, 1999). The Registry of Interpreters for the Deaf, founded in 1964, now provides various levels of certification that are nationally recognized in the United States and Canada (The Registry of Interpreters for the Deaf, 2013). Although there is no international or European legislation on interpreter provision in healthcare, many European regions and countries, such as Northern Ireland and Norway, have introduced regional and national laws to ensure anti-discrimination and equal access to healthcare services for all, including individuals who do not share the same language (Phelan, 2012).

The United States has established extensive federal and state legislative efforts to ensure language access in healthcare settings (Youdelman, 2008). At the federal level, Title VI of the 1964 Civil Rights Act prohibits discrimination on the basis of race, color, or national origin by any recipient of federal funding, including Medicaid and Medicare. The Americans with Disabilities Act of 1990 requires providers to provide auxiliary aids, including signed language interpreters, to patients with hearing impairment. The White House also issued an Executive Order on Improving Access to Services for Persons with Limited English Proficiency on August 11, 2000, which resulted in the Department of Health and Human

Services' written guidelines in 2003 requiring healthcare providers to provide reasonable accommodation to ensure access to care for patients with LEP. Although there are no federal requirements for the quality of interpreters in healthcare settings, many states have legislations to clarify or broaden federal requirements, providing language access for specific clinical contexts (Chen, Youdelman, & Brooks, 2007). For example, in 2001, Massachusetts passed a law mandating access to and use of trained interpreters in all emergency departments and acute psychiatric facilities. Some states also have state-level certification programs for interpreters and cultural competency training requirements for health professionals. Because the cost of interpreters cannot be transferred directly to patients by law, healthcare facilities often struggle to locate sufficient resources to fund interpreting services. In early 2009, California became the first state in the United States to require health insurance organizations to pay for interpreting and translating services.

The sociopolitical support within the country and/or region is essential to the burgeoning of professional healthcare interpreters because the professionalization of interpreters requires a stable and sizable demand in the market to attract and retain qualified interpreters (Meeuwesen, 2012). The recent anti-immigration pressure and economic recession in European countries have posed challenges to the maintenance of professional interpreter services in Europe (Phelan, 2012). Wadensjö (1998) argued that the instability of the labor market may also encourage interpreters to refrain from putting effort and time into developing professional skills. In short, the professionalization of healthcare interpreters requires institutional support, not just from interpreter organizations but also from the public, healthcare institutions, and from government agencies through the form of sociocultural values (e.g., multiculturalism and anti-discrimination), and legislation at the local, regional, and national levels. However, dependence on public support also leaves interpreters and interpreter practices vulnerable to the scrutiny and control of these social systems and institutions.

D. Problematic and Blind Preferences for Professional Interpreters

D.1. Problematic Assumptions of the Interpreter-as-conduit Model

As a result of the increasing professionalization of healthcare interpreters, the codes of ethics for healthcare interpreters emphasize the ideology of the interpreter-as-conduit model (Dysart-Gale, 2005). The interpreter-as-conduit model assumes that: (a) all participants are competent speakers who can communicate effectively and appropriately, (b) there are minimal differences between speakers' cultural knowledge and social practices, and (c) it is desirable to maintain the existing structure of relationships and patterns of communication (Hsieh, 2013). This assumption is also reflected in many guidelines for providers working with interpreters. For example, Launer (1978, p. 935) recommended providers "use the interpreter to tell the patient everything you would tell him if he could speak your language." This attitude may be fueled by the concept of Parsons' universalism, in which health professionals are obligated to treat all patients the same, thus avoiding the possibility of unequal services and discrimination.

These assumptions, however, are problematic in cross-cultural care. First, although there is a tendency to focus on language barriers, cross-cultural care involves many other challenges that are often not recognized or investigated. A recent review found five key predictors of communication problems in cross-cultural care: (a) cultural differences in explanatory models of health and illness, (b) differences in cultural values, (c) cultural differences in patients' preferences for doctor–patient relationships, (d) racism/perceptual biases, and (e) linguistic barriers (Schouten & Meeuwesen, 2006). Interactions with patients who do not share the same language always require crossing both linguistic and cultural boundaries. Failure to recognize these cultural boundaries may lead to miscommunication and reduced patient compliance (Harmsen, Meeuwesen, van Wieringen, Bernsen, & Bruijnzeels, 2003).

The differences in these cultural boundaries may have multidimensional impacts on provider–patient communication. In a large-scale study that examined the communicative patterns of 307 general practitioners and 5,820 patients from 10 different European countries (i.e., Belgium, Estonia, Germany, Great Britain, The Netherlands, Poland, Romania, Spain, Sweden, and Switzerland), Meeuwesen and colleagues (Meeuwesen, van den Brink-Muinen, & Hofstede, 2009) found that different countries have diverse norms of power distance (i.e., the extent to which an unequal distribution of power is accepted by members of a society) and uncertainty avoidance (i.e., the extent to which members of a society are motivated to reduce uncertainty), resulting in differences in their communicative patterns in medical encounters. For example, for countries with high power distance, providers and patients are more likely to assume a fixed communication role, follow an expected information exchange pattern, and have shorter medical encounters. In countries with high tolerance for uncertainty, providers and patients have more eye contact and pay more attention to rapport building. Providers are also more open to their patients' ideas and feedback. Finally, providers and patients from wealthy countries and from countries that have low tolerance for uncertainty are more likely to discuss psychosocial issues during medical encounters, with patients expressing their concerns and worries. In another study, researchers found that physicians in China and the United States follow very different clinical ethical practices, with Chinese physicians giving far greater weight to family preferences than US physicians (Feldman, Zhang, & Cummings, 1999). Unlike US physicians, who always inform cancer patients of their diagnoses, physicians in China and Japan often withhold a diagnosis of terminal illness from the patient and/or their family (Feldman et al., 1999; Parsons et al., 2007). Because Deaf culture prefers to obtain information quickly, they adopt some normative behaviors (e.g., blunt speech or telling a secret) that are generally considered rude or impolite among hearing people (Hall, 1983). Patients from different cultures may also have different expectations about communicative norms in medical encounters. For example, Korean Americans and Mexican Americans were less likely than African Americans and European Americans to believe that a patient should be told about their poor prognosis or that a patient (as opposed to his/her family members) should make decisions related to end-of-life care (Blackhall, Murphy, Frank, Michel, & Azen, 1995). These findings highlight the cultural differences in norms for provider–patient communication and indicate potential problems for intercultural medical encounters. More importantly, these differences influence not only individuals' patterns of behaviors but also the standards and criteria they adopt when evaluating the quality of provider–patient interactions.

The provider and the patient may be competent speakers and listeners in their own culture/language; however, in intercultural medical encounters, they (a) may share different expectations and norms about what constitutes a good interaction in healthcare settings, and (b) may not be able to anticipate, understand, and communicate about their cultural differences in various areas. "Communicate as if the other person shares the same language/culture" ignores the fact that the provider and the patient may not share the same sociocultural norms in intercultural medical encounters. As much as an American patient in Japan would experience anger and betrayal after learning his/her physician had withheld information about a diagnosis of a terminal illness, a Japanese patient might feel equally disrespected and harmed when such information is disclosed bluntly. The differences in the discursive norms in Deaf and hearing cultures can leave a deaf patient feeling that the hearing physician is talking down to them (Hall, 1983). The miscommunication is rooted in mismatched cultural norms. Cultural norms provide the larger interpretive frame for language users to derive meanings (e.g., Is my doctor rude or disrespectful?). Because cultural norms are often taken for granted and rarely referenced in our communicative processes, individuals are particularly vulnerable to miscommunication when there are mismatched norms in intercultural interactions.

In addition, the literature on provider–patient communication has long demonstrated that providers and patients are not on equal footing in medical interviews, with providers controlling the process and content of communication (Waitzkin, 1991). By providing services that are needed and desired, physicians possess legitimate, referent, and expert power in medical encounters, resulting in an asymmetrical provider–patient relationship (Beisecker, 1990). For interpreters who work in healthcare settings, their clients (i.e., institutional officials and laypeople) often involve two parties with significant power, educational, linguistic, sociocultural, and socioeconomic differences (e.g., [undocumented] immigrants and immigration officers or patients and physicians). It is not uncommon for patients to feel that their communicative needs are unfulfilled and to leave medical appointments feeling unsatisfied due to problematic provider–patient interactions. This situation is exacerbated by patients' low health literacy. In a study of

48,427 patients in California, researchers found that 44.9 percent of patients with LEP have low health literacy, versus 13.8 percent of English speakers (Sentell & Braun, 2012). While low health literacy and/or problematic provider–patient communication can be a problem for any patient, LEP patients suffer disproportionally from these problems. By enforcing the interpreter-as-conduit model in provider–patient interactions, interpreters inevitably maintain the imbalance of provider–patient relationship/communication and reinforce language-discordant patients' low health literacy.

In summary, the assumptions of the interpreter-as-conduit model cannot be supported by the literature. The significant cultural differences between providers and patients who do not share the same language make it difficult for them to understand each other's sociocultural norms and communicative behaviors. Their communicative process is likely to lead to misunderstanding or miscommunication. In addition, due to the asymmetrical relationship and communicative norms in provider–patient interactions, an interpreter-as-conduit is likely to maintain and reinforce the problematic communicative processes. In short, the communicative model that has been codified through codes of ethics for professional interpreters has failed to recognize the nature of interpreter-mediated medical encounters, which always involve cross-cultural care. As a result, while the model may appear reasonable from an ideological standpoint, researchers and practitioners have questioned its usefulness in actual practice (Dysart-Gale, 2005; Watermeyer, 2011).

D.2. Problems with the Unchallenged Preference for Professional Interpreters

Healthcare interpreters claim their professional status by establishing and upholding codes of ethics that emphasize the interpreter-as-conduit model. When the assumptions associated with the interpreter-as-conduit model cannot be supported by evidence, the significance and legitimacy of professional interpreters may face significant challenges.

Several reviews have provided concrete evidence of the benefits of using professional interpreters. For example, Flores (2005, p. 292) concluded that "trained interpreters generally result in better health processes, outcomes, and use of services." In another review, researchers concluded, "[P]rofessional interpreters are associated with an overall improvement of care for LEP patients. They appear to decrease communication errors, increase patient comprehension, equalize healthcare utilization, improve clinical outcomes, and increase satisfaction with communication and clinical services for limited English proficient patients" (Karliner, Jacobs, Chen, & Mutha, 2007). In short, the literature has provided ample evidence to suggest that when professional interpreters are provided, language-discordant patients can experience significant improvement of care. However, if the communicative model used by professional interpreters is not realistic or practical

(Dysart-Gale, 2007), how and why do professional interpreters have these positive impacts on patients' quality of care?

Even when researchers argue that professional interpreters often do better than nonprofessional interpreters in most areas (Flores, 2005; Karliner et al., 2007), there is no conclusive evidence to suggest that nonprofessional interpreters are universally worse than professional interpreters. The uncertainty is caused by the limited number of studies that directly compare the effectiveness and appropriateness of professional and nonprofessional interpreters. In addition, because there are significant variations in professionalism (e.g., from a 40-hour training program to a graduate degree in translation and interpreting) and workplace (e.g., hospital-based interpreters, agency-contracted interpreters, and telephone interpreters), professional interpreters still include a wide variety of people who may have differing impacts due to differences in their interpreting modality, workplace culture, or levels of training. In addition, depending on the types of illness and tasks involved, different types of interpreters (e.g., family members, bilingual nurses, telephone interpreters, and on-site professional interpreters) may be better in some areas/activities than in others.

The important question here is: What are the processes and pathways that allow (professional) interpreters to improve patients' quality of care? Understanding the processes and pathways is important, because it may be that the processes and pathways are not exclusive to professional interpreters. In addition, while concerns are raised about the use of nonprofessional interpreters in Flores' and Karliner et al.'s reviews, researchers also noted that there are studies that observed positive impacts from nonprofessional interpreters (see also Brisset et al., 2013). In other words, while researchers recognized the mixed impacts of nonprofessional interpreters, we know little about when, how, and why these impacts occur.

It is important to note that I do not advocate that nonprofessional interpreters are better than or should be used interchangeably with professional interpreters. The literature is clear that there are positive impacts on the quality of care when professional interpreters are present (Greenbaum & Flores, 2004; Lee et al., 2006). There are also good reasons to recommend and rely on professional interpreters as part of ethical practices (Hadziabdic, Albin, Heikkilä, & Hjelm, 2010; Jacobs, Diamond, & Stevak, 2010). However, I argue that the research community has not critically examined how or why professional interpreters can provide positive outcomes. Similarly, we need more studies to explore how and why nonprofessional interpreters influence the quality of care. Insisting that providers should only work with professional interpreters and condemning any other forms of interpreter as inappropriate, suboptimal, or even unethical without evidence-based claims ignores the reality of clinical practices and silences any meaningful discussions about best practices. Rather than resorting to common claims that have not been supported by evidence-based research (e.g., only professional interpreters can maintain neutrality), I propose that we should critically and empirically examine these issues. While it is unrealistic to expect all providers/

patients to have access to professional interpreters in all languages, regardless of the time or place of a medical encounter (Bischoff & Hudelson, 2010), it is essential to understand how providers can work effectively and appropriately with different types of interpreters (if they have to) without compromising the quality *and* ethics of clinical care (Bond, Bateman, & Nassrally, 2012; Seeleman, Essink-Bot, Selleger, & Bonke, 2012).

The key to advancing both theory and practice for bilingual/cross-cultural care should not be the restricted and/or exclusive investigation or use of professional interpreters. Rather, the aim should be to identify and investigate the various processes that facilitate the improvement of quality of care for language-discordant patients. By doing so, we will be able to provide evidence-based arguments about why certain types of interpreters are better than others (in specific contexts). We can also educate different types of interpreters to adopt the processes that are known to improve patients' quality of care. We can provide evidence-based guidelines to educate and regulate providers' use of interpreters. We can develop training programs to help providers and patients to work effectively and appropriately with different types of interpreters without compromising the quality of care. This is an issue that we will continue to revisit throughout this book.

In summary, rather than presuming that professional interpreters are universally better than nonprofessional interpreters, this book focuses on investigating the processes and pathways of effective interpreting practices, which may or may not be limited to professional interpreters. By doing so, I aim to identify specific practice guidelines that work across all types of interpreters for different types of healthcare providers in various clinical contexts.

Notes

1   In the process of the writing of this book, a few people have suggested using the term *interpreting*, rather than *interpretation*, when referring to interpreters' act of performing their tasks. The general argument is that interpretation is an outdated term and could suggest "subjective interpretation" of texts, data, or resources (e.g., literature, music, and medical records). The distinction is an important move in emphasizing interpreters' task in interpreting, rather than interpretation. Although the differences between interpreting/interpretation versus translation (which highlights the differences of speech vs. texts; interpreters work with spoken words while translators work with written texts) is widely accepted and emphasized, there appear to be some geographic differences in the use of interpreting versus interpretation. In the USA, the term interpretation is still quite common. There are still many universities and colleges that have departments, programs, or graduate degrees in "interpretation" (as opposed to interpreting; e.g., Middlebury Institute of International Studies at Monterey, the University of Arizona, and Gallaudet University). In contrast, in Europe, the consensus of the academic field has shifted to a preference for interpreting over interpretation. In this book, I honor this emerging trend. However, I kept the term interpretation when (a) this is how the organizations or individuals refer to themselves or describe their work, or (b) I emphasize the hermeneutic aspects of understanding the meaning(s) of texts, narratives, or resources. However, I want to note that I do not agree that interpreters can perform interpreting without subjective interpretation of the texts. Scheper-Hughes

(1992, p. 28) explained, "We cannot rid ourselves of the cultural self we bring with us into the field any more than we can disown the eyes, ears, and skin through which we take in our intuitive perceptions about the new and strange world we have entered." In other words, we cannot "objectively" interpret or understand the world, as our subjectivity is embedded in our consciousness. Discourse is always multivocal, full of (competing and possibility conflicting) meanings, and shaped by our consciousness (Ricoeur, 1976). One simply cannot reproduce "a" or "the" meaning of an utterance from one language to another without interpretation.

2   The field of interpreting studies still struggles somewhat with its categorization of interpreters and interpreting tasks. One can categorize interpreting by its medium (e.g., telephone interpreting or video interpreting), setting/context (e.g., court, conference, healthcare, or educational interpreting), temporal dimension of delivery (e.g., simultaneous vs. consecutive interpreting), speech modality (e.g., whispered interpreting), proxemics (e.g., in-person vs. remote interpreting). These are not mutually exclusive terms. A conference interpreter can work in simultaneous or consecutive modes. For more discussion on the variations of different forms and variations of interpreting, see Pöchhacker (2013).

3   In Chapter 4, I will review the available training and certification for professional healthcare interpreters.

References

Agich, G. J. (1980). Professionalism and ethics in health care. *Journal of Medicine and Philosophy*, 5, 186–199.

Alderete, J. F. (1967). The induction of hypnosis through an interpreter. *American Journal of Clinical Hypnosis*, 10, 138–140.

Andersen, M. R., Sweet, E., Zhou, M., & Standish, L. J. (2015). Complementary and alternative medicine use by breast cancer patients at time of surgery which increases the potential for excessive bleeding. *Integrative Cancer Therapies*, 14, 119–124.

Angelelli, C. V. (2003). The visible co-participant: The interpreter's role in doctor–patient encounters. In M. Metzger, S. Collins, V. Dively, & R. Shaw (Eds.), *From topic boundaries to omission: New research on interpretation* (pp. 3–26). Washington, DC: Gallaudet University Press.

Angelelli, C. V. (2004). *Revisiting the interpreters' roles: A study of conference, court, and medical interpreters in Canada, Mexico, and the United States*. Amsterdam, The Netherlands: John Benjamins.

Baker, D. W., & Hayes, R. (1997). The effect of communicating through an interpreter on satisfaction with interpersonal aspects of care. *Journal of General Internal Medicine*, 12, 117.

Bakhtin, M. M. (1981). *The dialogic imagination: Four essays by M. M. Bakhtin* (M. Holquist & C. Emerson, Trans.). Austin, TX: University of Texas Press.

Bancroft, M. (2005). The interpreter's world tour: An environmental scan of standards of practice for interpreters. Retrieved March 14, 2015, from www.hablamosjuntos.org/resources/pdf/The_Interpreter's_World_Tour.pdf.

Beisecker, A. E. (1990). Patient power in doctor-patient communication: What do we know? *Health Communication*, 2, 105–122.

Berkman, N. D., Sheridan, S. L., Donahue, K. E., Halpern, D. J., Viera, A., Crotty, K., Viswanathan, M. (2011, September 6, 2012). Health literacy interventions and outcomes: An updated systematic review. Retrieved March 14, 2015, from www.ncbi.nlm.nih.gov/books/NBK82434/.

Bischoff, A., & Hudelson, P. (2010). Access to healthcare interpreter services: Where are we and where do we need to go? *International Journal of Environmental Research & Public Health*, 7, 2838–2844.

Blackhall, L. J., Murphy, S. T., Frank, G., Michel, V., & Azen, S. (1995). Ethnicity and attitudes toward patient autonomy. *Journal of the American Medical Association*, 274, 820–825.

Bloom, M., Hanson, H., Frires, G., & South, V. (1966). The use of interpreters in interviewing. *Mental Hygiene*, 50, 214–217.

Bond, J., Bateman, J., & Nassrally, S. M. (2012). The role of ad-hoc interpreters in teaching communication skills with ethnic minorities. *Medical Teacher*, 34, 81.

Brisset, C., Leanza, Y., & Laforest, K. (2013). Working with interpreters in health care: A systematic review and meta-ethnography of qualitative studies. *Patient Education and Counseling*, 91, 131–140.

Bruce, W., & Anderson, R. (1976). Perspectives on the role of interpreter. In R. W. Brislin (Ed.), *Translation: Applications and research* (pp. 208–228). New York: Gardner.

Cegala, D. J., Street, R. L., Jr., & Clinch, C. (2007). The impact of patient participation on physicians' information provision during a primary care medical interview. *Health Communication*, 21, 177–185.

Chen, A. H., Youdelman, M. K., & Brooks, J. (2007). The legal framework for language access in healthcare settings: Title VI and beyond. *Journal of General Internal Medicine*, 22, S362–367.

Cohen, A. L., Rivara, F., Marcuse, E. K., McPhillips, H., & Davis, R. (2005). Are language barriers associated with serious medical events in hospitalized pediatric patients? *Pediatrics*, 116, 575–579.

David, R. A., & Rhee, M. (1998). The impact of language as a barrier to effective health care in an underserved urban Hispanic community. *Mount Sinai Journal of Medicine*, 65, 393–397.

Davidson, B. (2000). The interpreter as institutional gatekeeper: The social-linguistic role of interpreters in Spanish–English medical discourse. *Journal of Sociolinguistics*, 4, 379–405.

Davidson, B. (2001). Questions in cross-linguistic medical encounters: The role of the hospital interpreter. *Anthropological Quarterly*, 74, 170–178.

Drennan, G., & Swartz, L. (2002). The paradoxical use of interpreting in psychiatry. *Social Science & Medicine*, 54, 1853–1866.

Dysart-Gale, D. (2005). Communication models, professionalization, and the work of medical interpreters. *Health Communication*, 17, 91–103.

Dysart-Gale, D. (2007). Clinicians and medical interpreters: Negotiating culturally appropriate care for patients with limited English ability. *Family & Community Health*, 30, 237–246.

Feldman, M. D., Zhang, J., & Cummings, S. R. (1999). Chinese and US internists adhere to different ethical standards. *Journal of General Internal Medicine*, 14, 469–473.

Fenton, S. (1997). The role of the interpreter in the adversarial courtroom. In S. E. Carr, R. P. Roberts, A. Dufour, & D. Steyn (Eds.), *The critical link: Interpreters in the community* (pp. 29–34). Amsterdam, The Netherlands: John Benjamins.

Flores, G. (2005). The impact of medical interpreter services on the quality of health care: A systematic review. *Medical Care Research & Review*, 62, 255–299.

Flores, G., Abreu, M., & Tomany-Korman, S. C. (2005). Limited English proficiency, primary language at home, and disparities in children's health care: How language barriers are measured matters. *Public Health Reports*, 120, 418–430.

Flynn, P. M., Ridgeway, J. L., Wieland, M. L., Williams, M. D., Haas, L. R., Kremers, W. K., & Breitkopf, C. R. (2013). Primary care utilization and mental health diagnoses among adult patients requiring interpreters: A retrospective cohort study. *Journal of General Internal Medicine, 28,* 386–391.

Gaiba, F. (1998). *The origins of simultaneous interpretation: The Nuremberg Trial.* Ottawa, Canada: University of Ottawa Press.

Gavioli, L., & Baraldi, C. (2011). Interpreter-mediated interaction in healthcare and legal settings: Talk organization, context and the achievement of intercultural communication. *Interpreting, 13,* 205–233.

Gentile, A., Ozolins, U., & Vsilakakos, M. (1996). *Liaison interpreting: A handbook.* Victoria, Australia: Melbourne University Press.

Goffman, E. (1959). *The presentation of self in everyday life.* Garden City, NY: Doubleday.

Goffman, E. (1974). *Frame analysis: An essay on the organization of experience.* Cambridge, MA: Harvard University Press.

Goffman, E. (1979). Footing. *Semiotica: Journal of the International Association for Semiotic Studies/Revue de l'Association Internationale de Sémiotique, 25,* 1–29.

Goffman, E. (1983). The interaction order. *American Sociological Review, 48,* 1–17.

Greenbaum, M., & Flores, G. (2004). Lost in translation: Professional interpreters needed to help hospitals treat immigrant patients. *Modern Healthcare, 34,* 21.

Gregg, J., & Saha, S. (2007). Communicative competence: A framework for understanding language barriers in health care. *Journal of General Internal Medicine, 22,* S368–370.

Guercio, L. R. M. D. (1960). *The multilingual manual for medical interpreting.* New York: Pacific Print.

Hadziabdic, E., Albin, B., Heikkilä, K., & Hjelm, K. (2010). Healthcare staffs perceptions of using interpreters: A qualitative study. *Primary Health Care Research and Development, 11,* 260–270.

Hale, S. B. (2004). *The discourse of court interpreting: Discourse practices of the law, the witness, and the interpreter.* Amsterdam, The Netherlands: John Benjamins.

Hale, S. B. (2007). *Community interpreting.* London, UK: Palgrave Macmillan.

Hall, S. (1983). Train-gone-sorry: The etiquette of social conversations in American Sign Language. *Sign Language Studies, 41,* 291–309.

Harmsen, H., Meeuwesen, L., van Wieringen, J., Bernsen, R., & Bruijnzeels, M. (2003). When cultures meet in general practice: Intercultural differences between GPs and parents of child patients. *Patient Education and Counseling, 51,* 99–106.

Harris, B. (1997). Foreword: A landmark in the evolution of interpreting. In S. E. Carr, R. P. Roberts, A. Dufour, & D. Steyn (Eds.), *The critical link: Interpreters in the community* (pp. 1–3). Amsterdam, The Netherlands: John Benjamins.

Hatim, B., & Mason, I. (1990). *Discourse and the translator.* New York: Longman.

Hatton, D. C., & Webb, T. (1993). Information transmission in bilingual, bicultural contexts: A field study of community health nurses and interpreters. *Journal of Community Health Nursing, 10,* 137–147.

Hogue, C. J. R., Hargraves, M. A., Collins, K. S., & Fund, C. (2000). *Minority health in America: Findings and policy implications from the Commonwealth Fund Minority Health Survey.* Baltimore, MD: Johns Hopkins University Press.

Hsieh, E. (2002). Necessary changes in translation ideology. 翻譯學研究集刊 *Fan I Hsueh Yen Chiu Chi K'an [Studies of Translation and Interpretation], 7,* 399–435.

Hsieh, E. (2007). Interpreters as co-diagnosticians: Overlapping roles and services between providers and interpreters. *Social Science & Medicine, 64,* 924–937.

Hsieh, E. (2008). "I am not a robot!" Interpreters' views of their roles in health care settings. *Qualitative Health Research, 18,* 1367–1383.

Hsieh, E. (2013). Health literacy and patient empowerment: The role of medical interpreters in bilingual health communication. In M. J. Dutta & G. L. Kreps (Eds.), *Reducing health disparities: Communication intervention* (pp. 41–66). New York: Peter Lang.

Institute for Innovation in Health and Human Services. (2014). Blue Ridge Area Health Education Center. Retrieved March 14, 2015, from www.brahec.jmu.edu/index.html.

Jacobs, E. A., Chen, A. H., Karliner, L. S., Agger-Gupta, N., & Mutha, S. (2006). The need for more research on language barriers in health care: A proposed research agenda. *Milbank Quarterly*, 84, 111–133.

Jacobs, E. A., Diamond, L. C., & Stevak, L. (2010). The importance of teaching clinicians when and how to work with interpreters. *Patient Education and Counseling*, 78, 149–153.

Jiang, S., & Quave, C. (2013). A comparison of traditional food and health strategies among Taiwanese and Chinese immigrants in Atlanta, Georgia, USA. *Journal of Ethnobiology and Ethnomedicine*, 9, 1–14.

Jimenez, N., Moreno, G., Leng, M., Buchwald, D., & Morales, L. S. (2012). Patient-reported quality of pain treatment and use of interpreters in Spanish-speaking patients hospitalized for obstetric and gynecological care. *Journal of General Internal Medicine*, 27, 1602–1608.

Karliner, L. S., Hwang, E. S., Nickleach, D., & Kaplan, C. P. (2011). Language barriers and patient-centered breast cancer care. *Patient Education and Counseling*, 84, 223–228.

Karliner, L. S., Jacobs, E. A., Chen, A. H., & Mutha, S. (2007). Do professional interpreters improve clinical care for patients with limited English proficiency? A systematic review of the literature. *Health Services Research*, 42, 727–754.

Kaufert, J. M., & Koolage, W. W. (1984). Role conflict among 'culture brokers': The experience of native Canadian medical interpreters. *Social Science & Medicine*, 18, 283–286.

Kaufert, J. M., & Putsch, R. W., III. (1997). Communication through interpreters in healthcare: Ethical dilemmas arising from differences in class, culture, language, and power. *The Journal of Clinical Ethics*, 8, 71–87.

Kaufert, J. M., Putsch, R. W., III, & Lavallée, M. (1999). End-of-life decision making among Aboriginal Canadians: Interpretation, mediation, and discord in the communication of "bad news". *Journal of Palliative Care*, 15, 31–38.

Kelly, L. G. (1979). *The true interpreter: A history of translation theory and practice in the West.* New York: St. Martin's Press.

Lang, R. (1976). Orderlies as interpreters in Papua New Guinea. *Papua New Guinea Medical Journal*, 18, 172–177.

Launer, J. (1978). Taking medical histories through interpreters: Practice in a Nigerian outpatient department. *British Medical Journal*, 2, 934.

Leanza, Y. (2005). Roles of community interpreters in pediatrics as seen by interpreters, physicians and researchers. *Interpreting*, 7, 167–192.

Lee, K. C., Winickoff, J. P., Kim, M. K., Campbell, E. G., Betancourt, J. R., Park, E. R., … Weissman, J. S. (2006). Resident physicians' use of professional and nonprofessional interpreters: A national survey. *Journal of the American Medical Association*, 296, 1050–1053.

Lindholm, M., Hargraves, J. L., Ferguson, W. J., & Reed, G. (2012). Professional language interpretation and inpatient length of stay and readmission rates. *Journal of General Internal Medicine*, 27, 1294–1299.

Lion, K. C., Rafton, S. A., Shafii, J., Brownstein, D., Michel, E., Tolman, M., & Ebel, B. E. (2013). Association between language, serious adverse events, and length of stay among hospitalized children. *Hospital Pediatrics*, 3, 219–225.

McKee, M. M., & Paasche-Orlow, M. K. (2012). Health literacy and the disenfranchised: The importance of collaboration between limited English proficiency and health literacy researchers. *Journal of Health Communication*, 17, 7–12.

Meeuwesen, L. (2012). Language barriers in migrant health care: A blind spot. *Patient Education and Counseling*, 86, 135–136.

Meeuwesen, L., van den Brink-Muinen, A., & Hofstede, G. (2009). Can dimensions of national culture predict cross-national differences in medical communication? *Patient Education and Counseling*, 75, 58–66.

Mendoza, A. d. (1548). *Ordenanzas y copilación de leyes*. Mexico: Juan Pablos.

Metzger, M. (1999). *Sign language interpreting: Deconstructing the myth of neutrality*. Washington, DC: Gallaudet University Press.

Miller, K. E., Martell, Z. L., Pazdirek, L., Caruth, M., & Lopez, D. (2005). The role of interpreters in psychotherapy with refugees: An exploratory study. *American Journal of Orthopsychiatry*, 75, 27–39.

Morgan, L. (1998). Making the connection: Healthcare interpreters bridge the language gap. *Nurseweek (California Statewide Edition)*, 11, 9.

Morris, R. (1995). The moral dilemmas of court interpreting. *The Translator*, 1, 25–46.

National Council on Interpreting in Health Care. (2004). A national code of ethics for interpreters in health care. Retrieved March 14, 2015, from www.rwjf.org/content/dam/farm/toolkits/toolkits/2004/rwjf26946.

National Network of Libraries of Medicine. (2013). Health literacy. Retrieved March 14, 2015, from http://nnlm.gov/outreach/consumer/hlthlit.html.

Niska, H. (2007). From helpers to professionals: Training of community interpreters in Sweden. In C. Wadensjö, B. E. Dimitrova, & A.-L. Nilsson (Eds.), *The critical link 4: Professionalisation of interpreting in the community* (pp. 297–310). Amsterdam, The Netherlands: John Benjamins.

Parsons, S. K., Saiki-Craighill, S., Mayer, D. K., Sullivan, A. M., Jeruss, S., Terrin, N., ... Block, S. (2007). Telling children and adolescents about their cancer diagnosis: Cross-cultural comparisons between pediatric oncologists in the US and Japan. *Psycho-Oncology*, 16, 60–68.

Parsons, T. (1951). *The social system*. Glencoe, IL: The Free Press.

Phelan, M. (2012). Medical interpreting and the law in the European Union. *European Journal of Health Law*, 19, 333–353.

Pöchhacker, F. (1999). "Getting organized": The evolution of community interpreting. *Interpreting*, 4, 125–140.

Pöchhacker, F. (2007). Critical linking up: Kinship and convergence in interpreting studies. In C. Wadensjö, B. E. Dimitrova, & A.-L. Nilsson (Eds.), *The critical link 4: Professionalisation of interpreting in the community* (pp. 11–23). Amsterdam, The Netherlands: John Benjamins.

Pöchhacker, F. (2013). *Introducing interpreting studies*. New York: Routledge.

Pöchhacker, F., & Kadric, M. (1999). The hospital cleaner as healthcare interpreter: A case study. *Translator*, 5, 161–178.

Pöchhacker, F., & Shlesinger, M. (2002). Introduction. In F. Pöchhacker & M. Shlesinger (Eds.), *The interpreting studies reader* (pp. 1–12). New York: Routledge.

Pöchhacker, F., & Shlesinger, M. (2005). Introduction: Discourse-based research on healthcare interpreting. *Interpreting*, 7, 157–165.

Price, J. (1975). Foreign language interpreting in psychiatric practice. *Australian and New Zealand Journal of Psychiatry*, 9, 263–267.

Rawls, A. W. (1987). The interaction order sui generis: Goffman's contribution to social theory. *Sociological Theory, 5*, 136–149.

The Registry of Interpreters for the Deaf. (2013). About RID Overview. Retrieved March 14, 2015, from www.rid.org/about-rid/.

Richie, J. (1964). Using an interpreter effectively. *Nursing Outlook, 12*, 27–29.

Ricoeur, P. (1976). *Interpretation theory: Discourse and the surplus of meaning.* Fort Worth, TX: Texas Christian University Press.

Ricoeur, P. (1981). *Hermeneutics and the human sciences: Essays on language, action and interpretation* (J. B. Thompson, Trans. J. B. Thompson Ed.). Cambridge University Press.

Roat, C. E. (1996). *Bridging the gap: A basic training for medical interpreters.* Seattle, WA: Cross Cultural Health Care Program.

Roat, C. E., Putsch, R. W., III, & Lucero, C. (1997). *Bridging the gap over the phone: A basic training for telephone interpreters serving medical settings.* Seattle, WA: Cross Cultural Health Care Program.

Roberts, R. P. (1997). Community interpreting today and tomorrow. In S. E. Carr, R. P. Roberts, A. Dufour, & D. Steyn (Eds.), *The critical link: Interpreters in the community* (pp. 7–26). Amsterdam, The Netherlands: John Benjamins.

Scheper-Hughes, N. (1992). *Death without weeping: The violence of everyday life in Brazil.* Berkeley, CA: University of California Press.

Schmidt, S. J. (1984). The fiction is that reality exists: A constructivist model of reality, fiction, and literature. *Poetics Today, 5*, 253–274.

Schouten, B. C., & Meeuwesen, L. (2006). Cultural differences in medical communication: A review of the literature. *Patient Education and Counseling, 64*, 21–34.

Seeleman, C., Essink-Bot, M.-L., Selleger, V., & Bonke, B. (2012). Authors' response to letter from Bond et al. – The role of ad-hoc interpreters in teaching communication skills with ethnic minorities. *Medical Teacher, 34*, 81–82.

Sentell, T., & Braun, K. L. (2012). Low health literacy, limited English proficiency, and health status in Asians, Latinos, and other racial/ethnic groups in California. *Journal of Health Communication, 17*, 82–99.

Tang, J. (2008). Professionalization. In W. A. Darity, Jr. (Ed.), *International encyclopedia of the social sciences* (2nd ed., Vol. 6, pp. 515–517). New York: Macmillan.

Thornton, J. D., Pham, K., Engelberg, R. A., Jackson, J. C., & Curtis, J. R. (2009). Families with limited English proficiency receive less information and support in interpreted intensive care unit family conferences. *Critical Care Medicine, 37*, 89–95.

Todres, L., Galvin, K., & Dahlberg, K. (2007). Lifeworld-led healthcare: Revisiting a humanising philosophy that integrates emerging trends. *Medicine, Health Care and Philosophy, 10*, 53–63.

Tracy, K. (2013). *Everyday talk: Building and reflecting identities* (2nd ed.). New York: Guilford.

Treviño, A. J. (Ed.). (2001). *Talcott Parsons today: His theory and legacy in contemporary sociology.* Cumnor Hill, Oxford: Rowman & Littlefield.

Venuti, L. (2008). *The translator's invisibility: A history of translation* (2nd ed.). New York: Routledge.

Wadensjö, C. (1998). *Interpreting as interaction.* London: Longman.

Waitzkin, H. (1991). *The politics of medical encounters: How patients and doctors deal with social problems.* New Haven, CT: Yale University Press.

Washington Courts. (1989). Rule 11.2: Code of conduct for court interpreters. Retrieved March 14, 2015, from www.courts.wa.gov/court_rules/?fa=court_rules.rulesPDF&ruleId=gagr11.2&pdf=1.

Watermeyer, J. (2011). "She will hear me": How a flexible interpreting style enables patients to manage the inclusion of interpreters in mediated pharmacy interactions. *Health Communication, 26,* 71–81.

Woloshin, S., Schwartz, L. M., Katz, S. J., & Welch, H. G. (1997). Is language a barrier to the use of preventive services? *Journal of General Internal Medicine, 12,* 472–477.

Wong, W. W., Gabriel, A., Maxwell, G. P., & Gupta, S. C. (2012). Bleeding risks of herbal, homeopathic, and dietary supplements: A hidden nightmare for plastic surgeons? *Aesthetic Surgery Journal, 32,* 332–346.

Youdelman, M. K. (2008). The medical tongue: US laws and policies on language access. *Health Affairs, 27,* 424–433.

2

EMERGING TRENDS AND CORRESPONDING CHALLENGES IN BILINGUAL HEALTH RESEARCH

Individuals' language-discordant status and low health literacy are two important predictors of poor health outcomes, including patient satisfaction, resource utilization, healthcare delivery, provider–patient communication, and health status (Berkman, Sheridan, Donahue, Halpern, & Crotty, 2011; Ramirez, Engel, & Tang, 2008). In addition, individuals with limited English proficiency (LEP) in the United States often suffer disproportionally from low health literacy (McKee & Paasche-Orlow, 2012; Sentell & Braun, 2012). In two different studies, researchers found that individuals' language-discordant status is a stronger predictor than their low health literacy status for poor health communication and problematic health outcomes (Sentell & Braun, 2012; Sudore et al., 2009). These findings suggest that the impacts of language barriers are greater than the impacts of low health literacy for poor health outcomes.[1]

Understanding the correlations between language barriers and health outcomes, however, does not mean we understand how language barriers may influence health communication and health outcomes. After noting that health literacy level has no impact on language-discordant patients' experiences of poor communication, researchers were not sure whether the finding was "a result of the 'floor effect' (overall communication was poor for the entire Spanish discordant subgroup) or could suggest that interpreters, while not a panacea, level the playing field with respect to [health literacy] and verbal communication among Spanish discordant patient–physician dyads" (Sudore et al., 2009, p. 401). If interpreters were to "level the playing field," they would have to influence the process and content of provider–patient interactions, particularly for patients with low health literacy.

Some recent research findings suggest that there is some validity in the latter interpretation in Sudore et al.'s study. For example, in some studies, researchers found that the quality of healthcare services and health outcomes of interpreted patients are equivalent to and, at times, better than those of English-speaking patients (Bernstein et al., 2002; Gany, Leng, et al., 2007; Hampers & McNulty, 2002; Tocher & Larson, 1998). These findings are intriguing because language-concordant provider–patient interactions are often conceptualized as the gold standard for provider–patient interactions. However, low health literacy is a common problem in the United States, where 36 percent of the population has limited health literacy, and specific populations are at high risk (e.g., immigrants, low-income individuals, minorities, and the elderly) (National Network of Libraries of Medicine, 2013). An interpreter-as-conduit model is likely to maintain patients' barriers to care by replicating their low health literacy in provider–patient interactions because the model requires interpreters to adopt a passive, non-interfering role in medical encounters. However, interpreters as communicative experts in bilingual, cross-cultural care may be able to anticipate patients' communicative needs, convey providers' therapeutic goals, and facilitate provider–patient interactions in a way that enhances other speakers' abilities to seek, process, and utilize health information to make appropriate health decisions. It is possible for interpreter-mediated medical encounters to be comparable and even better than language-concordant medical encounters. The challenges faced by researchers and practitioners are to identify how such a process can take place effectively and appropriately.

Although researchers and practitioners generally agree on the positive impacts interpreters have on bilingual health care, little is known about the pathways and processes for accomplishing these positive outcomes. Somehow, the processes by which the interpreter shapes the quality and process of care are simply taken for granted and yet remain a mystery. To advance the theory and practice of bilingual health care, it is important that we move beyond the conduit model that has dominated the codes of ethics and professional training for healthcare interpreters.

A. Moving beyond the Conduit Model

The National Council on Interpreting in Health Care (NCIHC) noted that interpreter-as-conduit is defined "solely by the core function of 'message transmission,' performed by a third party, whose presence, ideally, is as 'invisible' as possible" (Avery, 2001, p. 6). Many researchers and practitioners traditionally have put great emphasis on the importance of and the necessity for interpreters to act as conduits (Launer, 1978; Singy & Guex, 2005). Several physician researchers have continued to categorize any discrepancy between the original and interpreted texts as errors (e.g., omission, addition, substitution, and editorialization; Flores, Abreu, Barone, Bachur, & Lin, 2012; Gany, Kapelusznik, et al., 2007). When any deviation to an original text is marked as an error, interpreters are confined in a conduit role, as the only "correct" interpreting is the one that provides a direct word-for-word linguistic relay of the original information. In other words, interpreters are conceptualized as and expected to be passive participants in the communicative process, providing a relay of information from one language to another with minimal interference or personal judgment. This conduit approach fails to recognize the nature of language and the reality of interpreting (Dysart-Gale, 2005; Hsieh, 2009).

As discussed in Chapter 1, the ideology of an interpreter as a neutral, faithful, non-thinking, and passive participant in provider–patient interactions is also reflected in the healthcare interpreters' codes of ethics and training (Dysart-Gale, 2005; Kaufert & Putsch, 1997). Healthcare interpreters even adopt unique communicative styles (e.g., reduced nonverbal interactions with other speakers and minimized emotional expression) to minimize their presence in medical encounters (Hsieh, 2006a, 2008). The prevalence of the conduit model is also reflected in the public's attitudes and expectations for interpreters, envisioning interpreters as neutral translating machines (Brämberg & Sandman, 2013; Fatahi, Hellstrom, Skott, & Mattsson, 2008; Rosenberg, Leanza, & Seller, 2007). In short, interpreter-as-conduit minimizes the complexity of interpreting processes by trivializing, if not ignoring, the complexity of interpreters' roles and functions.

The recent literature, however, indicates several important and emerging trends in conceptualizing bilingual health care. As researchers from a wide variety of disciplines successfully challenge the blind preference for interpreter-as-conduit, a new world is opened to researchers of healthcare interpreting. It is important to note that the identification of these emerging trends in this chapter is not a result of a quantitative analysis based on publication frequencies (cf. Brisset, Leanza, & Laforest, 2013). Rather, the trends highlighted here represent important shifts in conceptualizing bilingual health care, providing insights into research questions and directions that have been largely ignored in the past literature. While these trends may be interconnected, each promises distinctive and exciting research possibilities for theorists and practitioners.

The four emerging trends presented in this chapter are:

- Trend 1: Identifying the complexity of clinical demands
- Trend 2: Exploring contextual factors in bilingual health care
- Trend 3: Examining healthcare interpreting as a coordinated achievement
- Trend 4: Recognizing interpreters as active participants.

The chapter is largely formulated as a review that aims to provide a theoretical framework for bilingual health communication. The Model of Bilingual Health Communication (presented in Chapter 5) will be built according to these underlying principles of the latest research.

B. Trend 1: Complexity of Clinical Demands

The first trend in bilingual health care emerges as researchers and practitioners acknowledge the unique characteristics of healthcare interpreting that set it apart from other forms of interpreting. Rather than focusing on the values embedded in traditional views about interpreting (e.g., accuracy, faithfulness, and neutrality), researchers seek to examine how health services present distinctive demands and expectations that shape interpreting practices. By recognizing the complexity and reality of healthcare practices, researchers have begun to address two puzzles in bilingual health care, which I will discuss shortly. Two themes support the development of this trend: (a) the reality of interpreter diversity in healthcare settings, and (b) providers' clinical decision-making regarding interpreters.

The Reality of Interpreter Diversity in Healthcare Settings

The first puzzle is the conflicting findings about the impact of healthcare interpreters (Hsieh, 2006b). Up until the late 1990s, most studies treated healthcare interpreters as a single category, with minimal discussion about the types of interpreters included in the studies. Several studies have provided evidence of the benefits of providing interpreter services, arguing that when LEP patients have access to interpreters, their experiences with healthcare services and health outcomes are often equivalent to, if not better than, English-speaking patients (Andrulis, Goodman, & Pryor, 2002; Bernstein et al., 2002). However, other studies observed negative impacts, noting that interpreters were not sufficient in addressing LEP patients' experiences of health disparities as these patients often have their comments ignored, are less likely to receive referrals, and are less satisfied with their care even in areas unrelated to language (Baker & Hayes, 1997; Baker, Parker, Williams, Coates, & Pitkin, 1996; Sarver & Baker, 2000). Hsieh (2006b) argued that the conflicting findings were attributable to a failure to recognize the diversity of interpreters, noting that different types of interpreters have different impacts in the dynamics and processes of communication. Since then, there has been an increasing trend to identify specific types of interpreter and even to compare different types of interpreters in research publications (Brisset et al., 2013).

In recent years, several researchers and providers have shifted away from the argument that only professional interpreters should be used in healthcare settings as such an expectation is highly dependent on the patient's language and the service location/hours (Bischoff & Hudelson, 2010a). Rather, researchers and practitioners have argued that the ability of providers to work with different types of healthcare interpreter (e.g., family members, telephone interpreters, and in-person interpreters) is critical to the efficiency, quality, and informal economy of bilingual health care (Rosenberg, Seller, & Leanza, 2008). Although several recent reviews have noted the benefits of professional interpreters (Flores, 2005; Karliner, Jacobs, Chen, & Mutha, 2007), such observations do not equate to the conclusion that professional interpreters are universally better than nonprofessional interpreters.

There is evidence to suggest that professional interpreters and nonprofessional interpreters, such as family interpreters, do behave differently in medical encounters (Butow et al., 2011; Leanza, Boivin, & Rosenberg, 2010). However, these studies also demonstrate that professional interpreters are not necessarily better. For example, although professional interpreters are less likely to produce nonequivalent interpreting than family interpreters, their nonequivalent interpreting has a higher proportion of negative consequences than that of family interpreters (26 percent vs. 21 percent; Butow et al., 2012). In fact, several studies suggest that family interpreters may be better at performing certain tasks (e.g., patient advocacy, cultural brokering, taking medical history, and gaining patients' trust) depending on contexts and circumstances (Angelelli, 2010; Butow et al., 2011; Ho, 2008; Leanza et al., 2010).

By recognizing the variety of interpreters (e.g., in-person vs. telephone vs. family interpreters) available in healthcare settings, researchers can begin to explore the impacts of different types of interpreter on patient satisfaction, provider expectations, patient–interpreter relationships, institutional costs, and clinical consequences (MacFarlane et al., 2009; Messias, McDowell, & Estrada, 2009). As researchers begin to critically examine the types of interpreters and their corresponding impacts, researchers and practitioners can move beyond an ideological debate and preference for professional interpreters and provide evidence-based findings about *how* different types of interpreters can facilitate and/or compromise the delivery of care. Because this is still an early trend, the literature on comparing different types of interpreters has often been limited to interview data. As a result, little is known about the specific processes through which different types of interpreters influence provider–patient interactions, providers' or patients' communicative competence, and the quality of care during actual medical encounters. Because researchers have noted that participants' impressions about their own and others' performances in medical encounters often differ from their behaviors (Cegala, Gade, Broz, & McClure, 2004), it is important for researchers to examine data of actual interactions.

Some of the early findings are promising and exciting. For example, Rosenberg and colleagues found that not only do family interpreters and professional interpreters view their roles and functions differently in interpreter-mediated medical encounters, providers actually hold different expectations for family interpreters versus professional interpreters (Rosenberg et al., 2007, 2008). In addition, the research team found that when working with a professional interpreter (as opposed to a family interpreter), providers are (a) more likely to engage patients in emotion-related talk (Rosenberg, Richard, Lussier, & Shuldiner, 2011), but (b) are also more likely to interrupt a patient's disclosure about their Lifeworld concerns (Leanza et al., 2010). The findings are intriguing: While they do not suggest a consistent pattern, they provide early evidence of the different strategies and behaviors providers adopt when working with different types of interpreters. It is important for researchers to examine how and why providers develop different styles when working with different types of interpreters and how such practices impact the quality of care.

Providers' Clinical Decisions Regarding Interpreters

The second puzzle of bilingual health communication is the underutilization of professional interpreters despite the fact that since the late 1970s there have been various federal and state legal requirements for healthcare facilities to provide interpreters to LEP patients (Youdelman, 2008). If providers do not consider the use of (professional) interpreters necessary or valuable, they are unlikely to use them. Recognizing the importance of the provider's role in interpreter-mediated encounters, several researchers have examined providers' decision-making processes and the basis of their assessments. Some recent findings are alarming. For example, 56 percent of residents who self-reported to have non-proficient clinical Spanish reported comfort in using Spanish in straightforward clinical scenarios, and 10 percent reported comfort in clinical scenarios with legal implications (Lion et al., 2013). In another study, among the 83 percent of residents who reported less than conversational Spanish language skills, 53 percent had taken a history and/or provided medical advice directly to Spanish-speaking patients without any form of interpreting (Yawman et al., 2006). These findings are situated in the reality that although resident physicians recognize the value of intercultural training and the prevalence of language-discordant patients in their practice, about one-third to half of them, across various specialties, also reported little training in cross-cultural care (Thompson, Hernandez, Cowden, Sisson, & Moon, 2013; Weissman et al., 2005). Researchers have argued that providers often do not have accurate assessments about their ability to provide cross-cultural care (Chun, Jackson, Lin, & Park, 2010; Lion et al., 2013).

Multiple studies have demonstrated that providers continue to underutilize professional interpreters. In the United States, professional interpreters are consistently used for fewer than 20 percent of LEP patients (Ginde, Sullivan, Corel, Caceres, & Camargo, 2010; Schenker, Pérez-Stable, Nickleach, & Karliner, 2011). The literature reports that time pressure and lack of availability and/or accessibility were often cited as primary reasons for providers' underutilization of professional interpreters (Lee et al., 2006; Ramirez et al., 2008). However, although Massachusetts passed a state law in 2001 mandating access to professional healthcare interpreters for patients with limited English proficiency in emergency departments, researchers found little change in emergency physicians' likelihood of using professional interpreters, with 15 percent of LEP patients receiving professional interpreters in 2002 and 18 percent in 2008 (Ginde et al., 2010). The reality is that providers often underutilize professional interpreters even when they perceive benefits to using them and when they are readily available (Diamond, Schenker, Curry, Bradley, & Fernandez, 2009).

Instead, providers often rely on family/friend interpreters, ad hoc interpreters, and bilingual staff. Although some researchers argue that providers are "getting by" with other forms of interpreter (Diamond et al., 2009; Schenker et al., 2011), others suggest that providers' choice of interpreters may involve multiple factors (Diamond et al., 2009; Hsieh, 2015; Hsieh, Pitaloka, & Johnson, 2013; Locatis et al., 2010). In addition, providers' areas of expertise may also influence the type of interpreter they prefer to work with. For example, a provider in mental health care may prefer professional interpreters over family interpreters due to concerns about patient privacy and treatment efficacy; in contrast, an oncologist may feel that emotional support is more critical for the current tasks and decide that a family interpreter can serve multiple functions effectively (Hsieh et al., 2013). These findings demonstrate that in clinical practices, providers' decisions about the type of interpreter to use in different types of medical encounters would be a calculated process rather than an automatic response/preference for professional interpreters.

B.1. Addressing Challenges in Trend 1

In summary, this emerging trend highlights the complexity of healthcare practices and shifts attention away from interpreters' linguistic performances. Instead, researchers acknowledge the unique characteristics of healthcare settings that shape the processes and outcomes of healthcare interpreting. A crucial aspect of this perspective is researchers' willingness to challenge taken-for-granted assumptions to critically examine the practices of bilingual health care and to develop meaningful and practical solutions.

For example, rather than assuming that professional interpreters are universally superior to other types of interpreters, researchers aim to provide evidence-based arguments about the different impacts different types of interpreters have. In other words, this approach allows researchers and practitioners to develop meaningful practice guidelines for different types of interpreters by investigating (a) the communicative strategies that may be used by different types of interpreters, (b) effective strategies to coordinate with different interpreters, and (c) the limitations and ethical boundaries of different types of interpreters.

Similarly, rather than simply attributing the underutilization of professional interpreters to providers' mistakes or personal excuses, researchers should examine the interpersonal and organizational dynamics of bilingual medical encounters and explore the various factors that are critical in shaping the communicative process of healthcare interpreting. It is important to note that rather than presuming that certain types of interpreters or certain ways of interpreting are better, researchers who are influenced by this trend seek to generate evidence-based findings to support their claim.

Finally, because the quality of interpreting is situated in health contexts, researchers and practitioners can now consider various issues that may not be typically considered in other forms of interpreting. For example, even though family members are not typically considered to be primary participants in medical encounters, researchers have raised concerns that, compared to English-speaking patients' family members, LEP patients' family members receive less emotional support from the clinicians even when an interpreter is provided (Thornton, Pham, Engelberg, Jackson, & Curtis, 2009). Imposing professional interpreters on patients who express a preference for a family interpreter may be problematic, if not unethical, because it fails to respect the patient's cultural and interpersonal choices (Ho, 2008). On the other hand, physicians face unique concerns that involve institutional standards (e.g., medical ethics) as well as personal vulnerability (e.g., malpractice risks) that may motivate them to override patient preferences (Gadon, Balch, & Jacobs, 2007; Harshman, 1984). In short, the first emerging trend opens up various viewpoints to examine the quality and effectiveness of bilingual health care by highlighting the complexity and reality of healthcare practices. Identifying the complexity of clinical demands brings into focus various (new) criteria that are essential in evaluating the outcomes of interpreter-mediated medical encounters.

C. Trend 2: Contextual Factors in Bilingual Health Care

Contextual factors are critical in bilingual health communication. By raising the issue of context, researchers argued that

> the focal event cannot be properly understood, interpreted appropriately, or described in a relevant fashion, unless one looks beyond the event itself to other phenomena (for example cultural setting, speech situation, shared background assumptions) within which the event is embedded, or alternatively that features of the talk itself invoke particular background assumptions relevant to the organization of subsequent interaction.
>
> *(Goodwin & Duranti, 1992, p. 3)*

In other words, contexts provide the interpretive frame to understand the meanings that emerge during interpreter-mediated medical encounters.

While contextual factors appear to be a large category of issues, this emerging trend draws attention to larger contexts, including cultural, socioeconomic, interpersonal, environmental, organizational/institutional, legal, procedural, and ethical contexts. Although there are a wide variety of issues involved in this trend, it is important to note that these considerations would not arise in a world that assumes that the quality of interpreting is solely dependent on interpreters' abilities to provide word-to-word machine-like relay of information from one language to another. To recognize these factors in shaping meanings of cross-cultural care is to acknowledge the diverse forces that shape the content and process of interpreter-mediated medical encounters. Although this line of research has been growing rapidly, the specific factors that have been identified and systematically developed are still limited. Some of the contextual factors that have emerged in the literature include interpersonal trust (Brisset et al., 2013; Hsieh, Ju, & Kong, 2010; Robb & Greenhalgh, 2006), institutional policies (Jacobs, Diamond, & Stevak, 2010), and modes of interpreting (Locatis et al., 2010; Price, Pérez-Stable, Nickleach, Lopez, & Karliner, 2012). Rather than providing a comprehensive review of all contextual factors, I will focus on two factors that are likely to shape the future development of the field: (a) areas of medical specialty and (b) interpersonal relationships.

Areas of Medical Specialty

Although healthcare interpreting is a fledgling subfield within the larger field of (community) interpreting, the literature on bilingual health care has experienced exponential growth and has been challenging traditional thinking about interpreting studies since the early 2000s (Brisset et al., 2013). The first contextual factor mentioned here, area of medical specialty, is often implied but rarely systematically examined in this literature.

If interpreters were simply viewed as tools or translation machines, then their performance should not differ depending on context (Hsieh & Kramer, 2012). After all, a hammer will always be used as a hammer in all contexts. To consider that the areas of medical specialty can or should influence an interpreter's performance is to argue that the "preferred" interpreting style or performance may differ depending on the clinical context. Knowledge of the specialized vocabulary that marks various medical subfields, the types of patients involved, and the types of provider–patient dynamics and relationships expected is essential to high quality healthcare interpreting.

As researchers have become more sensitive to the types of interpreters included in their studies, they have also become more aware of the clinical settings in which they conduct their studies. Many studies specifically identify the clinical setting(s) in which their investigation took place, including pediatrics (Abbe, Simon, Angiolillo, Ruccione, & Kodish, 2006; Cunningham, Cushman, Akuete-Penn, & Meyer, 2008; DeCamp, Kuo, Flores, O'Connor, & Minkovitz, 2013; Flores et al., 2003; Kuo, O'Connor, Flores, & Minkovitz, 2007), emergency departments (Flores et al., 2012; Ginde, Clark, & Camargo, 2009; Grover, Deakyne, Bajaj, & Roosevelt, 2012; Hampers & McNulty, 2002; Meischke, Chavez, Bradley, Rea, & Eisenberg, 2010; Weissman et al., 2005), and palliative care (Kaufert, 1999; Roat, Kinderman, & Fernandez, 2011; Schenker, Fernandez, Kerr, O'Riordan, & Pantilat, 2012; Thornton et al., 2009). However, these studies fell short in exploring how the distinctive characteristics and provider–patient dynamics of pediatrics, emergency medicine, or palliative care may present special influences or challenges to interpreter-mediated medical encounters. Nevertheless, specifying types of clinical contexts raises the question as to whether and how the specific clinical context may influence participant expectations and performance in clinical encounters.

For example, family physicians or pediatric physicians often share long-term relationships with their patients, helping them to address health concerns based on patients' life choices and personal preferences (e.g., acne treatment, birth control, or treatment for erectile dysfunction). Provider–patient trust is essential to providers' ability to influence patients' decision-making and health management (e.g., a 13-year-old who wishes to have access to birth control). In contrast, a pathologist may rarely interact with a patient. But when they do, it's typically a one-time event to discuss the content of a pathology report (Gutmann, 2003). Although a patient may experience great anxiety, a pathologist can be generous and flexible with their time to help a patient understand diagnosis-related complexity or uncertainty. On the other hand, a paramedic may need to quickly assess a patient's condition in chaotic, traumatizing situations to provide accurate and appropriate treatment. The distinctive needs of the different specialties and their universal role as healthcare providers present researchers with challenges and opportunities to examine commonalities and differences in interpreting needs and delivery.

So far, in the field of bilingual health care, it appears that it is only in mental health care that researchers and practitioners have presented systematic discussions on how its clinical contexts impose unique challenges and expectations on interpreters (d'Ardenne & Farmer, 2009; Jackson, Zatzick, Harris, & Gardiner, 2008; Tribe & Lane, 2009). This is likely because mental health providers are particularly sensitive to individuals' use of language as well as cultural influences pertaining to the diagnostic and treatment process. Several researchers have argued that interpreting in mental health settings requires interpreters to adopt a much more active and aggressive role in assisting providers to understand patients' (culturally based) symptoms and provide culturally sensitive treatments (Tribe & Lane, 2009).

For example, it is common for Taiwanese and Japanese women who have had miscarriages or abortions to talk about haunting, menacing fetuses (i.e., their lost children) that follow them everywhere and demand their regular attention, such as temple offerings (Hardacre, 1997; Moskowitz, 2001). Without knowing this common folk belief, an American psychiatrist is likely to diagnose a Taiwanese or Japanese woman as having hallucinations (i.e., a psychotic disorder). However, few would diagnose an American patient with a psychotic disorder if he or she claimed to talk to a parent who died years ago or believed that certain events happened because the dead parent was "looking after" him/her.

From this perspective, culture is critical in shaping the meanings of one's experiences, defining what is ill or not (Castillo, 1997). For example, although sadness and suffering may be diagnosed as a symptom of depression in Western cultures, people from non-Western cultures may view these emotions as an empowerment of their cultural identities rather than an illness condition (Pitaloka, 2014; Thomas, Shabbir, & Yasmeen, 2010). Without realizing the cultural differences, a provider may mistakenly diagnose a cultural experience as a clinical symptom.

Nevertheless, in a large survey, mental health providers placed less value on the ability of interpreters to assist patients outside of medical encounters than providers in emergency medicine, obstetrics/gynecology (ob/gyn), and nursing. They also placed less value on interpreters' ability to advocate for patients than providers in emergency medicine and nursing (Hsieh et al., 2013). This reflects mental health providers' concerns about patient–interpreter bonding and its potential impact on patient–provider relationships and their therapeutic goals. By examining the specific contexts of mental health care and highlighting the potentially competing expectations held by providers, researchers are able to identify the specific behaviors that are essential to successful interpreter-mediated encounters and propose realistic expectations and guidelines to facilitate best practices in the field.

In addition, a recent topic to emerge in this set of literature concerns interpreters' emotion work when they work with refugees or patients who have had traumatic experiences (Green, Sperlinger, & Carswell, 2012; Johnson, Thompson, & Downs, 2009; Splevins, Cohen, Joseph, Murray, & Bowley, 2010), highlighting the potential emotional distress (e.g., burnout and trauma) experienced by interpreters in these settings. I find this topic particularly exciting because it signals that the field of bilingual health care is maturing. It is only when researchers and practitioners can actively acknowledge interpreters' active roles and presence in a medical encounter that we can begin to recognize and discuss the impacts and consequences of such practices.

Finally, it is important to remember that despite the attention to the unique needs, expectations, and conditions imposed by each medical specialty, there may still be universal needs and expectations across all healthcare subfields for bilingual health communication. In particular, researchers continue to report that physicians still hold the general expectation that interpreters should assume a neutral conduit role (Abbe et al., 2006; Fatahi et al., 2008). This finding is also supported by a recent survey in which providers from different specialties appeared to hold similar opinions about interpreters adopting a neutral, emotionally detached, and independent professional role (Hsieh et al., 2013). While the literature has argued that the interpreter-as-conduit model is unrealistic and problematic, researchers need to explore if there are universal expectations held by all providers and how these expectations may influence bilingual health care.

In other words, I believe that the complexity presented by diverse areas of medical specialty is a growing theme as researchers reflect critically on how differing clinical contexts impose different standards of "good" interpreting practices and expectations of appropriate interpreter performances. In addition, researchers can now reexamine how these different standards and expectations may influence interpreters' behaviors (and even patients' health status). Future research in this direction will need to further explore organizational and ethical guidelines for different medical specialties and to investigate to what extent interpreters can effectively respond to these different standards and expectations.

Interpersonal Relationships

The *ongoing relationship* between the provider, the interpreter, and the patient (and the patients' family members) is another contextual factor that is essential to the quality of bilingual health care. Although it has been neglected in the literature, several recent studies have suggested that this is an important contextual factor in bilingual health care. In a recent review, Brisset and colleagues concluded that "[b]uilding *trust* and *respect* (recognition) is a prerequisite to establishing a collaboration that allows all protagonists to find their place in the relational dynamic.... Trust and control issues take place within the relation (and its dynamics) between patients, interpreters and practitioners" (2013, p. 136).

Moving beyond an understanding of relationships as static phenomena, recent literature highlights the dynamic, emergent and changing nature of interpersonal relationships. For example, although a provider may have concerns about a family interpreter's lack of illness-related terminology and knowledge, he or she may eventually develop trust because the family interpreter has learned the relevant terms and knowledge by acting as a caregiver for the patient outside of the medical encounter (Hsieh et al., 2010). Although the industry traditionally tries to avoid assigning the same interpreter to the same patient multiple times, both providers and interpreters have argued that ongoing working relationships help to improve collaboration between the patient and the medical team (Hsieh et al., 2010). In a recent documentary, deaf breast cancer patients explained the importance and value of having interpreters who are familiar with their medical history as well as emotional needs as they navigate the complex medical system (Allen, 2011).

Professional interpreters' ability to develop trust with providers and patients over time is essential to their management of provider–patient interactions (Edwards, Temple, & Alexander, 2005; Robb & Greenhalgh, 2006). On the other hand, an in-person professional interpreter may not be trusted by a provider if they have been informed about that interpreter's alleged prior misconduct (Hsieh et al., 2010). Similarly, despite providers' preference for professional interpreters, researchers have argued that using family interpreters may be ethically necessary due to patients' long-term relationships and social obligations/responsibilities with the interpreter (Angelelli, 2010; Ho, 2008). Because the provider–patient–interpreter triad often works across many medical encounters, it is important to examine how such a relationship influences their coordination and collaboration over the course of an illness event.

Another aspect of the provider–patient relationship that has emerged in recent literature is a concern about gender pairing in cross-cultural care. Research about physician gender and quality of care is not new in the field of medicine (Weisman & Teitelbaum, 1985). For example, several studies found that female patients preferred to have a female physician in ob/gyn settings and reported higher satisfaction than with a male physician (Plunkett, Kohli, & Milad, 2002; Roter, Geller, Bernhardt, Larson, & Doksum, 1999). While having a female physician was positively associated with women's satisfaction in emergency care, physician gender is not associated with men's satisfaction (Derose, Hays, McCaffrey, & Baker, 2001). A recent study found that when interpreters were present, the differences in patient satisfaction between gender concordant and discordant doctor–patient pairs were minimal; however, when interpreters are not present, doctor–patient gender discordance was negatively associated with the quality of provider–patient interaction (Bischoff, Hudelson, & Bovier, 2008). From this perspective, interpreter presence may serve as a moderator for the impacts of provider–patient gender concordance.

In fields of intercultural research, researchers have recommended "matching" interpreters and interview participants by ethnicity, gender, age, and other potential confounding variables in order to obtain optimal data (Wallin & Ahlstrom, 2006). However, this practice may be difficult for healthcare interpreters due to limitations in available interpreters. For example, a Spanish-speaking interpreter from Columbia may have significant cultural differences from a Spanish-speaking patient from Spain. A Mandarin Chinese-speaking patient from China may have incompatible political views to a Mandarin Chinese-speaking interpreter from Taiwan. If finding a match between language and culture between a patient and an interpreter can be difficult, a match in all potential risk factors would be near impossible. A study found that while most physicians do not have a preference for interpreters to have the same gender as they do, 53.7 percent of patients reported such a preference (Kuo & Fagan, 1999); however, the same study noted that patient–interpreter gender concordance was not associated with patient satisfaction.

As I write this, I cannot help but think of a story an ob/gyn male physician shared with me. He said that he once asked a female resident to recommend a treatment plan to an American Indian elderly patient, thinking that the physician–patient gender concordance would make the patient receptive to his recommendation. "You know what?" he laughed and said, "She just said, 'NO! I don't trust WHITE people.' It was about my race, not my gender!" Rather than thinking of gender as a static variable that may directly influence the quality of interpreter-mediated medical encounters, it may be more useful to examine how and when specific contextual variables are invoked and the corresponding impact on the quality of care (e.g., provider/interpreter gender may be a more salient concern when a patient is discussing gender-specific concerns).

C.1. Addressing Challenges in Trend 2

Researchers need to explore and identify the various contextual factors that influence interpreter-mediated medical encounters. Compared to other trends, this trend is at a very early stage. Few contextual factors have been systematically examined and theorized. However, current research has suggested great potential. The literature on mental-healthcare interpreting has provided good examples and directions for researchers to explore other clinical contexts. Healthcare interpreting is thus viewed not simply as a generic form of interpreting but as a communicative activity situated in multiple contexts. Researchers' abilities to identify and investigate specific contexts and their corresponding influences on interpreter-mediated encounters are essential to the theoretical development and practical implications of this trend.

D. Trend 3: Healthcare Interpreting as Coordinated Achievement

All participants (e.g., the provider, the interpreter, the patient, and even family members) in interpreter-mediated medical encounters can influence the process and quality of bilingual health communication (Fatahi et al., 2008; Greenhalgh, Robb, & Scambler, 2006). This trend is critical because it recognizes the impacts of others in the interpreting process. Traditionally, interpreters are viewed as the ones who are solely responsible for the quality of interpreting. However, recent studies have challenged this presumption by noting: (a) the interdependence of participant performances, (b) participants' competition and coordination for control, and (c) healthcare interpreting as a goal-oriented activity.

The Interdependence of Participant Performances

Providers', patients', and interpreters' choices of communicative styles serve specific functions and are interdependent (Roy, 2000). The quality of interpreting of untrained interpreters can vary dramatically from one setting to another. For example, "A nurse [interpreter] could do an excellent job with one physician only to have difficulties with the next one.... Every physician ... had an individual style for relating to the patient, and the nurse [interpreter] had to accommodate that style" (Elderkin-Thompson, Silver, & Waitzkin, 2001, p. 1355). Interpreters are more likely to misinterpret or to ignore a physician's questions when they are structurally more complicated (Harrison, Bhatt, Carey, & Ebden, 1988). A study found that Latino patients who use interpreters receive significantly more verbal information when a new medication is prescribed than Latino patients who do not need an interpreter (Moreno, Tarn, & Morales, 2009). In other words, the presence of an interpreter changes the amount of information volunteered by a provider. These findings underline the importance of the physician's role and communicative strategies in achieving successful bilingual health communication.

It is important to note that the interdependence of participants' communicative competence is not unique to bilingual health care. Patient communicative competence (e.g., the ability to seek and provide information) is positively correlated with the quality of the information provided (Cegala & Post, 2009). When physicians interacted with high-participation patients, they provided more information overall, more information in response to questions, and volunteered more information than when they spoke with low-participation patients (Cegala, Street, & Clinch, 2007). The question here is whether interpreters should enhance or influence other speakers' communicative competence.

In bilingual health care, interpreters can play a significant role in this process by overtly and covertly enhancing the communicative competence of LEP patients and providers. For example, to ensure effective and appropriate provider–interpreter interactions, interpreters may conceal the providers' problematic behaviors or ask questions on behalf of the patient (Hsieh, 2008). A recent intervention program in the hematology/oncology care team of Minnesota Children's Hospitals and Clinics officially assigned healthcare interpreters the functions of advocates for the patient and family across the continuum of care, which led to improved efficiency and higher patient and provider satisfaction (MacPhail, 2014). Another study found that interpreters who work with patients with cancer also "sometimes felt the need to act as a cultural advocate, by intervening to encourage patients to ask questions, or to ask questions on their behalf... Many interpreters felt a responsibility to protect the patient from culturally inappropriate words or messages" (Butow et al., 2012, p. 238). While noting that such cultural/patient advocate roles may improve patients' quality of care, Butow and colleagues also warned readers about the potential conflicts between interpreters' functions in information provision and advocacy.

Providers' and patients' identities and relationships can also be influenced by the interpreter, resulting in clinical impacts. One study found that when interpreters are friendly and emotionally supportive, Latino patients are more receptive to providers' suggestions of amniocentesis (Preloran, Browner, & Lieber, 2005). A neutral/slightly cheerful interpreter can act as a buffer for the patient against the negative mood expressed by a despondent therapist (Brunson & Lawrence, 2002). Interpreters can actively provide emotional support by noting the need to bridge cultural differences and to ensure quality care (Hsieh, 2006a, 2008; Hsieh & Hong, 2010; Leanza, 2008). On the other hand, interpreters' behaviors may compromise other speakers' communicative competence. For example, when interpreters focus on medical information and ignore providers' rapport-building talk, providers may appear emotionally detached (Aranguri, Davidson, & Ramirez, 2006).

In summary, all participants' communicative behaviors can shape the quality of interpreting. Interpreters can significantly shape others' communicative competence, identity, and relationships, all of which may have significant clinical impacts. Alternatively, providers (and patients) can influence the quality of interpreters' performances through their ability to adapt, accommodate, and anticipate challenges in interpreter-mediated interactions.

Participants' Competition and Coordination for Control

Traditionally, interpreters are conceptualized as the only people who have control over the content and quality of interpreting. As a result, both the research and practice communities have directed attention to restricting and controlling interpreters' power, such as requiring them to perform the conduit role to limit their influences in provider–patient interactions. (Leanza, 2008). Zimányi (2013) found that mental health providers and interpreters often engage in delicate coordination about controlling the communicative flow during provider–patient interactions.

Researchers have noted that other participants are not passive in the interpreting process. A recent review identified the trust–control–power triangle when working with interpreters as one of the three major themes in healthcare interpreting (Brisset et al., 2013). Brisset et al. (2013, p. 136) explained,

> [t]rust and control issues take place within the relation (and its dynamics) between patients, interpreters and practitioners. These issues are notably the expression of power struggles occurring in broader contexts, such as healthcare institutions and the society at large, with its political choices that affect languages, minorities, refugees, etc.

The trust–control–power triangle highlights the inherent tension in the provider–patient–interpreter relationship as each individual holds a unique perspective and potentially competing objectives concerning the patient's illness event.

Researchers have examined the collaboration and competition of participants in interpreter-mediated interactions from different perspectives. For example, different participants' competing agendas and/or expectations may influence their communicative processes. The latest findings suggest that family interpreters and professional interpreters may be good at different tasks due to differences in their (personal) agendas and communicative styles (Leanza et al., 2010; Rosenberg et al., 2008). For example, a professional interpreter is likely to refrain from adopting cultural broker and advocate functions (as they are trained to be neutral conduits), whereas family interpreters are more likely to interject their personal perspectives in the medical discourse and to provide more complete information during medical history-taking sessions (Leanza et al., 2010). At the same time, researchers have found that a provider may also develop different expectations and adopt different communicative strategies when working with a family interpreter as opposed to a professional interpreter (Hsieh et al., 2010; Rosenberg et al., 2007). A provider may have a stronger sense of trust and alliance with a professional interpreter (compared to a family interpreter); however, they may choose to work with a family interpreter depending on the circumstances (e.g., clinical urgency; Hsieh, 2015). Researchers also found that physicians are more likely to interrupt a professional interpreter (as opposed to a family interpreter) when the patient discloses contextualized everyday narratives (Leanza et al., 2010). Finally, although some studies show that patients may prefer family interpreters (Green, Free, Bhavnani, & Newman, 2005), others suggest that patients may prefer professional interpreters (MacFarlane et al., 2009). These findings support the argument that individuals involved in bilingual health care may actively shape the communicative process based on their personal perspectives as well as their expectations of others' roles, functions, and performances.

Participants' perspectives, however, are not always compatible with each other. As a result, participants in bilingual health care often compete with each other to maintain or exert control over the communication processes. In Chapter 1, I noted that the conduit model is a way for the institution to control the interpreter's power and influence. However, providers also can exert control both inside and outside of the medical encounter. For example, a provider may question an interpreter if the interpreter fails to use a key term that the provider recognizes in the other language ("I did not hear you say *el glaucoma.*") or if the interpreter's narrative is significantly shorter or longer than the patient's narrative (e.g., "You said more. What did you say?"). Providers may also monitor a patient's nonverbal communication to ensure that the interpreter conveyed the intended emotional tone (e.g., hopefulness) or repeat a particular portion of talk because they suspect the interpreter did not interpret faithfully. Many interpreters and providers in my study also reported incidences in which a provider filed a complaint or even requested an interpreter to be fired due to problematic interpreting (Hsieh, 2010). In short, although interpreters are the only bilingual persons in the medical encounter, providers do not simply accept interpreters' control over the provider–patient communication. Rather, providers actively monitor the discursive process and revise their communicative strategies, using both discursive strategies and institutional power to ensure that interpreters' performances are subject to their control.

Although the literature has traditionally focused on interpreters' management of the discursive process, it is important to note that no one has full control over medical encounters. Each participant contributes to the dynamic, emergent communicative process through their competition over and resistance to control. More importantly, as researchers examine how individuals incorporate their perspectives and agendas into the discursive process, it appears that participants' values and practices are shaped by forces beyond their individual perspectives.

Healthcare Interpreting as a Goal-oriented Activity

Several researchers have suggested that organizational culture and environmental contexts are influential in shaping participants' evaluation of the quality of healthcare interpreting (Brisset et al., 2013), arguing that interpreters' performances are often shaped by system-level expectations and constraints (Bischoff & Hudelson, 2010b; Hsieh, 2006a). Interpreters often report frustration and conflicts when they feel that the conduit model fails to ensure satisfactory quality of care (Brisset et al., 2013; Hsieh, 2006a, 2008). In addition, providers may also find interpreters' conduit performances to be disruptive to the communicative process. Some of the latest studies suggest that healthcare settings present unique contexts that set healthcare interpreting apart from other forms of interpreting. For example, compared to court interpreters, professional healthcare interpreters adopt different interpreting strategies (e.g., suspended rendition), which are also favored by other participants, to encourage participation in medical dialogues (Gavioli & Baraldi, 2011). From this perspective, providers and interpreters seem to suggest that the criteria they use to evaluate the quality of their work are not based simply on the equivalence of the information conveyed in the different languages.

Unlike other forms of interpreting (e.g., court interpreting and conference interpreting), a healthcare interpreter is part of a larger healthcare team assembled with the purpose of improving patients' quality of care and health outcomes. In other words, the emphasis of neutrality and faithfulness upheld in traditional interpreting literature can be ancillary to larger healthcare goals. Healthcare interpreting thus becomes a goal-oriented activity that is situated in the context of successful provider–patient communication.

D.1. Addressing Challenges in Trend 3

By recognizing healthcare interpreting as a coordinated communicative activity, researchers open up theoretical possibilities and intervention points in bilingual health care. This is a revolutionary step in the theoretical development of interpreting studies. By doing so, researchers can move beyond a generic claim about how other participants are also important in the interpreting process or a simple encouragement for other participants to familiarize themselves with interpreters' styles. Instead, this emerging trend seeks to understand the process by which coordination occurs and the factors that shape such coordination.

For example, to achieve optimal bilingual health care, researchers need to understand how different individuals negotiate and coordinate their communicative needs, therapeutic objectives, and other concerns during dynamic, emergent provider–patient interactions. If interpreters are active participants, do they have their own personal goals and agendas in the medical encounter? How are those goals and agendas determined and how do they emerge during medical encounters? Are certain ways of negotiating these goals and agendas better than others? Researchers need to examine the theoretical, practical, clinical, and ethical consequences of the communicative strategies employed by participants.

E. Trend 4: Interpreters as Active Participants

While the third trend highlights the interdependence of the multi-party interactions in interpreter-mediated medical encounters, the fourth trend highlights interpreters' agency. By agency, I aim to highlight interpreters' ability *and* responsibility as problem-solvers in intercultural medical encounters. Conceptualizing interpreters as active participants within the multicultural and multilingual healthcare settings is one of the oldest trends shaping the recent paradigm shift in research in bilingual health communication. By recognizing interpreters' active roles, researchers can begin to examine the complexity of interpreting as a communicative process. The following arguments and research findings successfully validate this trend: (a) the reality of interpreters' performance and self-perceived visibility, (b) emerging evidence that the conduit role requires active judgment and intervention, and (c) emerging evidence that non-literal interpreting is necessary in healthcare settings.

Interpreters' Performance and Self-perceived Visibility

Although the conduit model defines the appropriate performance for interpreters based on their invisibility, such a conceptualization has been challenged as impractical, if not unrealistic (Dysart-Gale, 2005; Hsieh, 2009). Starting from the mid-1990s, researchers have noted that interpreters actively participate in the communicative process. Linell (1997, p. 55) suggested that "apart from being relayers (translators), interpreters must (and do) act as chairpersons and gatekeepers, monitoring the social and discursive situation" (see also Fenton, 1997; Wadensjö, 1998). Davidson (2000, 2001) and Angelelli (2002) also found that interpreters function as covert co-diagnosticians and informational gatekeepers in medical encounters. In short, when observing interpreters' practice, researchers consistently found interpreters adopting non-conduit behaviors. In fact, Angelelli (2002, 2004) argued that interpreters perceived their role to be visible across various settings (e.g., court, conference settings, and hospitals). Other researchers noted that interpreters often desire to assume a more visible presence in provider–patient interactions (Hsieh, 2008; Smith, Swartz, Kilian, & Chiliza, 2013), although they often move strategically between various levels of visibility.

Many researchers have examined interpreters' construction of interactional frames to structure provider–patient interactions (Metzger, 1999; Pöchhacker & Shlesinger, 2005); however, very few studies examine interpreters' behaviors outside of the medical encounter. This research design blind spot is partially attributable to the traditional emphasis of interpreter-as-conduit, which implies that interpreters do not have tasks or roles to perform when the primary speakers are not in the same settings. Healthcare interpreters often interact with language-discordant patients outside of medical encounters, helping them to navigate the complex medical systems (e.g., getting prescription medicine and making follow-up appointments). In fact, interpreters may intentionally interact with patients and providers outside of medical encounters as a strategy to manage the interactional frames and activities during medical encounters (Hsieh, 2006a, 2007).

Some recent studies argue that interpreters strategically move along the continuum of visibility by blurring and/or ignoring the boundaries of provider–patient interactions to manage competing roles and communicative goals. Researchers found that informal interpreters (e.g., hospital janitors) in a mental health facility in South Africa often volunteer patient information that they observed or acquired in other contexts (e.g., cleaning the room or overhearing conversations) when interpreting for the patient, assuming a co-clinician role in helping the providers to have access to not only the patients' language but also their everyday life (Smith et al., 2013). Phillips (2013) observed telephone interpreters engaging in meta-communication by sharing their personal experiences about survival and success in the host country as they resettled in the new environment. Phillips (2013, p. 12) concluded, "[t]he meta-communication about productive resettlement is established explicitly when the interpreter swaps information about their background with the patient, and implicitly through the background noises of the interpreter's life." For example, the background noises of a baby crying, children playing, a doorbell ringing, or a bird singing all suggest that life in the host country can be normalized again. By sharing their personal experiences and social identities (e.g., coming from the same region or being married with children), the telephone interpreter, while being anonymous and disembodied in the interpreting session, signaled to refugees about their own possible futures. By putting forward the concept of the interpreter's role-space, Llewellyn-Jones and Lee (2013) proposed that interpreters should strategically shift between the continuum of three different axes (i.e., alignment with provider versus patient, interpreter visibility, and control over interactions) to ensure successful interactions. In my own research, I have found healthcare interpreters strategically create environmental, interpersonal, and other contextual boundaries to actively denounce certain identities while claiming others when interacting with others to manage competing and/or conflicting goals (see Chapter 6).

In short, interpreters have a sophisticated understanding and management of their interactional frames, utilizing a wide variety of various resources (e.g., discourse pragmatics, interpersonal relationships, and environmental contexts) both inside and outside of a medical encounter to shape and influence others' communicative behaviors.

Conduit Role Requires Active Judgment and Intervention

Moving beyond the debate of interpreter (in)visibility, I have also argued that interpreters' conduit role is *not* a passive one that simply relays the voices of others. There are a couple of different ways in which an interpreter-as-conduit is actively involved in the process and content of provider–patient interactions. First, when discussing their conduit performances, interpreters talked about strategically adopting specific nonverbal behaviors to manipulate others' communicative behaviors and to reinforce the provider–patient relationship. For example, one interpreter, Sherry, explained:

What happens is when you stand here, the patient is going to look at you and you have to be doing this [looking down at the floor], "I'm the voice, just look at each other." So, if you stand behind the patient, then the patient can't [turn their head back], and they look at the physician, and then they are looking at each other.

Second, interpreters often refrain from interpreting when one of the participants responds in the other speaker's language. Watermeyer (2011) found that patients at times may prefer to establish direct communication with their physician, despite their limited language proficiency. Interpreters' ability and willingness to refrain from interpreting allows providers and patients to establish rapport. On the other hand, interpreters may need to monitor provider–patient interactions carefully so that they can jump into the communicative process when one or both sides experiences problematic communication. To do so, an interpreter must actively monitor the process of interaction, making real-time judgments about when and whether to interpret. In short, "interpreters' understanding of the conduit role is not a non-thinking, robotic way of interpreting but rather includes specific strategies to accomplish the communicative goal of reinforcing the provider–patient relationship" (Hsieh, 2008, p. 1381). In other words, even when interpreters enact the interpreter-as-conduit role, they are still active participants in provider–patient interactions as they adopt purposeful strategies to achieve specific goals.

Non-literal Interpreting as Necessity

A recent review of 61 studies concluded that "non-literal translation appears to be a prerequisite for effective and accurate communication" in healthcare settings (Brisset et al., 2013, p. 131). Two recent studies noted that interpreters' alterations to the original texts at times can lead to positive effects in clinical encounters (Butow et al., 2011; Jackson, Nguyen, Hu, Harris, & Terasaki, 2011). For example, an interpreter may change a patient's indirect information-seeking statement (e.g., "I always get sleepy after taking the pill.") to a direct information-seeking question (e.g., "Is it normal that I feel sleepy after taking the pill?"), which may be more effective in drawing the provider's attention to the patient's concerns. Interpreters are active participants who systematically adopt purposeful strategies to improve a patient's health literacy, to protect institutional resources (e.g., providers' time), to reduce the cultural gap between the provider and the patient, to reconcile provider–patient conflicts, and to ensure the quality of provider–patient interactions (Fatahi et al., 2008; Greenhalgh et al., 2006; Hsieh, 2007, 2009; Rosenberg et al., 2008). Metzger (1999) argued that an interpreter's ability to identify, assume, and negotiate other speakers' goals is crucial in fulfilling others' satisfaction.

As researchers noticed interpreters' active involvement in the communicative process, they also questioned interpreters' ethics and raised concerns over how some of their communicative strategies may infringe the authority of the providers or the autonomy of the patient (Hsieh, 2010; Hsieh et al., 2010). It is important not to romanticize interpreters' active role in interpreter-mediated medical encounters and to critically examine their performance and communicative strategies.

E.1. Addressing Challenges in Trend 4

Recognizing that interpreters are actively involved in the communicative process is one of the most important trends in interpreting studies, because such an approach highlights interpreters' agency, an issue that is largely ignored and undertheorized in the traditions of interpreting studies. Acknowledging interpreters' active roles in healthcare settings opens doors for researchers to critically examine (a) the specific process and impacts of interpreters' active involvement in healthcare delivery, and (b) other participants' understanding and evaluation of interpreters' active involvement.

For example, Brisset and colleagues (2013) questioned Karliner et al.'s (2007) conclusion that when compared to ad hoc interpreters, professional interpreters make fewer errors (i.e., deviations from the original texts) and enhance provider satisfaction. By noting that interpreters' deviation from original texts may serve functional, meaningful purposes and that patients may have different criteria in evaluating the quality of interpreting, Brisset et al. argued that Karliner's understanding of the quality of interpreting and its corresponding impact oversimplifies the discursive process of healthcare interpreting and is biased toward providers' perspectives. In fact, a study found that even though 31 percent of interpreted utterances are altered, only 5 percent were clinically significant, with 1 percent having a positive effect and 4 percent having a negative effect on the clinical encounter (Jackson et al., 2011). A different study found that 70 percent of nonequivalent interpretations were inconsequential or positive, 10 percent might result in misunderstanding, 5 percent adopted a more authoritarian tone than the original speech, and 3 percent conveyed more certainty (Butow et al., 2011). Another study found that 55 percent of professional interpreters' interpreting involves some form of alteration, among which 93 percent are likely to have negative effects and 7 percent are likely to have positive effects (Pham, Thornton, Engelberg, Jackson, & Curtis, 2008). The key questions here should not be whether or not interpreters actively shape the process and content of interpreting but *why*, *how*, and *what happens when* they do so. What are the kinds of alterations that lead to positive outcomes versus negative ones? And what kinds of outcomes do they have (e.g., health status, patient satisfaction, treatment adherence, and rapport building)?

To move beyond the argument of interpreters' agency in healthcare settings, researchers need to question the effectiveness and appropriateness of interpreters' strategic behaviors and to consider how these behaviors impact other participants' identities, relationships, and agency as well as the overall communicative activity. It is time for researchers and practitioners to question and examine the reality and boundaries of interpreters' active involvement in healthcare settings.

F. Conclusion

In this chapter, I have examined four emerging trends in the literature of bilingual health communication, highlighting their potential for theory advancement and practice implications. These trends are interconnected. For example, without recognizing other participants' influences in the interpreter-mediated encounter (Trend 3), one cannot truly understand and examine how providers' calculated use of interpreters might be dependent on specific clinical demands (Trend 1). Without seeing interpreters as active participants (i.e., an individual with agency in influencing the process and content of medical encounters; Trend 4), there is little possibility of examining how the provider–interpreter, interpreter–patient, or provider–patient–interpreter relationships may shape the delivery of bilingual health care (Trend 2).

After all, if interpreters are passive tools, like a computer, one would expect them to function the same as any other, regardless of context. In other words, a home computer should work and produce the same output as other computers in a lab, office, or library. Anyone who uses a computer would expect identical processes and results across times and places. A computer can be broken, but otherwise they work in the same way. Similarly, an interpreter who fails to assume the conduit role has been traditionally regarded as a "bad" interpreter; otherwise, all interpreters are the same. All providers and patients should expect the same "good" interpreting from all "unbroken" interpreters. This has been the traditional thinking in interpreter performances. But this belief is not supported by the reality of interpreting.

These emerging trends, supported by evidence-based studies, provide strong counterarguments to the traditional thinking. In addition, they are opening up new perspectives to conceptualize interpreter-mediated medical encounters. By moving beyond the comparisons between original and interpreted texts, researchers have demonstrated the value in viewing bilingual health communication as a goal-oriented, context-situated collaboration between multiple parties. These new trends also support a diverse methodological approach in examining interpreter-mediated medical encounters.

In the next chapter, I will provide a detailed background about the research designs of studies I have conducted. Readers will find that the studies that I have conducted in the last 15 years progressively address many concerns posed by these emerging trends and help formulate my Model of Bilingual Health Communication (Chapter 5).

Note

1 An earlier version of this chapter has been published elsewhere (i.e., Hsieh, 2014) and was named as one of the Top Three Papers in the Language and Social Interaction Division at the 2014 annual meeting of the National Communication Association, Chicago, IL.

References

Abbe, M., Simon, C., Angiolillo, A., Ruccione, K., & Kodish, E. D. (2006). A survey of language barriers from the perspective of pediatric oncologists, interpreters, and parents. *Pediatric Blood & Cancer*, 47, 819–824.

Allen, B. (Writer). (2011). Signing on: A documentary about Deaf breast cancer survivors [Motion picture]. United States: Screen Porch Films.

Andrulis, D., Goodman, N., & Pryor, C. (2002). What a difference an interpreter can make: Health care experiences of uninsured with limited English proficiency. Retrieved March 14, 2015, from www.accessproject.org/downloads/c_LEPreportENG.pdf.

Angelelli, C. V. (2002). *Deconstructing the invisible interpreter: A critical study of the interpersonal role of the interpreter in a cross-cultural linguistic communicative event.* University of Michigan, Ann Arbor. ProQuest database. (UMI No. AAT 302676)

Angelelli, C. V. (2004). *Revisiting the interpreters' roles: A study of conference, court, and medical interpreters in Canada, Mexico, and the United States.* Amsterdam, The Netherlands: John Benjamins.

Angelelli, C. V. (2010). A professional ideology in the making: Bilingual youngsters interpreting for their communities and the notion of (no) choice. *Translation and Interpretation Studies*, 5, 94–108.

Aranguri, C., Davidson, B., & Ramirez, R. (2006). Patterns of communication through interpreters: A detailed sociolinguistic analysis. *Journal of General Internal Medicine*, 21, 623–629.

Avery, M.-P. B. (2001). The role of the health care interpreter: An evolving dialogue. Retrieved March 14, 2015, from www.ncihc.org/mc/page.do?sitePageId=57022&orgId=ncihc.

Baker, D. W., & Hayes, R. (1997). The effect of communicating through an interpreter on satisfaction with interpersonal aspects of care. *Journal of General Internal Medicine*, 12, 117.

Baker, D. W., Parker, R. M., Williams, M. V., Coates, W. C., & Pitkin, K. M. (1996). Use and effectiveness of interpreters in an emergency department. *Journal of the American Medical Association*, 275, 783–788.

Berkman, N. D., Sheridan, S. L., Donahue, K. E., Halpern, D. J., & Crotty, K. (2011). Low health literacy and health outcomes: An updated systematic review. *Annals of Internal Medicine*, 155, 97–107.

Bernstein, J., Bernstein, E., Dave, A., Hardt, E., James, T., Linden, J., … Safi, C. (2002). Trained medical interpreters in the emergency department: Effects on services, subsequent charges, and follow-up. *Journal of Immigrant Health*, 4, 171–176.

Bischoff, A., & Hudelson, P. (2010a). Access to healthcare interpreter services: Where are we and where do we need to go? *International Journal of Environmental Research & Public Health*, 7, 2838–2844.

Bischoff, A., & Hudelson, P. (2010b). Communicating with foreign language-speaking patients: Is access to professional interpreters enough? *Journal of Travel Medicine*, 17, 15–20.

Bischoff, A., Hudelson, P., & Bovier, P. A. (2008). Doctor–patient gender concordance and patient satisfaction in interpreter-mediated consultations: An exploratory study. *Journal of Travel Medicine*, 15, 1–5.

Brämberg, E. B., & Sandman, L. (2013). Communication through in-person interpreters: A qualitative study of home care providers' and social workers' views. *Journal of Clinical Nursing*, 22, 159–167.

Brisset, C., Leanza, Y., & Laforest, K. (2013). Working with interpreters in health care: A systematic review and meta-ethnography of qualitative studies. *Patient Education and Counseling*, 91, 131–140.

Brunson, J. G., & Lawrence, P. S. (2002). Impact of sign language interpreter and therapist moods on deaf recipient mood. *Professional Psychology: Research and Practice*, 33, 576–580.

Butow, P. N., Goldstein, D., Bell, M. L., Sze, M., Aldridge, L. J., Abdo, S., ... Eisenbruch, M. (2011). Interpretation in consultations with immigrant patients with cancer: How accurate is it? *Journal of Clinical Oncology*, 29, 2801–2807.

Butow, P. N., Lobb, E., Jefford, M., Goldstein, D., Eisenbruch, M., Girgis, A., ... Schofield, P. (2012). A bridge between cultures: Interpreters' perspectives of consultations with migrant oncology patients. *Supportive Care in Cancer*, 20, 235–244.

Castillo, R. J. (1997). *Culture & mental illness: A client-centered approach.* Belmont, CA: Brooks/ Cole Publishing.

Cegala, D. J., Gade, C., Broz, S. L., & McClure, L. (2004). Physicians' and patients' perceptions of patients' communication competence in a primary care medical interview. *Health Communication*, 16, 289–304.

Cegala, D. J., & Post, D. M. (2009). The impact of patients' participation on physicians' patient-centered communication. *Patient Education and Counseling*, 77, 202–208.

Cegala, D. J., Street, R. L., Jr., & Clinch, C. (2007). The impact of patient participation on physicians' information provision during a primary care medical interview. *Health Communication*, 21, 177–185.

Chun, M. B. J., Jackson, D. S., Lin, S. Y., & Park, E. R. (2010). A comparison of surgery and family medicine residents' perceptions of cross-cultural care training. *Hawaii Medical Journal*, 69, 289–293.

Cunningham, H., Cushman, L. F., Akuete-Penn, C., & Meyer, D. D. (2008). Satisfaction with telephonic interpreters in pediatric care. *Journal of the National Medical Association*, 100, 429–434.

d'Ardenne, P., & Farmer, E. (2009). Using interpreters in trauma therapy. In N. Grey (Ed.), *A casebook of cognitive therapy for traumatic stress reactions* (pp. 283–300). New York: Routledge.

Davidson, B. (2000). The interpreter as institutional gatekeeper: The social-linguistic role of interpreters in Spanish–English medical discourse. *Journal of Sociolinguistics*, 4, 379–405.

Davidson, B. (2001). Questions in cross-linguistic medical encounters: The role of the hospital interpreter. *Anthropological Quarterly*, 74, 170–178.

DeCamp, L. R., Kuo, D. Z., Flores, G., O'Connor, K., & Minkovitz, C. S. (2013). Changes in language services use by US pediatricians. *Pediatrics*, 132(2), e396–406.

Derose, K. P., Hays, R. D., McCaffrey, D. F., & Baker, D. W. (2001). Does physician gender affect satisfaction of men and women visiting the emergency department? *Journal of General Internal Medicine*, 16, 218–226.

Diamond, L. C., Schenker, Y., Curry, L., Bradley, E. H., & Fernandez, A. (2009). Getting by: Underuse of interpreters by resident physicians. *Journal of General Internal Medicine*, 24, 256–262.

Dysart-Gale, D. (2005). Communication models, professionalization, and the work of medical interpreters. *Health Communication*, 17, 91–103.

Edwards, R., Temple, B., & Alexander, C. (2005). Users' experiences of interpreters: The critical role of trust. *Interpreting*, 7, 77–95.

Elderkin-Thompson, V., Silver, R. C., & Waitzkin, H. (2001). When nurses double as interpreters: A study of Spanish-speaking patients in a US primary care setting. *Social Science & Medicine*, 52, 1343–1358.

Fatahi, N., Hellstrom, M., Skott, C., & Mattsson, B. (2008). General practitioners' views on consultations with interpreters: A triad situation with complex issues. *Scandinavian Journal of Primary Health Care*, 26, 40–45.

Fenton, S. (1997). The role of the interpreter in the adversarial courtroom. In S. E. Carr, R. P. Roberts, A. Dufour, & D. Steyn (Eds.), *The critical link: Interpreters in the community* (pp. 29–34). Amsterdam, The Netherlands: John Benjamins.

Flores, G. (2005). The impact of medical interpreter services on the quality of health care: A systematic review. *Medical Care Research & Review*, 62, 255–299.

Flores, G., Abreu, M., Barone, C. P., Bachur, R., & Lin, H. (2012). Errors of medical interpretation and their potential clinical consequences: A comparison of professional versus ad hoc versus no interpreters. *Annals of Emergency Medicine*, 60, 545–553.

Flores, G., Laws, M. B., Mayo, S. J., Zuckerman, B., Abreu, M., Medina, L., & Hardt, E. J. (2003). Errors in medical interpretation and their potential clinical consequences in pediatric encounters. *Pediatrics*, 111, 6–14.

Gadon, M., Balch, G. I., & Jacobs, E. A. (2007). Caring for patients with limited English proficiency: The perspectives of small group practitioners. *Journal of General Internal Medicine*, 22, S341–346.

Gany, F., Kapelusznik, L., Prakash, K., Gonzalez, J., Orta, L. Y., Tseng, C.-H., & Changrani, J. (2007). The impact of medical interpretation method on time and errors. *Journal of General Internal Medicine*, 22, 319–323.

Gany, F., Leng, J., Shapiro, E., Abramson, D., Motola, I., Shield, D. C., & Changrani, J. (2007). Patient satisfaction with different Interpreting methods: A randomized controlled trial. *Journal of General Internal Medicine*, 22, S312–318.

Gavioli, L., & Baraldi, C. (2011). Interpreter-mediated interaction in healthcare and legal settings: Talk organization, context and the achievement of intercultural communication. *Interpreting*, 13, 205–233.

Ginde, A. A., Clark, S., & Camargo, C. A., Jr. (2009). Language barriers among patients in Boston emergency departments: Use of medical interpreters after passage of interpreter legislation. *Journal of Immigrant and Minority Health*, 11, 527–530.

Ginde, A. A., Sullivan, A. F., Corel, B., Caceres, J. A., & Camargo, C. A., Jr. (2010). Reevaluation of the effect of mandatory interpreter legislation on use of professional interpreters for ED patients with language barriers. *Patient Education and Counseling*, 81, 204–206.

Goodwin, C., & Duranti, A. (1992). Rethinking context: An introduction. In A. Duranti & C. Goodwin (Eds.), *Rethinking context: Language as an interactive phenomenon* (pp. 1–42). Cambridge, UK: Cambridge University Press.

Green, H., Sperlinger, D., & Carswell, K. (2012). Too close to home? Experiences of Kurdish refugee interpreters working in UK mental health services. *Journal of Mental Health*, 21, 227–235.

Green, J., Free, C., Bhavnani, V., & Newman, T. (2005). Translators and mediators: Bilingual young people's accounts of their interpreting work in health care. *Social Science & Medicine*, 60, 2097–2110.

Greenhalgh, T., Robb, N., & Scambler, G. (2006). Communicative and strategic action in interpreted consultations in primary health care: A Habermasian perspective. *Social Science & Medicine*, 63, 1170–1187.

Grover, A., Deakyne, S., Bajaj, L., & Roosevelt, G. E. (2012). Comparison of through-put times for limited English proficiency patient visits in the emergency department between different interpreter modalities. *Journal of Immigrant and Minority Health*, 14, 602–607.

Gutmann, E. J. (2003). Pathologists and patients: Can we talk? *Modern Pathology*, 16, 515–518.

Hampers, L. C., & McNulty, J. E. (2002). Professional interpreters and bilingual physicians in a pediatric emergency department: Effect on resource utilization. *Archives of Pediatrics and Adolescent Medicine*, 156, 1108–1113.

Hardacre, H. (1997). *Marketing the menacing fetus in Japan*. Berkeley, CA: University of California Press.

Harrison, B., Bhatt, A., Carey, J., & Ebden, P. (1988). The language of the bilingual medical consultation. In P. Grunwell (Ed.), *Applied Linguistics in Society: Papers from the Annual Meeting of the British Association for Applied Linguistics (20th, Nottingham, England, United Kingdom, September 1987)* (pp. 67–73). London: Centre for Information on Language Teaching and Research.

Harshman, P. (1984). A misinterpreted word worth $71 million. *Medical Economics*, 61, 298-292.

Ho, A. (2008). Using family members as interpreters in the clinical setting. *The Journal of Clinical Ethics*, 19, 223–233.

Hsieh, E. (2006a). Conflicts in how interpreters manage their roles in provider–patient interactions. *Social Science & Medicine*, 62, 721–730.

Hsieh, E. (2006b). Understanding medical interpreters: Reconceptualizing bilingual health communication. *Health Communication*, 20, 177–186.

Hsieh, E. (2007). Interpreters as co-diagnosticians: Overlapping roles and services between providers and interpreters. *Social Science & Medicine*, 64, 924–937.

Hsieh, E. (2008). "I am not a robot!" Interpreters' views of their roles in health care settings. *Qualitative Health Research*, 18, 1367–1383.

Hsieh, E. (2009). Bilingual health communication: Medical interpreters' construction of a mediator role. In D. E. Brashers & D. J. Goldsmith (Eds.), *Communicating to manage health and illness* (pp. 135–160). New York: Routledge.

Hsieh, E. (2010). Provider–interpreter collaboration in bilingual health care: Competitions of control over interpreter-mediated interactions. *Patient Education and Counseling*, 78, 154–159.

Hsieh, E. (2014). Emerging trends and the corresponding challenges in bilingual health communication. In B. Nicodemus & M. Metzger (Eds.), *Investigations in healthcare inter-preting* (pp. 70–103). Washington, DC: Gallaudet University Press.

Hsieh, E. (2015). Not just "getting by": Factors influencing providers' choice of interpret-ers. *Journal of General Internal Medicine*, 30, 75–82.

Hsieh, E., & Hong, S. J. (2010). Not all are desired: Providers' views on interpreters' emo-tional support for patients. *Patient Education and Counseling*, 81, 192–197.

Hsieh, E., Ju, H., & Kong, H. (2010). Dimensions of trust: The tensions and challenges in provider–interpreter trust. *Qualitative Health Research*, 20, 170–181.

Hsieh, E., & Kramer, E. M. (2012). Medical interpreters as tools: Dangers and challenges in the utilitarian approach to interpreters' roles and functions. *Patient Education and Counseling*, 89, 158–162.

Hsieh, E., Pitaloka, D., & Johnson, A. J. (2013). Bilingual health communication: Distinctive needs of providers from five specialties. *Health Communication*, 28, 557–567.

Jackson, J. C., Nguyen, D., Hu, N., Harris, R., & Terasaki, G. S. (2011). Alterations in medical interpretation during routine primary care. *Journal of General Internal Medicine*, 26, 259–264.

Jackson, J. C., Zatzick, D., Harris, R., & Gardiner, L. (2008). Loss in translation: Considering the critical role of interpreters and language in the psychiatric evaluation of non-English-speaking patients. In S. Loue & M. Sajatovic (Eds.), *Diversity issues in the diagnosis, treatment, and research of mood disorders* (pp. 135–163). New York: Oxford University Press.

Jacobs, E. A., Diamond, L. C., & Stevak, L. (2010). The importance of teaching clinicians when and how to work with interpreters. *Patient Education and Counseling*, 78, 149–153.

Johnson, H., Thompson, A., & Downs, M. (2009). Non-Western interpreters' experiences of trauma: The protective role of culture following exposure to oppression. *Ethnicity & Health*, 14, 407–418.

Karliner, L. S., Jacobs, E. A., Chen, A. H., & Mutha, S. (2007). Do professional interpreters improve clinical care for patients with limited English proficiency? A systematic review of the literature. *Health Services Research*, 42, 727–754.

Kaufert, J. M. (1999). Cultural mediation in cancer diagnosis and end of life decision-making: The experience of Aboriginal patients in Canada. *Anthropology & Medicine*, 6, 405–421.

Kaufert, J. M., & Putsch, R. W., III. (1997). Communication through interpreters in healthcare: Ethical dilemmas arising from differences in class, culture, language, and power. *The Journal of Clinical Ethics*, 8, 71–87.

Kuo, D., & Fagan, M. J. (1999). Satisfaction with methods of Spanish interpretation in an ambulatory care clinic. *Journal of General Internal Medicine*, 14, 547–550.

Kuo, D. Z., O'Connor, K. G., Flores, G., & Minkovitz, C. S. (2007). Pediatricians' use of language services for families with limited English proficiency. *Pediatrics*, 119, e920–927.

Launer, J. (1978). Taking medical histories through interpreters: Practice in a Nigerian outpatient department. *British Medical Journal*, 2, 934.

Leanza, Y. (2008). Community interpreter's power: The hazards of a disturbing attribute. *Journal of Medical Anthropology*, 31, 211–220.

Leanza, Y., Boivin, I., & Rosenberg, E. (2010). Interruptions and resistance: A comparison of medical consultations with family and trained interpreters. *Social Science & Medicine*, 70, 1888–1895.

Lee, K. C., Winickoff, J. P., Kim, M. K., Campbell, E. G., Betancourt, J. R., Park, E. R., … Weissman, J. S. (2006). Resident physicians' use of professional and nonprofessional interpreters: A national survey. *Journal of the American Medical Association*, 296, 1050–1053.

Linell, P. (1997). Interpreting as communication. In Y. Gambier, D. Gile, & C. Taylor (Eds.), *Conference interpreting: Current trends in research; Proceedings of the International Conference on Interpreting: What do We Know and How? (Turku, August 25–27, 1994)* (pp. 49–67). Amsterdam, The Netherlands: John Benjamins.

Lion, K. C., Thompson, D. A., Cowden, J. D., Michel, E., Rafton, S. A., Hamdy, R. F., … Ebel, B. E. (2013). Clinical Spanish use and language proficiency testing among pediatric residents. *Academic Medicine*, 88, 1478–1484.

Llewellyn-Jones, P., & Lee, R. (2013). Getting to the core of role: Defining interpreters' role-space. *International Journal of Interpreter Education*, 5, 54–72.

Locatis, C., Williamson, D., Gould-Kabler, C., Zone-Smith, L., Detzler, I., Roberson, J., … Ackerman, M. (2010). Comparing in-person, video, and telephonic medical interpretation. *Journal of General Internal Medicine*, 25, 345–350.

MacFarlane, A., Dzebisova, Z., Karapish, D., Kovacevic, B., Ogbebor, F., & Okonkwo, E. (2009). Arranging and negotiating the use of informal interpreters in general practice consultations: Experiences of refugees and asylum seekers in the west of Ireland. *Social Science & Medicine*, 69, 210–214.

MacPhail, S. L. (2014, July 2). Expanding interpreter role to include advocacy and care coordination improves efficiency and leads to high patient and provider satisfaction. Retrieved March 14, 2015, from https://innovations.ahrq.gov/profiles/expanding-interpreter-r ole-include-advocacy-and-care-coordination-improves-efficiency-and.

McKee, M. M., & Paasche-Orlow, M. K. (2012). Health literacy and the disenfranchised: The importance of collaboration between limited English proficiency and health literacy researchers. *Journal of Health Communication*, 17, 7–12.

Meischke, H., Chavez, D., Bradley, S., Rea, T., & Eisenberg, M. (2010). Emergency communications with limited-English-proficiency populations. *Prehospital Emergency Care*, 14, 265–271.

Messias, D. K. H., McDowell, L., & Estrada, R. D. (2009). Language interpreting as social justice work: Perspectives of formal and informal healthcare interpreters. *Advances in Nursing Science*, 32, 128–143.

Metzger, M. (1999). *Sign language interpreting: Deconstructing the myth of neutrality.* Washington, DC: Gallaudet University Press.

Moreno, G., Tarn, D. M., & Morales, L. S. (2009). Impact of interpreters on the receipt of new prescription medication information among Spanish-speaking Latinos. *Medical Care*, 47, 1201–1208.

Moskowitz, M. L. (2001). *The haunting fetus: Abortion, sexuality, and the spirit world in Taiwan.* Honolulu, HI: University of Hawai'i Press.

National Network of Libraries of Medicine. (2013). Health literacy. Retrieved March 14, 2015, from http://nnlm.gov/outreach/consumer/hlthlit.html.

Pham, K., Thornton, J. D., Engelberg, R. A., Jackson, J. C., & Curtis, J. R. (2008). Alterations during medical interpretation of ICU family conferences that interfere with or enhance communication. *Chest*, 134, 109–116.

Phillips, C. (2013). Remote telephone interpretation in medical consultations with refugees: Meta-communications about care, survival and selfhood. *Journal of Refugee Studies*, 26, 505–523.

Pitaloka, D. (2014). *The (passive) violence of harmony and balance: Lived experienced of Javanese women with type 2 diabetes.* (Ph.D.), University of Oklahoma. Retrieved September 16, 2015, from http://hdl.handle.net/11244/10430.

Plunkett, B. A., Kohli, P., & Milad, M. P. (2002). The importance of physician gender in the selection of an obstetrician or a gynecologist. *American Journal of Obstetrics & Gynecology*, 186, 926–928.

Pöchhacker, F., & Shlesinger, M. (2005). Introduction: Discourse-based research on healthcare interpreting. *Interpreting*, 7, 157–165.

Preloran, H. M., Browner, C. H., & Lieber, E. (2005). Impact of interpreters' approach on Latinas' use of amniocentesis. *Health Education & Behavior*, 32, 599–612.

Price, E. L., Pérez-stable, E. J., Nickleach, D., Lopez, M., & Karliner, L. S. (2012). Interpreter perspectives of in-person, telephonic, and videoconferencing medical interpretation in clinical encounters. *Patient Education and Counseling*, 87, 226–232.

Ramirez, D., Engel, K. G., & Tang, T. S. (2008). Language interpreter utilization in the emergency department setting: A clinical review. *Journal of Health Care for the Poor and Underserved*, 19, 352–362.

Roat, C. E., Kinderman, A., & Fernandez, A. (2011). Interpreting in Palliative Care. Retrieved March 14, 2015, from http://www.chcf.org/publications/2011/11/interpreting-palliative-care-curriculum.

Robb, N., & Greenhalgh, T. (2006). "You have to cover up the words of the doctor": The mediation of trust in interpreted consultations in primary care. *Journal of Health Organization & Management*, 20, 434–455.

Rosenberg, E., Leanza, Y., & Seller, R. (2007). Doctor-patient communication in primary care with an interpreter: Physician perceptions of professional and family interpreters. *Patient Education and Counseling*, 67, 286–292.

Rosenberg, E., Richard, C., Lussier, M.-T., & Shuldiner, T. (2011). The content of talk about health conditions and medications during appointments involving interpreters. *Family Practice*, 28, 317–322.

Rosenberg, E., Seller, R., & Leanza, Y. (2008). Through interpreters' eyes: Comparing roles of professional and family interpreters. *Patient Education and Counseling*, 70, 87–93.

Roter, D. L., Geller, G., Bernhardt, B. A., Larson, S. M., & Doksum, T. (1999). Effects of obstetrician gender on communication and patient satisfaction. *Obstetrics and Gynecology*, 93, 635–641.

Roy, C. B. (2000). *Interpreting as a discourse process*. New York: Oxford University Press.

Sarver, J., & Baker, D. W. (2000). Effect of language barriers on follow-up appointments after an emergency department visit. *Journal of General Internal Medicine*, 15, 256–264.

Schenker, Y., Fernandez, A., Kerr, K., O'Riordan, D., & Pantilat, S. Z. (2012). Interpretation for discussions about end-of-life issues: Results from a national survey of health care interpreters. *Journal of Palliative Medicine*, 15, 1019–1026.

Schenker, Y., Pérez-Stable, E. J., Nickleach, D., & Karliner, L. S. (2011). Patterns of interpreter use for hospitalized patients with limited English proficiency. *Journal of General Internal Medicine*, 26, 712–717.

Sentell, T., & Braun, K. L. (2012). Low health literacy, limited English proficiency, and health status in Asians, Latinos, and other racial/ethnic groups in California. *Journal of Health Communication*, 17, 82–99.

Singy, P., & Guex, P. (2005). The interpreter's role with immigrant patients: Contrasted points of view. *Communication & Medicine*, 2, 45–51.

Smith, J., Swartz, L., Kilian, S., & Chiliza, B. (2013). Mediating words, mediating worlds: Interpreting as hidden care work in a South African psychiatric institution. *Transcultural Psychiatry*, 50, 493–514.

Splevins, K. A., Cohen, K., Joseph, S., Murray, C., & Bowley, J. (2010). Vicarious post-traumatic growth among interpreters. *Qualitative Health Research*, 20, 1705–1716.

Sudore, R. L., Landefeld, C. S., Pérez-Stable, E. J., Bibbins-Domingo, K., Williams, B. A., & Schillinger, D. (2009). Unraveling the relationship between literacy, language proficiency, and patient–physician communication. *Patient Education and Counseling*, 75, 398–402.

Thomas, P., Shabbir, M., & Yasmeen, S. (2010). Language, culture, and mental health. *Arab Journal of Psychiatry*, 21, 102–111.

Thompson, D. A., Hernandez, R. G., Cowden, J. D., Sisson, S. D., & Moon, M. (2013). Caring for patients with limited English proficiency: Are residents prepared to use medical interpreters? *Academic Medicine*, 88, 1485–1492.

Thornton, J. D., Pham, K., Engelberg, R. A., Jackson, J. C., & Curtis, J. R. (2009). Families with limited English proficiency receive less information and support in interpreted intensive care unit family conferences. *Critical Care Medicine*, 37, 89–95.

Tocher, T. M., & Larson, E. B. (1998). Quality of diabetes care for non-English-speaking patients: A comparative study. *Western Journal of Medicine*, 168, 504–511.

Tribe, R., & Lane, P. (2009). Working with interpreters across language and culture in mental health. *Journal of Mental Health*, 18, 233–241.

Wadensjö, C. (1998). *Interpreting as interaction*. London: Longman.

Wallin, A.-M., & Ahlstrom, G. (2006). Cross-cultural interview studies using interpreters: Systematic literature review. *Journal of Advanced Nursing*, 55, 723–735.

Watermeyer, J. (2011). "She will hear me": How a flexible interpreting style enables patients to manage the inclusion of interpreters in mediated pharmacy interactions. *Health Communication*, 26, 71–81.

Weisman, C. S., & Teitelbaum, M. A. (1985). Physician gender and the physician–patient relationship: Recent evidence and relevant questions. *Social Science & Medicine*, 20, 1119–1127.

Weissman, J. S., Betancourt, J., Campbell, E. G., Park, E. R., Kim, M., Clarridge, B., … Maina, A. W. (2005). Resident physicians' preparedness to provide cross-cultural care. *Journal of the American Medical Association*, 294, 1058–1067.

Yawman, D., McIntosh, S., Fernandez, D., Auinger, P., Allan, M., & Weitzman, M. (2006). The use of Spanish by medical students and residents at one university hospital. *Academic Medicine*, 81, 468–473.

Youdelman, M. K. (2008). The medical tongue: US laws and policies on language access. *Health Affairs*, 27, 424–433.

Zimányi, K. (2013). Somebody has to be in charge of a session: On the control of communication in interpreter-mediated mental health encounters. *Translation and Interpreting Studies*, 8, 94–111.

3

INNOVATIVE RESEARCH DESIGNS TO ADVANCE THEORY AND PRACTICE

Becoming a professional interpreter was one of my earliest childhood aspirations. I was ecstatic to be accepted to the MA program (Mandarin Chinese–English) in Translation and Interpretation at the Monterey Institute of International Studies in 1997. During 1998–1999, I worked as a professional interpreter at UCSF Stanford Healthcare in California and as a telephone interpreter for AT&T Language Line. After moving to the University of Illinois at Urbana-Champaign in 1999 to pursue my doctoral degree, I remained active as a volunteer interpreter for local hospitals. At the same time, I became increasingly aware of the limitations of the training and codes of ethics for healthcare interpreters. Although my training was significantly more than that of average healthcare interpreters, who typically only require 40 hours' training to be considered professional interpreters (see Chapter 4.A), I constantly faced problematic situations and recognized that interpreter-mediated medical encounters involve much more than transferring information from one language to another.

For example, during my early days as a healthcare interpreter, I was walking with a patient who suffered from scoliosis to rehab services. His illness was so advanced that his spine was bent to an extent that he would look backward as he walked forward. Upon seeing the patient, a young resident who worked at the rehab could not contain his excitement and, with a big smile, he said out loud, "That's the worst case I've ever seen!" The comment caught me by surprise. I didn't know how to interpret the young resident's greeting. I supposed I could have interpreted it accurately and faithfully, with equal enthusiasm. Yet, it would have felt wrong to do so. My dilemma was not caused by my lack of linguistic skills but something else that I did not learn throughout my graduate program and professional training. In short, the frustration and constraint I experienced as an interpreter formed the early basis of my inquiries.

I have dedicated my research program to studying interpreter-mediated medical encounters. My research focus has evolved significantly over the last 15 years. However, I have always based my arguments on evidence-based research, involving data that were collected from practitioners (e.g., providers and interpreters) from various sources (e.g., participant observations, in-depth interviews, focus groups, and surveys).

A. Three-Phase Studies

Over the years, my research program has involved three large studies. The first study of my research took place in 2003–2004 during my doctoral program. Three data sets were collected during this period, including approximately 15 hours of medical encounters assisted by professional Mandarin Chinese interpreters. I focused on understanding interpreters' perspectives and practices of bilingual health communication. Details about this phase of the study are presented in Section B: Interpreters: Ethnography and Interviews.

The second study of my research program started in 2006, when I was awarded an NIH R03 grant on health literacy to examine providers' perspectives on interpreter-mediated interactions. The data were collected from 2006 to 2009. I examined whether providers from different clinical specialties share any similarities or differences in their attitudes and practices of bilingual health care. Details about this phase of study are presented in Section C: Providers: Interviews and Surveys.

The third study of my research program was conducted in 2012, with funding from the University of Oklahoma Health Sciences Center and Oklahoma Tobacco Settlement Endowment Trust. This larger study examined the illness experiences of patients who were newly diagnosed with gynecologic cancer and includes ethnographic observations, video-recorded medical encounters, and interviews. In this book, I only include interactions between 29 patients and 3 oncologists (i.e., MDs with gynecologic oncology specialty) during their first medical visits. Although the data involve only English-speaking medical encounters, they provide insights into the complexity of providers' management of communicative goals.

Findings from these three phases of my research program have been published in top-tiered journals, including *Journal of General Internal Medicine, Social Science & Medicine, Patient Education and Counseling, Health Communication,* and *Qualitative Health Research.* Details about the specific procedures used for each journal manuscript are located in the method sections of the published articles. All procedures reported in this book have been approved by the relevant institutional review boards.

B. Interpreters: Ethnography and Interviews

In the first phase of my research program, I collected data from 2003 to 2004. This phase included two parts: Part I (participant observation) and Part II (interview and theory development). Participants were recruited in both parts. There were three categories of participants in this study: (a) interpreters, (b) healthcare providers, and (c) patients with limited English proficiency (LEP) and their family members. I recruited healthcare interpreters from two interpreting agencies. *Agency A* was a nonprofit, healthcare interpreting agency in a large Midwestern city that required interpreters to have a minimum of 40 hours of training. It provided 120 healthcare interpreters for over 40 languages to hospitals in the area. *Agency B* was an interpreting agency that welcomes any volunteer interpreters. It provided healthcare interpreters for approximately ten languages to hospitals in a small Midwestern city. All interpreters recruited from Agency B passed a certification program for healthcare interpreters offered by a local hospital.

All interpreters included in this study were considered professional interpreters in healthcare settings, including the volunteer interpreters from Agency B. The majority of interpreters (n = 17) had participated in a 40-hour training course developed by the Cross Cultural Health Care Program (CCHCP), which has been viewed as an industry-recognized training program for professional interpreters. Those who had not attended the course had either passed certification programs offered by individual hospitals or had acted as trainers in education programs for healthcare interpreters. Some interpreters were even certified court interpreters, which generally required more training hours and a more rigorous certification process. Although none received other official training in addition to the 40-hour training program or the certification program for healthcare interpreting, all interpreters had consistently been receiving assignments in healthcare settings and gaining on-the-job experiences.

In Part I (participant observation; i.e., the first six months of the study), I recruited two Mandarin Chinese interpreters to be shadowed during their assignments and to participate in a series of informal interviews. Other participants (e.g., healthcare providers, patients, or patients' family members) were contacted before their scheduled appointment and asked for written consent to participate in the study. Four major hospitals in a large Midwestern city were included in this study. A total of 11 healthcare providers, 4 patients, and 1 family member were included. A total of 12 medical encounters, which generally lasted about 1–1.5 hours (i.e., the encounter includes the patient and the interpreter's conversation in the waiting room, the interpreter-mediated provider–patient interactions, and any follow-up conversations), were observed, audio-recorded, and transcribed.

In Part II (interview and theory development), I initiated a second round of recruitment for participants from the two interpreting agencies and managers of interpreting services from hospitals that participated in this study. A total of 26 participants from 17 languages (i.e., Arabic, Armenian, Assyrian, Mandarin Chinese, Cantonese, French, German, Hindi, Kurdish, Polish, Russian, Spanish, Turkish, Ukrainian, Urdu, Vietnamese, and Yoruba) were recruited, of whom 21 were practicing healthcare interpreters and 5 held management positions in

TABLE 3.1 Interpreters' demographic data

Category	Range	Number	Percentage
Interpreters		26	100.0
Agency	Agency A	19	73.1
	Agency B	7	26.9
	Total	**26**	**100.0**
Gender	Male	8	30.8
	Female	18	69.2
	Total	**26**	**100.0**
Age	18–30	2	7.7
	31–40	6	23.1
	41–50	12	46.2
	51–60	4	15.4
	61–70	2	7.7
	Total	**26**	**100.0**
Education	High school	1	3.8
	Undergraduate/vocational school	4	15.4
	Bachelor's degree	13	50.0
	Master's degree	2	7.7
	Doctorate degree	2	7.7
	MD	2	7.7
	Not reported	2	7.7
	Total	**26**	**100.0**
Ethnicity	White	5	19.2
	Hispanic	12	46.2
	Asian	5	19.2
	Azeri	1	3.8
	African	1	3.8
	Muslim	2	7.7
	Total	**26**	**100.0**
Experience	≤ 1 year	4	15.4
	2–5 years	6	23.1
	6–10 years	7	26.9
	11–15 years	7	26.9
	≥ 15 years	2	7.7
	Total	**26**	**100.0**

interpreting offices. All healthcare interpreters, regardless of their culture and language, were invited to participate in either an individual or dyadic in-depth interview, both of which lasted 1–1.5 hours. All dyadic interviews consisted of two healthcare interpreters. In total, 6 dyadic interviews and 14 individual interviews were conducted. Interpreter demographics are listed in Table 3.1.

B.1. Research Objectives

The study explores healthcare interpreters' communicative strategies in mediating the dynamics of provider–patient interactions. The objectives are to examine interpreters' communicative strategies in healthcare settings and to explore their accounts of their conduct. In essence, these two different issues require two different research methods. The first objective requires the researcher to investigate the practice of healthcare interpreting and the second objective seeks to understand the normative beliefs held by interpreters. The specific research questions are: First, what are the relevant categories of (a) role performances and (b) communicative goals for interpreters? Second, what are the relationships between (a) and (b)? Third, how do interpreters resolve conflicts in (a) and/or (b)? The study comprises two parts. In each part, different research methods and interviews are used.

B.2. Data Set I: Participant Observation

Procedure

To examine healthcare interpreters as the focus of the research and to develop theories for healthcare interpreting (i.e., theories that describe and explain the behaviors and beliefs of healthcare interpreting), I used participant observation. In adopting this observational technique, I assumed a peripheral membership role in two interpreting agencies and observed Mandarin Chinese interpreters' interactions with physicians and patients in medical settings. A peripheral membership (i.e., passively participating in the activities of the observed organization rather than being actively involved in the operation of the organization or activities) allows researchers to formulate an appraisal of the participants' daily practice from an insider's perspective while minimizing serious ethical problems or interfering with the investigated data (Adler & Adler, 1994; Mays & Pope, 1995).

In the first six months of the study, I shadowed the interpreters as they interacted with patients and healthcare-related personnel in medical settings (e.g., hospitals and clinics). I engaged in participant observation of the interpreters' daily assignments, such as interpreting for physicians during medical encounters, for nurses during medical history taking, or for administrative staff setting up future appointments. I also observed how interpreters interacted with patients outside the presence of other healthcare providers (e.g., waiting for physicians in the waiting room). I carried a portable recorder at all times when I was in the field, including at the agencies and other medical settings. If at any time a sensitive situation arose and the participants did not wish the conversation to be recorded, I turned off the recorder. I also asked the interpreters who I shadowed to carry a portable recorder. (In one incident, an interpreter told me that she turned off the recorder after I left the room with the provider because she was "just chitchatting with the patient and their discussion was not related to interpreting.") There are several reasons for having two portable audio-recorders in the field. First, individuals may move around in interpreting sessions. For example, a physician may ask a patient to sit on the exam chair or to go outside to check the x-ray results. As the physicians, patients, and interpreters move around in different spaces, a portable audio-recorder provided the best recording results. Second, with two portable recorders, I was able to position myself more strategically in recording sessions (e.g., stand in a corner to minimize my intrusion into the provider–patient interaction or step out of the room if necessary) and had a second tape to verify if confusion arose in transcription. Third, interpreters' portable recorders may provide important data on how they relate themselves to the patients. Interpreters often have informal conversations with patients in the waiting room. These conversations are essential to both the interpreter's and patient's understanding of their roles in healthcare settings. Having an interpreter carrying a portable recorder was much less intrusive than having a researcher standing near them and trying to record the conversations.

In addition to audio-recording during participant observations, I also took fieldnotes as I shadowed the interpreters. I later composed more detailed fieldnotes for each interpreter–patient pair. Because interpreting is conducted in various spaces, the movement and the setup of video-recording equipment would have been too intrusive. I therefore chose to audio-record interpreting sessions and to use fieldnotes to supplement the lack of visual data.

As to the organization of fieldnotes, the interpreter–patient pair was used for data recording (i.e., the fieldnotes were organized by the units of interpreter–patient pair rather than specific timeline or events). Because interpreters often interpret for the same patient in different settings (e.g., diabetic clinic and arthritis clinic) on multiple occasions, it is likely that they will develop relationships (e.g., friendships) and background knowledge (e.g., medical history) about their patients. By tracking the interpreter–patient unit, I was able to explore different issues. For example, I was able to examine the performances of an interpreter across different patients. I was also able to examine the interactions of an interpreter–patient unit across time and with different healthcare providers. These different dimensions gave valuable data for understanding interpreters' behavior and for evaluating their performance.

Rationale

Participant observation is a common technique for gathering ethnographic data as it allows researchers to participate in the daily routines of a particular setting and develop ongoing relations with the people within it, while observing what transpires in the setting (Emerson, Fretz, & Shaw, 1995). Jorgensen (1989) defined participant observation as having seven distinct features, including the insider's viewpoint, the here and now of everyday life, the development of interpretive theories, an open-ended process of inquiry, an in-depth case study approach, the researcher's direct involvement in the informant's life, and direct observation as a primary data-gathering device. These features made participant observation the method of choice for this study because I was interested in identifying the behavioral aspects of healthcare interpreting (i.e., the *how* questions) and in developing theories of healthcare interpreters' mediating interactions (i.e., the *why* questions; Bogdewic, 1992).

There are several reasons that participant observation (in the form of shadowing) and fieldnotes were likely to be the most effective and the least intrusive ways to examine the practice of healthcare interpreting. First, participant observation allows researchers to understand the world as the participants view it by participating in their daily routines, which is crucial to the investigator's interpretation of the participants' daily practice (Adler & Adler, 1994). Second, participant observation provides researchers with the opportunity to examine the discrepancies between interpreters' normative beliefs and their practices. Self-report information (e.g., data collected from interviews and surveys) are often at risk of participant biases (e.g., social desirability; Mays & Pope, 1995). More importantly, individuals may engage in complex routines without overt awareness of their behaviors or may have explicit theories that contradict their behaviors (Kulick, 1992). In these situations, self-report information, unlike participant observation, would not allow researchers to uncover the discrepancies between the participants' folk beliefs and their practice.

Finally, shadowing and fieldnote-taking are common in healthcare settings. Many hospitals offer shadowing programs for interns and pre-medical students to observe the daily routines of more experienced members such as physicians and nurses (Davis, Anderson, Stankevitz, & Manley, 2013). Shadowing is also often incorporated in the required training for healthcare interpreters (Hasbún Avalos, Pennington, & Osterberg, 2013; Ono, Kiuchi, & Ishikawa, 2013). Because they generally need to jot down key words or sentences for interpreting, healthcare interpreters often carry notepads and take notes during interpreting sessions. Therefore, as a researcher shadowing the interpreter and taking notes during interpreting sessions, I was able to minimize the impact of my presence and still obtain valid data without interrupting or interfering with the participants' daily routines.

In summary, to obtain data about interpreters' practices, I used participant observation and fieldnotes as observational methods. These methods provided realistic and naturalistic information on how interpreters mediate interactions between physicians and patients. More importantly, these methods allowed me to minimize interference in the interpreters' daily routines, obtain an insider's perspective to understand the relevant contexts of healthcare interpreting, and explore the discrepancies between translation beliefs and practices, all of which are crucial to the development of an interpretive theory.

B.3. Data Set II: Ethnographic Interviews

Procedure

In the early stage of the research, I observed and developed rapport with two Mandarin Chinese interpreters from Agency A. I also established relationships with interpreters of other languages, some of whom later became my informants on healthcare interpreting issues for other languages and cultures.

During Part I of the study, I conducted ethnographic interviews with Mandarin Chinese interpreters. In addition, if an interpreter-mediated conversation contained data that I wished to explore further, I interviewed all participants (e.g., the physician, the patient, and the interpreter) involved in the conversation. All interviews were recorded with portable audio-recorders. Ethnographic interviews were conducted in several formats, including as one-on-one interviews that were audio-recorded and casual conversations that happened in the field (Gilchrist & Williams, 1999). The ethnographic interviews in this part of the study were informal in nature, lasting from a few minutes to over an hour, depending on whether the interviewee was interested in further exploring the topics. For example, I had informal conversations with the interpreters by asking for memorable cases as they were taking a break in the agency or I asked a particular question after an interpreting session to explore why the interviewee (e.g., the physician, the patient, or the interpreter) acted in a specific way. As a researcher shadowing healthcare interpreters of a particular agency (i.e., using the method of participant observation), I had many opportunities to interview the participants in various settings (e.g., the agency, the waiting room, or other social occasions). My shared experience as a healthcare interpreter allowed these interpreters to develop a relationship with me and, perhaps, to be more open in discussing their experiences and thoughts.

Rationale

Interviews are very useful and valuable in conjunction with participant observation (Gilchrist & Williams, 1999). Because it is technically impossible to interview all individuals encountered in the field, informants become an important resource that allows a researcher to efficiently obtain information (Gilchrist & Williams, 1999). The interviews conducted in Part I were relatively unstructured and exploratory; the data provided rich information and vivid performances that aimed to socialize, educate, and enlighten me about the complicated practices of interpreters. The participants also had a greater voice in both the research process and the final report because these informal interviews were conducted as opportunities arose and sometimes consisted of multiple sessions over a period of time (Fontana & Frey, 1994).

B.4. Data Set III: Individual and Dyadic In-depth Interviews

Procedure

As my research progressed (3 months into Part I, the study entered Part II), I used more structured interviews, in which I presented the participants with specific theoretical concerns. In Part II, all healthcare interpreters, regardless of their culture and language, were invited to participate in individual or dyadic interviews. In total, 14 individual interviews and 6 dyadic interviews were conducted. Both types of interview lasted 1–1.5 hours. All dyadic interviews consisted of two interpreters from different languages (except one interview that included two Spanish interpreters). Because of the sensitive nature of the interview questions, it was important to make sure that the interpreters felt comfortable with the information and strategies they disclosed. I asked all interpreters not to share their actual names with each other and made sure that all discussions were done in a productive and friendly manner.

In these interviews, I relied on my knowledge about Mandarin Chinese culture/language, my experience as a healthcare interpreter, and my prior data collected through participant observation to navigate through the design, preparation, and interview process. The research questions included: How do interpreters present themselves in medical settings? What is their main task as healthcare interpreters? Why did they decide to be healthcare interpreters? How do they relate to physicians, healthcare providers, patients' family members, and patients? What were the most common challenges in their daily assignments? Had they ever had conflicts with physicians or patients? How did they resolve these conflicts? How do they handle their stress and emotions in interpreting sessions? What kind of training is needed for healthcare interpreters? The interview questions were developed with these theoretical concerns in mind.

Although the questions asked in dyadic interviews were the same as those in the individual in-depth interviews, the purposes of the interviews were different. The purpose of the individual interviews was to elicit detailed narratives of personal experiences and thoughts. The purpose of the dyadic interviews was to play off the diverse experiences and backgrounds of multiple participants, allowing these differences to stimulate and enrich the discussion. I presented research questions, solicited different opinions, and encouraged discussions between participants. The goal of the dyadic interviews was not to reach agreement among all participants but to uncover the diversity and variability of the practices and beliefs held by interpreters of different cultures and languages. Dyadic interviews conducted in this part allowed me to develop theories that had better external validity for healthcare interpreting in general.

Rationale

In-depth interviews were designed to generate narratives that focused on fairly specific research questions (Miller & Crabtree, 1999). Charmaz (1991, p. 385)

TABLE 3.2 Summary of data-collection information

Phase	Data-collecting methods	Participants	Location
Phase I: Participant observation	• Participant observation • Fieldnotes • Ethnographic interview	2 Mandarin Chinese interpreters (for participant observation; 12 medical encounters) 11 healthcare providers, 2 patients, and 1 patient's family member who used Mandarin Chinese interpreters' services	• Agency A • Other medical settings (e.g., hospitals)
Phase II: Theory development	• Individual interviews • Dyadic interviews	14 medical interpreters of various languages and cultures 12 medical interpreters of various languages and cultures	• Agency A • Agency B

suggested that in-depth interviews "elicit inner views of respondents' lives as they portray their worlds, experiences, and observations." Because the main objective of this study was to develop theories that explain healthcare interpreters' interpreting and mediating strategies and beliefs, the research questions for in-depth interviews focused on gaining insight into interpreters' interpretation and understanding of their roles.

On the other hand, the synergy, spontaneity, and stimulation of the group process are great advantages of group interviews as they facilitate exchanges among the participants (Barbour, 1995; Stewart & Shamdasani, 1990). I included interpreters from different cultures and had them discuss their experiences and thoughts about healthcare interpreting. In a heterogeneous group, differences in opinions may be explored from various perspectives as each participant is involved in the sense-making process (Schattner, Shmerling, & Murphy, 1993). Therefore, interpreters' shared experiences in healthcare interpreting and their diverse cultures and languages allowed them to have a common ground for discussion but at the same time explored the differences in their practices and beliefs about healthcare interpreting. Table 3.2 summarizes the data-collection methods and the number of participants in this phase of my research program.

C. Providers: Interviews and Survey

Although many researchers have examined the complexity of interpreter-mediated provider–patient interactions in recent years, most studies have centered on the interpreters' perspectives, soliciting information from only interpreters (e.g., Angelelli, 2004; Dysart-Gale, 2005). However, providers' communicative behaviors have significant influence over the quality of a medical encounter (Hsieh, 2006) and the interpreters' communicative strategies (Elderkin-Thompson, Silver, & Waitzkin, 2001). While many studies have explored how interpreters understand their roles, few studies examined providers' perceptions of, attitudes about, and expectations of the roles and performances of healthcare interpreters until the late 2000s. Considering the important role of providers in managing the content and the process of provider–patient interactions, it is critical that the providers' concerns and expectations of healthcare interpreters are reflected in the training and codes of ethics for interpreter-mediated medical encounters.

There are several reasons why providers' perspectives and needs are crucial in advancing the theory and practice of bilingual health care. First, providers assume a variety of roles which may require an interpreter to pay attention to different aspects of the interaction. Providers often need to perform different tasks (e.g., medical history taking and rapport building) and various roles (e.g., investigator and social supporter) during a medical encounter (Cegala & Broz, 2002; Putsch, 1985). If an interpreter fails to notice the changes in a provider's goals and roles, the provider may feel unsatisfied with the medical encounter (Metzger, 1999). Second, providers of different specialties may have different preferences for the interpreters' roles and communicative strategies. For example, a family physician may be more interested in developing long-term trust and rapport with the patient, whereas an emergency physician may want to focus only on the information that is relevant to the immediate diagnosis. In other words, because of the different communicative needs of providers, it is likely that the best practice for interpreter-mediated encounters in these contexts will be different. Third, providers may want an interpreter to assume the role of conduit, active participant, or a combination of the two, depending on the situations and/or their personal preferences. For example, a provider may want an interpreter to provide cultural information, discuss possible intercultural conflicts, or suggest treatment strategies that are culturally sensitive, but do it in ways that do not threaten the provider's goals. In summary, because providers' needs and goals can be context specific but also dynamically and emergently negotiated in medical encounters, it is important to investigate how providers manage interpreter-mediated medical encounters.

With my NIH funding in 2006–2009, I began a 3-year data collection of providers' perspectives about interpreter-mediated medical encounters. In Part I (i.e., interviews), I recruited 39 healthcare providers from 5 specialties (i.e., ob/gyn, emergency medicine, oncology, mental health, and nursing). By using a combination of focus groups and in-depth interviews, I explored providers' expectations and attitudes to interpreter-mediated medical encounters. By examining their specialty-specific needs and shared expectations as healthcare providers, I identified specific themes that provided the underlying principles for providers' utilization of healthcare interpreters.

Based on the qualitative analysis of Part I, I developed and executed a quantitative survey in Part II. The survey included 293 healthcare providers from the same

5 specialty areas. The objective of Part II (i.e., survey) was to generate external validity of the patterns observed in the interviews from Part I.

C.1. Research Objectives

The specific aims of this phase of my studies are (a) to assess providers' experiences with, perceptions of, attitudes about, and expectations for healthcare interpreters and (b) to explore differences in these dimensions across different medical specialties. The specific research questions were: (a) What are providers' experiences with and attitudes to the communicative strategies used by interpreters? (b) What are the criteria used by providers to evaluate the success of bilingual health communication? (c) What are providers' expectations for interpreters' roles and performances? and (d) Do providers in different specialties vary in their perceptions, attitudes, and expectations? These aims were addressed through qualitative formative work and a subsequent quantitative survey of healthcare providers.

The objective of this study was to generate a new communication theory that highlights providers' communicative goals during a medical encounter and educates interpreters to respond to these needs more effectively. The findings could significantly enhance the training for healthcare interpreters and the quality of bilingual provider–patient communication. Training can focus on educating interpreters to develop professional judgments on how to adopt appropriate communicative strategies that meet the providers' expectations during the course of provider–patient interactions. In other words, a professional interpreter will be expected to master different models of interpreting, including the conduit model and other communication models. The interpreters are "always judicious about how, when, and where any particular model is put into play" (Jacobs & Aakhus, 2002, p. 200). Research on bilingual health communication can identify the various interpreting strategies that are appropriate in different contexts and train interpreters to master these strategies. On the other hand, researchers can also develop training programs for providers to facilitate their use of healthcare interpreters. By identifying the providers' different needs and expectations, researchers can explore the effective ways for providers to inform interpreters about their expectations. The long-term goal of this line of research is to develop training models that make the best use of interpreters to help patients achieve improved health literacy and better healthcare interactions.

C.2. Data Set I: Interviews with Providers

Procedure

I recruited 39 providers from a major healthcare facility which also serves as a university teaching facility, in the southern United States. The providers are from five specialty areas: ob/gyn (n = 8), emergency medicine (n = 7), oncology

TABLE 3.3 Providers' demographic data

Variable		Interviews		Survey	
		N	%	N	%
Specialty areas					
	Emergency Medicine	7	17.9	88	30.6
	Mental Health	7	17.9	54	18.8
	Nursing	6	15.4	57	19.8
	OB/GYN	8	20.5	53	18.4
	Oncology	11	28.2	36	12.5
	Total	**39**	**100.0**	**288**	**100.0**
Gender					
	Male	14	35.9	119	41.3
	Female	25	64.1	169	58.7
	Total	**39**	**100.0**	**288**	**100.0**
Experience with interpreters					
	0–10 times	8	20.5	105	36.5
	10+ times	31	79.5	183	63.5
	Total	**39**	**100.0**	**288**	**100.0**
Age					
	18–30	8	20.5	98	34.0
	30–50	17	43.6	139	48.3
	50+	14	35.9	50	17.4
	Not reported	0	0.0	1	0.3
	Total	**39**	**100.0**	**288**	**100.0**
Native language					
	English			264	91.7
	Spanish			9	3.1
	Other			14	4.9
	Not reported			1	0.3
	Total			**288**	**100.0**

(n = 11), mental health (n = 7), and nursing (n = 6). I recruited providers through specialty-specific meetings held by clinics, sections, and departments. Participants in the nursing area were recruited through women and newborn services; all others were physicians of the corresponding specialties. The providers' demographics are listed in Table 3.3.

Because providers often have busy and variable schedules, I offered individual interviews to providers who were unable to attend the focus groups. The same semi-structured interview guide was used for both the focus groups and individual interviews. The interviews were conducted by a graduate research assistant who was not familiar with my theory of bilingual health communication. I also participated in the focus groups/interviews as an assistant moderator, monitoring the process of the interviews (Bowling, 1997). The interview guide explores providers' (a) expectations for healthcare interpreters' emotional support, (b) communicative needs in interpreter-mediated interactions, (c) criteria used to assess the success of bilingual health care, and (d) contextual factors that may influence their expectations.

Although professional interpreters are available in the healthcare facility, participants reported working with a variety of interpreters (e.g., telephone interpreter and family members). I encouraged providers to compare their experiences and expectations for different types of interpreters whenever possible. In total, my research team conducted 8 specialty-specific focus groups (each lasting 1–1.5 hours) and 14 individual interviews (each lasting 1–1.5 hours). I was present in all focus groups and individual interviews.

Rationale

For Part I (i.e., interview phase), only the providers who had experience working with interpreters were recruited. Because the objective of the focus group interviews was to explore the complexity and diversity in providers' attitudes and expectations for bilingual communication, providers' experiences with interpreters would give them the knowledge and ability to reflect on their experiences and provide more in-depth analysis. These five specialties represented providers with distinctive needs. For example, providers in the obstetrics-gynecology department often need to develop long-term relationships with their patients, helping them through the months of pregnancy. Providers in the emergency department may be less concerned about developing long-term rapport with their patients, but they face time constraints in making accurate diagnoses. Providers in the oncology department often deal with issues that are highly emotional and cultural (e.g., death and dying) and may need to interact with patients' family members regularly. Mental health providers may be particularly sensitive about language as talking is both the site of patient symptoms and their tool for treatment. Finally, nurses often interact with patients at a closer level than physicians and thus may have different communicative needs. The distinctive needs of the different specialties and their universal role as healthcare providers offer unique opportunities to examine the commonalities and the differences between providers.

Researchers have suggested that a minimum of 4–5 focus groups is required to reach data saturation (Brown, 1999; Morgan, 1988). With approximately ten providers from each specialty (i.e., eight focus groups), I was able to generate in-depth data that was sufficient to explore the variability and complexity of providers' understanding of interpreter-mediated interactions (Brown, 1999).

C.3. Data Set II: Survey

Procedure

I recruited 293 providers from five specialties (i.e., obstetrics-gynecology, emergency department, oncology, mental health, and nursing) to participate in the survey. After reviewing the survey responses, I dropped five surveys due to missing values, leaving a total of 288 participants. I recruited the providers through departmental meetings, through grand rounds, and from individual clinics. All participants included were physicians or residents who worked in the corresponding specialty areas, except nurses, who were recruited through hospital-wide, nursing-specific meetings. Providers completed the written survey on site or mailed the completed survey in a prepaid envelope. Each provider received a $15 gift card as an incentive for participating in the survey.

Materials

The survey was developed based on my previous qualitative studies and past literature to assess participants' evaluations of the importance of specific characteristics or issues related to healthcare interpreting. In addition to including items that explore interpreters' conduit and patient advocate roles, I also included several less well-known roles (e.g., co-diagnostician and information gatekeeper) and functions (e.g., providing emotional and informational support and other logistical services) that were identified in my previous qualitative studies. The survey used a 7-point Likert scale, ranging from 1 (extremely unimportant) to 7 (extremely important). I also measured five demographic variables, which included the providers' gender, experiences with interpreters, age, native language, and specialty area. These demographic variables were later used for a series of multivariate analyses of variance (MANOVAs).

Rationale

Newman and Benz (1998) proposed that qualitative and quantitative studies are not mutually exclusive or interchangeable; however, the relationship between the two approaches is one of many isolated events on the continuum of scientific inquiry. The application of survey questionnaires is part of the process in the continuum. This study of the providers' attitudes begins with a qualitative approach, using focus group interviews to generate an understanding of bilingual health communication from an insider's perspective. Although this approach guarantees a high level of internal validity (Morgan, 1988), external validity is neglected (LeCompte & Goetz, 1982). The survey aims to improve the external validity of this study.

D. Medical Encounters in Gynecologic Oncology

Procedure and Participants

The data included in this book is part of a larger longitudinal study conducted from January to October 2012, examining the illness experiences of patients who were newly diagnosed with gynecologic cancer. The larger study includes ethnographic observations, video-recorded medical encounters, and interviews. All video-recorded provider–patient interactions took place in counsel rooms and/or exam rooms in the gynecology-oncology clinic. Patients received a $10 Wal-Mart gift card for the video-recorded medical encounters. All research procedures have been approved by the appropriate institutional review boards.

In total, 29 patients and 3 oncologists (i.e., MDs with gynecologic oncology specialty) from a teaching hospital are included in this book. All participants are female and are native English speakers living in a large Midwestern city in the United States. The average age of the oncologists was 43.7 (standard deviation [SD] = 11.6). The age range of the patients was 42 to 89 (mean = 61.9; SD = 10.9). We assigned pseudonyms to all participants. Patients' pseudonyms start with C (e.g., Cara) and oncologists' start with P (i.e., Pam, Pearl, and Piper).

For this study, we examined data collected during the patient's *first* medical visit, including only interactions between the patients and the oncologists. In these first encounters, the patients and the oncologists often have multiple interactions. We treated each patient–oncologist interaction as a data segment. In total, 44 segments (553.25 minutes) of the first medical visits were included in the study. The average time per segment is 12.6 minutes (SD = 8.5), averaging 1.5 segments per patient. Of the 44 segments, 9 were with Pam, 33 were with Pearl, 1 was with Piper, and 1 was with Pearl and Piper together. We assigned pseudonyms to all participants, archived all segments, and anonymized the data. A professional transcription agency transcribed all medical encounters. All transcripts were then reviewed and edited to ensure accuracy prior to data analysis.

Rationale

A challenge faced by researchers in the field of bilingual health care is the difficulties in obtaining sufficient data for meaningful analysis. A review of 61 qualitative studies found that 75.4 percent of the studies (n = 46) used interviews/focus groups as primary data and only 19.6 percent (n = 12) used audio/video-recordings of the actual encounters (Brisset, Leanza, & Laforest, 2013). Many publications also share the same set of data derived from a parent study (Karliner, Jacobs, Chen, & Mutha, 2007). These findings are not unexpected as they reflect the challenges faced by researchers in this field: research design complexity and the limited number of interpreter-mediated medical encounters.

Compared to collecting data through interviews/focus groups, examining actual medical encounters represents a more complicated and difficult research design due to complexities in recruitment, equipment preparation, and concerns about potential litigation and privacy violations. It's not surprising that there are fewer studies based on actual medical encounters. However, researchers have found that participants' perceptions do not correlate with their or other participants' behaviors in the actual encounters (Cegala, Gade, Broz, & McClure, 2004). As a result, researchers have emphasized the importance of examining actual medical encounters, arguing that "connecting communication characteristics to difficulties and/or roles in future studies would give us better understanding of the communication process and help formulate relevant recommendations for different interpreting situations" (Brisset et al., 2013, p. 138).

Identifying communication characteristics of an emergent, dynamic medical encounter can be difficult due to the limited number of interpreter-mediated interactions. Individuals with LEP patients account for 9 percent of the total US population (Whatley & Batalova, 2013). Thus, compared to the English-speaking population in the United States, the LEP population represents a considerably smaller pool of participants. The number of interpreter-mediated encounters is further reduced by several other factors. First, LEP patients often prefer to visit language-concordant providers in their local communities (Simon et al., 2013). Second, providers often underutilize professional interpreters and communicate with LEP patients directly despite their limited proficiency in the patient's language (Diamond, Tuot, & Karliner, 2012). Two studies found that less than 20 percent of LEP patients received services from professional interpreters (Ginde, Sullivan, Corel, Caceres, & Camargo, 2010; Schenker, Pérez-Stable, Nickleach, & Karliner, 2011). Finally, researchers often need to limit the specific clinical contexts and language combination to ensure analytical rigor, which significantly reduces the number of eligible observations. Although researchers have stressed the need for comparative studies (e.g., Karliner et al., 2007), the limited number of interpreter-mediated medical encounters makes such research designs difficult, if not impossible.

I recognize the experimental nature of this approach as the data do not involve an interpreter or a bilingual component. Nevertheless, because providers generally have little training about working with interpreters (Brisset et al., 2014) and oncologists often maintain the same communicative script irrespective of patient differences (Gao, Burke, Somkin, & Pasick, 2009), physicians in our study are likely to adopt similar behaviors in both monolingual and bilingual medical encounters. By examining monolingual medical encounters, researchers can still identify the inherent challenges and barriers to interpreters' management of oncologist–patient interactions. These challenges are not a result of interpreters' problematic performances or lack of competence. Rather, these challenges are inherent to *all* (gynecologic) oncologist–patient interactions as they reflect the complex nature of human interactions in cancer care in the United States.

E. Data Analysis

Over the years, I have utilized data collected from these studies in multiple ways. I have examined data from interpreters and providers independently and have juxtaposed them to explore similarities and differences in their perspectives. I have examined interpreters' discursive strategies, role identities, and dilemmas in performing their tasks. Similarly, I have explored providers' attitudes and expectations of interpreters' roles and functions in healthcare settings. This book serves as a synthesis of prior findings of my work but also as an attempt to incorporate the latest research in the field. Because each chapter entails different analytical processes, rather than giving a generic account of the data analysis, I will include the details of the analysis in their corresponding sections.

F. Notations and Transcripts

The combination of data-collection methods allows us to obtain richer data by including more perspectives from participants with diverse expertise and communicative needs. The transcripts are CAPITALIZED when they are the speakers' emphasis and *italicized* when they are my emphasis. Each participant is assigned a pseudonym. I denote interpreters with a superscript I (i.e., ^{I}) and patients with a superscript P (i.e., ^{P}) after their pseudonyms. I denote healthcare providers' expertise with a superscript H (i.e., ^{H}) for data collected in Study 1. For provider data collected in Study 2, I indicate providers' areas of expertise: Obstetrics-gynecology is abbreviated as $^{OB/GYN}$, emergency medicine as ^{EM}, oncology as ^{ONC}, nursing as ^{NUR}, and mental health as ^{MH}. For Study 3, patients' pseudonyms start with C (e.g., Cara) and the three oncologists are Pam, Pearl, and Piper.

G. Limitations

There are three limitations based on these sets of data. First, although I recognize interpreter-mediated medical encounters as a coordinated achievement between multiple parties, the data lacks the patients' perspectives. The only patient perspectives included in the study were collected during the participant observations of the first and third studies. While I can examine what patients do in these medical encounters, the lack of self-report data prohibit me from making claims about their attitudes or preferences.

Although there is a wealth of research on minority health, most studies focused on language-discordant patients' barriers to care rather than their expectations, needs, and behaviors in interpreter-mediated medical encounters. The challenges in collecting data from the patients' perspectives in cross-cultural care stem from the difficulties in differentiating and reconciling the unique patient versus cultural perspectives. As patients' lives and experiences are culturally situated, their needs and perspectives are intertwined with unique illness-related needs and cultural perspectives. In other words, a Chinese patient may have very different expectations and needs than a Latino patient, even though both are patients with LEP. Examining these language-discordant patients' diverse needs and attitudes presents research design challenges as researchers face significant language and cultural barriers in collecting and analyzing the data. In contrast, because healthcare providers have been trained professionally, are well educated, and experience minimal language barriers in communicating their ideas, they often share similar worldviews and perspectives. The same is true for professional interpreters. As a result, researchers are able to effectively identify their belief systems and patterns of behavior by examining their commonalities. Nevertheless, by identifying providers' and interpreters' perspectives, researchers can generate meaningful future directions for patient-centered research in interpreter-mediated interactions. I will revisit this issue in later chapters.

A second limitation of the study is that the interpreters included in the studies are all professional interpreters. Healthcare providers have been found to consistently underutilize professional interpreters, who are generally only used for 20 percent of LEP patients (Ginde et al., 2010; Schenker et al., 2011). In other words, 80 percent of LEP patients work with a wide variety of nonprofessional interpreters. This poses a significant demand to examine and explore the functions and impacts of these nonprofessional interpreters in healthcare settings. While we did not collect data from nonprofessional interpreters, we have actively solicited professional interpreters and healthcare providers' perspectives about a wide variety of interpreters.

Finally, the third limitation is that all my data are collected in the United States. In addition, providers were recruited through large, comprehensive healthcare institutions, which generally have more resources and regulations for healthcare delivery for minority patients. Due to the differences in sociopolitical contexts in the host countries and organizational contexts in healthcare settings, it is possible that some of the arguments may not be applicable to different countries or healthcare institutions where these resources or social norms are not expected or available.

While these limitations present challenges, it is important to note that the amount and quality of data included in this book are unprecedented. For example, Roy's (2000) book has only 30 minutes of interactional data. Metzger's (1999) book on sign language interpreting contains less than 35 minutes of interactional data, including one mock and one actual provider–patient encounter. While Angelelli (2004) appeared to have a significant amount of data, a close look at the data shows that she has a total of 450 minutes of interpreter-mediated interactions, including 380 telephone interactions and 12 face-to-face interactions. This suggests that her data involved very short interactions, which limited the possibility of providing complex analysis.

In contrast, I have over 15 hours of face-to-face interpreter-mediated medical encounters (with Mandarin Chinese interpreters). The data allowed me to examine how interpreters manage provider–patient interactions both inside and outside of medical encounters. In addition, I also have interview data with 26 interpreters from 17 different cultures/languages and 39 healthcare providers from 5 clinical specialties, including emergency medicine, ob/gyn, mental health, oncology, and nursing. In addition, I surveyed 293 providers from 5 clinical specialties, including emergency medicine, ob/gyn, mental health, oncology, and nursing. This amount and quality of data is rare in bilingual health care. More importantly, this is the first book of its kind that includes not only interpreters' perspectives but also the needs and perspectives of providers from various clinical specialties.

References

Adler, P. A., & Adler, P. (1994). Observational techniques. In N. K. Denzin & Y. S. Lincoln (Eds.), *Handbook of qualitative research* (pp. 377–392). Thousand Oaks, CA: Sage.

Angelelli, C. V. (2004). *Medical interpreting and cross-cultural communication.* Cambridge, UK: Cambridge University Press.

Barbour, R. S. (1995). Using focus groups in general practice research. *Family Practice*, 12, 328–334.

Bogdewic, S. P. (1992). Participant observation. In B. F. Crabtree & W. L. Miller (Eds.), *Doing qualitative research* (pp. 45–69). Thousand Oaks, CA: Sage.

Bowling, A. (1997). *Research methods in health: Investigating health and health services.* Bristol, PA: Open University Press.

Brisset, C., Leanza, Y., & Laforest, K. (2013). Working with interpreters in health care: A systematic review and meta-ethnography of qualitative studies. *Patient Education and Counseling*, 91, 131–140.

Brisset, C., Leanza, Y., Rosenberg, E., Vissandjée, B., Kirmayer, L., Muckle, G., … Laforce, H. (2014). Language barriers in mental health care: A survey of primary care practitioners. *Journal of Immigrant and Minority Health*, 16, 1238–1246.

Brown, J. B. (1999). The use of focus groups in clinical research. In B. F. Crabtree & W. L. Miller (Eds.), *Doing qualitative research* (2nd ed., pp. 109–124). Thousand Oaks, CA: Sage.

Cegala, D. J., & Broz, S. L. (2002). Physician communication skills training: A review of theoretical backgrounds, objectives and skills. *Medical Education*, 36, 1004–1016.

Cegala, D. J., Gade, C., Broz, S. L., & McClure, L. (2004). Physicians' and patients' perceptions of patients' communication competence in a primary care medical interview. *Health Communication*, 16, 289–304.

Charmaz, K. (1991). *Good days, bad days: The self in chronic illness and time.* New Brunswick, NJ: Rutgers University Press.

Davis, J. M., Anderson, M. C., Stankevitz, K. A., & Manley, A. R. (2013). Providing premedical students with quality clinical and research experience: The Tobacco Science Scholars Program. *Wisconsin Medical Journal*, 112, 195–198.

Diamond, L. C., Tuot, D., & Karliner, L. (2012). The use of Spanish language skills by physicians and nurses: Policy implications for teaching and testing. *Journal of General Internal Medicine*, 27, 117–123.

Dysart-Gale, D. (2005). Communication models, professionalization, and the work of medical interpreters. *Health Communication*, 17, 91–103.

Elderkin-Thompson, V., Silver, R. C., & Waitzkin, H. (2001). When nurses double as interpreters: A study of Spanish-speaking patients in a US primary care setting. *Social Science & Medicine*, 52, 1343–1358.

Emerson, R. M., Fretz, R. I., & Shaw, L. L. (1995). *Writing ethnographic fieldnotes*. Chicago, IL: University of Chicago Press.

Fontana, A., & Frey, J. H. (1994). Interviewing: The art of science. In N. K. Denzin & Y. S. Lincoln (Eds.), *Handbook of qualitative research* (pp. 361–376). Thousand Oaks, CA: Sage.

Gao, G., Burke, N., Somkin, C. P., & Pasick, R. (2009). Considering culture in physician–patient communication during colorectal cancer screening. *Qualitative Health Research*, 19, 778–789.

Gilchrist, V. J., & Williams, R. L. (1999). Key informant interviews. In B. F. Crabtree & W. L. Miller (Eds.), *Doing qualitative research* (2nd ed., pp. 71–88). Thousand Oaks, CA: Sage.

Ginde, A. A., Sullivan, A. F., Corel, B., Caceres, J. A., & Camargo, C. A., Jr. (2010). Reevaluation of the effect of mandatory interpreter legislation on use of professional interpreters for ED patients with language barriers. *Patient Education and Counseling*, 81, 204–206.

Hasbún Avalos, O., Pennington, K., & Osterberg, L. (2013). Revolutionizing volunteer interpreter services: An evaluation of an innovative medical interpreter education program. *Journal of General Internal Medicine*, 28, 1589–1595.

Hsieh, E. (2006). Conflicts in how interpreters manage their roles in provider–patient interactions. *Social Science & Medicine*, 62, 721–730.

Jacobs, S., & Aakhus, M. (2002). What mediators do with words: Implementing three models of rational discussion in dispute mediation. *Conflict Resolution Quarterly*, 20, 177–203.

Jorgensen, D. L. (1989). *Participant observation: A methodology for human studies*. Newbury Park, CA: Sage.

Karliner, L. S., Jacobs, E. A., Chen, A. H., & Mutha, S. (2007). Do professional interpreters improve clinical care for patients with limited English proficiency? A systematic review of the literature. *Health Services Research*, 42, 727–754.

Kulick, D. (1992). *Language shift and cultural reproduction: Socialization, self, and syncretism in a Papua New Guinea village*. New York: Cambridge University Press.

LeCompte, M. D., & Goetz, J. P. (1982). Problems of reliability and validity in ethnographic research. *Review of Educational Research*, 52, 31–60.

Mays, N., & Pope, C. (1995). Qualitative research: Observational methods in health care settings. *British Medical Journal*, 311, 182–184.

Metzger, M. (1999). *Sign language interpreting: Deconstructing the myth of neutrality*. Washington, DC: Gallaudet University Press.

Miller, W. L., & Crabtree, B. F. (1999). Depth interviewing. In B. F. Crabtree & W. L. Miller (Eds.), *Doing qualitative research* (2nd ed., pp. 89–107). Thousand Oaks, CA: Sage.

Morgan, D. L. (1988). *Focus groups as qualitative research*. Newbury Park, CA: Sage.

Newman, I., & Benz, C. R. (1998). *Qualitative-quantitative research methodology: Exploring the interactive continuum*. Carbondale, IL: Southern Illinois University Press.

Ono, N., Kiuchi, T., & Ishikawa, H. (2013). Development and pilot testing of a novel education method for training medical interpreters. *Patient Education and Counseling*, 93, 604–611.

Putsch, R. W., III. (1985). Cross-cultural communication: The special case of interpreters in health care. *Journal of the American Medical Association*, 254, 3344–3348.

Roy, C. B. (2000). *Interpreting as a discourse process*. New York: Oxford University Press.

Schattner, P., Shmerling, A., & Murphy, B. (1993). Focus groups: A useful research method in general practice. *Medical Journal of Australia, 158,* 622–625.

Schenker, Y., Pérez-Stable, E. J., Nickleach, D., & Karliner, L. S. (2011). Patterns of interpreter use for hospitalized patients with limited English proficiency. *Journal of General Internal Medicine, 26,* 712–717.

Simon, M. A., Ragas, D. M., Nonzee, N. J., Phisuthikul, A. M., Luu, T. H., & Dong, X. (2013). Perceptions of patient-provider communication in breast and cervical cancer-related care: A qualitative study of low-income English- and Spanish-speaking women. *Journal of Community Health, 38,* 707–715.

Stewart, D., & Shamdasani, P. (1990). *Focus groups: Theory and practice*. Newbury Park, CA: Sage.

Whatley, M., & Batalova, J. (2013). Limited English proficient population of the United States. Retrieved February 8, 2015, from www.migrationpolicy.org/article/limited-english-proficient-population-united-states.

4

CONCEPTUALIZING INTERPRETERS IN BILINGUAL HEALTH COMMUNICATION

When I first started my research program in the early 2000s, the field of bilingual health care often failed to recognize the wide range of interpreters that work in healthcare settings. Empirical studies of the practices of healthcare interpreters have produced some conflicting findings. A review of different interventions to improve culturally and linguistically competent care (e.g., providing trained interpreters, training culturally sensitive healthcare staff, or using translated written materials) did not lead to clear conclusions due to a lack of both quantity and quality of comparative studies (Anderson et al., 2003).

Several studies have provided evidence of the benefits of providing interpreter services. For example, in Tocher and Larson's (1996) study, the treatment process and outcomes of diabetes care for patients receiving interpreting services were as good as, if not better than, those of English-speaking patients. In another study, uninsured patients who received interpreting services fared as well as or *better than* English-speaking uninsured patients in their satisfaction with healthcare services (Andrulis, Goodman, & Pryor, 2002). Other researchers have made similar observations, noting that the quality of healthcare services received by patients who received interpreting services was equivalent or similar to that of language-concordant provider–patient situations (Bernstein et al., 2002; Hampers & McNulty, 2002; L. J. Lee, Batal, Maselli, & Kutner, 2002). In addition, compared to patients who said an interpreter should have been used, patients with interpreters were more satisfied with their provider's friendliness, concern for the patient as a person, efforts to make the patient comfortable, and amount of time spent (Baker, Hayes, & Fortier, 1998). Also, compared to patients who did not receive interpreter services, patients who had an interpreter had a significantly greater increase in office visits, prescription writing, and prescription filling (Jacobs et al., 2001). These findings suggest that providing interpreter services improves patients'

TABLE 4.1 Comparisons between different types of interpreters

Type		Availability	Professionalism	Comfort to patient	Interpreting quality
Professional interpreters	In-person interpreters	Varied	High	Moderate–high	High
	Technology-based interpreters	High	Moderate–high	Moderate–high	Moderate–high
Bilingual medical professionals	Bilingual providers	Low	n/a	Moderate–high	w
	Bilingual medical staff	Varied	Low–moderate	Low–moderate	Varied
Nonprofessional interpreters	Chance interpreters	Moderate	Low	Low	Low
	Family interpreters	Moderate–high	Low	Moderate–high	Varied

quality of care, treatment process, health outcomes, satisfaction, and treatment adherence.

In other studies, however, the results of providing interpreter services were not all positive. For example, compared to English-speaking patients, Spanish-speaking patients who received interpreter services had less communication with their physicians, were less likely to receive facilitative comments from physicians (i.e., comments that encourage patients' further discussion), and were more likely to have their comments ignored (Rivadeneyra, Elderkin-Thompson, Silver, & Waitzkin, 2000). Compared to patients who thought an interpreter was necessary but were not provided with one, patients who received interpreting services were not significantly different in their objective understanding of diagnosis and treatment (Baker, Parker, Williams, Coates, & Pitkin, 1996). When compared to English-speaking patients, Spanish-speaking patients who communicated through an interpreter were significantly less likely to be given a referral for a follow-up appointment after an emergency department visit (Sarver & Baker, 2000) and were less satisfied with their provider–patient relationship even in areas unrelated to language (Baker & Hayes, 1997).

A closer examination of the literature suggests that many early studies did not report the sources and training of their interpreters. When faced with mixed findings about the impacts of interpreters in healthcare settings, researchers were unable to untangle the confounding influences of interpreter types, interpreter errors, clinical settings, or therapeutic complexities, among other potential factors that affect their findings. In 2006, I proposed a typology of healthcare interpreters (Hsieh, 2006), which was later adapted by the American Medical Association (American Medical Association, 2007). Since then, there has been significant progress in research designs and findings about interpreter types and their corresponding impacts. Based on these recent findings, I am proposing a revised typology of interpreters (Table 4.1). In the following section, I will examine the unique characteristics of each interpreter type, including the latest findings and the corresponding challenges.

A. Professional Interpreters

Several recent reviews have concluded that professional interpreters can significantly improve a patient's quality of care (Bischoff, 2012; Flores, 2005; Karliner, Jacobs, Chen, & Mutha, 2007). In particular, professional interpreters can significantly improve provider–patient communication, resource utilization, patient satisfaction, and health outcomes. Professional interpreters include a wide variety of interpreters with various levels of training. The Office of Minority Health, a branch of the US Department of Health and Human Services, has noted that a minimum training of 40 hours is recommended by the National Council on Interpretation in Health Care (IQ Solutions, 2001). A recent study found that interpreters with at least 100 hours of training are significantly less likely to commit interpreting errors than those with fewer than 100 hours of training (Flores, Abreu, Barone, Bachur, & Lin, 2012). There are also several undergraduate and graduate programs that offer majors in interpreting, some of which offer state-level certification in healthcare interpreting (Roat, 2006). It is important to note that there are no federal certifications for healthcare interpreting in the United States. The Registry of Interpreters for the Deaf (RID), the national association of signed language interpreters in the USA, offers specialized certification for legal and educational interpreters; however, it does not offer credentialing for healthcare interpreting. Although there are several national organizations promoting national certification programs and/or examinations for spoken language interpreters in the United States, none has been recognized as the official federal standard (International Medical Interpreters Association, 2014).

According to the US Bureau of Labor Statistics, the median annual wage for healthcare interpreters was $40,130 in May 2012, with self-employed interpreters paid at hourly rates (Bureau of Labor Statistics, 2014). However, actual income may vary significantly depending on the interpreter's language, specialty, skill, experience, education, and certification, as well as on the type of employer. As researchers and providers consider the level of training and professionalism needed for professional interpreters, it is important that the professionalism needed is commensurate with their compensation structure.

There has been tremendous progress in the professionalization of healthcare interpreters in recent years. Nevertheless, a review concluded that access to professional interpreters is dependent on national anti-discrimination legislation or on positive action at the national or local level (Phelan, 2012). In Europe, some countries that previously had high public support for interpreting services have suffered a recent decline. For example, in 2011, the Danish government announced that it would no longer cover interpreting costs for any patient who has lived in Denmark for more than seven years. Starting in 2012, the Dutch government stopped all subsidies for interpreter services. These government policies have had a significant impact on the health and survival of the industry of professional interpreting (Meeuwesen, 2012; Renée, 2013). In fact, a recent study found that physicians in states with reimbursement for interpreting services had twice the odds of utilizing professional interpreters compared with those in non-reimbursing states (DeCamp, Kuo, Flores, O'Connor, & Minkovitz, 2013).

The phenomenon of providers' underutilization of interpreters is true not only in countries and regions where there is no legal mandate to provide interpreters in healthcare settings but also in places where those mandates have been implemented for years. For example, in Massachusetts, USA, where legislative mandates to provide healthcare interpreters were passed in 2001, researchers found that there has been little change in emergency departments' (ED) utilization patterns, with 15 percent of limited English proficiency (LEP) patients in 2002 and 18 percent in 2008 ($p = 0.70$) receiving services from professional interpreters (Ginde, Sullivan, Corel, Caceres, & Camargo, 2010). Similar observations were found in other studies (DeCamp et al., 2013). In other words, compared to nonprofessional interpreters, professional interpreters represent a minority group of interpreters in interpreter-mediated medical encounters. As researchers investigate the complexity of interpreter-mediated medical encounters, it is important that we do not simply focus our investigation on professional interpreters. Rather, it is important to examine the real world and explore the causes and impacts of such phenomena.

A.1. In-person Interpreters

In several studies, in-person professional interpreters are reported as the preferred choice for patients, providers, and interpreters (Bagchi et al., 2011; Kuo & Fagan, 1999; Locatis et al., 2010; Nápoles et al., 2010). In-person interpreters, however, may include hospital interpreters or contract interpreters. Hospital interpreters are paid professionals/employees within the health organization who provide interpreting services in healthcare settings and may work in shifts to provide 24-hour services. Although they may have better job security and more stable income, they are subject to the specific institutional rules and norms of the healthcare facilities. They have the benefit of developing long-term working relationships with providers. In addition, depending on institutional policies, hospital interpreters may be able to coordinate with other colleagues so that each is responsible for specific clinics, allowing them to develop specialty-specific medical expertise over time. Because in-person interpreters often work in various clinics, they may need to prioritize one task/case over another, which can lead to provider frustration due to delayed care. Hospital interpreters often provide telephone interpreting in situations that involve short, simple interactions or medical emergencies (Angelelli, 2004).

Contract interpreters are professional interpreters hired through interpreting agencies as needed and are often paid hourly wages. They often provide interpreting services to different healthcare facilities. Because they are outside the organizational structure of the healthcare facility, they often do not have institutional badges/outfits and may be viewed as outsiders by providers in the healthcare institutions. In addition, because they are not considered hospital employees, they may not have access to certain resources (e.g., workspace) and information (e.g., patients' medical records). In short, although contract interpreters' work is similar to that of hospital interpreters, their work environment and provider–interpreter relationship can be drastically different, and this may also have a significant impact on their interpreting strategies. As future studies examine the practice of in-person interpreters, it may be useful to explore whether the types of employment impact in-person interpreters' behaviors and practices.

A.2. Technology-based Interpreters

In 2004, when I first proposed my typology of interpreters, I used the term telephone interpreters, rather than technology-based interpreters (Hsieh, 2006). As video remote interpreting (VRI) has become more common in healthcare settings in recent years, I have renamed this category of interpreters as technology-based interpreters. Technology has been central to the delivery of interpreting services for over 40 years. Australia was the first country to introduce telephone interpreting services in 1973 (Mikkelson, 2003), while the first telephone interpreting services in the United States were offered in 1981 (Kelly, 2007). VRI has been embraced by the Deaf and mute communities for sign language interpreting. VRI also allows both the interpreter and other speakers to assess others' nonverbal communication, providing a comparable experience to in-person interpreting. Researchers found that although VRI and telephone interpreting do not contribute to differences in participants' perceived quality of communication and interpretation, LEP parents who received VRI were better in more likely to name the child's diagnosis correctly (Lion et al., in press). While the literature on technology-based interpreting has often focused on its cost-effectiveness in relation to patient satisfaction, few studies have examined its impact on quality of care or health outcomes (e.g., Jacobs, Fu, & Rathouz, 2012; McLaughlin et al., 2013; Phillips, 2013).

There are several unique characteristics of these technology-based interpreters that may have an impact on the quality of interpreting. First, they are often employed by interpreting agencies, working from their home offices in remote locations (Phillips, 2013). Second, in order to maintain competitiveness, many interpreting agencies have set up call centers in foreign countries to reduce cost and to supplement interpreter shortage in the United States (Kelly, 2007). Third, interpreting agencies may have better control over the quality of interpreting services as they can maintain quality control by requiring regular web-based training as well as monitoring their performance through recorded and/or real-time interpreting.

While these characteristics may appear straightforward, they have significant implications that providers may not consider when working with technology-based interpreters. For example, because offshore interpreters are cheaper than US-based ones, the industry trend has been to establish call centers in other countries. This means technology-based interpreters may not only work in a time zone significantly different from that of the providers, they may also be unfamiliar with the norms and practices of healthcare settings in the United States. In addition, for many technology-based interpreters, interpreting provides supplemental, rather than primary, income. Kelly (2007) found that only 50 percent of the 2,000 interpreters employed by an interpreting agency are considered full-time employees. Interpreting agencies create various pay programs so that interpreters "can get paid by the hour or by the number of minutes they have taken calls in an hour" (LanguageLine Solutions, 2014). The limited income may prohibit an interpreter from developing advanced skills in healthcare interpreting. Finally, these technology-based interpreters generally provide interpreting services to a wide variety of clients (e.g., emergency call centers, banking industries, and police, among others). They may not be as specialized as hospital interpreters who work exclusively in healthcare settings. In addition, these interpreters are unlikely to develop long-term relationships with providers or patients as they are randomly assigned to different tasks as needed. This also means that unlike in-person interpreters, these interpreters are unlikely to have any background knowledge about provider–patient relationships/interactions based on prior interactions. In short, while technology-based interpreters are often considered and touted as professional interpreters, their unique characteristics suggest that they may have very different interpreting styles than in-person interpreters.

B. Bilingual Medical Professionals

Due to cost concerns, many healthcare facilities intentionally recruit bilingual providers and staff members to work with their language-discordant patients. These individuals are dual-role interpreters as their primary job responsibilities usually do not involve interpreting. Nevertheless, many bilingual providers and staff members have noted that they often are asked to serve as an interpreter for their colleagues (O'Leary, Federico, & Hampers, 2003).

In my earlier typology (Hsieh, 2006), bilingual providers were defined as healthcare providers who have learned the patients' native language as their second language whereas untrained interpreters are defined as bilingual support staff, including nurses and janitors, who do not have formal training. In this book, I have decided to revise and clarify these categorizations. In this larger category of bilingual medical professionals, I now include two types of medical professionals: (a) *bilingual providers* who work with patients directly and (b) *bilingual medical employees*, who are clinic-based medical professionals interpreting for their colleagues. Of equal importance is that untrained interpreters who do not have a medical background (e.g., clerks and janitors) are now in the category of chance interpreters. Bilingual medical professionals are a unique category of interpreters due to their medical expertise, in-clinic availability, and institutional roles in the healthcare settings.

Initially, as I reconsidered this category of interpreters, I had in mind three types of interpreters: bilingual providers who directly interact with patients, bilingual providers who serve as interpreters for their peers, and bilingual subordinate staff who interpret for a superior. Hospitals are full of hierarchies. The differences in rank may contribute to differences in individuals' communicative strategies and changes in provider–patient–interpreter dynamics. However, because there is limited research examining how hierarchies in healthcare settings influence these bilingual providers' and staff members' interpreting styles, there is not enough evidence to make such distinctions/claims. There is, however, sufficient evidence to support the distinction between providers who interact with patients directly and bilingual medical employees. I recognize that the differences between these two groups may be splitting hairs, as bilingual medical employees (e.g., nurses) may also interact with patients directly as bilingual providers. However, the distinction here is not based on their institutional title, but how their roles and functions in healthcare settings may shape their interactions and relationships with language-discordant patients.

B.1. Bilingual Providers

Because of their medical expertise and ability to communicate with patients directly, bilingual providers are often viewed as the gold standard for working with language-discordant patients. In several comparative studies of interpreting modalities in healthcare settings, bilingual attending providers are treated as one of the conditions (e.g., Crossman, Wiener, Roosevelt, Bajaj, & Hampers, 2010; Grover, Deakyne, Bajaj, & Roosevelt, 2012; L. J. Lee et al., 2002). The presumption is that if patients can communicate with the provider directly, they should have the best quality of care and health outcomes, similar to that of language-concordant pairs. Several studies have found that patients who had bilingual physicians received similar care when compared to language-concordant provider–patient interactions (Eamranond, Davis, Phillips, & Wee, 2009; Hampers & McNulty, 2002). A review concluded that bilingual providers can significantly improve patients' quality of care, satisfaction, and outcomes (Flores, 2005).

In the United States, medical students and residents often learn medical Spanish as a way to facilitate care of patients with limited English proficiency. A 10-week medical Spanish course for pediatric ED physicians was associated with decreased interpreter utilization and increased patient-family satisfaction (Mazor, Hampers, Chande, & Krug, 2002). However, it is important to recognize that a person with knowledge in multiple languages may not be equally proficient in all those languages. A person may use one language at home or as a child, but have received formal education in another. For example, although I am 100 percent Taiwanese and graduated from Taiwan as a college student, I speak very little Taiwanese. I understand it when spoken to if the discourse does not involve any sophisticated, complex understanding about the language or culture. On the other hand, I can read and write Mandarin Chinese very well as it was the official language throughout all my education in Taiwan. However, when it comes to writing a research manuscript, English is my language, as this is the language I used throughout my master's and doctoral programs. Thus, when we consider bilingual providers who interact with patients directly, it is important to consider their level of language proficiency and their ability to use that language in healthcare settings.

In fact, not all findings about bilingual providers are positive. While a true bilingual provider can be extraordinarily valuable, it is important to recognize that being able to speak a second language does not necessarily mean that a provider has the language skills to interact with patients across different clinical contexts (e.g., patient education, discharge instructions, and informed consent). Providers often overlook the threat posed by bilingual providers' limited language proficiency due to the benefits of bilingual providers' medical expertise and in-clinic availability (Hsieh, Ju, & Kong, 2010). In fact, physicians and nurses with limited Spanish proficiency regularly communicated with patients directly, even in important clinical circumstances (Diamond, Tuot, & Karliner, 2012; Lion et al., 2013; Yawman et al., 2006), a finding that was also supported by other studies even when hospital interpreters are available (O'Leary et al., 2003). In addition, providers' self-reports of their linguistic skills do not always reflect their true ability (Diamond, Luft, Chung, & Jacobs, 2012; Lion et al., 2013).

Although many studies have noted that language-concordant providers result in higher ratings for patient satisfaction (Carrasquillo, Orav, Brennan, & Burstin, 1999; Gany et al., 2007; A. R. Green et al., 2005), patient compliance (Manson, 1988), and perceived quality of care (Ngo-Metzger et al., 2007), researchers need to recognize that this may be a function of rapport rather than an indicator of quality care. Patients' illness experiences and concerns are socially and culturally situated in their everyday life. A short-term class on medical Spanish, while valuable, is unlikely to replace the need for professional interpreters. In fact, researchers found that ED physicians with medical Spanish training make minor errors in 50 percent of their consultations and major errors (e.g., misunderstanding duration of symptoms and misunderstanding of vocabulary) in 14 percent of their consultations (Prince & Nelson, 1995). Another study found that although short-term language courses allow providers to develop better inquiry skills and higher confidence during medical encounters, there is little change in their ability to provide emotional support (Farnill, Todisco, Hayes, & Bartlett, 1997). In other words, medical Spanish may give providers false confidence that they are able to communicate directly with their patient, resulting in problematic assessments of quality of care. Diamond and Jacobs (2010, p. s189) concluded that "teaching 'Medical Spanish' or related courses may actually contribute to health care disparities if clinicians begin using these non-English language skills inappropriately with patients."

This may also help address some intriguing findings in the literature, in which bilingual providers are not always perceived to be the most desirable form of communication for language-discordant patients. For example, Kuo and Fagan (1999) found that patients are more satisfied with family interpreters (85.1 percent) and in-person interpreters (92.4 percent) than bilingual providers (75 percent). In Crossman's study (2010), patients in the bilingual provider group were less satisfied with their language service than those in the in-person or telephone interpreter groups. Simon et al. (2013) found that bilingual providers gave different information to English-speaking versus Spanish-speaking patients, with less medical terminology in Spanish-speaking consultations. While bilingual providers may be satisfied with their information needs for diagnostic purposes, they may not be able to communicate with the patients effectively about illness-related concerns (Diamond & Reuland, 2009). For example, compared to physicians, a higher percentage of patients consider interpreters' ability to offer assistance after a doctor's visit to be important (94 percent vs. 45.1 percent; $p < 0.01$; Kuo & Fagan, 1999). A patient may not feel comfortable asking for a professional interpreter even when they recognize that the bilingual provider does not have sufficient skills to communicate with them directly due to concerns about rapport with or face-threat to the provider (Fryer, Mackintosh, Stanley, & Crichton, 2013).

It is therefore essential for researchers and practitioners to develop a meaningful assessment of and clear institutional guidelines for providers' language fluency. This is especially important when various studies continue to demonstrate that physicians and nurses who self-report to have low language proficiency frequently rely on their limited language skills when delivering care. In addition, future studies should expand beyond the investigation of patient satisfaction and examine the specific processes and impacts that bilingual providers, especially those who use their non-native language skills for care delivery, have on patients' quality of care and health outcomes (e.g., Fernandez et al., 2011).

B.2. Bilingual Medical Employees

I use the term bilingual medical employees to include any medical professional who serves as an interpreter in healthcare settings, including bilingual residents, physicians, and nurses. Bilingual medical employees often offer higher availability and convenience than professional interpreters because they are readily available within the clinic. Several studies have found that bilingual staff are one of the most frequently used types of interpreter, often second only to family interpreters (Bischoff & Hudelson, 2010; Gill, Beavan, Calvert, & Freemantle, 2011; Ginde et al., 2010; Kuo, O'Connor, Flores, & Minkovitz, 2007). Bilingual medical employees share similar challenges with bilingual providers. For example, one study found one in five dual-role staff interpreters do not have adequate language skills to serve as interpreters (Moreno, Otero-Sabogal, & Newman, 2007). While many hospitals encourage bilingual staff members to be registered in their language banks, individual facilities often have different testing and training requirements.

However, in addition to their language proficiency, bilingual medical employees face other challenges when serving as dual-role interpreters. First, they may not assume a neutral role in medical encounters as their primary responsibilities often align with the physician and/or the healthcare team. For example, bilingual nurses' interpreting is more likely to align with providers' preferences and clinical expectations rather than with patients' needs (Elderkin-Thompson, Silver, & Waitzkin, 2001; Mueller et al., 2011). Bilingual medical employees often assume the co-provider role with the tacit approval of the provider (Bridges et al., 2015). This can be particularly problematic because providers often have strong, implicit trust of bilingual medical employees due to their medical expertise (Hsieh et al., 2010), failing to recognize that their institutional role and hierarchy may prompt these bilingual medical employees to be biased, resulting in compromised care. For example, because these interpreters are locally based, they may feel pressured to provide interpreting services, even when they feel uncomfortable or inadequate for the task at hand (Yang & Gray, 2008). Refusing to interpret when asked may make these bilingual medical employees appear selfish, unsupportive, or unprofessional as a member of the healthcare team. Thus, to ensure quality of care, providers need to be aware of these interpersonal dilemmas and allow bilingual medical employees to refuse assignments for tasks that they are not prepared for or qualified to take on.

Second, because they are bilingual medical professionals rather than trained interpreters, there appears to be more variation in their interpreting styles. The literature suggests that the quality of their interpreting can easily be influenced by others' communicative styles (Elderkin-Thompson et al., 2001). Researchers have argued that the complexity of language used and the interpersonal dynamics in medical encounters may contribute to the variation in interpreting quality for these dual-role interpreters (Ebden, Bhatt, Carey, & Harrison, 1988; Mueller et al., 2011). For example, because providers are likely to assume that bilingual medical employees are familiar with medical knowledge and procedure, they may not recognize the fact that complex questions (e.g., "Does she know what the diagnosis is?") or serial questions (e.g., "Would she describe this pain as a sharp, dull, or burning pain? Can she describe it at all?") may present challenges for interpreters. (Nonprofessional interpreters are likely to face similar challenges.)

Finally, despite the popularity of bilingual medical employees as a solution to the shortage or inconvenience of professional interpreters, many studies have noted that dual-role interpreters face significant challenges in balancing their workload with their interpreting responsibilities (Engstrom, Piedra, & Min, 2009). For example, one study found that bilingual residents estimated that they spent a mean of 2.3 hours per week interpreting for other residents although hospital interpreters were readily available (O'Leary et al., 2003). This can pose a significant challenge to bilingual providers' workload. If organizations recruit bilingual providers with the intention of having them serve as stationed interpreters for specific clinics, it is essential that organizational policies are developed to address the allocation and expectations of their responsibilities and workload. If this is done, other providers would feel more comfortable requesting their assistance and this would thus decrease the likelihood of them avoiding or minimizing communication with LEP patients.

C. Nonprofessional Interpreters

Nonprofessional interpreters, also known as ad hoc, untrained, or informal interpreters, include a wide variety of interpreters, usually those who do not have formal training in interpreting in healthcare settings. In this book, I use this larger category to include any individual who has neither training in interpreting nor medical expertise. If they have no training in interpreting but have medical expertise, they are considered bilingual medical employees.

It is important to note that nonprofessional interpreters are extremely common in healthcare settings, often used more frequently than professional interpreters. One study found that 86 percent of physicians reported using family interpreters within the 12 months prior to the survey, compared to 71 percent for bilingual staff, 41 percent for in-person interpreters and 21 percent for telephone interpreters (Rose et al., 2010). A national survey in the United States found that when facing language barriers, 77 percent of residents reported using professional interpreters; in contrast, 84 percent reported using adult family interpreters, and 22 percent (including 37 percent of pediatric and emergency medicine residents) reported using children (K. C. Lee et al., 2006). After Massachusetts passed a law mandating access to and use of professional interpreters for LEP patients in 2001, researchers found that while there were negligible changes in ED providers' use of professional interpreters between 2002 and 2008 (from 18 percent to 15 percent; $p = 0.70$), there was a significant increase in the use of family interpreters (from 24 percent to 59 percent; $p < 0.001$; Ginde et al., 2010). In short, nonprofessionals are often the norm, rather than the exception, in interpreter-mediated medical encounters, even in places where there is legislation mandating language access to language-discordant patients (Ginde et al., 2010; Gray, Hilder, & Donaldson, 2011; Papic, Malak, & Rosenberg, 2012; Schenker, Pérez-Stable, Nickleach, & Karliner, 2011).

This is a common practice that has rarely been studied systematically. The challenge in studying these nonprofessional interpreters is that there have been a plethora of commentaries, case studies, and anecdotal observations highlighting the problems of working with nonprofessional interpreters (Cambridge, 1999; Lehna, 2005; Pöchhacker, 2007; Pöchhacker & Kadric, 1999). However, many other studies have also demonstrated that professional interpreters make plenty of (similar) interpreting errors. In other words, without comparative studies, identifying the problems with nonprofessional interpreters is an inadequate claim for the exclusive use or superiority of professional interpreters. The same is true for the recent reviews that reported the positive impacts of professional interpreters (Flores, 2005; Karliner et al., 2007). The lack of comparative studies and the limited number of larger-scale, evidence-based studies on nonprofessional interpreters make it difficult to make any conclusive arguments about the positive or negative impacts of nonprofessional interpreters.

The few comparative studies between professional and nonprofessional interpreters have reported conflicting findings. For example, Flores et al. (2003) found that although there were no significant differences in the frequency of interpreting errors (e.g., omission, substitution, addition, editorialization, and false fluency) committed by nonprofessional as compared to professional interpreters, the percentage of nonprofessional interpreters' errors that had potential clinical consequences was significantly higher (77 percent versus 55 percent, $p < 0.001$).

A more recent study by Flores et al. (2012) found that a significantly lower proportion of interpreting errors had potential clinical consequences (18 percent), while the nonprofessional interpreters' errors were still more likely to have potential clinical consequences (22 percent versus 12 percent, $p < 0.01$). In contrast, Butow, Goldstein et al. (2011) found that while professional interpreters are less likely to produce nonequivalent speech than family interpreters ($p = 0.02$), they have a higher (but statistically non-significant) proportion of negative alterations than family interpreters (26 percent vs. 21 percent; $p = 0.2$). Pham and colleagues found that 55 percent of professional interpreters' interpreting involves some form of alteration, among which 93 percent have negative impacts (Pham, Thornton, Engelberg, Jackson, & Curtis, 2008). Part of the challenge in this line of research is that researchers still differ in how they define interpreting errors and/or measure clinical impacts. In short, there have been some mixed findings about whether professional interpreters and family interpreters differ in the frequencies and types of interpreter alterations and their corresponding positive/negative consequences.

Another problem faced in systematic investigations of nonprofessional interpreters is research ethics. Despite the prevalence of nonprofessional interpreters, including child interpreters, institutional review boards are likely to raise concerns about providing substandard care if family interpreters, and child interpreters in particular, are used as a comparative condition against other types of interpreters (e.g., professional interpreters or bilingual providers). As a result, studies on the use of nonprofessional interpreters are often limited to individuals' self-reports (e.g., Rosenberg, Leanza, & Seller, 2007; Rosenberg, Seller, & Leanza, 2008) or case studies rather than actual interpreter-mediated interactions across multiple sessions. Greenhalgh, Robb, and Scambler (2006, p. 1186) argued, "Interpreting by family members (and other ad hoc contacts) is probably the most widespread and also the most under-researched of all the models in use in UK health care." This is likely to be true in any other country as well. Without evidence-based research to systematically identify the patterns and processes of nonprofessional interpreters, the arguments to support or reject the use of nonprofessional interpreters are likely to be ideological rather than evidence based.

Finally, it is important to note that providers' use of nonprofessional interpreters does not appear to be a random decision or a choice of convenience. By examining providers' choice of interpreters at the Geneva University Hospitals, Bischoff and Hudelson (2010) argued that providers' choice between professional and nonprofessional interpreters appears to be influenced by the availability of bilingual staff, perception of interpreting quality, and cost concerns. Rose et al. (2010) found that organizational contexts can influence providers' choice of interpreters. For example, compared with physicians in health management organizations, physicians in county governments, medical school/university settings, solo practice settings, or single-specialty medical groups were all significantly less likely to use professional interpreters. Diamond, Tuot, et al. (2012) found that providers with different levels of language proficiency differ in their strategies in communicating with patients; in addition, their choice also reflects their consideration for the task at hand. For example, although 100 percent of physicians with high Spanish proficiency would communicate to a patient directly to update him/her about clinical conditions, only 15 percent of physicians with low Spanish fluency would do so. However, when it comes to discussing end-of-life issues, 33 percent of physicians with high Spanish proficiency and 90 percent with low Spanish proficiency would use a professional interpreter. In other words, providers' use of interpreters is a calculated choice (Diamond, Schenker, Curry, Bradley, & Fernandez, 2009; Hsieh, 2015).

In summary, the use of nonprofessional interpreters is a reality for a large portion of interpreter-mediated medical encounters. By identifying their unique characteristics and examining their communicative practices and corresponding impacts, researchers can develop evidence-based arguments for the effective and appropriate use of nonprofessional interpreters. For example, despite the fact that providers appear to have specific criteria when choosing methods for communicating with language-discordant patients, there is little research examining whether such criteria are appropriate or whether nonprofessional interpreters do perform adequate interpreting in these chosen contexts.

In the category of nonprofessional interpreters, I decided to create two subcategories: (a) chance interpreters, and (b) family interpreters. Although these two subgroups of interpreters have traditionally been viewed as one, recent studies have highlighted the importance of considering them separately. After all, a bilingual bystander in the waiting room who happens to work as an interpreter would have very different communicative styles than a bilingual daughter who also serves as the primary caretaker for an elderly parent.

C.1. Chance Interpreters

Chance interpreters are untrained individuals who provide interpreting services by chance (e.g., bilingual bystanders). For example, in an emergency room, providers may ask a bilingual janitor or even call a local ethnic restaurant in the hope of finding a person to help with the interpreting task (Pöchhacker, 2007; Weaver & Sklar, 1980). The use of chance interpreters raises concerns about misinterpretation, patient privacy, and litigation risks, as such interpreters have minimal training in medical knowledge and interpreting skills (MacFarlane et al., 2009; Meeuwesen, Twilt, ten Thije, & Harmsen, 2010). It is important to note that I do not wish to underplay the problems of chance interpreters, as many studies have demonstrated that they often are prone to problematic interpreting styles and poor patient outcomes (L. J. Lee et al., 2002; Meeuwesen, 2012). However, as I indicated earlier, we need more comparative studies to illustrate whether these problems are inherent in all types of interpreters or if they are unique to nonprofessional interpreters, including chance and family interpreters.

One issue worth noting about chance interpreters is that this category acts somewhat as a catch-all category. Many studies counted nursing/office staff and bilingual employees as chance interpreters, some counted family members and friends as chance interpreters, and others considered any nonprofessional interpreters as chance interpreters. However, the literature has provided sufficient evidence to support the distinction between bilingual medical employees and family interpreters. Without a medical background, chance interpreters do not share the professional courtesy bilingual medical employees have. Without an existing relationship with or knowledge about the patient, chance interpreters do not have the kinds of responsibilities and obligations that a family interpreter might have. These unique characteristics are likely to shape chance interpreters' performances in healthcare settings. By conceptualizing interpreter typology in a more sophisticated theoretical framework, researchers can examine how the unique characteristics associated with each type of interpreter shape their performances, functions, and impacts in provider–patient interactions. Maybe as research progresses we will be able to identify other unique types of interpreters that warrant their own categories.

C.2. Family Interpreters

Family interpreters are patients' family members or friends who also serve as interpreters in healthcare settings. Although providers do share concerns about using family interpreters, including bilingual children (Cohen, Moran-Ellis, & Smaje, 1999; Rosenberg et al., 2007), family interpreters continue to be one of the most common types of interpreters in healthcare settings. Researchers have also argued that respecting patients' preferences, cultural expectations, and the larger decision-making contexts for family interpreters may be more appropriate in certain situations than imposing the Western biomedical ideology of professional interpreters (Ho, 2008). Recent findings highlight the need to situate family interpreters as a unique category due to their distinctive relationship with and knowledge about patients.

Family interpreters share many of the problems of chance interpreters, but with some additional issues. In particular, although it is not uncommon for physicians to use bilingual children as interpreters (K. C. Lee et al., 2006; Pöchhacker, 2007), researchers have argued that such children may not have adequate medical knowledge or the emotional maturity to ensure the patient's quality of care or their own personal well-being (Cohen et al., 1999; Jacobs, Kroll, Green, & David, 1995; Levine, 2006). Although few studies have examined actual medical encounters mediated through child interpreters, several researchers have explored this issue through examining participants' perceptions and attitudes. For example, bilingual youngsters (aged 10–18) did not view their experiences as family interpreters as inadequate translators or exploited children; rather, they took pride in their ability to provide skillful mediation as a contributing member of the family (Angelelli, 2010; Green, Free, Bhavnani, & Newman, 2005). Researchers have argued that these bilingual children's experiences as interpreters have enriched their experiences and professionalism. In particular, they not only learn to bridge communicative barriers between the minority and majority communities for their family members but also develop exceptional abilities in memory, analytical skills, speech comprehension and production, and stress tolerance that set them apart from their peers (Valdés, 2003).

Clearly, the benefits of allowing these bilingual youngsters to develop professionalism and valuable skills as interpreters should not overshadow the dangers of compromised care. However, we actually know very little about the ways in which child interpreters compromise care. The limited number of studies on child interpreters' actual practices is likely to be a result of ethical concerns for research design rather than limited data in healthcare settings as child interpreters are not uncommon in such settings (K. C. Lee et al., 2006). To advance this area of literature, we will need innovative research design to further identify the impacts of child interpreters on the quality of care.

Recent studies also have highlighted that family interpreters and professional interpreters differ in systematic ways. For example, family interpreters do not separate their other social roles (e.g., caregiver and family member) when acting as an interpreter, prompting them to adopt advocacy roles to facilitate understanding and ensure quality care (Meeuwesen et al., 2010; Rosenberg et al., 2008; Valdés, 2003). They actively engage in provider–patient interactions, controlling the process and content of communication. Compared to professional interpreters, family interpreters are also more likely to initiate talk on their own behalf, promoting their own agenda (Butow et al., 2011; Leanza, Boivin, & Rosenberg, 2010). In addition, providers appear to interact with family interpreters differently than with professional interpreters, relying on them to report symptoms that the patient does not mention, provide interpreting services after the visit, and establish relationships with the whole family (Rosenberg et al., 2007).

While there are concerns about the quality of interpreting from family interpreters, several studies have provided important findings. For example, although family interpreters have a significantly higher rate of nonequivalent interpreting than professional interpreters, the nonequivalent interpreting appears to be mostly inconsequential (Butow et al., 2011). After comparing the specific interpreting strategies, Leanza et al. (2010, p. 1893) concluded, "[A]dult family interpreters might be considered, at a linguistic level, as reliable as trained interpreters." Because family interpreters are not professionally trained, it is unlikely that they would share the same ethics and/or interpreting strategies as professional interpreters. However, family interpreters' understanding of their roles often entails "a sense of linguistic advocacy between speakers of minority languages and a society that struggles to accommodate the linguistic needs of its members" (Angelelli,

2010, p. 95), which is likely to shape their communicative strategies as interpreters. In addition, if they are serving as a long-term caretaker, they may in fact develop better knowledge and vocabularies of the patient's illness condition than a professional interpreters who is working with the patient for the first time.

In summary, when conceptualizing and examining family interpreters, researchers should not use professional interpreters as the gold standard, hoping that the "best" family interpreters would act the same. They do not because they are not the same. Family interpreters know a lot more background information about the patient, share a stronger trust and bond with the patient, and can be a great ally for the provider to derive an accurate diagnosis and shared decision-making. Nevertheless, they also lack certain quality or professional training (e.g., neutrality) that a professional interpreter would have. The challenges for researchers and healthcare providers are to identify the specific conditions, processes, and functions family interpreters can serve in a medical encounter and to develop meaningful and ethical boundaries for collaboration.

D. Implications for Theory Development and Healthcare Practice

While the cost of different interpreting modalities and interpreter types will continue to be an important topic for healthcare institutions, it is likely to be an issue that is highly dependent on locations of the healthcare facilities, patient demographics, resource availability, and national and regional policies. The concerns for cost, however, should not supersede concerns about quality and equality of care.

A meaningful typology of interpreters is the foundation for research in bilingual health care. Our understanding and conceptualization of interpreters should move beyond ideological claims. By presenting this typology, I hope to highlight and clarify some of the conflicting findings in the literature. The revised typology of interpreters reflects some of the latest understanding about the unique characteristics and different impacts of each type of interpreter.

Different types of interpreters have unique strengths and weaknesses. They are not interchangeable. Providers are inherently aware of these differences, resulting in calculated choices of different types of interpreter depending on the task at hand (Diamond et al., 2009; Diamond, Tuot, et al., 2012; Hsieh, 2015). However, it is unclear whether these choices are appropriate as we still know little about how different types of interpreters influence the processes, content, and outcomes of interpreter-mediated medical encounters. Rigorous, systematic identification of the types of interpreters involved in research studies is necessary to advance the theory and practice of the interpreter-mediated medical encounter. By identifying the specific types of interpreters involved in the research design, researchers can effectively compare and contrast findings from different studies, developing insights beyond a single study. Otherwise we will continue to be plagued by conflicting or confounding findings riddled with research design flaws.

From this perspective, the important question to ask is: In what ways do different types of interpreters shape the processes, content, and outcomes of interpreter-mediated medical encounters? The goal of identifying the unique communicative patterns is not to demonstrate whether one type of interpreter is categorically better than others. This approach ignores the reality of health-care delivery. Effective and meaningful utilization of interpreters cannot be completely dependent on a single type of interpreter since each type of interpreter has distinctive strengths and weaknesses. In other words, identifying when and how best to utilize each type of interpreter to achieve optimal care would allow researchers and practitioners to develop meaningful guidelines for best practices for language-discordant patients.

By recognizing that different types of interpreters entail distinct interpersonal dynamics, institutional relationships, and social responsibilities (beyond the immediate medical encounters), researchers can further explore how providers' and patients' expectations and behaviors may differ in response to the unique characteristics of the interpreters. This approach highlights providers' and patients' agency, preferences, and needs in the communicative process, emphasizing the collaborative and coordinated nature of interpreter-mediated provider–patient interactions. Rather than placing the success of bilingual health communication as the sole responsibility of the interpreters' "professionalism" and/or "accurate" interpreting, this approach allows researchers to examine a variety of strategies that providers and patients can adopt to ensure the quality of care.

References

American Medical Association. (2007). Official guide to communicating with limited English proficient patients. 2nd edition. Retrieved March 30, 2008, from www.ama-assn.org/ama1/pub/upload/mm/433/lep_booklet.pdf.

Anderson, L. M., Scrimshaw, S. C., Fullilove, M. T., Fielding, J. E., Normand, J., & Task Force on Community Preventive Services. (2003). Culturally competent healthcare systems: A systematic review. *American Journal of Preventive Medicine*, 24, 68–79.

Andrulis, D., Goodman, N., & Pryor, C. (2002). What a difference an interpreter can make: Health care experiences of uninsured with limited English proficiency. Retrieved March 14, 2015, from http://www.accessproject.org/downloads/c_LEPreportENG.pdf.

Angelelli, C. V. (2004). *Medical interpreting and cross-cultural communication*. Cambridge, UK: Cambridge University Press.

Angelelli, C. V. (2010). A professional ideology in the making: Bilingual youngsters interpreting for their communities and the notion of (no) choice. *Translation and Interpretation Studies*, 5, 94–108.

Bagchi, A. D., Dale, S., Verbitsky-Savitz, N., Andrecheck, S., Zavotsky, K., & Eisenstein, R. (2011). Examining effectiveness of medical interpreters in emergency departments for Spanish-speaking patients with limited English proficiency: Results of a randomized controlled trial. *Annals of Emergency Medicine*, 57, 248–256.

Baker, D. W., & Hayes, R. (1997). The effect of communicating through an interpreter on satisfaction with interpersonal aspects of care. *Journal of General Internal Medicine*, 12, 117.

Baker, D. W., Hayes, R., & Fortier, J. P. (1998). Interpreter use and satisfaction with interpersonal aspects of care for Spanish-speaking patients. *Medical Care*, 36, 1461–1470.

Baker, D. W., Parker, R. M., Williams, M. V., Coates, W. C., & Pitkin, K. M. (1996). Use and effectiveness of interpreters in an emergency department. *Journal of the American Medical Association*, 275, 783–788.

Bernstein, J., Bernstein, E., Dave, A., Hardt, E., James, T., Linden, J., ... Safi, C. (2002). Trained medical interpreters in the emergency department: Effects on services, subsequent charges, and follow-up. *Journal of Immigrant Health*, 4, 171–176.

Bischoff, A. (2012). Do language barriers increase inequalities? Do interpreters decrease inequalities? In D. Ingleby, A. Chiarenza, W. Devillé, & I. Kotsioni (Eds.), *COST series on health and diversity. Volume 2: Inequalities in health care for migrants and ethnic minorities* (pp. 128–143). Philadelphia, PA: Garant.

Bischoff, A., & Hudelson, P. (2010). Communicating with foreign language-speaking patients: Is access to professional interpreters enough? *Journal of Travel Medicine*, 17, 15–20.

Bridges, S., Drew, P., Zayts, O., McGrath, C., Yiu, C. K. Y., Wong, H. M., & Au, T. K. F. (2015). Interpreter-mediated dentistry. *Social Science & Medicine*, 132, 197–207.

Bureau of Labor Statistics. (2014). Occupational outlook handbook, 2014–15 edition. Retrieved March 14, 2015, from www.bls.gov/ooh/media-and-communication/interpreters-and-translators.htm.

Butow, P. N., Goldstein, D., Bell, M. L., Sze, M., Aldridge, L. J., Abdo, S., ... Eisenbruch, M. (2011). Interpretation in consultations with immigrant patients with cancer: How accurate is it? *Journal of Clinical Oncology*, 29, 2801–2807.

Cambridge, J. (1999). Information loss in bilingual medical interviews through an untrained interpreter. *Translator*, 5, 201–219.

Carrasquillo, O., Orav, E. J., Brennan, T. A., & Burstin, H. R. (1999). Impact of language barriers on patient satisfaction in an emergency department. *Journal of General Internal Medicine*, 14, 82–87.

Cohen, S., Moran-Ellis, J., & Smaje, C. (1999). Children as informal interpreters in GP consultations: Pragmatics and ideology. *Sociology of Health & Illness*, 21, 163–186.

Crossman, K. L., Wiener, E., Roosevelt, G., Bajaj, L., & Hampers, L. C. (2010). Interpreters: Telephonic, in-person interpretation and bilingual providers. *Pediatrics*, 125, e631–638.

DeCamp, L. R., Kuo, D. Z., Flores, G., O'Connor, K., & Minkovitz, C. S. (2013). Changes in language services use by US pediatricians. *Pediatrics*, 132(2), e396–406.

Diamond, L. C., & Jacobs, E. A. (2010). Let's not contribute to disparities: The best methods for teaching clinicians how to overcome language barriers to health care. *Journal of General Internal Medicine*, 25, S189–193.

Diamond, L. C., Luft, H. S., Chung, S., & Jacobs, E. A. (2012). "Does this doctor speak my language?" Improving the characterization of physician non-English language skills. *Health Services Research*, 47, 556–569.

Diamond, L. C., & Reuland, D. S. (2009). Describing physician language fluency: Deconstructing medical Spanish. *Journal of the American Medical Association*, 301, 426–428.

Diamond, L. C., Schenker, Y., Curry, L., Bradley, E. H., & Fernandez, A. (2009). Getting by: Underuse of interpreters by resident physicians. *Journal of General Internal Medicine*, 24, 256–262.

Diamond, L. C., Tuot, D., & Karliner, L. (2012). The use of Spanish language skills by physicians and nurses: Policy implications for teaching and testing. *Journal of General Internal Medicine, 27*, 117–123.

Eamranond, P. P., Davis, R. B., Phillips, R. S., & Wee, C. C. (2009). Patient–physician language concordance and lifestyle counseling among Spanish-speaking patients. *Journal of Immigrant and Minority Health, 11*, 494–498.

Ebden, P., Bhatt, A., Carey, O., & Harrison, B. (1988). The bilingual medical consultation. *The Lancet, 331*, 347.

Elderkin-Thompson, V., Silver, R. C., & Waitzkin, H. (2001). When nurses double as interpreters: A study of Spanish-speaking patients in a US primary care setting. *Social Science & Medicine, 52*, 1343–1358.

Engstrom, D. W., Piedra, L. M., & Min, J. W. (2009). Bilingual social workers: Language and service complexities. *Administration in Social Work, 33*, 167–185.

Farnill, D., Todisco, J., Hayes, S. C., & Bartlett, D. (1997). Videotaped interviewing of non-English speakers: Training for medical students with volunteer clients. *Medical Education, 31*, 87–93.

Fernandez, A., Schillinger, D., Warton, E. M., Adler, N., Moffet, H. H., Schenker, Y., … Karter, A. J. (2011). Language barriers, physician-patient language concordance, and glycemic control among insured Latinos with diabetes: The Diabetes Study of Northern California (DISTANCE). *Journal of General Internal Medicine, 26*, 170–176.

Flores, G. (2005). The impact of medical interpreter services on the quality of health care: A systematic review. *Medical Care Research & Review, 62*, 255–299.

Flores, G., Abreu, M., Barone, C. P., Bachur, R., & Lin, H. (2012). Errors of medical interpretation and their potential clinical consequences: A comparison of professional versus ad hoc versus no interpreters. *Annals of Emergency Medicine, 60*, 545–553.

Flores, G., Laws, M. B., Mayo, S. J., Zuckerman, B., Abreu, M., Medina, L., & Hardt, E. J. (2003). Errors in medical interpretation and their potential clinical consequences in pediatric encounters. *Pediatrics, 111*, 6–14.

Fryer, C. E., Mackintosh, S. F., Stanley, M. J., & Crichton, J. (2013). "I understand all the major things": How older people with limited English proficiency decide their need for a professional interpreter during health care after stroke. *Ethnicity & Health, 18*, 610–625.

Gany, F., Leng, J., Shapiro, E., Abramson, D., Motola, I., Shield, D. C., & Changrani, J. (2007). Patient satisfaction with different interpreting methods: A randomized controlled trial. *Journal of General Internal Medicine, 22*, S312–318.

Gill, P. S., Beavan, J., Calvert, M., & Freemantle, N. (2011). The unmet need for interpreting provision in UK primary care. *PLoS One, 6*, 1–6.

Ginde, A. A., Sullivan, A. F., Corel, B., Caceres, J. A., & Camargo, C. A., Jr. (2010). Reevaluation of the effect of mandatory interpreter legislation on use of professional interpreters for ED patients with language barriers. *Patient Education and Counseling, 81*, 204–206.

Gray, B., Hilder, J., & Donaldson, H. (2011). Why do we not use trained interpreters for all patients with limited English proficiency? Is there a place for using family members? *Australian Journal of Primary Health, 17*, 240–249.

Green, A. R., Ngo-Metzger, Q., Legedza, A. T. R., Massagli, M. P., Phillips, R. S., & Iezzoni, L. I. (2005). Interpreter services, language concordance, and health care quality: Experiences of Asian Americans with limited English proficiency. *Journal of General Internal Medicine, 20*, 1050–1056.

Green, J., Free, C., Bhavnani, V., & Newman, T. (2005). Translators and mediators: Bilingual young people's accounts of their interpreting work in health care. *Social Science & Medicine*, 60, 2097–2110.

Greenhalgh, T., Robb, N., & Scambler, G. (2006). Communicative and strategic action in interpreted consultations in primary health care: A Habermasian perspective. *Social Science & Medicine*, 63, 1170–1187.

Grover, A., Deakyne, S., Bajaj, L., & Roosevelt, G. E. (2012). Comparison of throughput times for limited English proficiency patient visits in the emergency department between different interpreter modalities. *Journal of Immigrant and Minority Health*, 14, 602–607.

Hampers, L. C., & McNulty, J. E. (2002). Professional interpreters and bilingual physicians in a pediatric emergency department: Effect on resource utilization. *Archives of Pediatrics and Adolescent Medicine*, 156, 1108–1113.

Ho, A. (2008). Using family members as interpreters in the clinical setting. *The Journal of Clinical Ethics*, 19, 223–233.

Hsieh, E. (2006). Understanding medical interpreters: Reconceptualizing bilingual health communication. *Health Communication*, 20, 177–186.

Hsieh, E. (2015). Not just "getting by": Factors influencing providers' choice of interpreters. *Journal of General Internal Medicine*, 30, 75–82.

Hsieh, E., Ju, H., & Kong, H. (2010). Dimensions of trust: The tensions and challenges in provider–interpreter trust. *Qualitative Health Research*, 20, 170–181.

International Medical Interpreters Association. (2014). National certification. Retrieved March 14, 2015, from www.imiaweb.org/advocacy/nationalcertificatereport.asp.

IQ Solutions. (2001). *National standards for culturally and linguistically appropriate services*. Washington, DC: US Department of Health and Human Services. Retrieved September 16, 2015, from http://minorityhealth.hhs.gov/assets/pdf/checked/finalreport.pdf.

Jacobs, B., Kroll, L., Green, J., & David, T. J. (1995). The hazards of using a child as an interpreter. *Journal of the Royal Society of Medicine*, 88, 474P–475P.

Jacobs, E. A., Fu, P. C., Jr., & Rathouz, P. J. (2012). Does a video-interpreting network improve delivery of care in the emergency department? *Health Services Research*, 47, 509–522.

Jacobs, E. A., Lauderdale, D. S., Meltzer, D., Shorey, J. M., Levinson, W., & Thisted, R. A. (2001). Impact of interpreter services on delivery of health care to limited-English-proficient patients. *Journal of General Internal Medicine*, 16, 468–474.

Karliner, L. S., Jacobs, E. A., Chen, A. H., & Mutha, S. (2007). Do professional interpreters improve clinical care for patients with limited English proficiency? A systematic review of the literature. *Health Services Research*, 42, 727–754.

Kelly, N. (2007). *Telephone interpreting: A comprehensive guide to the profession*. Victoria, BC: Trafford.

Kuo, D., & Fagan, M. J. (1999). Satisfaction with methods of Spanish interpretation in an ambulatory care clinic. *Journal of General Internal Medicine*, 14, 547–550.

Kuo, D. Z., O'Connor, K. G., Flores, G., & Minkovitz, C. S. (2007). Pediatricians' use of language services for families with limited English proficiency. *Pediatrics*, 119, e920–927.

LanguageLine Solutions. (2014). Interpreter FAQ. Retrieved March 14, 2015, from www.languageline.com/company/careers/interpreter-careers/faq/#LL2.

Leanza, Y., Boivin, I., & Rosenberg, E. (2010). Interruptions and resistance: A comparison of medical consultations with family and trained interpreters. *Social Science & Medicine*, 70, 1888–1895.

Lee, K. C., Winickoff, J. P., Kim, M. K., Campbell, E. G., Betancourt, J. R., Park, E. R., ... Weissman, J. S. (2006). Resident physicians' use of professional and nonprofessional interpreters: A national survey. *Journal of the American Medical Association*, 296, 1050–1053.

Lee, L. J., Batal, H. A., Maselli, J. H., & Kutner, J. S. (2002). Effect of Spanish interpretation method on patient satisfaction in an urban walk-in clinic. *Journal of General Internal Medicine*, 17, 641–645.

Lehna, C. (2005). Interpreter services in pediatric nursing. *Pediatric Nursing*, 31, 292–296.

Levine, C. (2006). Use of children as interpreters. *Journal of the American Medical Association*, 296, 2802.

Lion, K. C., Brown, J. C., Ebel, B. E., Klein, E. J., Strelitz, B., Gutman, C. K., ... Mangione-Smith, R. (in press). Effect of telephone vs video interpretation on parent comprehension, communication, and utilization in the pediatric emergency department: A randomized clinical trial. *JAMA Pediatrics*.

Lion, K. C., Thompson, D. A., Cowden, J. D., Michel, E., Rafton, S. A., Hamdy, R. F., ... Ebel, B. E. (2013). Clinical Spanish use and language proficiency testing among pediatric residents. *Academic Medicine*, 88, 1478–1484.

Locatis, C., Williamson, D., Gould-Kabler, C., Zone-Smith, L., Detzler, I., Roberson, J., ... Ackerman, M. (2010). Comparing in-person, video, and telephonic medical interpretation. *Journal of General Internal Medicine*, 25, 345–350.

MacFarlane, A., Dzebisova, Z., Karapish, D., Kovacevic, B., Ogbebor, F., & Okonkwo, E. (2009). Arranging and negotiating the use of informal interpreters in general practice consultations: Experiences of refugees and asylum seekers in the west of Ireland. *Social Science & Medicine*, 69, 210–214.

Manson, A. (1988). Language concordance as a determinant of patient compliance and emergency room use in patients with asthma. *Medical Care*, 26, 1119–1128.

Mazor, S. S., Hampers, L. C., Chande, V. T., & Krug, S. E. (2002). Teaching Spanish to pediatric emergency physicians: Effects on patient satisfaction. *Archives of Pediatrics & Adolescent Medicine*, 156, 693–695.

McLaughlin, M., Nam, Y., May, W., Baezconde-Garbanati, L., Georgiou, P., & Ahn, Z. (2013). Technology-based medical interpretation for cross-language communication: In person, telephone, and videoconference interpretation and their comparative impact on Limited English Proficiency (LEP) patient and doctor. In P. L. P. Rau (Ed.), *Cross-cultural design: Cultural differences in everyday life* (Vol. 8024, pp. 137–146). New York: Springer; Berlin: Heidelberg.

Meeuwesen, L. (2012). Language barriers in migrant health care: A blind spot. *Patient Education and Counseling*, 86, 135–136.

Meeuwesen, L., Twilt, S., ten Thije, J. D., & Harmsen, H. (2010). "Ne diyor?" (What does she say?): Informal interpreting in general practice. *Patient Education and Counseling*, 81, 198–203.

Mikkelson, H. (2003). Telephone interpreting: Boon or bane? In L. P. González (Ed.), *Speaking in tongues: Language across contexts and users* (pp. 251–269). Valencia, Spain: Universidad de València.

Moreno, M. R., Otero-Sabogal, R., & Newman, J. (2007). Assessing dual-role staff-interpreter linguistic competency in an integrated healthcare system. *Journal of General Internal Medicine*, 22, S331–335.

Mueller, M.-R., Roussos, S., Hill, L., Salas, N., Villarreal, V., Baird, N., & Hovell, M. (2011). Medical interpreting by bilingual staff whose primary role is not interpreting: Contingencies influencing communication for dual-role interpreters. In J. J.

Kronenfeld (Ed.), *Access to care and factors that impact access, patients as partners in care and changing roles of health providers* (pp. 77–91). Bingley, UK: Emerald.

Nápoles, A. M., Santoyo-Olsson, J., Karliner, L. S., O'Brien, H., Gregorich, S. E., & Pérez-Stable, E. J. (2010). Clinician ratings of interpreter mediated visits in underserved primary care settings with ad hoc, in-person professional, and video conferencing modes. *Journal of Health Care for the Poor and Underserved*, 21, 301–317.

Ngo-Metzger, Q., Sorkin, D. H., Phillips, R. S., Greenfield, S., Massagli, M. P., Clarridge, B., & Kaplan, S. H. (2007). Providing high-quality care for limited English proficient patients: The importance of language concordance and interpreter use. *Journal of General Internal Medicine*, 22, S324–330.

O'Leary, S. C. B., Federico, S., & Hampers, L. C. (2003). The truth about language barriers: One residency program's experience. *Pediatrics*, 111, e569–573.

Papic, O., Malak, Z., & Rosenberg, E. (2012). Survey of family physicians' perspectives on management of immigrant patients: Attitudes, barriers, strategies, and training needs. *Patient Education and Counseling*, 86, 205–209.

Pham, K., Thornton, J. D., Engelberg, R. A., Jackson, J. C., & Curtis, J. R. (2008). Alterations during medical interpretation of ICU family conferences that interfere with or enhance communication. *Chest*, 134, 109–116.

Phelan, M. (2012). Medical interpreting and the law in the European Union. *European Journal of Health Law*, 19, 333–353.

Phillips, C. (2013). Remote telephone interpretation in medical consultations with refugees: Meta-communications about care, survival and selfhood. *Journal of Refugee Studies*, 26, 505–523.

Pöchhacker, F. (2007). Giving access – or not: A developing-country perspective on healthcare interpreting. In F. Pöchhacker, A.-L. Jakobson, & I. M. Mees (Eds.), *Interpreting studies and beyond* (pp. 121–137). Frederiksberg, Denmark: Samfundslitteratur.

Pöchhacker, F., & Kadric, M. (1999). The hospital cleaner as healthcare interpreter: A case study. *Translator*, 5, 161–178.

Prince, D., & Nelson, M. (1995). Teaching Spanish to emergency medicine residents. *Academic Emergency Medicine*, 2, 32–37.

Renée, M. (2013). The death of healthcare interpreting in The Netherlands. Retrieved March 14, 2015, from http://aiic.net/page/6612.

Rivadeneyra, R., Elderkin-Thompson, V., Silver, R. C., & Waitzkin, H. (2000). Patient centeredness in medical encounters requiring an interpreter. *American Journal of Medicine*, 108, 470–474.

Roat, C. E. (2006). Certification of healthcare interpreters in the United States. Retrieved March 14, 2015, from http://www.calendow.org/uploadedFiles/certification_of_health_care_interpretors.pdf.

Rose, D. E., Tisnado, D. M., Malin, J. L., Tao, M. L., Maggard, M. A., Adams, J., … Kahn, K. L. (2010). Use of interpreters by physicians treating limited English proficient women with breast cancer: Results from the provider survey of the Los Angeles Women's Health Study. *Health Services Research*, 45, 172–194.

Rosenberg, E., Leanza, Y., & Seller, R. (2007). Doctor-patient communication in primary care with an interpreter: Physician perceptions of professional and family interpreters. *Patient Education and Counseling*, 67, 286–292.

Rosenberg, E., Seller, R., & Leanza, Y. (2008). Through interpreters' eyes: Comparing roles of professional and family interpreters. *Patient Education and Counseling*, 70, 87–93.

Sarver, J., & Baker, D. W. (2000). Effect of language barriers on follow-up appointments after an emergency department visit. *Journal of General Internal Medicine*, 15, 256–264.

Schenker, Y., Pérez-Stable, E. J., Nickleach, D., & Karliner, L. S. (2011). Patterns of interpreter use for hospitalized patients with limited English proficiency. *Journal of General Internal Medicine*, 26, 712–717.

Simon, M. A., Ragas, D. M., Nonzee, N. J., Phisuthikul, A. M., Luu, T. H., & Dong, X. (2013). Perceptions of patient-provider communication in breast and cervical cancer-related care: A qualitative study of low-income English- and Spanish-speaking women. *Journal of Community Health*, 38, 707–715.

Tocher, T. M., & Larson, E. B. (1996). Interpreter use and the impact of the process and outcome of care in type II diabetes. *Journal of General Internal Medicine*, 11, 150.

Valdés, G. (2003). *Expanding definitions of giftedness: The case of young interpreters from immigrant communities*. Mahwah, NJ: Erlbaum.

Weaver, C., & Sklar, D. (1980). Diagnostic dilemmas and cultural diversity in emergency rooms. *The Western Journal of Medicine*, 133, 356–366.

Yang, C.-F., & Gray, B. (2008). Bilingual medical students as interpreters – What are the benefits and risks? *New Zealand Medical Journal*, 121, 15–28.

Yawman, D., McIntosh, S., Fernandez, D., Auinger, P., Allan, M., & Weitzman, M. (2006). The use of Spanish by medical students and residents at one university hospital. *Academic Medicine*, 81, 468–473.

5

MODEL OF BILINGUAL HEALTH COMMUNICATION

Many researchers have proposed communication models for interpreter-mediated provider–patient interactions. Since the late 1990s, various scholars have proposed viewing interpreter-mediated medical encounters as a triangle in which providers, patients, and interpreters occupy each corner (see Figure 5.1a). Such an understanding moves beyond the conduit model of communication, which conceptualizes interlocutors as merely encoders and decoders of messages (see Figure 5.1b). In addition, this conceptual model draws attention to the interactions between pairs (i.e., provider–patient, patient–interpreter, and interpreter–provider dyads). By noting the interpersonal dynamics, researchers emphasize that interpreter-mediated medical encounters are not accomplished through the interpreter acting as a passive medium, but rather they involve the delicate balance of the three dyadic relationships in the communicative processes. The triangular positioning in space is even recommended for seating arrangements in provider–patient interactions (Hilliard, 2013; Phelan & Parkman, 1995), with "three parties seated in an equilateral triangle" (Westermeyer, 1990, p. 747).

However, the triangular conceptualization limits our understanding of interpreter-mediated interactions in certain ways. For example, the triangle envisions the interpreter as a third party who holds equal distance/power with other parties. By doing so, it fails to acknowledge the wide range of contextual factors that shape the interpersonal dynamics and processes of communication in interpreter-mediated interactions. In addition, the dyadic communications envisioned in the triangular formation are not independent from each other. While patients may have limited language proficiency, their hearing and speaking abilities may vary significantly. Patients from different cultures and/or educational

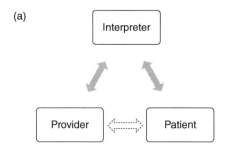

FIGURE 5.1a   Interpreter-mediated medical encounters

FIGURE 5.1b   Interpreter-as-conduits model of communication

backgrounds may also have varied desires to communicate with the provider directly despite their limited language proficiency. As a result, patients may actively monitor and interject their opinions during provider–interpreter talk. Thus, the triadic formation of the three dyadic pairs fails to account for the interactions in which all participants are actively engaged in one single interaction. In other words, in interpreter-mediated interactions, it's not a rotation between dyadic conversations as each dyad takes a turn in their communicative space. Rather, the multiple communicative parties form and overlap with each other's communicative turns, much like how a family member interjects his/her narratives during a provider–patient interaction.

Therefore, I propose that interpreter-mediated interactions should be conceptualized as in the following diagram, where each party creates conversational spaces within the larger communicative event (i.e., provider–patient communication; see Figure 5.2). In this model, interpreters are conceptualized as active participants in provider–patient interactions. The processes of communication are not necessarily linear (e.g., a patient talks first, followed by the interpreter's interpreting and the provider's acknowledgment and response, and vice versa). Rather, all individuals in the communicative event actively negotiate the communicative process through their understanding of these conversational spaces.

I use the term conversational space to highlight the participatory aspects of these interactions in which all individuals are capable of creating or denying access for others to participate in the interaction. In other words, each participant can define and draw the boundaries of a space to engage in conversations with their chosen others. For example, to establish rapport with the provider, a patient may choose to communicate with the provider directly and only seek the

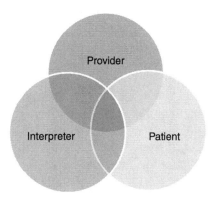

FIGURE 5.2 Interpersonal dynamics in interpreter-mediated medical encounters

interpreter's assistance for specific words or phrases. Similarly, a provider may say to an interpreter in English, "Do you think I should ask her if she'd like her son in here when I tell her she has cancer?" The question is not meant to be relayed to the patient; rather, it is directed to the interpreter-as-cultural-broker. These are intentional, purposeful communicative strategies to create dyadic conversations. Conversational spaces can be challenged. For example, a provider may feel frustrated or confused by an enthusiastic patient's limited language skills and ask the interpreter to interpret everything. A patient may ask the interpreter about the side talk that the physician had with the interpreter that was not relayed to him or her. All participants are able to choose to include or exclude conversational others in the medical encounter. These conversational spaces can be created through both verbal and nonverbal means, such as code-switching (e.g., speaking in a language that excludes the participation of certain others) or through physical boundaries (e.g., talking directly to the provider privately). *Who* gets to communicate *what* to *whom* is a collaborative and coordinated communicative activity among all participants.

This conceptualization also allows for additional parties (e.g., another family member or a nurse) to participate in the interpreter-mediated interactions (see Figure 5.2a). For example, a family member may ask the interpreter to tell the physician that the patient should not be informed about his or her poor prognosis. A patient may ask the physician to use the family member as an interpreter rather than the in-person interpreter. A nurse may have a side conversation with the provider that is not relevant to the patient or the interpreter. Different individuals may actively create or demand specific conversational spaces with the participant of their choice. In other words, this model views each person as an active participant in the dynamic, emergent processes of medical encounters. While all participants share similar goals in improving the patient's health through quality care, each participant may also have different goals and agendas that create tension in their collaboration.

(a)

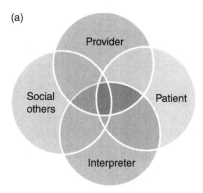

FIGURE 5.2a Interpersonal dynamics in interpreter-mediated medical encounters: with social others

Finally, it is important to note that not all participants have the same power or ability to negotiate conversational spaces in interpreter-mediated mediated medical encounters. For example, a patient who has higher language proficiency, self-advocacy, or education is more likely to have direct conversations with the provider than a patient who does not have those qualities. An in-person interpreter who has more job security and professional courtesy in a healthcare facility is more likely to challenge providers' communicative styles and preferences than a chance or telephone interpreter. Figure 5.2b presents an example in which a patient has little voice in the conversational spaces and an interpreter who actively and aggressively creates conversational spaces in the medical encounter. This is most likely to happen when a family interpreter assumes the caretaking and patient advocate role for a patient who has no knowledge of the language spoken by the provider. In other words, I do not see the circle of each individual to be static in the interpreter-mediated interaction. Rather, each participant's circle and their overlapping conversational spaces can expand or contract depending on various factors (that we will explore in later chapters). Not all overlapping areas exist in every medical encounter either. For example, patients with sufficient language proficiency may communicate directly with the physician while the interpreter maintains a silent observer presence (Figure 5.2c).

Some readers may notice the similarities between this conceptualization of the interpreter role and the concept of interpreters' role-space proposed by Llewellyn-Jones and Lee (2013). They argued that interpreters should strategically shift between the continuum of three different axes (i.e., alignment with provider versus patient, interpreter visibility, and control over interactions) to ensure successful interactions. However, whereas interpreters' role-space centers on interpreters' management and decision-making, my conceptualization highlights the

(b)

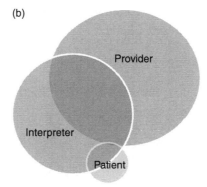

FIGURE 5.2b Interpersonal dynamics in interpreter-mediated medical encounters: family interpreters with patients with no language proficiency

(c)

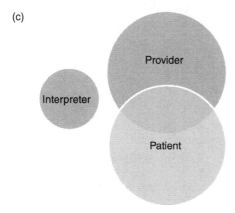

FIGURE 5.2c Interpersonal dynamics in interpreter-mediated medical encounters: professional interpreters with patients with high language proficiency

coordinated and collaborative nature of interpreter-mediated interactions. In other words, conversational spaces can be created, negotiated, and resisted by *any* participants in the medical encounter. Successful interactions depend on the ability of individuals to coordinate and collaborate with one another.

In summary, the Venn diagram aims to demonstrate the flexible, interactive nature of interpersonal dynamics in interpreter-mediated medical encounters. It sets the foundation of how I conceptualize interpersonal relationships and interactions in interpreter-mediated medical encounters. In the following chapters, I will situate this provider–patient–interpreter Venn diagram in healthcare contexts, exploring a wide variety of factors that shape the process and dynamics of multi-party interactions and influence how these conversational spaces are created, negotiated, and contested.

A. Providers' Diversity, Expectations, and Agenda

In Chapter 4, I examined how interpreters' diversity may shape their agenda and communicative strategies in medical encounters. One of the most important elements highlighted by Figure 5.2 is the individual agents in interpreter-mediated medical encounters. Each participant is conceptualized as an independent, active participant in the communicative process, though each will have his/her unique characteristics and agenda. Although the literature on interpreter-mediated medical encounters has traditionally focused on interpreters, providers' unique characteristics and agendas can also have a significant impact on the discursive processes of bilingual health communication. Many researchers have explicitly identified the clinical contexts in which the studies took place, including pediatrics (Kuo, O'Connor, Flores, & Minkovitz, 2007), emergency medicine (Flores, Abreu, Barone, Bachur, & Lin, 2012), oncology (Butow, Bell, et al., 2011), and mental health (Flynn et al., 2013); however, few have examined how these unique clinical contexts may shape interpreter-mediated medical encounters.

In one of my recent studies, I focused on identifying how the diversity of providers may shape their agenda and expectations when working with interpreters. The data reported in the following section is based on an 18-item survey I developed through funding from National Institutes of Health (see also Hsieh, Pitaloka, & Johnson, 2013). The survey was developed based on my previous qualitative studies and past literature to assess participants' evaluation of the importance of specific characteristics or issues related to medical interpreting. The 18 items use a 7-point Likert scale, ranging from 1 (extremely unimportant) to 7 (extremely important). Table 5.1 provides a list of the items. I also measured five demographic variables, including provider's gender, experiences with interpreters, age, native language, and specialty area. These demographic variables were later used for a series of MANOVAs (see Table 3.3). Detailed descriptions of the instruments and methods have been published elsewhere (Hsieh et al., 2013).[1]

A.1. Components Shaping Providers' Views

Three dimensions effectively measured providers' views of interpreters: (a) interpreter as patient ally ($\alpha = 0.874$), (b) interpreter as health professional ($\alpha = 0.792$), and (c) interpreter as provider proxy ($\alpha = 0.763$). Because the principal component analysis (PCA) demonstrated significant loading on all three components, each with a high α value (i.e., high internal validity among items), the items effectively measured providers' attitudes toward healthcare interpreters through these dimensions (see Table 5.1).

TABLE 5.1 Providers' expectations and needs for medical interpreters

Item	Content	Component loading		
		Patient Ally	Health Professional	Provider Proxy
8	Interpreter's ability to provide emotional support to the patient	.799		
12	Interpreter's familiarity with the patient's needs	.739		
11	Interpreter's ability to help the patient seek information (e.g., such as asking about treatment alternatives or more affordable medication)	.719		
10	Interpreter's willingness to assist the patient outside of the medical encounter	.691		
2	Interpreter's ability to read the patient's nonverbal behaviors	.644	.340	
9	Interpreter's ability to develop rapport between the provider and the patient	.635	.322	
14	Interpreter's ability to advocate for the patient	.555		.351
13	Interpreter's ability to help patients to navigate the healthcare system	.549		
4	Interpreter's ability to not take sides (i.e., neutrality)		.821	
6	Interpreter's ability to remain emotionally detached		.746	
3	Interpreter's ability to offer literal (i.e., word-for-word) translation		.739	
1	Interpreter's medical knowledge and medical terminology		.577	.329
17	Interpreter's ability to ensure the quality of care			.743
16	Interpreter's ability to keep the medical interview on track		.402	.655
18	Interpreter's familiarity with the patient's medical history			.630
15	Interpreter's ability to facilitate the provider's agenda (e.g., treatment) in medical encounters		.311	.578
5	Interpreter's ability to anticipate and minimize cultural differences between the provider and the patient			
7	Interpreter's ability to put patients at ease			

Interpreter as Patient Ally

The first component, interpreter as patient ally (Patient Ally), comprises eight items: interpreter's ability to provide emotional support to the patient (item 8), interpreter's familiarity with the patient's needs (item 12), interpreter's ability to help the patient seek information (item 11), interpreter's willingness to assist patients outside of the medical encounter (item 10), interpreter's ability to read the patient's nonverbal behaviors (item 2), interpreter's ability to develop rapport between the provider and the patient (item 9), interpreter's ability to advocate for the patient (item 14), and interpreter's ability to help patients navigate the healthcare system (item 13). Several items within this component are traditionally viewed as problematic behaviors to be avoided (e.g., advocating for patients, assisting patients outside of medical encounters, and providing emotional support to others) (see Dysart-Gale, 2007; Hsieh, 2006; Hsieh & Hong, 2010). Others (e.g., helping patients seek information or navigate the healthcare system, reading the patient's nonverbal cues, facilitating provider–patient rapport, being familiar with patients' needs) may be irrelevant when all speakers are competent at communicating with one another.

Interpreter as Health Professional

The second component, interpreter as health professional (Professional), includes: interpreter's ability to not take sides (item 4), interpreter's ability to remain emotionally detached (item 6), interpreter's ability to offer literal translation (item 3), and interpreter's medical knowledge and medical terminology (item 1). This component is similar to the conduit role (Dysart-Gale, 2007; Kaufert & Putsch, 1997), which highlights interpreters' responsibilities to relay neutral, faithful, and accurate information from one language to another. Some items extend beyond the conduit role, requiring interpreters to be independent (e.g., to remain emotionally detached) and to have a certain level of medical expertise (e.g., to have medical knowledge and terminology).

Interpreter as Provider Proxy

The third component, interpreter as provider proxy (Provider Proxy), includes: interpreter's ability to ensure the quality of care (item 17), interpreter's ability to keep the medical interview on track (item 16), interpreter's familiarity with the patient's medical history (item 18), and interpreter's ability to facilitate the provider's agenda in medical encounters (item 15). This component situates interpreters as members of the healthcare team, sharing responsibilities to ensure the quality of care and being familiar with patients' medical histories. However, it also views interpreters as being in a subordinate, auxiliary role in assisting providers' control over the medical encounter (e.g., keeping the medical interview on track and facilitating the provider's agenda).

A.2. Demographic Variables Influencing Providers' Attitudes

The only two demographic variables that have a significant impact on providers' attitudes are gender and experiences with interpreters.

Providers' Gender

Providers' gender has a significant impact on their views of interpreters ($F_{(3,284)} = 4.277$, Wilks' $\lambda = 0.957$, $\eta_p^2 = 0.043$, $p = 0.006$). Providers' gender shows significant differences in Patient Ally ($F_{(1,286)} = 4.201$, $\eta_p^2 = 0.41$, $p = 0.041$) and Professional ($F_{(1,286)} = 6.412$ $\eta_p^2 = 0.22$, $p = 0.012$,) but not in Provider Proxy ($F_{(1,286)} = .014$, $\eta_p^2 = 0.00$, $p = 0.905$). Female providers value Patient Ally ($M = 41.19$, $SD = 7.28$, 95% CI [40.05, 42.33]) and Professional ($M = 23.40$, $SD = 3.46$, 95% CI [22.83, 23.96]) more highly than male providers ($M = 39.34$, $SD = 7.85$, 95% CI [37.99, 40.70] and $M = 22.27$, $SD = 4.06$, 95% CI [21.60, 22.94], respectively).

Providers' Experiences with Interpreters

Providers' experience with interpreters does not have a significant impact on their overall views of interpreters ($F_{(3,284)} = 1.255$, Wilks' $\lambda = 0.987$, $\eta_p^2 = 0.013$, $p = 0.290$). Among the three dimensions, however, Professional was marginally significant ($F_{(1,286)} = 3.324$, $\eta_p^2 = 0.011$, $p = 0.069$). Follow-up tests revealed that providers with more experience working with interpreters (i.e., more than 10 times) placed higher importance on interpreters' ability to offer literal translation (item 3; $F_{(1,286)} = 3.959$, $\eta_p^2 = 0.014$, $p = 0.048$), to anticipate and minimize cultural differences between the provider and the patient (item 5; $F_{(1,286)} = 3.984$, $\eta_p^2 = 0.014$, $p = 0.047$), to advocate for the patient (item 14; $F_{(1,286)} = 5.698$, $\eta_p^2 = 0.020$, $p = 0.018$), to keep the medical interview on track (item 16; $F_{(1,286)} = 6.035$, $\eta_p^2 = 0.021$, $p = 0.015$), and to ensure the quality of care (item 17; $F_{(1,286)} = 4.027$, $\eta_p^2 = 0.014$, $p = 0.046$) (see Table 5.2).

A.3. Similarities and Differences between Specialties

Providers' specialty does not have a significant impact on their views of interpreters ($F_{(12,744)} = 1.078$, Wilks' $\lambda = 0.955$, $\eta_p^2 = 0.015$, $p = 0.375$).

Interpreter as Patient Ally

Pairwise comparisons, however, suggest that nurses ($M = 42.35$, $SD = 1.00$, 95% CI [40.38, 44.33]) place more significance on Patient Ally than oncologists ($M = 38.92$, $SD = 1.26$, 95% CI [36.45, 41.39]) and mental health providers ($M = 39.32$, $SD = 1.06$, 95% CI [37.23, 41.41]) (see Table 5.3 for significance levels and 95% CI for differences). No other specialty differences were observed in

TABLE 5.2 Pairwise comparisons between different experiences

Item	(I) Exp.	(J) Exp.	Mean Difference (I-J)	Std. Error	Sig.	95% CI for Difference	
						Lower bound	Upper bound
3: Interpreter's ability to offer literal translation	High	Low	.286*	.144	.048	.003	.570
5: Interpreter's ability to anticipate and minimize cultural differences between the provider and the patient	High	Low	.281*	.141	.047	.004	.558
14: Interpreter's ability to advocate for the patient	High	Low	.416*	.174	.018	.073	.758
16: Interpreter's ability to keep the medical interview on track	High	Low	.281*	.141	.047	.004	.558
17: Interpreter's ability to ensure the quality of care	High	Low	.392*	.195	.046	.008	.777

* The mean difference is significant at the 0.05 level.

TABLE 5.3 Pairwise comparisons across specialties: principal component

Dimension	(I) Exp.	(J) Exp.	Mean Difference (I-J)	Std. Error	Sig.	95% CI for Difference	
						Lower bound	Upper bound
Patient Ally	Nursing	Ob/Gyn	2.035	1.436	.158	−.792	4.863
		Mental health	3.170*	1.429	.027	.356	5.983
		Emergency medicine	1.519	1.280	.236	−1.000	4.039
		Oncology	3.364*	1.603	.037	.210	6.518

* The mean difference is significant at the 0.05 level.

the other two dimensions. We conducted MANOVA with the other four demographic variables and did not find any significant results.

MANOVA was used to test items loaded on Patient Ally. Providers from different specialties have significantly different views on items loaded on Patient Ally ($F_{(32, 1019)} = 1.675$, Wilks' $\lambda = 0.828$, $\eta_p^2 = 0.46$, $p = 0.011$). Providers from different specialty areas differ significantly in their expectations of an interpreter's ability (a) to assist patients outside of medical encounters (item 10; $F_{(4, 283)} = 3.625$, $\eta_p^2 = 0.49$, $p = 0.007$) and (b) to advocate for the patient (item 14; $F_{(4, 283)} = 4.216$, $\eta_p^2 = 0.56$, $p = 0.002$). The least significant difference pairwise comparisons (see Tables 5.3 and 5.4) show that compared to both mental health providers and oncologists, nurses place significantly more importance on (a), (b), and interpreter's ability to offer emotional support to patients. Mental health providers place less value on (a) than all other specialties (except oncology), and on (b) than emergency medicine and nursing. Oncologists place less importance on (a) and (b) than nurses and less importance on (b) than physicians in emergency medicine.

Providers' Shared Attitudes

When using the three principal components as dependent variables, we did not find any significant differences between specialties. While providers from different specialties may have different expectations and needs, we also recognize that providers in general may share common attitudes toward the roles of healthcare interpreters. Because no individual items in the Professional and Provider Proxy dimensions showed significant results in pairwise comparisons, our data would suggest that they may be common beliefs shared by diverse types of providers.

TABLE 5.4 Pairwise comparisons across specialties: survey items

Item	(I) Specialty areas	(J) Specialty areas	Mean Difference (I–J)	Std. Error	Sig.	95% Confidence Interval for Difference	
						Lower bound	Upper bound
8. Interpreter's ability to provide emotional support to the patient	Nursing	Ob/Gyn	.153	.234	.514	–.307	.613
		Mental health	.580*	.233	.013	.122	1.038
		Emergency medicine	.285	.208	.172	–.125	.695
10. Interpreter's willingness to assist patient outside of the medical encounter	Mental health	Oncology	.534*	.261	.042	.020	1.047
		Ob/Gyn	–.561*	.278	.045	–1.109	–.013
	Oncology	Emergency medicine	–.555*	.249	.027	–1.045	–.065
		Oncology	–.259	.310	.403	–.869	.351
		Nursing	–.996*	.273	.000	–1.534	–.458
		Ob/Gyn	–.302	.311	.333	–.914	.310
		Mental health	.259	.310	.403	–.351	.869
		Emergency medicine	–.295	.285	.301	–.856	.265
14. Interpreter's ability to advocate for the patient	Mental Health	Nursing	–.737*	.307	.017	–1.340	–.133
		Ob/Gyn	–.424	.271	.119	–.958	.110

	Emergency medicine	−.803*	.242	.001	−1.280	−.325
	Oncology	−.213	.302	.481	−.807	.381
	Nursing	−.887*	.266	.001	−1.411	−.363
Oncology	Ob/Gyn	−.211	.303	.486	−.808	.385
	Mental health	.213	.302	.481	−.381	.807
	Emergency medicine	−.590*	.278	.034	−1.136	−.043
	Nursing	−.674*	.299	.025	−1.262	−.086

* The mean difference is significant at the 0.05 level.

A.4. Universalities and Distinctiveness of Providers' Expectations

If each participant in an interpreter-mediated medical encounter has his/her unique needs and perspectives, it is important not to limit our investigation to interpreters. This survey was one of the first studies to document how provider diversity may shape the desired processes of bilingual health communication. In particular, several patterns were particularly important for the Model of Bilingual Health Communication.

First, there are shared expectations across all healthcare providers. I did not find any specialty-specific differences in two of the three dimensions (i.e., Professional and Provider Proxy). While one cannot prove a null hypothesis, the lack of significant findings was not surprising. After all, researchers have consistently found that healthcare providers often expect interpreters to assume a neutral conduit role (Abbe, Simon, Angiolillo, Ruccione, & Kodish, 2006; Brämberg & Sandman, 2013; Fatahi, Hellstrom, Skott, & Mattsson, 2008), a default role in interpreters' codes of ethics and training (Dysart-Gale, 2007) represented by the Professional dimension in the survey. On the other hand, it is interesting that providers do not necessarily recognize their competing (and conflicting) demands for interpreters, as these three dimensions are not necessarily compatible with one another. For example, if an interpreter were a neutral conduit, he/she would not be able to pursue the provider's agenda (i.e., Provider Proxy); yet these two dimensions are both shared expectations for all providers. From this perspective, it is important to examine how the shared attitudes and competing expectations influence providers' behaviors and evaluations of interpreter-mediated medical encounters.

The other pattern that has significant potential to advance theory development of bilingual health communication is the identification of specialty-specific differences in the Patient Ally dimension. This is a research area that has been implied but not systematically examined before. While there have been many studies exploring interpreter roles in providing emotional support and advocacy functions both inside and outside of medical encounters, this survey provides the first quantitative evidence that highlights providers' distinctive differences in their evaluation on this particular dimension. In other words, interpreters may need to assume different levels of Patient Ally, as the best or desired interpreting style may differ depending on the clinical setting.

The provider differences in Patient Ally also help to refocus our future research directions. For example, Patient Ally involves behaviors that are traditionally considered problematic (e.g., advocating for patients, assisting patients outside of medical encounters, providing emotional support) (see Dysart-Gale, 2007; Hsieh, 2006; Hsieh & Hong, 2010). The fact that some providers value these behaviors suggests that there may be some positive impacts or desirable outcomes related to these behaviors (at least for these providers). It is important to further examine the corresponding consequences and implications of these behaviors.

In addition, because Patient Ally also involves interpreter performances that would be irrelevant when all speakers are competent at communicating with one another (e.g., helping patients seek information or navigate the healthcare system, reading patients' nonverbal cues, facilitating provider–patient rapport, and familiarity with patients' needs), this highlights the interactive and dynamic nature of provider–patient interactions. In other words, this suggests that certain interpreter performances may emerge (intermittently) during interpreter-mediated medical encounters in response to interactional dilemmas that arise. Interpreters' roles and functions should not be fixed but flexible and responsive to the dynamics of provider–patient interactions.

Finally, the fact that provider gender and providers' experiences with interpreters have significant impacts on their expectation of interpreter roles and functions suggests that certain variables can shape the interpersonal dynamics and preferred interpreter performances. This is an important issue because if interpreters are conduits and robot-like, then they are interchangeable. As long as they are competent, one interpreter is no different from another. However, our findings suggest that, depending on a number of factors (provider–interpreter relationship, providers' familiarity with interpreters, providers' unique characteristics), providers may hold different standards in evaluating the appropriateness and effectiveness of interpreter performance. This is an issue we will explore throughout this book. For now, as far as the Model of Bilingual Health Communication is concerned, this finding highlights the importance of recognizing individual characteristics and interpersonal history in interpreter-mediated medical encounters.

B. A Normative Approach to Interpreter-Mediated Medical Encounters

While some of the earliest publications by healthcare practitioners date back to the 1960s (e.g., Bloom, Hanson, Frires, & South, 1966; Richie, 1964), before the late 1980s most studies provided anecdotal observations and often focused on working with informal interpreters. The emergence of professional interpreters in the 1990s facilitated the development of systematic and evidence-based studies, with findings highlighting the respective discipline-specific interests, such as clinical impacts for medical researchers, discourse pragmatics for applied linguists, and interpreter performance/visibility for researchers of interpreting studies. By the 2000s, a wide variety of interdisciplinary publications and reviews, including studies with sophisticated research designs and large sample sizes, began to address *both* the clinical/medical and the sociopolitical/sociocultural dimensions of healthcare interpreting (Bischoff, 2012).

The field of interpreter-mediated interactions, however, appears to have plateaued in terms of its theoretical development. Since the important breakthrough in recognizing interpreters as active participants in discursive events (Metzger, 1999; Pöchhacker & Shlesinger, 2005; Roy, 2000; Wadensjö, 1998), researchers have examined interpreters' visibility (Angelelli, 2004), strategic management of medical encounters (Greenhalgh, Robb, & Scambler, 2006; Leanza, Boivin, & Rosenberg, 2010), and impacts on patients' health outcomes (Butow, Goldstein, et al., 2011; Flores et al., 2012). What is implied in these lines of research is the recognition that interpreters influence the process, content, and outcome of provider–patient interactions. However, they do not provide theoretical explanations of how or why interpreters choose to influence medical encounters in one way or another. Similarly, both researchers and practitioners increasingly emphasize the role of other speakers (e.g., physicians and patients) in interpreter-mediated medical encounters in ensuring quality of care, but little has been done to incorporate these conversational others in the theoretical conceptualization of interpreter-mediated medical encounters.

These two issues prompted me to consider interpreter-mediated medical encounters from a different angle. Rather than focusing on interpreter behaviors, I am interested in examining how the interpersonal dynamics may shape the processes and content of bilingual health communication. If interpreters act as active participants in medical encounters along with at least two other speakers (i.e., the provider and the patient), researchers should conceptualize interpreter-mediated medical encounters as triadic interactions.

In a review of physician–adult patient–adult companion (triadic) communication, Laidsaar-Powell et al. (2013) found that adult companions assume a variety of roles and are often perceived as helpful. Nevertheless, they also present specific challenges, with some behaviors considered more helpful than others (e.g., information support versus demanding behaviors) and varying preferences for companion involvement. To manage triadic communication, Laidsaar-Powell et al. (2013, p. 11) recommended specific strategies for providers:

- Encourage, welcome, and involve companions in consultations.
- Ascertain from the patient and/or the companion why the companion has accompanied the patient to the consultation.
- Highlight helpful companion behaviors.
- Clarify and agree upon the role preferences of patients and companions at the start of the consultation.
- Be aware of, and respect, the patient's preference for companion involvement.
- Take opportunities to discuss sensitive information privately with the patient alone.
- Be aware that companions are involved in decision-making discussion outside of the consultation.
- Reflect upon your own behaviors toward companions.

It is important to note that I do not believe that all interpreters are (or should be treated as) adult companions. However, the recommendations would be particularly helpful for providers who work with family interpreters. In addition, the findings highlight some unique aspects of triadic communication. First, each participant may have his/her unique concerns and agenda. Second, individuals' understanding, interpretation, and evaluation of the appropriateness and effectiveness of certain behaviors is contextually situated (e.g., can be influenced by their interpersonal relationships and cultural norms). Third, effective triadic interactions require providers to actively coordinate and manage others' roles and performances and be reflexively adaptive to situational or individual needs that emerge during interactions.

The examination of the interpreter-mediated medical encounter thus should explore how the participants coordinate with one another throughout the emergent and dynamic processes of cross-cultural care, responding to challenges and tensions in provider–patient interactions. In other words, the focus of our analysis should be on how each participant can best coordinate and collaborate with the others as a communicative accomplishment during medical encounters.

It is from this perspective that I adopt a normative approach to interpreter-mediated medical encounters (Baumslag, 1998). By normative I mean a theoretical account designed to predict and explain the meanings and evaluations of communicative responses during interpreter-mediated medical encounters. Goldsmith (2001, p. 515) explained, "One important goal of a normative theory is to provide a basis for recommendations about how communicators can achieve desirable outcomes." Rather than focusing on the accuracy and fidelity of interpreted texts, I ask, "How do different participants coordinate with each other during the communicative event of provider–patient interactions?" This approach also takes into account the variations in communicative practices and their corresponding impacts. By assuming individuals coordinate their competing goals through communicative practices, I propose that certain practices can be more effective and appropriate than others due to the unique values and preferences within specific contexts, including clinical contexts (e.g., end-of-life care) and sociocultural contexts (e.g., organizational hierarchy and cultural preferences). Goldsmith (2001, p. 518) explained,

Both speech community and speech event are defined by expectations about how communication is structured (e.g., who speaks to whom, how, in what setting, for what purposes?) and about how communication is evaluated (e.g., what is the purpose of the episode, what are the appropriate identities and relational definitions for carrying out such an episode, what values are enacted in these episodes?). Any particular individual may be more or less attuned to these expectations and the degree to which particular episodes embody these expectations may vary; nonetheless, it is possible to abstract from observed practice and from participants' articulation of their expectations a description of the social norms that define speech communities and speech events.

Taking inspiration from Goldsmith's normative approach (Goldsmith, 2001; Goldsmith & Fitch, 1997), I propose to ask (a) how individuals should behave if they wish to achieve desired outcomes and why, and (b) when people behave in a particular way, how will they be evaluated?

The meanings, significance, and processes of interpreter-mediated medical discourse in a particular context may evoke multiple and potentially conflicting goals. Following the traditions of dialectic theorists (Bakhtin, 1981; Baxter & Montgomery, 1996; Houtlosser & van Rees, 2006), I conceptualize interpreter-mediated medical encounters within the contexts of potentially conflicting goals and the dilemmas these can create. By recognizing that each participant in an interpreter-mediated encounter may have distinct goals regarding tasks, identity, and relationships and that these goals are often (a) implicitly coordinated between participants and (b) mediated by an interpreter (Tracy, 2013), I explore situations in which the tensions between individuals' management of these goals are high, in order to understand how communication serves as a way to manage these competing goals.

This new approach allows researchers to ask interesting research questions regarding: (a) the meanings and functions of interpreter-mediated medical encounters within specific contexts and the potentially conflicting goals speakers may have as they seek to honor competing values, such as control over the discursive process, patient autonomy, and shared decision-making; (b) the interrelationships among communicative behaviors that are related to individuals' management of these goals and the ways in which these form meaningful practices, and (c) the ways in which the meanings and functions of interpreter-mediated medical encounters provide an account for why certain behaviors are judged to be more appropriate and effective than others.

Goldsmith (2001, p. 530) explained:

> A normative theory poses questions such as the following: When a social actor wishes to accomplish some purpose in a particular kind of social context, what are the constraints to accomplishing that purpose, what are the discursive resources that are available for addressing those constraints, and what are the evaluative criteria by which the effectiveness and appropriateness of the actor's efforts may be judged?

This line of questioning presents two major shifts in research focus, moving away from the text-centered, interpreter-oriented approach to interpreter-mediated medical encounters. The first shift is to focus attention not simply on the frequency of individual communicative behaviors (e.g., interpreter alterations or mistakes) but on the *meanings* of such practices. The end goal of a normative approach is to account for judgments that some communicative practices in interpreter-mediated medical encounters are "better" than others. These judgments are embedded in cultural systems of meaning and belief, including individual assumptions about the competing goals and values, as well as the expected norms in managing them. By identifying the cultural systems that facilitate the interpretation and evaluation of these practices, researchers can explain and predict why certain practices would be preferred over others.

For example, most people feel that it is appropriate and effective for interpreters to reenact other speakers' exaggerated performance of positive emotions (e.g., a physician showing great enthusiasm when congratulating a mom with a newborn) because it facilitates provider–patient bonding and promotes quality of care (see also Chapter 8.C). As a result, we could predict that interpreters are likely to relay positive emotions, which would also be evaluated positively by other participants. However, what about negative emotions?

When a patient exhibits abusive behaviors (e.g., cursing or mocking the provider), most people would find it inappropriate for an interpreter to reenact in a verbatim fashion with equal affective intensity because such behaviors do not promote the provider–patient relationship or quality of care. As a result, the normative model predicts that interpreters are likely to adopt non-conduit behavior (e.g., provide a summary report or downplay the intensity of the negative emotion) rather than an embodied performance of the negative emotions. By downplaying the intensity of emotion, the interpreter aims to maintain providers' positive attitude toward the patient and to protect provider–patient trust. By providing a summary report, the interpreter makes the provider aware of the patient's dissatisfaction and thus gives them the opportunity to address problematic interactions. There are purposeful strategies to maintain and support values in healthcare settings (e.g., provider–patient trust, provider's control, and quality of care). In addition, the model would predict that providers would prefer interpreters' modified display over a word-by-word relay of the abusive behavior. No one likes to be abused twice, even when it is in different languages. Being congratulated twice in different languages is a different story.

However, if the patient's abusive behavior takes place during a talk therapy in a mental health clinic, I suspect that an interpreter may reenact it. This is because an interpreter may view such behaviors as clinically relevant (e.g., the abusive behavior is part of the symptoms rather than the patient's poor character or communicative style) and do not want to disrupt the therapeutic flow of provider–patient interaction. The normative model also predicts that a provider would prefer the enacted display over the interpreter's summarized report or downplay of negative emotions. This is because, rather than viewing the abusive behavior as a threat to the provider–patient relationship or the provider's face, the provider also views it as a clinical symptom that requires accurate assessment of its intensity to determine the best course of treatment. In addition, by minimizing their presence through enacted relay, the interpreter reinforces the provider–patient relationship as the primary relationship, an important value in healthcare settings. In fact, a provider may feel betrayed or angry if an interpreter "modifies" what s/he perceives to be a clinically relevant behavior in order to protect the provider–patient relationship. In short, our different attitudes about whether and how an interpreter should relay or perform others' abusive behavior or negative attitudes depend on our evaluation of the meanings and impacts of those behaviors as situated in the larger communicative context. In other words, by identifying the values that shape individuals' interpretations and drive their communicative behaviors, researchers can prescribe communicative interventions and practices that are likely to be adopted as they are consistent with the values or goals of the participants.

The second shift in research focus is to move from a linear, positivistic view in prescribing appropriate behaviors in interpreter-mediated medical encounters to an interpretive, heuristic approach to predict and explain evaluations of behaviors as more or less appropriate and effective. From this perspective, my goal is not to define, identify, or regulate the particular behavior that is deemed appropriate or effective in a given provider–patient interaction in a top-down manner. Rather, I aim to explore why certain behaviors are evaluated more favorably than others by examining how well these practices adapt to the potentially conflicting values which emerge in provider–patient interactions. To understand the conflicting values to which participants in interpreter-mediated medical encounters orient, we need to identify the meanings and functions of interpreter-mediated medical encounters. To understand the wide range of communicative strategies that can be employed to respond to interactional dilemmas, we need to first identify the communicative practices within the specific contexts.

By examining the underlying values and principles that shape participants' evaluation and interpretation of communicative behaviors, we can identify some basic features of discourse that can serve as resources to address conflicting goals. Because discursive resources are often language specific and contextually situated, this approach allows researchers to explore the socially defined contexts (e.g., linguistic, cultural, political, and clinical contexts) that shape individuals' evaluations and interpretations. This approach also provides opportunities for researchers to hypothesize how and why certain discursive practices are associated with situated evaluations, investigating both the correlation and the processual links that connect the two.

C. The Model of Bilingual Health Communication

The normative approach to interpreter-mediated medical encounters forms the basis of my Model of Bilingual Health Communication (the BHC Model). In this section, I will explore (a) the individual-level constructs, (b) the interpersonal-level constructs, and (c) the propositions of the BHC Model.[2]

C.1. Individual-level Constructs within the Model of Bilingual Health Communication

Individual-level constructs are factors that shape individual behaviors and evaluations of the interpreter-mediated medical encounter (see Figure 5.3). The

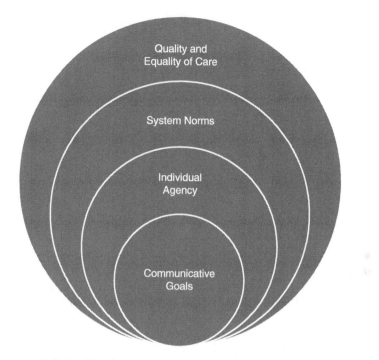

FIGURE 5.3 Individual-level constructs within the Model of Bilingual Health Communication

four constructs are: Communicative Goals, Individual Agency, System Norms, and Quality and Equality of Care (QEC). It is important to note that all these constructs are applicable to all participants in the medical encounter. However, individuals' understanding, assessment, and skill level for these constructs may differ. In addition, individuals may hold competing (and potentially conflicting) understandings of these constructs, resulting in tensions and challenges in interpreter-mediated medical encounters.

Communicative Goals

Fundamental to the BHC Model is the fact that I view interpreter-mediated medical encounters as a goal-oriented communicative activity. In everyday talk, individuals hold multiple goals (e.g., task, identity, and relationship goals) that are often negotiated and coordinated rather than explicitly discussed (Tracy, 2013). All participants in interpreter-mediated interactions, including the interpreter, have communicative goals. For example, a professional interpreter may wish to appear neutral, maintain job security, or ensure the quality of care. A provider may want to be friendly and supportive, maintain efficient time management, and engage in shared decision-making. The communicative goals may be inherent in the communicative activity but can also emerge during the dynamic discursive process. For example, although an interpreter may wish to maintain neutrality in medical encounters, a patient's lack of communicative competence may prompt the interpreter to address the imbalance of provider–patient communication by adopting a more active role in mediating provider–patient interactions. A provider may wish to be friendly and supportive but if a patient continues to chat about family activities and non-health-related issues, a provider may decide to end the conversation to ensure good time management.

Although individuals in interpreter-mediated interactions may share some goals (e.g., improving a patient's health), they also have unique individual goals. For example, providers may hold specific interpersonal goals (e.g., developing trust and rapport) in addition to their therapeutic goals. Individuals' multiple goals may not be compatible with each other, or with others' goals. For example, patients may wish to receive Western biomedical care without giving up their cultural health practices (e.g., taking herbal medicine). On the other hand, a provider may refuse to offer treatment to a patient who insists on continuing to take herbal medicine for fear of potential interactions with the prescribed medication.

Individuals' interpretation and evaluation of the meaning and quality of interpreter-mediated medical encounters are fundamental to their understanding of their goals. A provider who wishes to show empathy with a patient may feel frustrated with an interpreter who focuses on biomedical information while neglecting rapport talk (Aranguri, Davidson, & Ramirez, 2006; Hsieh & Hong, 2010). An interpreter may initiate communicative activities to independently accomplish specific tasks (e.g., offer emotional support by telling a patient "Don't be scared.") with the tacit approval of the clinician, treating the delivery of care as part of her responsibility (Bridges et al., 2015).

Finally, an individual's ability to fulfill their communicative goals may be dependent on their and others' communicative competence as well as other contextual factors during the communicative event. For example, an interpreter who believes that the quality of interpreter-mediated communication is dependent on a passive, neutral conduit interpreting style may feel frustrated when a provider lacks sufficient intercultural competence to "ask the right question" (Hsieh, 2006). When a provider responds to a Jehovah's Witness's refusal of blood transfusion by saying, "We are not going to allow it and we are going to do it anyway. But you tell them that's okay," an interpreter is put in an impossible position to honor provider–interpreter trust without compromising patient autonomy and informed decision-making (Hsieh, 2006, p. 723).

In summary, although individuals are motivated to fulfill their communicative goals, they may need to reconcile their own and others' competing goals. Failure to achieve their intended goals may result in problematic outcomes (e.g., frustration, dissatisfaction, and miscommunication). Nevertheless, because goals are dynamic and can be interactively constructed/negotiated, all individuals can actively collaborate and coordinate with each other to identify and fulfill each other's communicative goals.

Individual Agency

Whereas communicative goals emphasize differences between individuals in their agendas, they do not address their ability to fulfill those goals. In the BHC Model, I view individual agency as the condition needed for the fulfillment of communicative goals. I conceptualize individual agency as a socially constructed and contextually situated self that is rooted in "everyday practices and sites that call forth and supply its meanings" (Gubrium & Holstein, 1995, p. 566). The meanings and functions of individual agency cannot be separated from its actors or the participants of the communicative event. Individual agency is not just an inherent or fixed ability that the human agent holds but a quality that can be interactively negotiated and socially enacted (De Jaegher & Froese, 2009).

Why is this important to BHC? In healthcare settings, not all individuals have the same agency. From an institutional perspective, individual agency can be shaped by power structure, institutional hierarchy, access to resources, and professionalism. For example, physicians are likely to have more individual agency than nurses as they are the head of a healthcare team, imbued with higher institutional power. In contrast, compared to nurses, interpreters may have even less individual agency as they do not always have an institutionalized office (e.g., interpreter services), can be outsourced to external agencies, or are considered to be low-ranked or low-priority workers. As a result, a physician is likely to exert his/her own communicative goals over those of an interpreter when their goals conflict with one another. On the other hand, because interpreters are often trained to assume a neutral, passive presence in provider–patient interactions, an interpreter may actively refrain from intervening in the medical discourse even when they have observed problematic interactions.

At an individual level, individual agency can also be derived through individuals' educational background, self-efficacy skills, communicative competence, emotional status, and motivational relevance (Bandura, 2001). A patient with high health literacy is more likely to participate actively in the medical discourse than a patient who has minimal education and is terrified about seeking care in a cultural system that is completely foreign to him or her (Shaw, Huebner, Armin, Orzech, & Vivian, 2009; Sudore et al., 2009). A family interpreter who also serves as the primary caregiver is motivated to ensure the patient gets a high quality of care and may be more likely to intervene in the provider–patient communication and exert their communicative goals than a telephone interpreter at a remote location (Greenhalgh et al., 2006). Physicians with low self-efficacy admitted that they avoid communicating with language-discordant patients (O'Leary, Federico, & Hampers, 2003); fortunately, physician self-efficacy can be enhanced through training and experiences of working with language-discordant patients (Hernandez et al., 2014; Thompson, Hernandez, Cowden, Sisson, & Moon, 2013).

At an interpersonal level, individual agency can be shaped through interpersonal relationships, social obligations, and interactional dynamics. For example, an interpreter who is familiar with and trusted by the provider is likely to have higher individual agency to pursue his or her communicative goals than an interpreter who does not know anyone in the clinic. A family interpreter may feel more obligated to insist on specific ways of communication (e.g., do not disclose a poor prognosis to the patient) than a professional interpreter. An interpreter may become more aggressive in seeking information upon a patient's request (e.g., "I don't know what questions to ask. Can you help me? Ask whatever is important.")

Similarly, a provider may feel reluctant to rely on a family interpreter when working with a new patient for fear of losing control over the interaction or uncertainty about the quality of interpreting. However, the same provider may feel comfortable relying on a family interpreter in a simple follow-up visit with a long-time patient with diabetes or arthritis. Or a provider may feel pressured to use a family interpreter because the patient shows extreme anxiety in a new environment and resists sharing his/her medical information with a professional interpreter who belongs to the same small immigrant community as the patient.

Finally, it is important to note that individual agency can also be challenged. For example, a provider may ask an interpreter to just interpret what the patient has said and not to add additional personal opinions when conducting interpreting. An interpreter may inform a provider that the line of questioning is culturally inappropriate and unlikely to get a truthful answer from the patient. In other words, although individual agency is about individuals' ability and willingness to exert their communicative goals, the appropriateness and effectiveness of individuals' enactment or embodiment of individual agency is still subject to others' evaluation.

In summary, I view individual agency as a necessary condition for individuals involved in the medical encounter to pursue their communicative goals. Individual agency can be inherent in institutional structure as well as in individuals' skills and competence. However, it can also be socially constructed through interpersonal interactions. A successful communicator can leverage others' support and contextual factors to gain more individual agency; in contrast, a less successful communicator may fail to utilize the resources available to secure their individual agency.

System Norms

System norms move the understanding of interpreter-mediated interactions beyond the examination of individual performances and behaviors. Each individual in an interpreter-mediated medical encounter assumes certain roles, functions, and behaviors under the influences and frames of the system(s). I view the system as the social systems and cultures in which there are specific norms, values, and worldviews that are imposed upon individuals within the system. In other words, individuals interpret meaning through the system to which they subscribe. From this perspective, we can argue that providers are within the culture of medicine, in which there are specific views about conceptualizing health and illness (e.g., principle of verification, germ theory, and Cartesian dualism) that make a patient's cultural illness ideology (e.g., an illness caused by spirits stealing one's souls) incompatible if not incomprehensible.

System norms guide the behaviors of individuals within the system. For example, because professional interpreters are trained to value neutrality and to view the provider–patient relationship as the primary relationship in medical encounters, they adopt specific behaviors (e.g., interpreting in first-person style and avoiding eye contact with others) to minimize their presence. Providers expect to assume the leading and controlling role in provider–patient interactions as they are trained to take charge of the flow of medical discourse. From this perspective, individuals' behaviors are always coherent and consistent within the meaning structure of the system.

However, because not all individuals share the same system, participants in bilingual/cross-cultural medical encounters may experience problematic interactions. For example, a provider may have a hard time understanding why an interpreter insists on avoiding eye contact when providing interpreting services or why a patient continues to complain about haunting spirits when seeking biomedical care. In other words, miscommunication can arise as a result of competing systems.

Because individuals in interpreter-mediated medical encounters are not necessarily regulated by the same systems and the systems involved may not be compatible with each other, individuals may struggle to (a) identify the systems at play during the medical encounter, and (b) prioritize and negotiate the systems that give meaning to the current interaction. For example, a patient may choose to ignore a provider's treatment recommendation if s/he believes the provider has failed to provide an accurate diagnosis. Just as an American patient would scoff at a shaman's effort to dispel an evil spirit, a Hmong parent who believes that his child's epilepsy is caused by a lost soul is unlikely to accept an American physician's explanation that the illness is caused by an "electrical storm" in the brain (Fadiman, 1997). However, a provider can contact child protective services and remove a pediatric patient if s/he suspects that the parent has endangered the child by providing substandard care (Fadiman, 1997). In other words, not all systems are of equal footing. Although the parents are considered dutiful parents in their own ethnic culture, a physician using the biomedical system to identify a parent's failure to provide the proper dosing for treatment can access the legal system to exert his/her control, not just over the child patient's illness experiences but also over the parents' control over the child. Miscommunication due to incompatibilities between systems can thus result in problematic outcomes, including intense conflicts.

The identification and prioritization of systems may prompt individuals to ignore or overrule other participants' needs and preferences. For example, a provider may decide that the legal obligation for informed consent supersedes a patient's family members' preferences about end-of-life disclosure. An interpreter may choose to editorialize other participants' narratives if they feel obligated to act as institutional gatekeepers to conserve limited resources (Davidson, 2000) or as moral mediators to ensure the quality of care (Seale, Rivas, Al-Sarraj, Webb, & Kelly, 2013). By aligning themselves with a system of higher power/value (e.g., moral values and ethical standards), those with a lower institutional ranking (e.g., interpreter) may feel legitimized to adopt behaviors that override the values of other systems (e.g., organizational guidelines) or attitudes of superior others (e.g., physicians). Similar examples can be found in nurses' management of nurse–physician conflicts in which a nurse is willing and even feels justified to disagree with, object to, even undermine a physician's practices if s/he believes that such behaviors are unethical (Peter, Lunardi, & Macfarlane, 2004; Simpson & Lyndon, 2009).

Finally, although all systems have their internal values and structures, systems can also be adaptive to changes as well as influences and impositions from other systems. Granted, not all systems are equally adaptive. For example, the legal system is much more rigid as any changes require legislative efforts to modify laws and regulations. However, a provider who originally subscribed to the values and norms of a biomedical system may become aware of and even appreciate the patient's cultural understanding of their illness. In fact, providers' ability to incorporate patients' cultural worldviews in the treatment process is essential in gaining patient compliance and improving health outcomes (Dutta, 2007; Dutta & Basu, 2007).

This does not mean that the provider abandons his/her original system norms. The best provider is not the one who embraces a patient's cultural norm by abandoning his own. Rather, as individuals come into contact with different system norms and cultural values, successful communicators are able to add the new norms and values to their cultural repertoires (Kramer, 2013). A successful provider learns to integrate two different systems by developing skills to communicate with the patient, using the system norms that construct meanings and guide behavior for the patient (Dutta, 2007). This is a form of cultural fusion (Kramer, 2000). In some ways we can even argue that the provider becomes "acculturated" in the patient's cultural norm, which gives them greater resources to influence and persuade the patient as they negotiate the differences in their (meaning/cultural) systems.

In cross-cultural care, an interpreter is presumed to be aware of the diverging system norms that guide both the provider's and the patient's understanding and behavior in the medical encounter. As a result, interpreters are encouraged to serve as cultural brokers in cross-cultural care (Butow et al., 2012; Dohan & Levintova, 2007).

What happens when individuals' system norms conflict with one another in interpreter-mediated medical encounters? Which system gets to be prioritized over other systems? Answers to these questions come from a higher guiding value for provider–patient communication and cross-cultural care: Quality and Equality of Care.

Quality and Equality of Care

I list Quality and Equality of Care as the overarching value of the BHC Model. Although QEC can be a communicative goal when applied in context, it also serves as an all-encompassing value that integrates differences between systems, providing an ultimate value that guides the interpretation of competing systems. In other words, when individuals experience conflict due to competing or conflicting system norms, they rely on the guiding value of QEC to resolve their differences.

Traditionally, quality of care has been conceptualized using three components: structure (i.e., the organizational factors that define the healthcare system under which care is provided), process (i.e., the clinical and interpersonal care given to the user), and outcomes (i.e., consequences of care) (Donabedian, 1980). Individuals' quality of care can be evaluated through their access to (i.e., whether individuals can access the healthcare structures and process of care which they need) and the effectiveness (i.e., the extent to which care delivers its intended outcome or results in a desired process, in response to needs) of the structure, process, and outcomes (Campbell, Roland, & Buetow, 2000). Within the BHC Model, I am particularly interested in process as an indicator of quality care. Interpreters are essential to ensure access (e.g., making information and resources available to patients) and effectiveness (e.g., allowing providers to provide culturally sensitive care to achieve optimal outcomes) of clinical and interpersonal care, in which other participants rely on interpreters to communicate needs, coordinate tasks, and perform identities.

I recognize that quality of care can be a cultural (and system) construct (Harmsen, Bernsen, Bruijnzeels, & Meeuwesen, 2008). Individuals from different systems are likely to define and perceive quality of care differently (Campbell et al., 2000). For example, for Jehovah's Witnesses, not accepting blood transfusions even in life-or-death situations is essential to their faith and does not constitute a threat to the quality of care. A Chinese patient may consider Chinese food therapy (i.e., consuming food that has specific medical effects) to be a dietary health practice that defines their cultural identity and cannot be separated from their everyday life (Kong & Hsieh, 2012). Quality of care cannot be separated from one's understanding of well-being, which is always culturally and socially situated (Ryan & Deci, 2011; Williams, Teixeira, Carraça, & Resnicow, 2011). In other words, it is possible that a patient, a provider, and/or an interpreter do not share the same understanding of quality of care.

For example, in the United States, the meanings and functions of quality of care are defined in medical education, socialized in clinical practices, and legislated through professional and institutional regulations and laws. For instance, medical schools provide informed consent training to residents, arguing that appropriate and effective consent processes are essential to provider–patient relationships, patient satisfaction, quality of care, and minimizing one's legal liability (Angelos, DaRosa, Bentram, & Sherman, 2002; Maclean, 2009; McClean & Card, 2004). Despite numerous studies showing that patients lack understanding even when there is a rigorous informed consent process (Gattellari, Voigt, Butow, & Tattersall, 2002; Joffe, Cook, Cleary, Clark, & Weeks, 2001; Tam et al., 2015) or concerns about nocebo effects (e.g., warning patients about potential negative side effects can lead to actual experiences of these side effects; Wells & Kaptchuk, 2012), informed consent remains a core value in medical ethics and clinical practices. Western medicine, rooted in individualistic cultures, values patient autonomy and self-determinism (Ryan & Deci, 2011; Williams et al., 2011). Maclean explained, "Because consent is predicated on autonomy, the patient must be competent, the decision must be made voluntarily and the patient should have sufficient knowledge to enable a rational decision" (2009, p. 264). Patient empowerment, another core value of Western medicine, is accomplished through providing necessary information that allows a patient to make autonomous decisions. An ideal patient is an informed patient who is capable and willing to assume *all* responsibilities in their illness events (Kapp, 2007; Ulrich, 2001). These values and expectations also directly or indirectly shape other core values of Western medicine (e.g., patient confidentiality) and are further reinforced through federal/state legislation and professional standards (e.g., The Patient Self-Determinism Act [PSDA] and Health Insurance Portability and Accountability Act [HIPAA]) (Maclean, 2009; Ulrich, 2001).

It is important to note that these system values in Western medicine (e.g., informed consent, self-determinism, and patient confidentiality) are highly formalized because they are regulated through legislation and enforced through legal liability toward individual healthcare providers as well as healthcare institutions. As such, these values can become extremely rigid and completely internalized by healthcare providers. For example, when asked to find a way to balance family preferences and truth-telling to a dying patient, a physician responded, "When I was in medical school, it was driven home to us that autonomy was the lynchpin concept. You're destroying my moral compass" (Solomon, 1997, p. 90). I can only imagine how vulnerable the physician may feel about the legal liability that he would be exposed to and the potential devastating consequences (e.g., becoming an unethical person) had he agreed to such a compromise. This is the power of a system. It powerfully structures our consciousness, guiding our behaviors (e.g., self-sanction) and ethical standards.

However, some bioethicists and physicians have argued that imposing Western biomedical values on patients who do not share those values can be problematic, if not unethical (Gostin, 1995; Ho, 2008). For example, European-American and African-American patients were more likely to view truth-telling as empowering, enabling the patient to make choices; in contrast, Korean-American and Mexican-American patients were more likely to see truth-telling as cruel, even harmful, to patients (Blackhall, Frank, Murphy, & Michel, 2001). The differences in the functions and meanings of "truths" in various communities can result in diverging practices. For example, Korean-American and Mexican-American populations are more likely to shelter patients from information about a poor prognosis and adopt a family-centered model of medical decision-making; in contrast, European-American and African-American populations emphasize the individual autonomy and informed decision-making of the patient (Blackhall, Murphy, Frank, Michel, & Azen, 1995). If a physician insists on disclosing a poor prognosis to a Korean-American or Mexican-American patient, despite his/her family's objection, the physician is likely to increase the patient's suffering and distress, causing disruption in the patient's social network. This is because such practices ignore the cultural meanings, functions, and practices of truth-telling.

In cross-cultural care, interpreters are faced with challenges regarding cultural differences in disclosure practices and information management, which are fused with meanings about identity and relationships. For example, in Chinese culture, if a son fails to assume the responsibility of information management for the patient (e.g., seeking information about treatment options or concealing information from the patient), he may face public criticism that he is an inadequate son (Muller & Desmond, 1992). On the other hand, if a Chinese father gives permission to his son to take over the responsibility of information management and to be a proxy decision-maker (e.g., making decisions about treatments), he is demonstrating his commitment to his family and community (Ellerby, McKenzie, McKay, Gariepy, & Kaufert, 2000). Rees and Bath (2000) found that when mothers with breast cancer withheld information from their daughters, it was often motivated by a desire to protect the daughters. Miller and Zook (1997) noted that AIDS patients' care partners negotiated and legitimized their roles through actively seeking information from physicians. Therefore, information management in a family is not just about patient autonomy but also about family members' identities as part of the family (Blackhall et al., 2001). Failing to respect these cultural meanings of health practices can result in major disruptions to a patient's well-being. From this perspective, quality of care cannot be accomplished without considering the cultural construction and meanings of a patient's sense of well-being.

I will revisit these issues about incompatibility between providers' and patients' understanding about quality of care later in Chapter 9, where I will also provide practice guidelines for healthcare delivery based on the BHC Model. For now, I just want to demonstrate that both providers' and patients' understanding of their social systems will guide their expectations of appropriate performances in healthcare settings. Both can be equally passionate about their system values and expectations, which always entail symbolic and pragmatic consequences.

For marginalized and underserved populations, including language-discordant populations, quality of care cannot be separated from equality of care (Aligning Forces for Quality, 2010). For the BHC Model, I define equality as the extent to which language-discordant populations share comparable access to and effectiveness of care with language-concordant populations. More importantly, equality of health is "conditional upon a respect for personal preferences [or in medical ethics, the principle of 'autonomy'] and upon a prohibition on reductions in current health" (Culyer & Wagstaff, 1993, p. 455). From this perspective, like quality of care, equality of care is not beyond the influence of system, as individual preferences are often shaped by their cultural norms.

In reality, all participants in interpreter-mediated medical encounters often need to manage a potentially delicate and complicated balance between personal preference and health outcomes. Despite the fact that QEC cannot escape the influences of (cultural) systems, individuals within different systems can learn to recognize and acknowledge its transcending values. For example, a provider can recognize and respect a parent's desire to provide the best care for a child patient, despite their disagreement on the treatment procedures. Similarly, interpreters can educate providers, patients, and their family members about the cultural differences in the meanings and functions of truth-telling in end-of-life care, allowing all participants to become aware of other participants' legal and social obligations. Therefore, rather than advocating universal values or standards of quality of care (Beauchamp, 2004), I propose that individuals from different (cultural) systems can generate an integrated value of QEC.

Within the integrated value meta-system, values within different systems (from the participants) are not always consistent or compatible with each other. As a result, what really constitutes the integrated value of QEC is not a fixed value. Rather, it is constantly co-constructed and negotiated between multiple parties. Such an approach also echoes the argument that interpreters' and providers' practices should be guided by valued principles situated in interactional contexts, rather than a set of predetermined, context-free rules (Dean, 2014; Dean & Pollard, 2011). All participants collaborate to develop a prioritized list of diverse values, accessing resources to strengthen their claim and control over the definition of QEC.

For example, an American physician may adopt different disclosure strategies for poor prognosis with a German patient versus a Japanese patient in response to differences in the patient's cultural norms. In addition, an American physician may have different communicative patterns when talking to a Japanese patient who has lived in the USA for decades, a German exchange student on a summer program, or a Syrian refugee who recently arrived in the United States out of fear of genocidal threats. Differences in providers' communicative behaviors are not causes for inequality in healthcare delivery (i.e., treating everyone the same does not equate to quality care). Rather, a physician's ability to understand, empathize, adapt, and respond to a patient's unique needs and expectations can give the provider more resources to provide QEC. This requires a provider to be *mindful* about the specific criteria and contexts that shape a patient's understanding of QEC.

Similarly, a professional interpreter may work with a language-discordant patient for years while maintaining a neutral, detached professional persona. However, after working as the interpreter when the female patient loses a newborn, the interpreter may choose to actively provide emotional support and shift to a more intimate relational footing (Hsieh, 2006). This does not compromise the quality or equality of care. Rather, the interpreter's ability to detect and respond to a critical moment without holding on to a rigid definition of and preference for neutral interpreter is the definition of professionalism and quality care.

In summary, I view QEC as a value system that guides the practices of all involved in interpreter-mediated medical encounters. This value is not universally recognized. Rather, it is contextually situated, interactionally managed, and locally defined in the communicative process. Nevertheless, it allows individuals with competing system norms to acknowledge others' perspectives and forces all participants to subject themselves to the meta-value of quality of care that is co-constructed by all involved in the medical encounter.

C.2. Interpersonal-level Constructs within the Model of Bilingual Health Communication

While individual-level constructs shape individual behaviors and evaluations of the interpreter-mediated medical encounter, interpersonal-level constructs delineate the dimensions through which these individual-level constructs operate. Based on the literature and my own research, I have included two interpersonal-level constructs: (a) Trust–Control–Power, and (b) Temporal Dimension.

Trust–Control–Power

Trust–control–power has been identified as a major theme in bilingual health care. This dynamic can exist at the micro, interpersonal level of provider–patient–interpreter interactions and at the macro, system/cultural level of healthcare institutions and the society at large (Brisset, Leanza, & Laforest, 2013). By recognizing the interpreter's active role in bilingual health care, recent studies have highlighted the importance of *relational contexts* (e.g., interpersonal trust and therapeutic alliances) in shaping providers' and interpreters' collaboration (Gray, Hilder, & Donaldson, 2011; Hsieh, Ju, & Kong, 2010; Robb & Greenhalgh, 2006). In addition, providers and interpreters often compete for control over the communicative process by monitoring others' performances, setting boundaries of time, space, and content of provider–patient interactions, and adopting specific verbal and nonverbal strategies to control others' behaviors (Hsieh, 2010; Mason & Ren, 2012; Zimányi, 2013).

Trust–control–power as a dimension shapes how participants negotiate the various individual-level constructs with one another. For example, when individuals have diverging communicative goals, individual agency, or system norms, who gets to control the provider–patient interaction? Does the person with the most power get to control the interaction? But what kinds of power? The provider has legitimate power (i.e., institutional hierarchy) and expert power (i.e., medical expertise); in contrast, the interpreter has the expert power in language and culture and informational power as they control the content and process of communication through their interpretation (Mason & Ren, 2012; Nugus, Greenfield, Travaglia, Westbrook, & Braithwaite, 2010; Raven, 1993). On the other hand, a patient has reward power and coercive power as they can always choose to find a different provider if the provider fails to respect the patient's request to use a family interpreter, who maintains social power with the patient through long-term relational trust. In other words, trust–control–power is not a fixed understanding of interpersonal dynamics; rather, it is constantly enacted and resisted in the communicative process.

Trust–control–power as a dimension reflects individuals' efforts and competition in defining their interactional (and professional) boundaries. This can be particularly tricky in cross-cultural care, as the boundaries of medicine, language, and culture are often overlapping and blurred. Patients' understanding of their illness and illness symptoms is situated in their Lifeworld (Lo & Bahar, 2013; Todres, Galvin, & Dahlberg, 2007), which is infused with their cultural beliefs, social experiences, and folk ideologies. A patient's illness experiences cannot be separated from their culture or language. For example, a Chinese patient may use the term "腎虛" (pronounced as shen xu) to describe his illness, which literally means 'weak kidney' in English. But for a male patient, this term can be used for various symptoms, including bodily coldness, poor memory, defective cognition, palpitations, dizziness, premature ejaculation, poor erectile function, back pain, urinary frequency, and weakness (Hinton, Nguyen, Tran, & Quinn, 2005). As a result, as interpreters assist in cross-cultural care, they inevitably need to tread in the boundaries of medicine as they bridge the blurry boundaries of medicine, language, and culture. Despite the provider's claim and power over medical expertise, they face challenges in sharing their control over the process of care and meanings of medicine with interpreters in cross-cultural care. For example, because patients from different cultures often have different symptoms/signs of their mental illness (Westermeyer, 1985), a mental healthcare provider needs to rely on an interpreter's assessment of whether the patient's mood display or word choice is appropriate in the patient's cultural norms.

In addition, the three components (i.e., trust, control, and power) are interdependent and intertwined with each other. For example, as an interpreter develops more trust with the provider, the interpreter will have more power to control the process and content of provider–patient interactions (Hsieh, 2010). On the other hand, a provider who insists on maintaining absolute control over the interpreter-mediated interaction can develop a utilitarian view of the interpreter's role and function in which even the interpreter's interpersonal care (e.g., emotional support) is viewed as a tool for therapeutic objectives (Hsieh & Kramer, 2012). In other words, even interpreters' communicative goals are subject to providers' control.

Temporal Dimension

Time is a theoretical dimension that has rarely been discussed in the literature of bilingual health care. This can be partially attributed to the conduit model of interpreting. After all, if interpreters are no more than conduits, providing mechanical and faithful relay of information from one language to another, time would not have made any difference in the quality of interpreting or the quality of care. After all, a hammer remains the same tool regardless of the time elapsed. A user is unlikely to develop a closer bond or relationship with a certain tool, resulting in different usage patterns when using an old hammer versus a new one. In other words, in the traditional literature of healthcare interpreting, the temporal dimension in interpreter-mediated health care is irrelevant and thus undertheorized.

Nevertheless, we know that even the analogy of a hammer is problematic. Even with a tool as rigid as a hammer, we do become more comfortable with the one we have grown accustomed to. We learn its unique characteristics and develop tricks that make the specific hammer work better in different situations.

However, when researchers and practitioners do consider the temporal dimension in interpreter-mediated interactions, time is often perceived to be an enemy, a point of human weakness, of interpreter-mediated medical encounters. The temporal dimension of interpreter-mediated healthcare makes it possible for interpreters to develop relationships with their clients, making them susceptible to the corruption and pressure of interpersonal relationships. Traditionally, the industry has developed specific strategies to prevent potential problems as a result of the temporal dimension of interpreter-mediated health care. For example, to avoid interpreter–patient bonding, some interpreting agencies establish internal rules to minimize repeatedly pairing the same interpreter with the same patient. In contrast, there seems to be less anxiety about and no internal rules against pairing the same interpreter with the same provider. From this perspective, the preferences for provider–interpreter bonding over patient–interpreter bonding also highlight the physician-centered biases in traditional conceptualizations of interpreter-mediated medical encounters.

Time is an important dimension in any system. Most systems are open systems that develop adaptive changes in response to outside influences as well as internal tensions. Because interpreter-mediated provider–patient interactions involve several different systems, each of which entails its own unique values and norms, the participants are likely to face tensions, challenges, and conflicts due to their diverse systems, including practices and values. However, time as a dimension makes integration of diverging systems possible, at individual, organizational, and even cultural levels. For example, interpreters intentionally develop a particular way of speaking (e.g., first-person interpreting styles and avoiding eye contact when interpreting) to systematically reinforce the provider–patient relationship and to claim an invisible role (Hsieh, 2009). For a person who is not aware of the meanings of such practices, an interpreter's performance may appear strange, rude, or even disruptive. However, when a provider learns the meanings and functions of such practices in the interpreter's speech community, he or she may learn to appreciate the interpreter's performance.

Similarly, time makes it possible for people who are initially unfamiliar with each other's behaviors and intentions to develop rapport and trust, allowing them to be more flexible and adaptive to each other's needs and expectations. For example, as physicians become more familiar with patients' cultural values, they may be more willing to modify their communicative practices to accommodate patients' needs. This is the basis of interpreters' cultural broker role. We assume that as providers become knowledgeable about different cultural norms and values, other speakers would be better at understanding and interacting with one another.

It is important to note that recent literature on acculturation[3] has demonstrated that individuals are unlikely to abandon their own cultural values once they become familiar with or even adaptive to the new cultural practices (Kramer, 2013; Wade, Chao, & Kronenberg, 2007). Rather, individuals tend to develop layers of consciousness and pluralistic approaches in managing different areas of life. In other words, time does not make a person forget or abandon his or her original cultural norms. Several studies have demonstrated that acculturation level does not predict the extent to which an individual might abandon prior health beliefs and health practices (Ma, 1999; Wade et al., 2007); rather, interactions between systems allow individuals to develop multiple repertoires. For example, a Chinese patient may prefer to adopt a biomedical model for acute conditions but rely on traditional Chinese medicine for chronic illnesses (Chung et al., 2012). An American physician may welcome shamanistic practices for patients' spiritual well-being but feel strongly about ensuring accurate medication and dosing practices (Brown, 2009).

Finally, rather than portraying a rosy picture of time as a theoretical dimension, researchers also need to recognize that, without meaningful interactions, time may perpetuate miscommunication. For example, patients may become increasingly agitated when a provider fails to acknowledge or accommodate their cultural practices and values after repeated interactions. Such feelings may prompt a patient to avoid care and minimize interactions with outside members. Failure to address provider–interpreter conflicts may result in widespread distrust for interprofessional collaboration within the organization. In short, the temporal dimension within interpreter-mediated health care does not guarantee improved interactions over time.

C.3. Propositions of the Model of Bilingual Health Communication

By adopting a heuristic approach, my goal is to generate a theoretical framework to conceptualize interpreter-mediated medical encounters as an interactive, goal-oriented communicative activity that is situated in the larger communicative event of provider–patient interaction. In addition, the theory presumes that QEC is a shared value that guides all participants' interpretation of and practices in interpreter-mediated medical encounters.

Given the individual-level and interpersonal-level constructs proposed in the BHC Model, I offer the following general propositions that guide the understanding and interpretation of interpreter-mediated medical encounters:

1. Successful BHC is dependent on individuals' ability and agency to negotiate and adapt to competing and/or emerging goals. Moving away from the focus on interpreter performances, this proposition views interpreter-mediated medical encounters as a collaborative achievement among all participants.
2. The desired interpreting style is dependent on contexts. Rather than adopting a positivist stance on pursuing the ideal interpretation through equivalences between two languages, the BHC Model acknowledges that contexts are essential in participants' understanding and preference of interpreting performances. The contexts include but are not limited to clinical, interpersonal, and sociocultural contexts.[4]
3. Evaluation of the appropriateness and effectiveness of interpreters' interpreting strategies requires consideration of the corresponding short-term and long-term impacts. One strategy may have desirable short-term impacts in clinical care but problematic consequences for long-term provider–patient trust.

In the following chapters, I will examine these propositions through the constructs proposed in the BHC Model. By doing so, I aim to demonstrate that the BHC Model advances the literature by presenting a comprehensive theoretical framework to conceptualize and evaluate the quality of interpreter-mediated medical encounters. Finally, I will explore the multiple intervention points identified through the BHC Model that have been largely neglected in the literature.

Notes

1   *Analysis.* We used PASW Statistics 18 for principal component analysis (PCA) and ANOVA to examine the different needs and expectations for interpreters across five demographic variables. For PCA, we first examined the factorability of the 18-item survey. The finding was positive, with Kaiser-Meyer-Olkin Measure of Sampling (MSA) = 0.909 and Bartlett's Test of Sphericity χ^2 [df = 153] = 2527.032, $p < 0.05$.

Univariate MSA values also showed good signs with all items greater than 0.60. As a result, all 18 items were retained for the PCA. To determine the number of components to be extracted, a scree plot and a 95th percentile parallel analysis were used. In order to give a clear interpretation of the components, direct oblimin rotation was utilized. We extracted 3 components based on all 18 items, according to the convergence of scree plot criteria and eigenvalues. The 95th percentile parallel analysis was not taken into consideration because the communality values of all 18 variables were good (above 0.40). Items 5 and 7 were eliminated because their loading on two components were $> \approx |.40|$ and are thus considered crossloaders. After deleting items 5 and 7, we reran the PCA on the remaining 16 items. The MSA and communality values were very strong for the 16 items (> 0.60), providing a clear picture of how each item correlates with the others in each component. This model had no loading less than 0.55 for any item of the three components. We created new variables representing the three dimensions identified through PCA by summing the items of each dimension. We then conducted one-way ANOVA and pairwise comparisons to explore how the five contextual variables (i.e., providers' gender, experiences with interpreters, age, native language, and specialty area) influence their perception in these three dimensions. If we did not obtain significant findings, we proceeded with one-way ANOVA with individual items on the survey as dependent variables.

2   An earlier version of this section has been published elsewhere (Hsieh, in press).

3   Acculturation explains the process by which individuals adapt to a new culture through familiarizing, learning, and eventually internalizing the new cultural norms and values. Different disciplines have operationalized acculturation differently according to their theoretical interests (Thomson & Hoffman-Goetz, 2009). Some common proxy measures used to measure acculturation include: primary language, nativeness, length of residence, language of the interview, generational status, age at immigration, and language proficiency. Different measures entail different assumptions. For example, some of the measures assume that acculturation increases as one increases one's exposure to the host culture (e.g., length of residence), others uses functional measures (e.g., language proficiency and language of interviews), and some assume the importance of formative experiences (e.g., nativeness or age at immigration). It is important to note that one does not necessarily become more acculturated simply because of exposure to the host culture (e.g., a Chinese person can live in Chinatown in New York without speaking a word of English for years).

4   Some of the contexts may be salient and inherent in a medical encounter. For example, interpreters need to consider clinical urgency when interpreting in emergency care, or an elderly male patient may feel uncomfortable discussing impotence through a young female interpreter. Other contexts may be invoked during an emergent interaction. For example, a provider may become suspicious that a female patient's injury is caused by intimate partner violence, thus starting to question the quality of interpreting by a friendly male family interpreter.

References

Abbe, M., Simon, C., Angiolillo, A., Ruccione, K., & Kodish, E. D. (2006). A survey of language barriers from the perspective of pediatric oncologists, interpreters, and parents. *Pediatric Blood & Cancer, 47*, 819–824.

Aligning Forces for Quality. (2010). Quality & equality in US health care: A message handbook. Retrieved March 14, 2015, from www.rwjf.org/content/dam/farm/reports/reports/2010/rwjf69340.

Angelelli, C. V. (2004). *Medical interpreting and cross-cultural communication.* Cambridge, UK: Cambridge University Press.

Angelos, P., DaRosa, D. A., Bentram, D., & Sherman, H. (2002). Residents seeking informed consent: Are they adequately knowledgeable? *Current Surgery*, 59, 115–118.

Aranguri, C., Davidson, B., & Ramirez, R. (2006). Patterns of communication through interpreters: A detailed sociolinguistic analysis. *Journal of General Internal Medicine*, 21, 623–629.

Bakhtin, M. M. (1981). *The dialogic imagination: Four essays by M. M. Bakhtin* (M. Holquist & C. Emerson, Trans.). Austin, TX: University of Texas Press.

Bandura, A. (2001). Social cognitive theory: An agentic perspective. *Annual Review of Psychology*, 52, 1–26.

Baumslag, D. (1998). Choosing scientific goals: The need for a normative approach. *Studies in History and Philosophy of Science*, 29, 81–96.

Baxter, L. A., & Montgomery, B. M. (1996). *Relating: Dialogues and dialectics*. New York: Guilford Press.

Beauchamp, T. L. (2004). Does ethical theory have a future in bioethics? *Journal of Law, Medicine & Ethics*, 32, 209–217.

Bischoff, A. (2012). Do language barriers increase inequalities? Do interpreters decrease inequalities? In D. Ingleby, A. Chiarenza, W. Devillé, & I. Kotsioni (Eds.), *COST series on health and diversity. Volume 2: Inequalities in health care for migrants and ethnic minorities* (pp. 128–143). Philadelphia, PA: Garant.

Blackhall, L. J., Frank, G., Murphy, S., & Michel, V. (2001). Bioethics in a different tongue: The case of truth-telling. *Journal of Urban Health*, 78, 59–71.

Blackhall, L. J., Murphy, S. T., Frank, G., Michel, V., & Azen, S. (1995). Ethnicity and attitudes toward patient autonomy. *Journal of the American Medical Association*, 274, 820–825.

Bloom, M., Hanson, H., Frires, G., & South, V. (1966). The use of interpreters in interviewing. *Mental Hygiene*, 50, 214–217.

Brämberg, E. B., & Sandman, L. (2013). Communication through in-person interpreters: A qualitative study of home care providers' and social workers' views. *Journal of Clinical Nursing*, 22, 159–167.

Bridges, S., Drew, P., Zayts, O., McGrath, C., Yiu, C. K. Y., Wong, H. M., & Au, T. K. F. (2015). Interpreter-mediated dentistry. *Social Science & Medicine*, 132, 197–207.

Brisset, C., Leanza, Y., & Laforest, K. (2013). Working with interpreters in health care: A systematic review and meta-ethnography of qualitative studies. *Patient Education and Counseling*, 91, 131–140.

Brown, P. L. (2009, September 20). A doctor for disease, a shaman for the soul. *The New York Times*, p. A20. Retrieved from http://www.nytimes.com/2009/09/20/us/20shaman.html.

Butow, P. N., Bell, M., Goldstein, D., Sze, M., Aldridge, L., Abdo, S., … Eisenbruch, M. (2011). Grappling with cultural differences; Communication between oncologists and immigrant cancer patients with and without interpreters. *Patient Education and Counseling*, 84, 398–405.

Butow, P. N., Goldstein, D., Bell, M. L., Sze, M., Aldridge, L. J., Abdo, S., … Eisenbruch, M. (2011). Interpretation in consultations with immigrant patients with cancer: How accurate is it? *Journal of Clinical Oncology*, 29, 2801–2807.

Butow, P. N., Lobb, E., Jefford, M., Goldstein, D., Eisenbruch, M., Girgis, A., … Schofield, P. (2012). A bridge between cultures: Interpreters' perspectives of consultations with migrant oncology patients. *Supportive Care in Cancer*, 20, 235–244.

Campbell, S. M., Roland, M. O., & Buetow, S. A. (2000). Defining quality of care. *Social Science & Medicine*, 51, 1611–1625.

Chung, V. C. H., Ma, P. H. X., Lau, C. H., Wong, S. Y. S., Yeoh, E. K., & Griffiths, S. M. (2012). Views on traditional Chinese medicine amongst Chinese population: A systematic review of qualitative and quantitative studies. *Health Expectations*, n/a-n/a.

Culyer, A. J., & Wagstaff, A. (1993). Equity and equality in health and health care. *Journal of Health Economics*, 12, 431–457.

Davidson, B. (2000). The interpreter as institutional gatekeeper: The social-linguistic role of interpreters in Spanish–English medical discourse. *Journal of Sociolinguistics*, 4, 379–405.

De Jaegher, H., & Froese, T. (2009). On the role of social interaction in individual agency. *Adaptive Behavior*, 17, 444–460.

Dean, R. K. (2014). Condemned to repetition? An analysis of problem-setting and problem-solving in sign language interpreting ethics. *Translation & Interpreting*, 6, 60–75.

Dean, R. K., & Pollard, R. Q. (2011). Context-based ethical reasoning in interpreting. *The Interpreter and Translator Trainer*, 5, 155–182.

Dohan, D., & Levintova, M. (2007). Barriers beyond words: Cancer, culture, and translation in a community of Russian speakers. *Journal of General Internal Medicine*, 22, S300–305.

Donabedian, A. (1980). *The definition of quality and approaches to its assessment*. Michigan, MI: Health Administration Press.

Dutta, M. J. (2007). Communicating about culture and health: Theorizing culture-centered and cultural sensitivity approaches. *Communication Theory*, 17, 304–328.

Dutta, M. J., & Basu, A. (2007). Health among men in rural Bengal: Exploring meanings through a culture-centered approach. *Qualitative Health Research*, 17, 38–48.

Dysart-Gale, D. (2007). Clinicians and medical interpreters: Negotiating culturally appropriate care for patients with limited English ability. *Family & Community Health*, 30, 237–246.

Ellerby, J. H., McKenzie, J., McKay, S., Gariepy, G. J., & Kaufert, J. M. (2000). Bioethics for clinicians: 18. Aboriginal cultures. *Canadian Medical Association Journal*, 163, 845–850.

Fadiman, A. (1997). *The spirit catches you and you fall down: A Hmong child, her American doctors, and the collision of two cultures*. New York: Farrar, Straus and Giroux.

Fatahi, N., Hellstrom, M., Skott, C., & Mattsson, B. (2008). General practitioners' views on consultations with interpreters: A triad situation with complex issues. *Scandinavian Journal of Primary Health Care*, 26, 40–45.

Flores, G., Abreu, M., Barone, C. P., Bachur, R., & Lin, H. (2012). Errors of medical interpretation and their potential clinical consequences: A comparison of professional versus ad hoc versus no interpreters. *Annals of Emergency Medicine*, 60, 545–553.

Flynn, P. M., Ridgeway, J. L., Wieland, M. L., Williams, M. D., Haas, L. R., Kremers, W. K., & Breitkopf, C. R. (2013). Primary care utilization and mental health diagnoses among adult patients requiring interpreters: A retrospective cohort study. *Journal of General Internal Medicine*, 28, 386–391.

Gattellari, M., Voigt, K. J., Butow, P. N., & Tattersall, M. H. N. (2002). When the treatment goal is not cure: Are cancer patients equipped to make informed decisions? *Journal of Clinical Oncology*, 20, 503–513.

Goldsmith, D. J. (2001). A normative approach to the study of uncertainty and communication. *Journal of Communication*, 51, 514–533.

Goldsmith, D. J., & Fitch, K. (1997). The normative context of advice as social support. *Human Communication Research*, 23, 454–476.

Gostin, L. O. (1995). Informed consent, cultural sensitivity, and respect for persons. *Journal of the American Medical Association*, 274, 844–845.

Gray, B., Hilder, J., & Donaldson, H. (2011). Why do we not use trained interpreters for all patients with limited English proficiency? Is there a place for using family members? *Australian Journal of Primary Health*, 17, 240–249.

Greenhalgh, T., Robb, N., & Scambler, G. (2006). Communicative and strategic action in interpreted consultations in primary health care: A Habermasian perspective. *Social Science & Medicine*, 63, 1170–1187.

Gubrium, J. F., & Holstein, J. A. (1995). Individual agency, the ordinary, and postmodern life. *Sociological Quarterly*, 36, 555–570.

Harmsen, J. A. M., Bernsen, R. M. D., Bruijnzeels, M. A., & Meeuwesen, L. (2008). Patients' evaluation of quality of care in general practice: What are the cultural and linguistic barriers? *Patient Education and Counseling*, 72, 155–162.

Hernandez, R. G., Cowden, J. D., Moon, M., Brands, C. K., Sisson, S. D., & Thompson, D. A. (2014). Predictors of resident satisfaction in caring for limited English proficient families: A multisite study. *Academic Pediatrics*, 14, 173–180.

Hilliard, R. (2013). Using interpreters in healthcare settings. Retrieved March 14, 2015, from www.kidsnewtocanada.ca/care/interpreters.

Hinton, D. E., Nguyen, L., Tran, M., & Quinn, S. (2005). Weak kidney and panic attacks in a traumatized Vietnamese male. *Culture, Medicine and Psychiatry*, 29, 125–135.

Ho, A. (2008). Using family members as interpreters in the clinical setting. *The Journal of Clinical Ethics*, 19, 223–233.

Houtlosser, P., & van Rees, A. (Eds.). (2006). *Considering pragma-dialectics*. Mahwah, NJ: Erlbaum.

Hsieh, E. (2006). Conflicts in how interpreters manage their roles in provider–patient interactions. *Social Science & Medicine*, 62, 721–730.

Hsieh, E. (2009). Bilingual health communication: Medical interpreters' construction of a mediator role. In D. E. Brashers & D. J. Goldsmith (Eds.), *Communicating to manage health and illness* (pp. 135–160). New York: Routledge.

Hsieh, E. (2010). Provider–interpreter collaboration in bilingual health care: Competitions of control over interpreter-mediated interactions. *Patient Education and Counseling*, 78, 154–159.

Hsieh, E. (in press). The Model of Bilingual Health Communication: Theorizing interpreter-mediated medical encounters. In E. A. Jacobs & L. C. Diamond (Eds.), *Providing health care in the context of language barriers: International perspectives*. Bristol, UK: Multilingual Matters.

Hsieh, E., & Hong, S. J. (2010). Not all are desired: Providers' views on interpreters' emotional support for patients. *Patient Education and Counseling*, 81, 192–197.

Hsieh, E., Ju, H., & Kong, H. (2010). Dimensions of trust: The tensions and challenges in provider–interpreter trust. *Qualitative Health Research*, 20, 170–181.

Hsieh, E., & Kramer, E. M. (2012). Medical interpreters as tools: Dangers and challenges in the utilitarian approach to interpreters' roles and functions. *Patient Education and Counseling*, 89, 158–162.

Hsieh, E., Pitaloka, D., & Johnson, A. J. (2013). Bilingual health communication: Distinctive needs of providers from five specialties. *Health Communication*, 28, 557–567.

Joffe, S., Cook, E. F., Cleary, P. D., Clark, J. W., & Weeks, J. C. (2001). Quality of informed consent in cancer clinical trials: A cross-sectional survey. *The Lancet*, 358, 1772–1777.

Kapp, M. B. (2007). Patient autonomy in the age of consumer-driven health care: Informed consent and informed choice. *Journal of Legal Medicine*, 28, 91–117.

Kaufert, J. M., & Putsch, R. W., III. (1997). Communication through interpreters in healthcare: Ethical dilemmas arising from differences in class, culture, language, and power. *The Journal of Clinical Ethics*, 8, 71–87.

Kong, H., & Hsieh, E. (2012). The social meanings of traditional Chinese medicine: Elderly Chinese immigrants' health practice in the United States. *Journal of Immigrant and Minority Health*, 14, 841–849.

Kramer, E. M. (2000). Cultural fusion and the defense of difference. In M. K. Asante & J. E. Min (Eds.), *Socio-cultural conflict between African and Korean Americans* (pp. 182–223). New York: University Press of America.

Kramer, E. M. (2013). Dimensional accrual and dissociation: An introduction. In J. Grace & E. M. Kramer (Eds.), *Communication, comparative cultures, and civilizations* (Vol. 3, pp. 123–184). New York: Hampton.

Kuo, D. Z., O'Connor, K. G., Flores, G., & Minkovitz, C. S. (2007). Pediatricians' use of language services for families with limited English proficiency. *Pediatrics*, 119, e920–927.

Laidsaar-Powell, R. C., Butow, P. N., Bu, S., Charles, C., Gafni, A., Lam, W. W. T., … Juraskova, I. (2013). Physician–patient–companion communication and decision-making: A systematic review of triadic medical consultations. *Patient Education and Counseling*, 91, 3–13.

Leanza, Y., Boivin, I., & Rosenberg, E. (2010). Interruptions and resistance: A comparison of medical consultations with family and trained interpreters. *Social Science & Medicine*, 70, 1888–1895.

Llewellyn-Jones, P., & Lee, R. (2013). Getting to the core of role: Defining interpreters' role-space. *International Journal of Interpreter Education*, 5, 54–72.

Lo, M. C., & Bahar, R. (2013). Resisting the colonization of the lifeworld? Immigrant patients' experiences with co-ethnic healthcare workers. *Social Science & Medicine*, 87, 68–76.

Ma, G. X. (1999). Between two worlds: The use of traditional and Western health services by Chinese immigrants. *Journal of Community Health*, 24, 421–437.

McClean, K. L., & Card, S. E. (2004). Informed consent skills in internal medicine residency: How are residents taught, and what do they learn? *Academic Medicine*, 79, 128–133.

Maclean, A. (2009). *Autonomy, informed consent and medical law: A relational challenge*: Cambridge, UK: Cambridge University Press.

Mason, I., & Ren, W. (2012). Power in face-to-face interpreting events. *Translation and Interpreting Studies*, 7, 234–253.

Metzger, M. (1999). *Sign language interpreting: Deconstructing the myth of neutrality*. Washington, DC: Gallaudet University Press.

Miller, K., & Zook, E. G. (1997). Care partners for persons with AIDS: Implications for health communication. *Journal of Applied Communication Research*, 25, 57–74.

Muller, J. H., & Desmond, B. (1992). Ethical dilemmas in a cross-cultural context: A Chinese example. *Western Journal of Medicine*, 157, 323–327.

Nugus, P., Greenfield, D., Travaglia, J., Westbrook, J., & Braithwaite, J. (2010). How and where clinicians exercise power: Interprofessional relations in health care. *Social Science & Medicine*, 71, 898–909.

O'Leary, S. C. B., Federico, S., & Hampers, L. C. (2003). The truth about language barriers: One residency program's experience. *Pediatrics*, 111, e569–573.

Peter, E., Lunardi, V. L., & Macfarlane, A. (2004). Nursing resistance as ethical action: Literature review. *Journal of Advanced Nursing*, 46, 403–416.

Phelan, M., & Parkman, S. (1995). How to do it: Work with an interpreter. *British Medical Journal*, 311, 555–557.

Pöchhacker, F., & Shlesinger, M. (2005). Introduction: Discourse-based research on healthcare interpreting. *Interpreting*, 7, 157–165.

Raven, B. H. (1993). The bases of power: Origins and recent developments. *Journal of Social Issues*, 49, 227–251.

Rees, C. E., & Bath, P. A. (2000). Meeting the information needs of adult daughters of women with early breast cancer: Patients and health care professionals as information providers. *Cancer Nursing*, 23, 71–79.

Richie, J. (1964). Using an interpreter effectively. *Nursing Outlook*, 12, 27–29.

Robb, N., & Greenhalgh, T. (2006). "You have to cover up the words of the doctor": The mediation of trust in interpreted consultations in primary care. *Journal of Health Organization & Management*, 20, 434–455.

Roy, C. B. (2000). *Interpreting as a discourse process*. New York: Oxford University Press.

Ryan, R. M., & Deci, E. L. (2011). A self-determination theory perspective on social, institutional, cultural, and economic supports for autonomy and their importance for well-being. In V. I. Chirkov, R. M. Ryan, & K. M. Sheldon (Eds.), *Human autonomy in cross-cultural context* (Vol. 1, pp. 45–64). New York: Springer.

Seale, C., Rivas, C., Al-Sarraj, H., Webb, S., & Kelly, M. (2013). Moral mediation in interpreted health care consultations. *Social Science & Medicine*, 98, 141–148.

Shaw, S. J., Huebner, C., Armin, J., Orzech, K., & Vivian, J. (2009). The role of culture in health literacy and chronic disease screening and management. *Journal of Immigrant and Minority Health*, 11, 460–467.

Simpson, K. R., & Lyndon, A. (2009). Clinical disagreements during labor and birth: How does real life compare to best practice? *MCN: The American Journal of Maternal/Child Nursing*, 34, 31–39.

Solomon, M. Z. (1997). From what's neutral to what's meaningful: Reflections on a study of medical interpreters. *The Journal of Clinical Ethics*, 8, 88–93.

Sudore, R. L., Landefeld, C. S., Pérez-Stable, E. J., Bibbins-Domingo, K., Williams, B. A., & Schillinger, D. (2009). Unraveling the relationship between literacy, language proficiency, and patient–physician communication. *Patient Education and Counseling*, 75, 398–402.

Tam, N. T., Huy, N. T., Thoa, L. T. B., Long, N. P., Trang, N. T. H., Hirayama, K., & Karbwang, J. (2015). Participants' understanding of informed consent in clinical trials over three decades: Systematic review and meta-analysis. *Bulletin of the World Health Organization*, 93, 186–198H.

Thompson, D. A., Hernandez, R. G., Cowden, J. D., Sisson, S. D., & Moon, M. (2013). Caring for patients with limited English proficiency: Are residents prepared to use medical interpreters? *Academic Medicine*, 88, 1485–1492.

Thomson, M. D., & Hoffman-Goetz, L. (2009). Defining and measuring acculturation: A systematic review of public health studies with Hispanic populations in the United States. *Social Science & Medicine*, 69, 983–991.

Todres, L., Galvin, K., & Dahlberg, K. (2007). Lifeworld-led healthcare: Revisiting a humanising philosophy that integrates emerging trends. *Medicine, Health Care and Philosophy*, 10, 53–63.

Tracy, K. (2013). *Everyday talk: Building and reflecting identities* (2nd ed.). New York: Guilford.

Ulrich, L. P. (2001). *The patient self-determination act: Meeting the challenges in patient care*. Washington, DC: Georgetown University Press.

Wade, C., Chao, M. T., & Kronenberg, F. (2007). Medical pluralism of Chinese women living in the United States. *Journal of Immigrant and Minority Health*, 9, 255–267.

Wadensjö, C. (1998). *Interpreting as interaction*. London: Longman.

Wells, R. E., & Kaptchuk, T. J. (2012). To tell the truth, the whole truth, may do patients harm: The problem of the nocebo effect for informed consent. *American Journal of Bioethics*, 12, 22–29.

Westermeyer, J. (1985). Psychiatric diagnosis across cultural boundaries. *American Journal of Psychiatry*, 142, 798–805.

Westermeyer, J. (1990). Working with an interpreter in psychiatric assessment and treatment. *Journal of Nervous and Mental Disease*, 178, 745–749.

Williams, G., Teixeira, P., Carraça, E., & Resnicow, K. (2011). Physical wellness, health care, and personal autonomy. In V. I. Chirkov, R. M. Ryan, & K. M. Sheldon (Eds.), *Human autonomy in cross-cultural context* (Vol. 1, pp. 133–162). New York: Springer.

Zimányi, K. (2013). Somebody has to be in charge of a session: On the control of communication in interpreter-mediated mental health encounters. *Translation and Interpreting Studies*, 8, 94–111.

6

INTERPRETERS' PERCEPTION AND MANAGEMENT OF COMPETING GOALS

Professional interpreters are meticulously trained about the legitimacy, functions, and parameters of different roles (e.g., conduit, clarifier, cultural broker, and advocate) (Dysart-Gale, 2005). Are their performances motivated and regulated by interpreter roles? If they consider their roles to be visible, as suggested by Angelelli (2004b), why do they experience frustration when deviating from the conduit role? Why do they still experience role dissonance (e.g., feeling conflicted about assuming certain roles during medical encounters) and struggle with blurred boundaries between roles (Brua, 2008; Hsieh, 2008; Messias, McDowell, & Estrada, 2009)? On the other hand, would it be appropriate to use interpreter roles to examine nonprofessional interpreters' performances? Nonprofessional interpreters are unlikely to understand their functions and behaviors through interpreter roles due to their lack of training (Brua, 2008). Their communicative strategies and performances are likely to adopt a more heuristic approach, following their normative patterns as a layperson rather than a top-down understanding of interpreter roles (Meeuwesen, Twilt, ten Thije, & Harmsen, 2010; Rosenberg, Seller, & Leanza, 2008).

Conceptualizing interpreter-mediated medical encounters through interpreter roles allows researchers to identify interpreters' systematic behaviors based on certain identities they assume during the medical encounter (see Chapter 1). However, "role" also limits the development of the field in certain ways (Lee & Llewellyn-Jones, 2011). Role, as a theoretical concept, suggests that there is a consistent, stable identity that a person steps in and out of in a structured performance.

Interpreter performance in a medical encounter is dynamic and emergent. Their behaviors are adaptive and responsive to others' performances. In other words, interpreters rarely stay in a single role across multiple interactions or even within a single interaction. Although researchers were able to identify a wide range of roles adopted by interpreters (Brisset, Leanza, & Laforest, 2013), little is known about how, when, or why interpreters move between these roles. Let me rephrase this. Based on self-report data (e.g., interviews and focus groups), we do know that interpreters' concerns about job security, litigation risks, or quality of care can influence their choice of roles (Hsieh, 2008; Rosenberg et al., 2008). Self-report data provide insights into interpreters' justifications of their choices but also facilitate thinking in treating interpreter roles as stable identities to be carefully chosen and performed. However, such an approach fails to account for the contextualization cues that emerge during a medical encounter that prompt an interpreter to shift between roles. In other words, our analysis of roles often leads to interpreters' reactive responses and claims to interactional dynamics rather than proactive understanding about best practices.

In short, conceptualizing interpreters' management of interpreter-mediated medical encounters through interpreter roles fails both to account for the dynamic shifts of interpreters' communicative strategies and to incorporate the perspectives of nonprofessional interpreters.

In this chapter, I will discuss the following issues:

- a paradigm shift to focus on the interactive management of communicative goals
- interpreters' management of interactional dilemma
- provider–interpreter differences in their normative frameworks.

A. Communicative Goals in Interpreter-Mediated Medical Encounters

An implicit claim in the literature on interpreter roles is that interpreters are aware of the diversity of roles and make specific decisions related to their performance accordingly. However, such an approach does not provide insights into how specific roles and functions may be challenged or co-constructed during a medical encounter. Rather than focusing on interpreter roles, I propose to examine individuals' management and collaboration of communicative goals.

I do not presume interpreters and other participants are necessarily aware of the complexity of their communicative goals. This is because at an individual level, individuals often have multiple goals (e.g., task, identity, and relational goals; Tracy, 2013) that may or may not be consistent or compatible with one another. At an interpersonal level, individuals may share certain goals but differ on others. As a result, individuals in interpreter-mediated medical encounters may need to collaborate with others on some goals while competing with one another to assert their communicative goals as potential differences and conflicts emerge during the dynamic interaction. By focusing on communicative goals (as opposed to interpreter roles), the paradigm shift allows researchers to recognize the interactive

TABLE 6.1 Interpreters' role performances, communicative goals, and strategies

Role performances	Communicative goals and the corresponding strategies
Conduit	Transferring complete information • Including all comments (i.e., no information screening) • Representing nonverbal messages (e.g., emotion) Reinforcing provider–patient relationship • Interpreting in first-person singular style • Using verbal and nonverbal strategies to claim an invisible role
Advocate	Empowering patients • Acting on behalf of the patient (overt advocate) • Providing means for self-advocacy (covert advocate) • ★ Assuming a conduit role (★ see discussion in Chapter 8.A.2 and Hsieh [2008])
Manager	Conserving medical resources • Performing tasks that are not related to interpreting • Assuming roles that are complementary and/or supplementary to other healthcare providers Regulating appropriate and ethical performances • Managing problematic behaviors of other speakers • Providing a framework to interpret and evaluate performances Managing optimal exchange of information • Enhancing the speakers' understanding of information • Managing the content and flow of information to be culturally appropriate and to provide optimal care
Professional	Being perceived as a professional • Maintaining and claiming professionalism • Disguising interpreters' nonprofessional performances

★ Adapted from Hsieh, E. (2008). "I am not a robot!" Interpreters' views of their roles in health care settings. *Qualitative Health Research*, 18, 1367–1383.

and dynamic nature of provider–patient interactions and to explore the specific incidents, contextualization cues, and frames that orient participants' understanding of interpreter-mediated medical encounters.

I do not wish to trivialize the research community's understanding about and interest in interpreter roles and functions; however, interpreters' role performance is motivated by their understanding of communicative goals (for themselves, for others, for the organizations, and for the communicative event) (Hsieh, 2008, 2009), which are implicitly framed in the communicative contexts (Goffman, 1959, 1983). In an earlier publication, I have explored interpreters' understanding of the distinct goals associated with specific interpreter roles (Hsieh, 2008; see Table 6.1). The understanding of interpreter roles has allowed researchers to examine interpreters' goals and functions indirectly.

While interpreter roles highlight the issues of *contexts* and *others* (see Chapter 1.B.2), this approach does not provide the necessary tools to examine others' perspectives and performances. Providers and patients are viewed as participants of interpreters' communicative frames. However, the communicative frame is dynamically and interactively co-constructed by all participants. Recognizing the complexity and interrelationships of communicative goals is essential to a normative approach to interpreter-mediated medical encounters. By focusing on communicative goals, individual agency is brought to the foreground. Every individual has specific communicative goals that require them to collaborate, coordinate, and compete with others in order to control the communicative activity (Hsieh, 2010).

In the following section, I will examine how communicative goals may influence the process and content of bilingual health communication. Although I may rely on some of my published data, the analysis and arguments here are not a simple repetition of my previous findings. Rather, I aim to develop an in-depth synthesis and analysis based on my previous research.

A.1. Participants' Competing Goals

One of the issues that is rarely examined in interpreter-mediated interactions is providers' (and patients') communicative goals. This is partially attributed to the traditional emphasis on interpreter performances. However, in interpreter-mediated interactions, all participants have their own communicative goals. In addition, these goals are not necessarily consistent or compatible with one another. This can create problems in provider–patient communication for the following reasons.

First, participants may or may not be aware of their competing demands. For example, when discussing the importance of the conduit model of interpreting, Gloria[OB/GYN] explained,

> I rely on the fact that the PROFESSIONAL interpreter is supposed to be working for ME, as a go-between with the patient. [...] The interpreter's ROLE is to be neutral and to communicate both sides. [...] Professional interpreters should not have a hidden agenda.

Gloria's[OB/GYN] desire for a neutral conduit is not uncommon, as many studies have repeatedly found that interpreter-as-conduit is a commonly shared expectation among healthcare providers (Brämberg & Sandman, 2013; Fatahi, Hellstrom, Skott, & Mattsson, 2008). Despite the desire for interpreter neutrality, both providers and interpreters have commented on the expectations for interpreters to take charge of provider–patient interactions. For example, Vicky[I] said, "Sometimes, doctors say, 'Okay, I am going to ask a question, you give me the answer. *If it doesn't deal with my question, I don't want to hear it.*' I have that kind of doctors before." Eli[EM] noted, "The interpreter should at least have a capacity to be able to redirect the patient and kind of filter what they say, if the response is completely unrelated to the question."

As another example, Vicky[I] mentioned that patients from her culture (i.e., Vietnam) are often not knowledgeable about the appropriate content and sequence of a medical encounter. Vicky[I] explained:

> If [the patients] feel comfortable with you, they will tell you, "Please tell the doctor this, this, this." [I would tell them,] "Okay. Slow down. Let's talk about today's symptoms. Not the symptoms we have a week ago, a month ago. […] *Don't bother him with too much information.*"

Vicky[I] manages the patient's narrative by informing the patient about what information should be given to the provider. Vicky (rather than the provider) is the person who filters information for medical purposes. While her performance is consistent with providers' expectations, she not only editorializes the patients' narratives but also exerts control over others' performances (i.e., informing the patient about what to say and what *not* to say and deciding what the provider should hear). It is important to note that providers' desire for an interpreter to take control of the flow and content of communication is not compatible with the expectation of a neutral, invisible interpreter performance. Nevertheless, providers do not appear to be aware of their conflicting demands.

Interpreters may also experience conflicts due to their own competing goals. In this regard, perhaps due to their training, professional interpreters seem to be much more aware of and conflicted about their competing desires. One of the most common conflicts is rooted in the interpreters' codes of ethics, which conceptualizes the conduit role as the default (Dysart-Gale, 2005). Contrary to an earlier study (Angelelli, 2002), which concluded that interpreters perceived their role as visible across various settings, the interpreters in Study 1 (see Chapter 3 for details of the three studies) strove to be invisible (i.e., to minimize their presence) in provider–patient interactions. In fact, conduit was the role that was identified most explicitly and frequently by the interpreters (i.e., 21 of 26 participants in Study 1 claimed various forms of a conduit role). For example, Selena[I], an interpreter with 32 years of experience, stated, "I am sort of in the background, I am the voice, I try to be faceless. That way, I don't interfere with their communication or their rapport between the patient and the provider." Often, interpreters who identify with a conduit role claim that all that they do is "just interpret everything" and they are "just interpreters." The constant use of "just" in their narratives reflects their effort to claim a limited role (i.e., they are nothing more than a conduit). Claire[I] explained:

> Because when I went through the training, we have to interpret everything exactly as what the doctor said, even have to interpret exactly the same tone, and same expression, and the same use of words. So, I just did the same. I would always try to follow what I learned in the class. So, I did the same thing. I just interpreted in Chinese, just equivalent what he said in English.

The pursuit of neutrality challenges interpreters to justify their performances. Their physical presence in the medical encounter and their functions in eliminating language and cultural barriers between providers and patients make it difficult for interpreters to claim that they are truly faceless or nonexistent. Some interpreters claim a *non-thinking* status to justify their interpreting strategy. In other words, if their performances do not require them to think in the communicative process, they cannot interfere with the process or the content of provider–patient communication. Peter[1] explained, "No matter what my judgment or my opinion, or my feelings [are], in a healthcare provider setting, I interpreted everything." Roger[1] shared a similar attitude, "You cannot adjust [information] the way you like it or how you think. *You are here to work, not to think.* Remember."

As a result, when the communicative context requires an interpreter to step out of a conduit role, they can experience significant distress as they lose their invisibility and neutrality. Several interpreters talked about incidents in which they witnessed inadequate care but felt constrained to rectify the situation. For example, Stella[1] said:

> There was one situation that the doctor could have explained things a little bit better and they just chose not to. [...] The patient went home so confused. And I said to myself, "This is not my place. I cannot do this [i.e., advocate for the patient]." I could have resolved it. *I was in such turmoil because I didn't know what to do.*

Interpreters may feel conflicted about the problematic consequences of their conduit performances. Silvia[1] explained, "*Something is not right.* I keep thinking about this interpreting. This interpreting is very robotic. You know, you are a human being. You are a person. And you are not supposed to show emotions?" The emotionless aspects of the conduit role troubled many interpreters as they faced their emotions and compassion and realized that they are expected to assume the role of an emotionless professional.

Shirley[1], director of the interpreter services in a major hospital, described an incident when she told a trainee that interpreters should not have any physical or emotional interactions with the patient (i.e., they are only the voices of others); however, when she and the trainee entered the exam room, the mother immediately gave Shirley[1] a hug. Later, she told the trainee, "I was the interpreter the night her baby died. To not to let her hug me or not hug her back would have been unfeeling." In other words, interpreters struggle to maintain a balance between their competing (and potentially conflicting) goals. This finding is supported by Messias et al. (2009) who concluded, "Far from being a neutral conduit, interpreters found themselves *stuck* in the middle of competing expectations of technical neutrality, linguistic comprehensiveness, and cultural appropriateness" (p. 133).

Second, providers may intentionally (or unintentionally) create narratives with competing goals. It is important to note that provider–patient communication may inherently entail competing communicative goals. Providers' conflicting narratives may be a result of their desire to honor competing (and potentially conflicting) goals. For example, when Cadence[P] expressed concerns about hormone deficiency if her healthy ovary was removed, Pam[ONC] responded:

> Well, *your hormones probably are pretty not working* so much anymore because you're after 50. [...] So after menopause, these ovaries, they're not dead, *so you're right, they still do make some hormones*. It shifts, and so they make different hormones, more androgen type hormones.

On the surface, it would appear that Pam was inconsistent in the information she provided. However, a closer look at the surrounding talk suggests that Pam's agenda was to encourage Cadence to remove both ovaries. Pam's strategic omission of information (i.e., the ovary's hormone production) was initially used as a strategy for persuasion. However, as she tried to balance her goals in pursuing her agenda while being accurate (or truthful) about medical facts, Pam may appear to be deceptive (i.e., not informing the patient about the truths) or incompetent (i.e., not knowing the facts). In this particular interaction, Pam's goals include: (a) providing accurate medical information, (b) suggesting to Cadence that she have both ovaries removed, and (c) respecting Cadence's autonomy and decision-making. These are not compatible goals, especially when Cadence was reluctant to remove her healthy ovary.

Similarly, when Piper[ONC] explained to Candie[P] about removing her omentum, she said, "We'll take that out and basically *you don't use it for much. It walls off infections and kind of is considered the watchdog of the abdomen*, trying to protect your intra-abdominal organs but is not super important for your life." Piper's description about the omentum was contradictory. However, such a contradiction reflects the inherent tensions between a provider's treatment agenda and the patient's right to autonomous, informed decision-making.

A provider may struggle to maintain a hopeful attitude while providing information about a poor prognosis. For example, Pam[ONC] explained to Cailey[P]:

> The report doesn't see anything big, spread, *which is good. They don't even see that cancer that's there.* [...] CAT scans are a little bit- I mean *they're helpful, and then they're not helpful* because we know you have a cancer and they don't even comment on it.

In another example, when discussing Candie[P]'s prognosis, Pearl[ONC] said:

> So I think what my examination says is that you're better than average in terms of the way, you know, your exam is. And *I'm not seeing anything scary*. Okay? So *the only thing scary is the biopsy result*, not anything about your physical exam at all, so *that's awesome*, okay?

These narratives provide conflicting information. In addition, because these conflicting statements appear to follow one another, the inconsistency embedded in the narrative structure can present unique challenges for an interpreter to effectively identify and accurately convey the true meanings of these conflicting remarks. What does it mean to say something is "helpful but not helpful?" How about "Not seeing anything scary, except one scary thing. So that's awesome!"

It is important to note that these self-conflicting remarks may not be the speaker's failure or mistake in providing a coherent meaning. In fact, it is not uncommon for providers to give both optimistic and pessimistic statements in a single medical encounter (Robinson et al., 2008). Strategic ambiguity has been identified as a communicative behavior utilized by many to manage conflicting goals (Bavelas, Black, Chovil, & Mullett, 1990). In other words, these structural and informational inconsistencies may be intended to "cover all grounds." Ambiguity can result from intended or unintended speech. While seeking clarification is an effective strategy to resolve unintended ambiguity by the speaker, an interpreter who wishes to clarify the meaning by asking the speaker to commit to a single meaning fails to recognize the speaker's complex strategies in navigating the semantic and pragmatic fields of speech.

In summary, participants' competing communicative goals are common in provider–patient interactions as providers and interpreters manage a wide range of issues related to task, identities, and relationships. As interpreters manage the competing goals that are inherent in the complexity and multivocality of human interactions, they face unique challenges in identifying and prioritizing various goals, managing ambiguity in discourse pragmatics, and coordinating with other speakers about multilayered meanings in medical encounters.

A.2. Communication as an Emergent Activity

A major strength in shifting research focus from interpreter roles to communicative goals is the opportunity to adopt a normative approach in examining the dynamic shifts in communicative goals in provider–patient communication. Goodwin (2007) advanced Goffman's (1979) conceptualization of footing by demonstrating that interactional others are essential in the communicative processes in co-constructing the footing, meanings, and processes of an interaction. By recognizing that communicative goals can be interactively negotiated during medical encounters, researchers can begin to explore how participants manage their goals during the emergent interactions, examine how these communicative goals are communicated and coordinated, and investigate whether certain strategies are more effective and appropriate than others.

Participants' shifts in communicative goals (and footing) can be a response to others' behavior (Goodwin, 2007). For example, patient-centered care and shared decision-making are both central values to healthcare delivery in the United

States. Providers are cautioned against manipulating a patient's decision-making process by offering incomplete or inaccurate information (Karnieli–Miller & Eisikovits, 2009; Maclean, 2009). However, providers' therapeutic agenda and patient autonomy are not just two competing goals. As providers enact these two valued identities (i.e., a medical expert who respects patient autonomy), an interpreter inevitably needs to face the tensions embedded in these identities. At times, it may be difficult to assess which is the providers' desired identity and which is the one that is "for show" only.

For example, when meeting Charmaine[P], a 76-year-old patient, Pearl[ONC] explained, "We're trying to figure out who you are, what your daily life is like, what you're able to do, what you're able to function, *whether you're willing to be disabled, you know, by surgery and everything else in order to live for three years.*" This appeared to be an effort to portray an objective, patient-centered, expert identity. However, although patient preference is noted here, Pearl's description about the potential negative complications and the minimal gain suggests that she is discouraging the surgical option. Later, when Charmaine[P] expressed her desire to have the surgery, Pearl[ONC] commented, "I wasn't expecting that answer. So, that's interesting." Pearl[ONC] then left the room and asked Piper[ONC], an oncology fellow, to step in and explain the surgical procedures. Piper[ONC] provided extensive details about the surgery and the anticipated long recovery. When Pearl[ONC] returned later, Charmaine[P] had changed her mind and indicated that she would prefer to have chemotherapy instead. Pearl[ONC] responded, "I thought *if we got real specific with you*, you might understand. So, I think at your age – then we usually try to be gentler." In these examples, providers strategically omitted or added information to manipulate patient uncertainty, prompting the patient to change their preferred choice to the provider's proposed option (Hsieh, Bruscella, Zanin, & Kramer, in press).

This example illustrates the dilemma faced by interpreters. The challenge of multilayered identities is that although each identity may be equally genuine and sincere (Goffman, 1959), the provider's enacted identity is dependent on the emergent, dynamic communicative process. If the patient had agreed with the physician's assessment, the physician identity that honors patient autonomy would have been the prioritized performance. However, as soon as the patient disagreed with the physician, the physician quickly shifted into an authoritative expert identity, emphasizing her medical expertise and providing technical details, and persuaded Charmaine[P] to abandon her original decision. Once the persuasion was successful, Pearl[ONC] quickly shifted back to the identity that values patient autonomy. As interpreters manage providers' various communicative goals (and identities), they will have to be responsive to the emergent changes in providers' performance and goals.

Shifts in communicative goals can also be a result of participants' strategies in managing potentially problematic interactions. For example, Sara[I] talked about an incident when a patient's father was frustrated by the two doctors who were discussing possible treatments for the child in English during the middle of a medical encounter.

> [The father said], "If they don't know what they are doing, why don't they look for another doctor? Bring someone who knows." I'm just saying it the same way. "BRING SOMEONE who knows, why don't you do that?" And the doctors kept looking at me, but kept talking to the other doctor. And all of a sudden, when I said, "If you don't know what you are doing, why don't you look for someone else?" And I said that and I go like [pointing to the father]. And the doctor went and looked at the patient and *realized that it wasn't me.*

Interpreters also talked about situations in which they shift from an invisible presence to a visible identity during medical encounters:

> **Vicky**[1]: If the patient is told she has cancer, I am not going to tell her, "You have cancer." [...] I would tell the patient, "*The doctor says it MIGHT be.* So, in order to prevent the tumor from getting bigger, *he* would like you to undergo chemo."
>
> **Ulysses**[1]: What I would do is I try to be polite and say, "The doctor is asking for HIS information, do you smoke?" "NO, Sir, how can you smoke, you know it's prohibited in our religion." "Yes, but even then, it is the *American* way."

By shifting from a first-person interpreting style to a third-person style, the interpreters managed to differentiate their (cultural) identities from those of the providers. The interpreters' changes in footing during the medical encounter are thus attempts to manage potential miscommunication or conflicts as they emerge during the provider–patient interactions.

In summary, interpreter-mediated interactions are multi-party communicative activities in which all participants actively enact and negotiate their communicative goals. In addition, these goals do not remain static during the interaction but can emerge interactively in response to others' behaviors or problematic interactions. Interpreters' ability to recognize and respond to the subtle shifts in footing and communicative goals is essential to their management of the meanings of provider–patient communication.

B. Managing of Interactional Dilemmas

In the literature on bilingual health care, interpreters are often conceptualized as individuals without communicative goals as they are only the voices of others.[1] However, if this were the case, one would not expect interpreters to experience frustration during interpreter-mediated medical encounters. After all, if they were linguistic robots without personal agendas, they should not have any feelings or opinions about the process and content of interpreter-mediated interactions. Nevertheless, researchers have found that interpreters can experience significant frustration and conflicts when managing provider–patient interactions.

In the following section, I will first examine the sources of interpreters' frustration and explore the strategies for managing these problematic interactions. In particular, I will explore how communicative goals and other constructs of BHC may facilitate our understanding of the phenomenon. Finally, I will discuss how these findings provide insights about interpreters' communicative goals in bilingual health care. I will explore providers' management of communicative goals in Chapter 7.

B.1. Sources of Conflict in Interpreter Performances

Messias et al. (2009, p. 140) argued that interpreters experience role dissonance because they "found themselves situated in an uncomfortable position *in the middle*, witnessing the need for cultural brokering, agency, and advocacy, yet constrained by their technical role definition." This finding is consistent with my earlier observations (Hsieh, 2006a). However, such an explanation also overlooks the complex environment of interpreter-mediated interactions and the fact that professional interpreters are trained to assume a wide variety of roles, not just the conduit role. In other words, the question here is: Why would a frustrated interpreter choose not to adopt other legitimate non-conduit roles that s/he learned during the training?

A key issue here is that the interactional dilemmas faced by interpreters are not always under their control and cannot be resolved through their choice of roles. For example, interpreters in Study 1 experienced four sources of conflict in their role performances during medical encounters: (a) others' communicative practices, (b) changes in participant dynamics, (c) institutional constraints, and (d) unrealistic expectations (for detailed discussion, see Hsieh, 2006a).

Others' Communicative Practices

When others construct competing communicative frames that conflict with that of the interpreter, the interpreter loses control of the communicative frame of the interpreter-mediated medical encounter. For example, a provider may make comments that are directed to the interpreter or other providers without expecting the patient to hear or be told about those comments. Sandra[1] explained, "[I think providers] feel more freedom and they speak more. And they say things in front of the patient because they know that [the patients] are not aware of what they are saying." She talked about an incident where she was concerned about the legal consequences:

[The patients] were Jehovah's Witnesses, and I know, for instance, that they are not allowed to get blood transfusions. [...However, the doctor said,] "When the time comes, if the patient will die if he does not receive the transfusion, *we are not going to allow it and we are going to do it anyway. But you tell them that's okay.*"

In this incident, the provider's utterances were no longer directed to the patients but to the interpreter, and they projected a role expectation that was different from a conduit role. The conflict arose because the provider viewed the interpreter as a confidant, who was able to take sides and receive information without relaying it. If Sandra[1] had actually relayed *everything* the provider said, she would have challenged and violated the provider's communicative frame (i.e., the conversation excludes the patient as a participant).

Similarly, when a participant lacks individual agency (e.g., due to low health literacy or a lack of communicative competence), an interpreter may find it difficult to mediate provider–patient interactions without making their own communicative goals salient. For example, cultural differences can make a speaker less than competent. Several interpreters talked about incidents in which a patient was not familiar with the information-seeking patterns of American providers and thus was unable to provide the appropriate answer. Roland[1] explained:

[The patient has] a problem with his leg. I was asked to go with him. [After a full physical, the doctor did not check his leg but she asked,] "Is there anything else?" He said, "No, I'm fine." And I would kind of *hint* to him, like, "Before we came, you mentioned something about your leg." I don't want to sort of push him, but I sort of hinted. He said, "Oh, by the way, yes, I have a problem with my leg." He showed the leg.

Yetta[1] explained that in Nigerian culture, even a common illness (e.g., high blood pressure) can be used as a personal attack against an individual. As a result, Nigerian people go to great lengths to hide their symptoms. She explained:

The secrecy of not exposing what they have. [...] I have to let the patients know that they are here to be treated, "TELL THEM, what's wrong with you. How you are going to get help." [...] They are not used to revealing what's wrong with them.

A patient who fails to disclose his or her problem certainly cannot have meaningful provider–patient communication. To facilitate provider–patient interaction requires an interpreter to actively negotiate with the patient about the appropriate communicative goals.

It is important to note that healthcare providers can also experience reduced communicative competence. Sara[1] explained, "[Sometimes a patient's answer] sounds kind of like, 'What?' And the doctor would say, 'What is she saying?' And you have to repeat the same thing, but you know that the problem is *the provider is not asking the right question*." Stella[1] talked about how the speaker's communicative skills may have a significant influence on the patient's satisfaction:

> [The patient could not decide whether to receive an amniocentesis, and the doctor said], "I cannot make this decision for you. You have to make it for yourself." And the patient went home confused. And that's where it stood. [...] And a week later, I had the very same situation with another doctor and the doctor simply said, "You know what, this is what I tell my patients. My wife never had the amnio, because she said, 'Whatever the baby is I'm still having it.' So, she never had the amnio." So, the patient went home so happy. [...] You want me to say something? I can't say anything. I'm not supposed to be saying anything. I know what to say. I have to tie up my tongue so that I didn't say anything.

Stella[1] was aware of what needed to be asked and what information should be given; however, for her to *initiate* information-seeking or information-giving behaviors would require her to depart from a conduit role. But why would departing from a conduit role create such frustration for an interpreter?

In these cases, other participants' individual agency has failed to support their communicative goals. Patients in a medical encounter clearly wish to have their illness treated (i.e., communicative goals), yet their lack of communicative competence (i.e., an aspect of individual agency) make it difficult to accomplish those goals. Similarly, a provider who is unable to ask the appropriate questions is unlikely to solicit the needed information to accomplish their therapeutic objectives. This can be a major problem in bilingual health care. In fact, a recent study found that residents reporting high self-efficacy (a major contributor to individual agency) have a 4.5 times greater likelihood of reporting high satisfaction in caring for limited English proficiency (LEP) patients; however, a majority of residents reported lacking self-efficacy with regard to their ability to deliver care to LEP patients (Hernandez et al., 2014). Another study found most residents (91 percent) perceived their quality of communication with a hospitalized LEP patient as worse than with their English-speaking counterparts (Tang, Kruger, Quan, & Fernandez, 2014).

When other speakers' individual agency fails to support their *own* communicative goals, interpreters inevitably are faced with the challenge of choosing to respect others' (lack of) agency or to honor their communicative goals. In other words, the interpreter's struggle is not a simple binary choice of roles (i.e., conduit versus non-conduit), but the extent to which they choose to infringe on others' individual agency (i.e., autonomy) or to disregard the speakers' communicative goals. In addition, an interpreter faces competing values within Quality and Equality of Care in these scenarios. If they choose to refrain from interfering they can honor patient autonomy and provider authority, two important values in Western medicine;

however, such practices would inevitably lead to compromised care, which contradicts another important value of Western medicine (i.e., do no harm).

Changes in Participant Dynamics

A change in the participant dynamics often reflects a change in the communicative frame. For example, an additional participant (e.g., a nurse or a family member) in a provider–patient interaction may challenge the assumptions of dyadic provider–patient communication (e.g., all conversations are between the provider and the patient and center on the patient's illness). It is not uncommon for two providers to discuss issues irrelevant to the current case or for family members to have a private discussion with the patient during a medical encounter. In these situations, the spoken utterances may not be directed to the primary speakers (i.e., the provider or the patient); however, if the interpreter does not relay the information, the primary speakers would be excluded from understanding the ancillary interactions. On the other hand, speakers may decide to have these conversations precisely because they know that the bystanders will not understand their comments. For an interpreter, interpreting those comments would violate the speaker's assumption about the privacy of the conversation. I asked interpreters how they would respond if a resident and a supervisor argued about the diagnosis in front of a patient, an actual event experienced by one of my interviewees. An interpreter must decide the extent to which s/he is going to include the clients in a conversation that (a) is not directed to them and (b) may or may not concern them. Several participants explained their responses:

> **Ulysses**[I]: In this type of situation, it is best tell the physicians politely that they should not talk in front of the patient about their diagnosis. […] They should not fight in front of the patient. Otherwise, my job is to interpret everything and I have to tell the patient that they are talking about the diagnosis, they have not come to the conclusion. I will inform the patient when the doctors have come to the conclusion, it's a different thing. Otherwise, if they are just talking between themselves, I would never disclose the diagnosis. Or at the end of the session, I may ask the doctor, "Doctor, you were talking about the diagnosis. Should I tell?"
>
> **Albert**[I]: I would stop the interpreting and tell both providers that they don't have to argue in front of the patient, *especially* if the patient KNOWS a little bit English. So, "Can you stop it or take your time, or go some other places and discuss this." I'd want the main provider to speak to the patient.
>
> **Rachel**[I]: What are you going to do? Are you going to confuse the patient? And the patient should know that even doctors didn't know what's going on, right? I don't know.

These three interpreters adopted very different strategies. Ulysses' comments reflected his uncertainty about the change in participant dynamics. Ulysses first talked about an interpreter's role in controlling the conversational context ("It is best tell the physicians politely that they should not talk in front of the patient about their diagnosis"), highlighting his role as a conduit ("My job is to interpret everything"). However, his later solution appeared to accept the provider's expectation of privacy ("If they are just talking between themselves, I would never disclose the diagnosis.") and relegated the management responsibilities to the providers (i.e., asking providers whether he should interpret or not). The shift in his response suggests that he was aware of the two competing communicative frames but allowed the provider to control the meanings, participants, and access to the frames.

Albert's focus was to maintain the integrity of the providers' communicative frame. A provider's effort to exclude the patient from the communicative frame through language may not be successful if the patient's limited English proficiency still allows them to understand (partial) information. A similar example would be if the providers went to an adjoining room to discuss their disagreement about the diagnosis only to find that the facility has thin walls and the patient can hear their muffled conversations. From this perspective, Albert acknowledged the changes in the provider's communicative frame, recognized potential threats, and recommended strategies to protect the provider's new frame. At the same time, Albert took control of the communicative frame of the interpreter-mediated medical encounter, ensuring that a potentially overlapping and competing frame would not bleed into the triadic communication between providers, the patient, and the interpreter.

Rachel's comment suggests that she was aware of how changes in participant dynamics can not only create competing frames but may have potential consequences that compromise important principles of healthcare delivery. On one hand, if she interprets the conversation between the two providers, the patient may become more confused and even distrust the providers. On the other hand, if she chooses not to interpret the conversation, her act may constitute medical paternalism (e.g., shielding certain information from the patient) by infringing on patients' control and access to the communicative event. From this perspective, Rachel's concern was more than just the competing frames, but also included her understanding about system norms and quality of care (e.g., the need for patient empowerment through informed decision-making).

In summary, the changes in participant dynamics require interpreters to adapt. In certain cases, a conduit role would actually violate other speakers' communicative goals/frames (e.g., expectation of privacy or empowerment strategies). Interpreters need to decide how to manage participant dynamics while honoring system norms and quality of care.

Institutional Constraints

Institutional constraints come from several sources: Institutional culture, hierarchy, policies, regulations, and environment may all present challenges to an interpreter's management of bilingual health care. I view institutional constraints as issues related to system norms. For example, several interpreters stated that they would not do the simplest tasks (e.g., reading the instructions on the prescription, helping a patient to complete a questionnaire, or writing down a provider's instructions) outside the presence of providers because of their concerns about legal liability. The institutional hierarchy may also make it difficult for interpreters to adopt certain roles (e.g., to challenge providers' behaviors). For example, the institutional culture often treats the provider's time as a scarce resource and pressures the interpreter to conserve it. Several interpreters talked explicitly about possible conflicts. Rachel explained, "You are between the doctor who is in a hurry, who wants to leave, and the patient who wants to talk, who needs time. You know, that's a really difficult situation." In these situations, the provider and the patient may have very different expectations of the interpreter. Interpreters' management of the provider–patient interaction reflects their understanding of the values, principles, and norms of the dominating system.

Interpreters in the study also talked about how environmental constraints limit their performance. For example, a conduit role does not allow an interpreter to have direct communication with the speakers; therefore, the interpreter is instructed not to be alone with a patient at any time. However, this expectation may not be feasible or realistic. Claire[1] explained:

> You cannot remain in the same room with the patient alone. [...but any interpreter will tell you that after the initial check-up, the nurses] just leave you alone in the [exam] room! Where else can you go? I tried. I tried to not to stay in the same room, and then, I stepped out of the room and stayed in the hallway, and the nurse would tell me, "Don't stay in the hallway, you are not allowed here. Stay in the room!" I said, "Can I sit out in the waiting area?" They said, "NO! You have wait with the patient. The doctor is coming." I think this is not possible, you know, in all situations.

Space is a scarce resource in medical facilities. The power hierarchy within the healthcare system, the interpreter's outsider status, the limited numbers of patients with LEP, and the pressure to conserve the provider's time all present difficulties in establishing a space dedicated to interpreters. The discrepancies between training for interpreters and the reality of medical encounters lead to interpreters being aware of their lower status in the healthcare system and their inability to correct the situation. In short, when the system norms cannot support the desirable communicative frame (e.g., interpreter-as-conduit), an interpreter may find it difficult to have successful performances (even when they have high individual agency).

Unrealistic Expectations

When delineating the importance of frame, Goffman (1959, p. 13) explained:

> When an individual projects a definition of the situation and thereby makes an implicit or explicit claim to be a person of a particular kind, he

automatically exerts a moral demand upon the others, obliging them to value and treat him in the manner that persons of his kind have a right to expect. He also implicitly forgoes all claims to be things he does not appear to be and hence forgoes the treatment that would be appropriate for such individuals. The others find, then, that the individual has informed them as to what is and as to what they ought to see as "is."

The challenge faced by interpreters is that participants may impose frames that are inconsistent, incompatible, or problematic. For example, an interpreter may decide to elaborate on clinical information because the patient may not have the medical knowledge to understand the physician's comment (Angelelli, 2004a); however, such behaviors may violate the provider's expectation of the communicative frame in which the interpreter serves as a passive conduit. Sandra[1] talked about an incident in which the physician was upset and asked her why she used the term "pressure in the eye" to replace his term "glaucoma." She realized that she had violated the provider's role expectation but felt that it was important for the patient "to know more what he was going to be tested for than the terminology for the procedure." In such cases, in order to ensure a patient's comprehension of their diagnosis (i.e., an important component of quality of care), an interpreter may intentionally contradict the role expectation (and communicative frame) imposed by a provider.

Interpreters can experience problematic, if not unrealistic, role expectations due to the limitations of a specific frame. In their training, interpreters are told to adopt a conduit role that emphasizes a robotic view of interpreting; however, if an interpreter were to choose the neutral, emotionally detached role as their identity goal, they inevitably lose the ability to provide emotional support. Selena[1] explained, "The code of ethics says that you cannot establish an emotional rapport with the patient. But it's very hard to do, when you know if you hold a patient's hand, that's going to convey, 'I sympathize with you.'" What Selena expressed here is the conflicting norms between two systems. Whereas the medical system constructs an emotionless professional as the desirable performance in healthcare settings, the social norms of everyday life demand an empathetic, compassionate performance when witnessing others' crisis or suffering. Selena is thus unclear about what would be an appropriate performance as she is caught in the middle of the conflicting expectations of two system norms.

Communication is an activity that requires the participants to coordinate behaviors, understanding the implicit and explicit meanings of their behaviors. Interpreters are constantly required to evaluate the process of coordination, to monitor miscommunication, and to ensure successful interactions. This task is made difficult by these sources of conflict. Nevertheless, interpreters have developed specific strategies to resolve these conflicts.

B.2. Solutions to Perceived Conflicts

In this section, I will report the strategies practicing interpreters adopt to reconcile the various role conflicts they encounter in provider–patient communication. More importantly, these strategies allow them to take control over the communicative frame by redefining the communicative context, along with the tasks, identities, and relationships implied in the frame. The strategies that interpreters utilize include: (a) creating boundaries, (b) (re)defining relationships and identities, and (c) manipulating communicative strategies.[2]

These strategies highlight interpreters' strategic use of diverse resources in (re)negotiating and (re)defining the communicative frame(s) at work during the medical encounter. By utilizing organizational norms/structures and environmental cues, interpreters create operational boundaries to justify their communicative behaviors. By (re)defining identities for themselves and other patients, they project a communicative frame that obligates others to respond (if not to conform) to the frame they make salient. Finally, by manipulating communicative strategies, they resort to their informational power to control who, what, how and where information is shared, through which they can resist others' communicative frame(s) and exert control over the frame under question. These are strategies that manage different types of resources; however, they share a similar outcome in allowing the interpreter to maintain control of the communicative context, providing them the ability to define the communicative frame and control others' behaviors.

Creating Boundaries

There are several ways that interpreters create boundaries as a strategy to control the communicative frame. First, because several interpreters have other jobs (e.g., case manager and patient representative) in healthcare settings, they choose their roles based on the source of the assigned interpreting task. Stella[1] explained that because she is given different instructions, she acts as an advocate when she serves as the staff interpreter for a hospital and as a conduit when she takes freelance assignments from interpreter agencies.

This strategy can be particularly relevant to dual-role interpreters (e.g., bilingual medical professionals or family interpreters). Because dual-role interpreters have several "official" roles, they may face conflicts between these roles. Sharon[1], director of a major interpreting agency, mentioned an incident in which she found that a case manager, who also acted as the interpreter for his clients, had the attitude of "I am going to go with my client to every appointment and I'm going to be the interpreter. *I am going to lie if I have to, to get my clients their benefits.*" The case manager chose the advocate role because he felt that his responsibility to obtain the client's benefits superseded the need to provide neutral interpreting. Messias et al. (2009) found that some dual-role interpreters readily admit to purposely adopting a non-conduit role by viewing their interpreting responsibilities as ancillary to their other roles (e.g., social worker or primary caregiver).

The second way that interpreters in this study created boundaries was to narrow the definition of a medical encounter. In other words, although they feel obligated to act as a conduit *during* medical encounters (i.e., appointments), they are not constrained to the conduit role outside of the medical encounter. Sophia[1] explained:

> I am going to be an advocate when that family finishes [the appointment]. I would take them to the clinic and I am not going to interpret. I ask for the bill statement and I can go and make the claim for them. [...]. [I am an interpreter] when I am in the room, but when I am outside and they come to see me, then I'm an advocate.

Creating boundaries allows interpreters to justify their choices of roles, which is projected by the communicative contexts they highlighted. Whereas creating boundaries seems to define roles through static factors (e.g., the source and location of an assignment), the next strategy (i.e., redefining relationships and identities) is to define roles through dynamic interactions.

(Re)defining Relationships and Identities

An interpreter is in a privileged position to be aware of the dynamic shifts and changes of communicative contexts. At times, an interpreter needs to let other speakers know that the dynamics and meanings of the interpreter-mediated interaction have changed, so that they can respond accordingly. Some interpreters *claim* specific roles as they change their communicative behavior. To a certain degree, interpreters strategically claim specific roles to navigate through the potential conflicts in communicative frames. It is important to note that these are roles and identities strategically claimed in response to emergent contexts, allowing the interpreter to define and control the communicative event as well as others' behaviors. Stacey[1] noted:

> When I assume the role of advocate, I let the doctor know that I am assuming the role. I am not just interpreting. I am advocating for the patient. So, he knows where I am coming from. I said, "*I am a friend of the family*. And I know the situation. Let me explain to you the issues around this." So, they understand.

When I asked Stacey[1] if she was truly a friend of the family, it was clear that it was only a claim for the role because she does not have any social interactions with her clients outside of healthcare settings. Interpreters claim roles to justify their behaviors. Sophia[1] explained that when she interpreted for her mother, she assumed the role of a daughter (rather than a professional interpreter) and thus was justified in taking care of her mother by modifying the provider's disclosure of a poor prognosis. Christie[I] explained that when she provided assistance that was not permitted in a conduit model, she did not do it as an interpreter but as a "volunteer for a charity organization." In short, by claiming certain roles, interpreters in the study redefined their relationships with others, identified the essential communicative frame, and thus justified their behaviors.

Some interpreters also talked about (re)defining their relationships and roles *with* others. For example, they talked about incidents in which they made sure that the patient was aware of their roles and identities. Yetta[I] noted:

> I would explain to the patient that "I am here just to make sure that you understand what the doctor's saying and the doctor understands what you are saying. *I am not interested in your case at all.*" Because in my community, [… people do not want others to know about their illness.] So, I give them the confidence that I'm here to interpret and once we get out of here, there's no discussion.

Yetta[I] chose to highlight certain aspects of her roles in response to specific concerns that patients from her culture would have. On the other hand, an interpreter may rebuff others' request for certain performances by asserting their specific roles. Steve[I] explained, "I have had one situation that the provider said, 'Well, you don't need to interpret that.' And I said, 'Actually, I do. It's my job.'" By asserting his responsibility as a conduit, Steve[I] implicitly informed the provider that he is an independent professional (as opposed to a physician's aide).

Some interpreters use various strategies to directly or indirectly define roles *for* others. For example, an interpreter may make speakers aware of their identities as a strategy to rectify problematic communication; in other situations, an interpreter may choose to use a third-person interpreting style to differentiate himself/herself from the actual speaker. Certain methods of information giving may be problematic in different cultures. Interpreters in the study talked about the ways that they made it clear that the message is not from them but from others:

> **Vicky**[I]: If the patient is told to have cancer, I am not going to tell her, "You have cancer." […] I would tell the patient, "*The doctor says it MIGHT be.* So, in order to prevent the tumor from getting bigger, *he* would like you to undergo chemo."
> **Ulysses**[I]: What I would do is I try to be polite and say, "The doctor is asking for HIS information, do you smoke?" "NO, Sir, how can you smoke, you know it's prohibited in our religion." "Yes, but even then, it is the *American* way."

Interpreters also may implicitly remind others about their roles and identities, a strategy to highlight the primary communicative frame during a provider–patient interaction. Shirley[I] noted that when a speaker makes an inappropriate comment (e.g., profanity), she would hint to the speaker that *he or she* is the person who makes the comment, not the interpreter. She explained, "What we have done is we will say something like, 'You sure you want me to interpret that?' DON'T USE ME as a camouflage." Interpreters may also choose to explicitly define roles and relationships for speakers. For example, when Vicky[I] felt that a staff member's comments were inappropriate, she defined the patient's identities, forcing the staff member to back down:

> A staff was looking at the client, "ARE YOU SURE YOU WANT TO GO THROUGH THAT ROUTE? Are you sure you want to waste your time?" So, I told the lady, "You know, you are dealing with a person who is a refugee, who has been in the States for 3 days. He doesn't even have his own social security card. He is still fighting the jetlag. So, if you ask if he is sure or not, he doesn't know. So, please, understand his situation." So the lady said, "All right" and she backed off.

In summary, when interpreters (re)define their roles and identities, they justify their communicative behaviors. On the other hand, when interpreters (re)define roles for *others*, they influence others' perception about the dynamics, contexts, and content of the medical encounter. The process of (re)defining relationships and identities, however, can be a constant negotiation and coordination between all participants. Nevertheless, by identifying the footing within the communicative contexts, participants can (re)align their communicative frames, obligating others to conform to their definition(s) of the communicative event.

Manipulating Communicative Strategies

Finally, interpreters may opt to manipulate linguistic and communicative strategies to resolve role conflicts. For example, interpreters talked about how they manipulate the message for specific communicative goals. As noted earlier, Vicky[I] explained that she would disclose a poor prognosis or diagnosis by prefacing it with "*The doctor THINKS it MIGHT be…*" By doing so, Vicky[I] not only differentiates herself from the doctor (i.e., using third-person interpreting style), but also softens the blow by using hedges. An interpreter may also intentionally choose a different corresponding term to avoid the negative implications that often are associated with the provider's term (e.g., cancer). Roland[I] noted:

> In that particular case, *I wouldn't say the word cancer*. He had leukemia. So, I asked him about how his *leukemia* doing, you know. […] He knew that he had leukemia, but he didn't want to hear the word cancer. So, you just name it more specifically. So, he would be relaxed. Maybe he didn't know that it means cancer. He thought that leukemia is not cancer, for example. But it's not my point to educate him about that.

Roland's concerns highlight the cultural difference in speech practices about illnesses. In the USA, oncologists often stress the importance of open communication (Rogg, Aasland, Graugaard, & Loge, 2010) and believe that providing complete information is necessary for patient empowerment and informed decision-making (Parsons et al., 2007). However, other cultures are likely to question the provider's assertion on "facts" that are based on probability (as opposed to reality). In Asian cultures, being blunt about a patient's physical condition or chances of survival would be considered presumptuous, arrogant, insensitive, and even malicious, rather than being objective and professional (Blackhall, Frank, Murphy, & Michel, 2001; Yum, 1988). When telling a provider about how the cultural framework of *informing about a poor prognosis* would be understood in his culture, Roland[I] explained, "Well, this is really not the way it's done there. Because he would collapse by talking about it. He would just die in front of your eyes and his relatives would be suing you."

Interpreters' manipulation of linguistic strategies in an ideal world (i.e., both speakers have no knowledge of the other's language) is always covert because they are the only ones who understand both languages. As a result, interpreters have tremendous power to influence the content and the process of communication. Through covert strategies, interpreters are able to remain invisible, enacting the conduit role that is valued in provider–patient interactions while performing other types of roles. For example, some of the interpreters talked about how they covertly hinted to patients to discuss symptoms that they had mentioned earlier with the interpreter but had not told the provider about, or coached the patient about appropriate information-seeking skills. These communicative strategies allow patients to advocate for themselves, which presents a more competent and assertive patient identity without compromising a provider's expectation of a neutral interpreter.

Several interpreters also talked about how they purposefully employ specific strategies to influence others' communicative practices and role expectations. For example, interpreters in my study talked about explicitly informing others about appropriate ways to communicate (e.g., using short sentences and establishing eye contact with the other speaker rather than the interpreter) at the beginning of a medical encounter. Interpreters also talked about employing nonverbal strategies (e.g., avoiding eye contact) to prompt others to modify their communicative behaviors. By forcing others to modify their behaviors in a way that is consistent with the conduit model, interpreters were able to change the communicative contexts and others' role expectations. For example, Roger[I] explained, "You look down and you just [looking down]. I am not here. […] Sometimes, you go down [looking down], he looks at you and your ear, one time, two times, and he turns around and he looks at the patient."

In summary, interpreters' manipulation of communicative strategies functions in two ways to resolve conflicts of role expectations. Through a covert manipulation of their communicative strategies, interpreters are able to perform various roles while appearing to be a conduit (or in the roles that are expected by others). On the other hand, by using strategies that influence others' communicative behaviors, interpreters are able to reshape others' role expectations and thus reduce possible conflicts.

Finally, two issues are worth noting about interpreters' solutions to role conflicts. First, the roles I discussed throughout this section should not be conceptualized as nor limited to the roles professional interpreters learn during their training. Rather, the roles presented here should be understood through a normative approach to include everyday social roles that can be claimed by a wide variety of interpreters. For example, a professional interpreter may claim the social role of a daughter when interpreting for her parent, allowing her to draw the lines between personal/private and professional/public identities. A family interpreter may highlight her role as a primary caregiver, providing additional details to enrich a patient's narrative. A bilingual medical employee (e.g., a bilingual resident) may question if the primary physician has misspoken the necessary dosage, which implicitly highlights the interpreter's medical expertise. This conceptualization of roles provides researchers with richer analytical perspectives to examine the social contexts of interpreter-mediated interactions.

Second, it is important to note that these three strategies are not mutually exclusive. For example, when an interpreter provides support outside of the medical appointment as a volunteer with a local charity, rather than as an interpreter, the role boundaries she proposes also allow her to redefine her identity. Similarly, when an interpreter adopts a third-person interpreting style, s/he makes an implicit claim about the differences between her own and other participants' identities. The important insights of these findings are not just about the specific strategies an interpreter adopts to resolve role conflicts. Rather, collectively, these strategies highlight the importance of communicative frames and interpreters' resourcefulness in generating salient frames to control the process and content of provider–patient interactions.

B.3. Implications for Theory Development and Healthcare Delivery

Several studies have identified interpreters' anxiety, frustration, and sense of conflict when they are unable to assume the conduit role. While many researchers, including me, have examined this issue from the perspectives of interpreter roles, I have proposed reconceptualizing this phenomenon from the perspectives and constructs of BHC. While communicative goals are inherent in the interpreter role, the relationships are often implicit and obscure. In addition, the focus on interpreter role fails to recognize other participants' abilities to impose and challenge the communicative frame(s) of interpreter-mediated medical encounters. In short, I aim to untangle the interrelationship between interpreter roles and communicative goals and to account for other participants' influences on bilingual health communication.

A closer examination of interpreters' solutions to role conflicts shows that interpreters are extremely resourceful in defining the communicative frame. Organizational structures (e.g., job responsibilities) and external environments (e.g., exam rooms) allow them to create boundaries that shape their communicative frame. As they control and define their and others' identities and relationships (e.g., nurses versus refugees), they control the footing that provides meaning to the communicative context and project moral demands on others to treat them accordingly. By controlling the framing of and access to information, they exert control of the communicative frame and deny others' negotiation or imposition of competing frames.

These issues are often undertheorized in the traditional literature as these behaviors are viewed as interpreting errors rather than interpreters' attempts to control and manage communicative frames. However, such an approach presumes that the only accurate interpreting style is the conduit model, which ignores the wide variety of healthcare interpreters who may not be aware of the conduit model, and oversimplifies the complexity of interpreters' management of provider–patient interactions. These findings highlight important issues and perspectives that have been neglected in the literature.

First, interpreters' use of resources, including linguistic, spatial, nonverbal, environmental, and organizational resources, is not limited to the immediate interaction. When conceptualizing and examining interpreters' performance in and control of medical encounters, researchers should not be limited to the immediate provider–patient interactions but should also consider the utilization, impacts, limitations, and meanings of these resources in shaping interpreters' management of communicative frames. In other words, when researchers examine interpreters' management of provider–patient interactions, it is important to consider the varieties of resources that are used to invoke the contextual frame(s). This approach allows researchers to move beyond the text-oriented analysis of interpreter performance and to recognize the diversity and complexity of communicative contexts that can be emphasized, negotiated, or mitigated in medical encounters.

Second, interpreters' understanding and strategic claims of identities are important in shaping their management of communicative frames through footing. For example, an interpreter who also serves as a social worker or a primary caregiver has the flexibility to claim different identities in response to tensions and challenges that emerge during the communicative process. *When, how,* and *why* the interpreter claims these identities may have important implications for the quality and process of provider–patient interactions. For example, several researchers have suggested that family interpreters can be valuable patient advocates (e.g., Meeuwesen et al., 2010; Rosenberg et al., 2008). However, researchers found that family interpreters do not simply act as patient advocates. Instead, while they provide extra biomedical and Lifeworld information about the patient, they also actively integrate their voices and perspectives in provider–patient communication, interjecting their personal agenda in medical encounters and controlling patients' Lifeworld perspectives (Leanza, Boivin, & Rosenberg, 2010, 2013). In fact, providers often view family interpreters as primary caregivers (even when they are not) and expect them "to report symptoms the patient does not mention, to arrange further contacts with healthcare services and to translate/explain their statements to the patient after the visit" (Rosenberg, Leanza, & Seller, 2007, p. 290). In other words, both family interpreters and providers *collaboratively* co-construct the interactional frame in which family interpreters can be (and are expected to be) more than a passive conduit. From this perspective, one can recognize the significant differences in the footing and communicative contexts that guide the practices of professional versus family interpreters, resulting in different criteria in evaluating the quality of interpreting and interpreter performance.

In clinical practice, providers can readily recognize how the dual-role nature of a family interpreter can influence the quality of care (Hsieh, Ju, & Kong, 2010; Rosenberg et al., 2007). Without a clear discussion about the boundaries of these different social roles (e.g., patient advocate, healthcare interpreter, and caregiver) between participants in medical encounters, interpreters' emergent shifts between these roles can become problematic and hidden, allowing them to avoid potential scrutiny from others. However, I am concerned that most providers do not think twice when working with bilingual medical employees, many of whom are highly trusted due to their roles as in-clinic nurses or technicians (see Chapter 7.C.1). As healthcare institutions actively recruit bilingual nurses to manage the quality of care for language-discordant patients, it is critical that we tackle this issue head-on.

At an organizational level, institutions need to provide clear ethical and professional guidelines about the boundaries of different roles. For dual-role interpreters, they will need to develop appropriate and effective strategies to manage their potentially competing goals (Meyer, Bührig, Kliche, & Pawlack, 2010). For example, when a bilingual resident who is serving as an interpreter notices an error in prescription or diagnosis, are there some ways of resolving potential miscommunication that are better than others? What about if the interpreter is a nurse? Due to the differences in their institutional roles, they are likely to prefer different strategies. (We will revisit this issue in Chapter 9.)

Finally, it is important for providers to be mindful when working with dual-role interpreters. For example, Nacia[NUR] commented about the common claim of an interpreter as family member, "Sometimes I don't even know who that family member is. And if that person is a FAMILY member or not." By being mindful about identity claims as well as potential conflicts of interests (e.g., patient confidentiality or desire to fulfill the provider's agenda due to institutional hierarchy), providers will be more successful in avoiding the potential pitfalls of dual-role interpreters.

Third, by shifting the analytical focus to the co-construction of communicative frames, researchers open up opportunities to investigate how interpreters and other participants can collaborate, compete, or negotiate control over medical encounters. Many studies have found that interpreters experience challenges and frustrations during medical encounters (Angelelli, 2004a; Butow et al., 2012; Wros, 2009), noting conversational others' behaviors as a potential contributor. Why is it then that these conversational others' behaviors are overlooked when researchers aim to generate theories about interpreter-mediated medical encounters? Rather than seeing providers' or patients' behaviors as mistakes or challenges, recognizing their communicative goals marks the first step in theorizing other participants' influences and management of interpreter-mediated medical encounters.

For example, the two providers who chose to speak in English while arguing about the patient's diagnosis in the exam room did so because they believed that language barriers were sufficient to create a separate conversational space that excluded patient participation. An interpreter feels problematic in this situation because if s/he chooses to interpret all the information said by the physicians, s/he would, in fact, violate the physicians' communicative frame which excludes the patient as a participant. On the other hand, if an interpreter does not interpret the information, a patient can challenge the interpreters' control of information (e.g., "The doctors are talking about something. What is it?"), asserting his/her right to have access to information that is exchanged during the medical encounter.

It is important to note that it is others' communicative *goals* (and frames) rather than their communicative *behaviors* that can create interactional dilemmas (e.g., should the interpreter honor the provider's expectation of privacy or the patient's right to know) with regard to interpreters' understanding and management of communicative frames. For example, if an interpreter believes that the providers expect the patient to understand that they disagree with one another, the interpreter is unlikely to experience any frustration when interpreting the providers' discussion. The interpreter perceived an interactional dilemma because arguing about the patient's diagnosis is inconsistent with the norms of provider–patient interactions in the United States. By not directing the conversation to the patient and speaking in a language that the patient cannot understand, the providers are implicitly suggesting that the patient is not the intended participant or even audience of the conversation. It is the provider's communicative goals (e.g., discussing the patient's diagnosis without the patient's knowledge) that create an interactional dilemma for the interpreter because such a communicative goal is incompatible with the interpreter's understanding and definition of the communicative event (i.e., provider–patient interactions in which the interpreter provides both parties access to all information discussed).

Finally, the temporal dimension is important to the investigation of interpreters' management of competing goals. Interpreters' strategies may have different short-term and long-term impacts (Hsieh, 2007, 2010). For example, covert strategies (e.g., providing an editorialized statement) ensure the flow of provider–patient interaction. These strategies, however, effectively remove others' control over the communicative process. In contrast, seeking clarification, informing the provider about potential misunderstandings, and educating the provider about cultural differences inevitably disrupts the flow of communication and challenges the provider's authority and control over the medical encounter. However, these strategies not only provide immediate resolutions to interpreting challenges but also enhance providers' communicative and cultural competence, which will be valuable for future healthcare delivery (Hsieh & Kramer, 2012b). When examining the impacts of interpreters' strategies in managing competing goals in provider–patient communication, researchers therefore need to consider both the short-term and long-term impact on quality of care as well as other participants' individual agency and communicative competence (e.g., understanding of system norms).

C. Provider–Interpreter Differences in a Normative Framework

The challenge of the interpreter-mediated medical encounter is that participants need to negotiate meanings across various *languages*, *cultures*, and *expertise*, which often entail differences in worldviews and values. Providers are the medical experts who are well acquainted with Western biomedical culture and knowledge (Gawande, 2002). However, they are laymen in their understanding of patients' cultures and the complexity of interpreter-mediated interactions (Abbe, Simon, Angiolillo, Ruccione, & Kodish, 2006). Unlike professional interpreters who are trained to generate specialized communicative frames for interpreter-mediated medical encounters, most providers have little training in working with any type of interpreter (Flores et al., 2008; Thompson, Hernandez, Cowden, Sisson, & Moon, 2013). In contrast, healthcare interpreters are the linguistic and cultural experts who often engage in complex management of interpreter-mediated interactions (Hsieh, 2006b). Nevertheless, the latter are novices when it comes to medical knowledge and procedures as a typical 40-hour training program for professional interpreters does not provide in-depth understanding of clinical practices (Abbe et al., 2006). Although the differences in the providers' and interpreters' expertise may appear to be complementary, their co-construction of meanings in interpreter-mediated medical encounters is a complicated process that warrants further investigation.

In the following section, I will examine how healthcare interpreters' communicative strategies may create problems with their clients, focusing on how interpreters and providers may share different understandings of the communicative frames. Here, however, my analysis centers on provider–interpreter differences in recognizing, understanding, and responding to interpreters' communicative frames.[3]

C.1. Interpreter-mediated Medical Encounter as a Specialized Genre

Interpreter-mediated interaction requires interpreters to speak in a way that situates itself as a specialized speech genre. In this section, I will briefly summarize findings from my data which echo with many studies that have identified interpreters' specialized speech practices.

Interpreters are trained to adopt a first-person speech style. Sophia[1] explained: "For example, 'I believe you have hepatitis.' I just repeat. I don't say the doctor said that he believes that. I just said, 'Creo que usted tiene hepatitis.' I don't use third-person." The use of a first-person style is important. It places interpreters in an invisible role. Sara[1] explained: "When I'm interpreting, I speak in first person. *I am not there*. I'm the doctor, I'm the patient." The interpreter's management of the textual transformation is hidden and they appear to be neutral as they relay the voices of others.

Typically, in healthcare settings, interpreters use consecutive interpreting, meaning that the interpreter and the speakers take turns after each other's talk (Bot, 2005). Some interpreters, however, talked about adopting simultaneous interpreting (i.e., interpreting while the speaker is speaking). Because there is minimal time lag between the speeches, such an interpreting style creates an illusion of monolingual talk and creates smoother transitions between speakers (e.g., the length of speech in simultaneous interpreting is closer to that of monolingual talk). Roger[1] echoed, "I found that simultaneous interpreting is very helpful. [The other speakers] don't stop. They don't waste the energy to stop, wait, and then focus again on what he was trying to say. *It just flows*. It goes with the flow."

Interpreters also reported adopting other verbal and nonverbal strategies to create the role of an invisible conduit. For example, Sally[1] said, "We are advised to just look at the floor or just look down and just be as out of the conversation as possible, to just be a voice." Rachel[1] mentioned that she positioned herself in the room in a way that made her invisible to others, "What I do is I stay a little bit behind [the doctor and the patient]… When I take that position, […] I know that I am at the back side, like I'm not in the room, so they just look at each other and they talk to each other." Thus, interpreters utilize not only verbal and nonverbal messages but also their positioning in the space to construct meanings (i.e., the invisible conduit) in healthcare settings.

Although interpreters' concern about adopting an invisible role is mostly tied to provider–patient interactions, their desire to maintain the invisible presence may extend beyond the medical encounter. For example, Sophia [1] said, "Sometimes, I just go sit down and take a magazine to avoid talking. Or start to write my time sheets. Things that you do just to avoid [talking with the patient]." Colin[1] used a similar strategy, "I would have my book and I just read. That's one way for me to avoid conversation with the patient also. Even if they are sitting next to you, they respect the fact that you are reading and they don't bother you." These strategies allow interpreters to present themselves as invisible machines as opposed to human beings who are obligated to be sociable to others.

It is important to point out that these strategies employed by interpreters also allow interpreters to control *others'* communicative behaviors. At times, interpreters realized that their institutional hierarchy does not allow them to give providers instructions, but then they used verbal and nonverbal resources to control others' behaviors. Selena[1] explained:

> I always tell the patient, you look at [the doctors] and I will interpret. Don't look at me. But sometimes, you cannot tell that to the provider. Because YOU DON'T tell them that. THEY ARE IN CHARGE. And they don't like to be bossed around. So, what I do is I go towards the back of the patient, as far back as I can, so that when they are looking at me, then, I look at the patient, so that I don't look at them, *I lower my eyes, that forces them to talk to the patient.*

By adopting these specific strategies, interpreters obligate other participants in the interpreter-mediated interaction to respond to the communicative contexts that situate interpreters in an invisible role.

C.2. Provider–Interpreter Differences in Speech Conventions

Providers' Lack of Knowledge of the Specialized Frame

Individuals who are not familiar with the speech genre of interpreter-mediated interactions would have a hard time anticipating or understanding the role performances of a medical interpreter. Steve[1] explained:

> From the provider's perspective, if a patient needs an interpreter, they would get an interpreter for them, but beyond that, *they don't really understand our role. It's not a very well-defined profession, I suppose.* It's not really like an official position, like a nurse or a doctor, or one of the health providers. We almost could have just been the family members, as far as they are concerned.

In addition, the communicative contexts that interpreters carefully construct are often interrupted by other speakers' behaviors. Claire[1] explained:

> [For interpreters,] it's like a daily job, they know how [the interaction] goes, between the two parties. But *always, the patient or the healthcare providers they are not familiar with working with interpreters, they are not familiar with how it goes.* Sometimes, they just need some kind of hints from the interpreter, like they have to stop frequently, speak in short sentences, to let the interpreter have enough time to interpret.

Working with an interpreter requires other speakers to change their speech style to ensure quality interpreting. Several interpreters mentioned that when others fail to talk in an appropriate way (e.g., lengthy or overlapping talk), they are forced to step out of the invisible conduit role and give explicit instructions to the speakers. In other words, others' problematic performances can disrupt the interpreter's effort in constructing the image of an invisible conduit.

If interpreters are to reinforce provider–patient relationships and assume an invisible role, it is important that the other speakers maintain direct eye contact with each other when the interpreter is speaking. Sophia[1] explained:

> "[Providers] don't know, when they are talking, who to look at, or how to do it. They probably never have done it and they get nervous too. Because they think they should be looking at the interpreter and I tell them look at your patient. I am just here to be the voice. … We tried to tell them to make that eye contact with the patient."

The problem here is that in interpreter-mediated talk, the interpreter often is the only person who is trained and familiar with the specific speech style and role performances of this speech activity. Such confusions are common when the participants are not familiar with this speech genre as it projects specific expectations for the performance of different speakers (e.g., the interpreter should be invisible and the provider and the patient should interact with each other directly). Interpreters often commented on their frustration about others' failure to maintain appropriate performances in interpreter-mediated interactions.

From other speakers' perspectives, however, they may not be aware of their lack of knowledge about the genre of interpreter-mediated interactions, which can cause problematic interactions. Researchers of speech acts have pointed out that individuals interpret the meanings and functions of speech acts through conventions and cultural norms (Grice, 1975). The conventionalized use of language can be culture and language specific (Searle, 1979; Wierzbicka, 1985). Failure to recognize the cultural or linguistic aspects of speech acts may lead to miscommunication as the speakers use their cultural and linguistic conventions to interpret others' speech acts (Lu, 2001).

Differences in the Frames of References for Meanings

To a layperson, these behaviors entail specific meanings in their normative, communicative frame. For example, Stella[1] mentioned that one of her patients once told her, "You get shy. You get embarrassed when you interpret. Because you always close your eyes and look away. Like you get shy." Stella's effort to assume an invisible role in the medical encounter was interpreted in the conventions of monolingual interactions. Even interpreters have doubts about the training they receive:

> **Vicky**[1]: They wanted us to be sitting or standing by the patient, not even looking at the doctor. Not even looking at the patient. But just translating

what we were hearing. Spacing us out. And the doctor is talking and we should simultaneously interpret. It would not work. We have done it but we think *it's so impersonal.*

Claire[1]: They said, when you arrived at the clinic, do not speak with the patient. Stay away from the patient, until the nurse calls. This is HARD! […] I mean, for Chinese culture, it is very rude if you don't talk to people, if you just sit at a separate place. *Patients would find you rude.* You know, if you don't talk to them. I don't know. It's hard. It's hard.

Interpreters recognized that the specialized communicative frame they constructed can be interpreted differently by other laymen who are not familiar with the purposes of this behavior. In fact, our interviews with providers suggest that interpreters' concerns are not unfounded.

Some providers suggested that they find the interpreter's invisible conduit role counterproductive to the treatment process because it appears to be impersonal to the patient. Gillian[OB/GYN] explained:

You know, you've got somebody on the bed, naked, and the legs opened. And everything right there in front of everybody. And there's this strange interpreter, who has said nothing but blah, blah, blah [dull tone]… as opposed to somebody who is willing to laugh with you, kind of gets that you are trying to bond while doing all of these.

Several providers also commented on how the interpreter's behavior made them uncomfortable even when they suspected that interpreters were trained to adopt such behavior. For example, because simultaneous interpreting requires the interpreter and the other speaker (e.g., the doctor or the patient) to speak at the same time, the continuous overlapping talk can be hard to understand, if not annoying or disrespectful, for some people who are not familiar with that particular type of speech activity. Cory[ONC] noted:

Before you finish your sentence, they are already speaking. That really bugs the tar out of me. Okay. But maybe they are supposed to do it that way. … And not looking at the person and not looking at me. And like looking straight ahead like they are inanimate objects, just rotate, you know those kinds of things. *It is distracting to everybody in the room.*

Right after Cory's comment about the interpreter's style, Cleo[ONC] concluded: "Because she's kind of like a robot. Language robot." Cara[ONC] echoed: "Because the translator is a PERSON, for better or worse there, a person. And *for them to act like they are not. It just doesn't work.* I mean, it just doesn't work." Claudia[ONC] concluded: "It's a *human interaction* that you are having with the patient."

From this perspective, the specialized frame that interpreters were trained in takes on new meanings when understood through other participants' normative understanding. As a result, both the interpreters and other participants experience frustration and miscommunication because they do not share the same communicative frame and conventions that construct meanings for their communicative behaviors.

The challenge here is that interpreters are imposing a very particular type of context on provider–patient interactions. Essentially, the providers and patients use the conventions that are familiar to them to understand the interpreter's effort, which can be problematic. For most people, lack of eye contact does not mean professionalism but an uncaring attitude (if not deceiving) (Knapp & Hall, 2006). In our interviews, providers consistently pointed out that the quality of care is their utmost concern, and interpreters' behaviors should be flexible and adaptive to accomplish such goals. As Camila[ONC] put it, "I don't think patients are really thinking about the interpreter. I think they are thinking about their health care." Providers do not put much thought into the communicative contexts that are carefully and meticulously constructed by interpreters. In addition, because such communicative contexts can be so foreign to laymen, providers (and patients) may feel more confused rather than appreciative of the interpreter's communicative strategies.

Finally, it is important to note that as they became more acquainted with the style of interpreter-mediated encounters, some providers in our study became more appreciative of the functions and values of these particular forms of speech. For example, Candice[ONC] said, "[The interpreter] would be talking AS I was talking and there was NO emotional reaction. Once *I got used to that style*, I kind of liked it. Because the parents are looking at ME and reading MY nonverbal and MY emotions." Camila[ONC] said, "[With simultaneous interpreting,] you are actually having a conversation with that person." One can argue that if providers learn to use frames that are consistent with the interpreter's style, they can interpret the meanings of interpreters' behaviors better and become more appreciative of their management of contexts.

Challenges in Defining the Meanings of Patients' Talk

A fundamental challenge faced by providers and interpreters in resolving the clashes between their management and control over the medical dialogue is to have a defined boundary for their expertise so that the linguistically and culturally knowledgeable interpreter and the medically knowledgeable physician can collaborate effectively. However, in everyday practice, the boundary is not always clear. For example, Yetta[1] talked about her effort in helping Nigerian patients to understand US providers' use of drug names:

> [For] patients from Nigeria, we don't use the medical terms [in the United States]. So, mentioning [those drug names], don't mean anything to the

patient. So, what I always do is explain, I try to tell them, Dulcolax is like water pills. Okay, because [laxatives over there] is not Dulcolax in Nigeria. They are from Europe, from Germany, from London. So, being bicultural, I can always tell them this kind of medicine, this is what it does.

The problem here is that Dulcolax is *not* like water pills and laxatives are *not* the same as water pills. More importantly, Yetta[1] viewed this as information that requires her cultural expertise to facilitate provider–patient interaction when in fact she has overstepped the boundary that separates interpreting medical information and dispensing medical knowledge. Vicky[1], a Vietnamese interpreter, also commented on how American physicians often provide too many options for the patient (e.g., various treatments available and their corresponding risks), which often confuses Asian patients even more. As a result, rather than giving patients the option to hear various treatment options, she asked the doctor:

"So, according to your expertise, doctor, if this patient would be your own flesh and blood, what would your decision be?" He said, "Oh, this. If I were her, I would do that." I said, "Good. That's okay. So, why don't you choose this option then?"

Clearly, Vicky's cultural intervention has a direct impact on the content and process of provider–patient interactions. Although her judgment was based on her cultural understanding of Asian patients, it is unclear whether these strategies may have legal consequences (e.g., informed consent) or may ignore individual differences (e.g., some Asian patients may still desire patient autonomy).

Interpreters are in a difficult position as any talk can be perceived as medically *meaningful*. Gloria[OB/GYN] mentioned an incident she had with an English-speaking patient:

I had a patient walk in one day, who had 40 complaints and always wanted to tell me *they are turning off the husband from the ventilator that night and that he's going to die.* And we spent time on that. I got her into a psychiatrist after that too. *But that's not a pap smear.*

Gloria[OB/GYN] used this example to illustrate how patients may go off track during a medical encounter, and concluded:

The interpreter needs to know how *to keep the patient focused* if the patient is not focusing. So that the time management in the interaction is efficient as well. […] If the interpreter is going to sit there and tell me all about the dog and the cat and the everything else, no, I don't need to know those things. And they are really irrelevant. *What we need to stay focused on is the PROBLEM.*

The challenge presented by Gloria is that for interpreters to keep the patient focused, they need to make active judgments about whether certain information is medically relevant to the encounter at hand. As a result, comments such as "turning off the husband from the ventilator" may be medically meaningful in a psychiatric appointment but not in an ob/gyn appointment. However, Gloria[OB/GYN] also mentioned that she referred the patient to a psychiatrist, which is a medical intervention. Had the interpreter kept the patient focused, these issues would not have been brought up and a needed medical intervention might not have been provided.

Another challenge faced by interpreters is that the provider–patient relationship is perceived as bonded to therapeutic objectives and the interpreter's interactions with the patient may interfere with those objectives. For example, Mira[MH], a psychologist, commented, "if the patient opens up so much to the interpreter that they become so emotional or have an emotional breakdown, that can interfere with the treatment process tremendously." Michael[MH], a psychologist, also indicated that he'd rather interpreters not have interactions with patients without his presence. He explained:

> Cause I'm not there to participate in guiding that interaction. Should the family or the patient have a lot of angst or anxiety about seeing us, the interpreter won't be able to regulate that as well as if I was there. *So that may impact patient care* cause they are not gonna talk with us. Or they'll become too anxious and they'll kick us out or they're paranoid or afraid or angry.

From Michael's perspective, even everyday talk may lead to issues that need to be dealt with in the medical encounter. As a result, even though in earlier discussions, some interpreters have argued that not greeting or chitchatting with patients may be perceived as being rude in their cultures, these behaviors risk compromising the therapeutic process in provider–patient interactions.

As medicine becomes increasingly specialized and each physician has his or her area of expertise, providers learn to focus their patients on what is medically relevant *and* also what is relevant to their area of specialty. In other words, physicians have learned to filter patients' talk through their areas of specialty (i.e., not anything medically relevant would do). In contrast, a healthcare interpreter's frame for understanding a patient's talk in healthcare settings is holistic because s/he is involved in all aspects of that talk (e.g., the medical talk with providers and the financial talk with social workers).

In summary, in Chapter 6, I have explored bilingual health communication through the perspectives of interpreters, highlighting the value and importance of shifting our focus of analysis from interpreter roles to communicative goals. Such an approach gives researchers tools to examine and conceptualize the emergent, dynamic interactions in medical encounters, providing opportunities to advance theories in interpreter-mediated encounters. In addition, by exploring how individuals manage and manipulate discursive strategies in medical encounters, researchers can adopt a normative approach to bilingual health care and explore why certain communicative strategies may be more or less effective in defining communicative frames and controlling others' performances, including the process and content of interpreter-mediated interactions.

Notes

1   For this section, I relied heavily on the data analysis of a study I published in *Social Science & Medicine* (i.e., Hsieh, 2006a). In the original analysis, I framed the discussion through the tensions between interpreters' understanding of roles and other participants' role expectations for interpreters. Rather than simply repeating my previous findings, my goal here is to connect and reframe previous findings and to incorporate the latest literature through the theoretical framework of BHC. I used grounded theory (Charmaz, 2006; Glaser & Strauss, 1967) to identify the thematic categories presented in this section.

2   I want to emphasize that I do not endorse the strategies presented here. In fact, some of the strategies presented here are considered "errors" by some researchers (e.g., Flores, Abreu, Barone, Bachur, & Lin, 2012). I will examine the appropriateness and ethical considerations for interpreters' communicative strategies in Chapter 9.

3   Some of the themes identified here have also been reported elsewhere (e.g., Hsieh, 2010; Hsieh & Kramer, 2012a), in which we focused our analysis on providers' and interpreters' efforts in maintaining control and in managing the dynamic, emergent frames in medical encounters.

References

Abbe, M., Simon, C., Angiolillo, A., Ruccione, K., & Kodish, E. D. (2006). A survey of language barriers from the perspective of pediatric oncologists, interpreters, and parents. *Pediatric Blood & Cancer, 47,* 819–824.

Angelelli, C. V. (2002). *Deconstructing the invisible interpreter: A critical study of the interpersonal role of the interpreter in a cross-cultural linguistic communicative event.* University of Michigan, Ann Arbor. ProQuest database. (UMI No. AAT 302676).

Angelelli, C. V. (2004a). *Medical interpreting and cross-cultural communication.* Cambridge, UK: Cambridge University Press.

Angelelli, C. V. (2004b). *Revisiting the interpreters' roles: A study of conference, court, and medical interpreters in Canada, Mexico, and the United States.* Amsterdam, The Netherlands: John Benjamins.

Bavelas, J. B., Black, A., Chovil, N., & Mullett, J. (1990). *Equivocal communication.* Thousand Oaks, CA: Sage.

Blackhall, L. J., Frank, G., Murphy, S., & Michel, V. (2001). Bioethics in a different tongue: The case of truth-telling. *Journal of Urban Health, 78,* 59–71.

Bot, H. (2005). Dialogue interpreting as a specific case of reported speech. *Interpreting, 7,* 237–261.

Brämberg, E. B., & Sandman, L. (2013). Communication through in-person interpreters: A qualitative study of home care providers' and social workers' views. *Journal of Clinical Nursing, 22,* 159–167.

Brisset, C., Leanza, Y., & Laforest, K. (2013). Working with interpreters in health care: A systematic review and meta-ethnography of qualitative studies. *Patient Education and Counseling, 91,* 131–140.

Brua, C. (2008). Role-blurring and ethical grey zones associated with lay interpreters: Three case studies. *Communication & Medicine*, 5, 73–79.

Butow, P. N., Lobb, E., Jefford, M., Goldstein, D., Eisenbruch, M., Girgis, A., ... Schofield, P. (2012). A bridge between cultures: Interpreters' perspectives of consultations with migrant oncology patients. *Supportive Care in Cancer*, 20, 235–244.

Charmaz, K. (2006). *Constructing grounded theory: A practical guide through qualitative analysis*. Thousand Oaks, CA: Sage.

Dysart-Gale, D. (2005). Communication models, professionalization, and the work of medical interpreters. *Health Communication*, 17, 91–103.

Fatahi, N., Hellstrom, M., Skott, C., & Mattsson, B. (2008). General practitioners' views on consultations with interpreters: A triad situation with complex issues. *Scandinavian Journal of Primary Health Care*, 26, 40–45.

Flores, G., Abreu, M., Barone, C. P., Bachur, R., & Lin, H. (2012). Errors of medical interpretation and their potential clinical consequences: A comparison of professional versus ad hoc versus no interpreters. *Annals of Emergency Medicine*, 60, 545–553.

Flores, G., Torres, S., Holmes, L. J., Salas-Lopez, D., Youdelman, M. K., & Tomany-Korman, S. C. (2008). Access to hospital interpreter services for limited English proficient patients in New Jersey: A statewide evaluation. *Journal of Health Care for the Poor and Underserved*, 19, 391–415.

Gawande, A. (2002). *Complications: A surgeon's notes on an imperfect science*. New York: Metropolitan Books.

Glaser, B. G., & Strauss, A. L. (1967). *The discovery of grounded theory: Strategies for qualitative research*. Hawthorne, NY: Aldine de Gruyter.

Goffman, E. (1959). *The presentation of self in everyday life*. Garden City, NY: Doubleday.

Goffman, E. (1979). Footing. *Semiotica: Journal of the International Association for Semiotic Studies/Revue de l'Association Internationale de Sémiotique*, 25, 1–29.

Goffman, E. (1983). The interaction order. *American Sociological Review*, 48, 1–17.

Goodwin, C. (2007). Interactive footing. In E. Holt & R. Clift (Eds.), *Reporting talk: Reported speech in interaction* (pp. 16–46). Cambridge: Cambridge University Press.

Grice, H. P. (1975). Logic and conversation. In P. Cole & J. L. Morgan (Eds.), *Syntax and semantics: Speech acts* (Vol. 3, pp. 41–58). Cambridge, MA: Harvard University Press.

Hernandez, R. G., Cowden, J. D., Moon, M., Brands, C. K., Sisson, S. D., & Thompson, D. A. (2014). Predictors of resident satisfaction in caring for limited English proficient families: A multisite study. *Academic Pediatrics*, 14, 173–180.

Hsieh, E. (2006a). Conflicts in how interpreters manage their roles in provider–patient interactions. *Social Science & Medicine*, 62, 721–730.

Hsieh, E. (2006b). Understanding medical interpreters: Reconceptualizing bilingual health communication. *Health Communication*, 20, 177–186.

Hsieh, E. (2007). Interpreters as co-diagnosticians: Overlapping roles and services between providers and interpreters. *Social Science & Medicine*, 64, 924–937.

Hsieh, E. (2008). "I am not a robot!" Interpreters' views of their roles in health care settings. *Qualitative Health Research*, 18, 1367–1383.

Hsieh, E. (2009). Bilingual health communication: Medical interpreters' construction of a mediator role. In D. E. Brashers & D. J. Goldsmith (Eds.), *Communicating to manage health and illness* (pp. 135–160). New York: Routledge.

Hsieh, E. (2010). Provider–interpreter collaboration in bilingual health care: Competitions of control over interpreter-mediated interactions. *Patient Education and Counseling*, 78, 154–159.

Hsieh, E., Bruscella, J., Zanin, A., & Kramer, E. M. (in press). "It's not like you need to live 10 or 20 years": Challenges to patient-centered care in gynecologic oncologist-patient interactions. *Qualitative Health Research*.

Hsieh, E., Ju, H., & Kong, H. (2010). Dimensions of trust: The tensions and challenges in provider–interpreter trust. *Qualitative Health Research*, 20, 170–181.

Hsieh, E., & Kramer, E. M. (2012a). The clashes of expert and layman talk: Constructing meanings of interpreter-mediated medical encounters. In C. Callahan (Ed.), *Communication, comparative cultures and civilizations* (Vol. 2, pp. 19–44). New York: Hampton.

Hsieh, E., & Kramer, E. M. (2012b). Medical interpreters as tools: Dangers and challenges in the utilitarian approach to interpreters' roles and functions. *Patient Education and Counseling*, 89, 158–162.

Karnieli-Miller, O., & Eisikovits, Z. (2009). Physician as partner or salesman? Shared decision-making in real-time encounters. *Social Science & Medicine*, 69, 1–8.

Knapp, M. L., & Hall, J. A. (2006). *Nonverbal communication in human interaction* (6th ed.). New York: Wadsworth.

Leanza, Y., Boivin, I., & Rosenberg, E. (2010). Interruptions and resistance: A comparison of medical consultations with family and trained interpreters. *Social Science & Medicine*, 70, 1888–1895.

Leanza, Y., Boivin, I., & Rosenberg, E. (2013). The patient's Lifeworld: Building meaningful clinical encounters between patients, physicians and interpreters. *Communication & Medicine*, 10, 13–25.

Lee, R. G., & Llewellyn-Jones, P. (2011). *Re-visiting "role": Arguing for a multi-dimensional analysis of interpreter behaviour* Paper presented at Supporting Deaf People 2011: An online conference from Direct Learn. http://clok.uclan.ac.uk/5031/1/Lee%20and%20 L-J%202011.pdf.

Lu, D. (2001). Cultural features in speech acts: A Sino-American comparison. *Language Culture and Curriculum*, 14, 214–223.

Maclean, A. (2009). *Autonomy, informed consent and medical law: A relational challenge.* Cambridge University Press.

Meeuwesen, L., Twilt, S., ten Thije, J. D., & Harmsen, H. (2010). "Ne diyor?" (What does she say?): Informal interpreting in general practice. *Patient Education and Counseling*, 81, 198–203.

Messias, D. K. H., McDowell, L., & Estrada, R. D. (2009). Language interpreting as social justice work: Perspectives of formal and informal healthcare interpreters. *Advances in Nursing Science*, 32, 128–143.

Meyer, B., Bührig, K., Kliche, O., & Pawlack, B. (2010). Nurses as interpreters? Aspects of interpreter training for bilingual medical employees. In B. Meyer & B. Apfelbaum (Eds.), *Multilingualism at work: From policies to practices in public, medical and business settings* (pp. 163–184). Amsterdam, The Netherlands: John Benjamins.

Parsons, S. K., Saiki-Craighill, S., Mayer, D. K., Sullivan, A. M., Jeruss, S., Terrin, N., ... Block, S. (2007). Telling children and adolescents about their cancer diagnosis: Cross-cultural comparisons between pediatric oncologists in the US and Japan. *Psycho-Oncology*, 16, 60–68.

Robinson, T. M., Alexander, S. C., Hays, M., Jeffreys, A. S., Olsen, M. K., Rodriguez, K. L., ... Tulsky, J. A. (2008). Patient–oncologist communication in advanced cancer: Predictors of patient perception of prognosis. *Supportive Care in Cancer*, 16, 1049–1057.

Rogg, L., Aasland, O. G., Graugaard, P. K., & Loge, J. H. (2010). Direct communication, the unquestionable ideal? Oncologists' accounts of communication of bleak prognoses. *Psycho-Oncology*, 19, 1221–1228.

Rosenberg, E., Leanza, Y., & Seller, R. (2007). Doctor-patient communication in primary care with an interpreter: Physician perceptions of professional and family interpreters. *Patient Education and Counseling, 67*, 286–292.

Rosenberg, E., Seller, R., & Leanza, Y. (2008). Through interpreters' eyes: Comparing roles of professional and family interpreters. *Patient Education and Counseling, 70*, 87–93.

Searle, J. R. (1979). *Expression and meaning: Studies in the theory of speech acts.* Cambridge, UK: Cambridge University Press.

Tang, A. S., Kruger, J. F., Quan, J., & Fernandez, A. (2014). From admission to discharge: Patterns of interpreter use among resident physicians caring for hospitalized patients with limited English proficiency. *Journal of Health Care for the Poor and Underserved, 25*, 1784–1798.

Thompson, D. A., Hernandez, R. G., Cowden, J. D., Sisson, S. D., & Moon, M. (2013). Caring for patients with limited English proficiency: Are residents prepared to use medical interpreters? *Academic Medicine, 88*, 1485–1492.

Tracy, K. (2013). *Everyday talk: Building and reflecting identities* (2nd ed.). New York: Guilford.

Wierzbicka, A. (1985). Different cultures, different languages, different speech acts: Polish vs. English. *Journal of Pragmatics, 9*, 145–178.

Wros, P. (2009). Giving voice: Incorporating the wisdom of Hispanic RNs into practice. *Journal of Cultural Diversity, 16*, 151–157.

Yum, J. O. (1988). The impact of Confucianism on interpersonal relationships and communication patterns in East Asia. *Communication Monographs, 55*, 374–388.

7

CLINICAL DEMANDS AND INTERPERSONAL RELATIONSHIPS IN BILINGUAL HEALTH CARE

Despite the tremendous growth of research on interpreter-mediated medical encounters in recent years, little is known about providers' needs and perspectives in bilingual health care. This can partly be attributed to an earlier focus on the conduit model of interpreting, which centers on the accuracy and faithfulness of the conduit. As such, the only point that is worth investigating is interpreters' ability to provide equivalent relays of information from one language to another. After all, all other participants are encouraged to keep their communicative behavior the same (i.e., providers should talk as if they are talking to language-concordant patients). However, recent studies have revealed important issues that warrant a closer examination of providers' perspectives and needs in bilingual health care.

First, there is little explanation to account for providers' underuse of professional interpreters. The provider's choice of interpreter should be guided by institutional regulations/guidelines as well as ethical standards. This is why many researchers and practitioners continue to advocate the use of professional interpreters (Papic, Malak, & Rosenberg, 2012; VanderWielen et al., 2014). However, studies of different clinical contexts (e.g., primary care, emergency medicine, and inpatient settings), countries (e.g., the United States and Australia), and longitudinal designs (e.g., before and after state mandates for language access) found that providers consistently underutilize professional interpreters, generally using them for less than 20 percent of language-discordant patients (Ginde, Sullivan, Corel, Caceres, & Camargo, 2010; Gray, Hilder, & Donaldson, 2011; Meischke, Chavez, Bradley, Rea, & Eisenberg, 2010; Schenker, Pérez-Stable, Nickleach, & Karliner, 2011). Providers regularly underutilize professional interpreters even in situations in which interpreters are easily accessible (Schenker et al., 2011; Schenker, Wang, Selig, Ng, & Fernandez, 2007), when they perceive benefits of using professional interpreters (Diamond, Schenker, Curry, Bradley, & Fernandez, 2009), and in states that have legislation mandating interpreters and/or cultural competency in healthcare settings (Flores et al., 2008; Ginde et al., 2010). Although such patterns are often treated as providers' error or negligence, these findings suggest that there are other factors shaping providers' patterns of interpreter utilization. It would be a disservice to the research on and practice of bilingual health care to categorically claim all these normative practices as unethical or substandard. Instead, we need to explore further why providers consistently and continuously adopt such practices, investigate the corresponding clinical consequences and ethical implications, and identify potential intervention points.

Second, although many studies have explicitly identified the clinical contexts in which they are conducted, little is known about how these contexts may shape interpreter performances or provider needs. It is somewhat intriguing that researchers have neglected the impact of clinical specialties on provider needs despite their explicit references to clinical settings, including pediatrics (Abbe, Simon, Angiolillo, Ruccione, & Kodish, 2006; Cunningham, Cushman, Akuete-Penn, & Meyer, 2008; DeCamp, Kuo, Flores, O'Connor, & Minkovitz, 2013; Flores et al., 2003; Kuo, O'Connor, Flores, & Minkovitz, 2007), oncology (Butow, Goldstein, et al., 2011; Butow et al., 2012; Lubrano di Ciccone, Brown, Gueguen, Bylund, & Kissane, 2010), emergency departments (Flores, Abreu, Barone, Bachur, & Lin, 2012; Ginde, Clark, & Camargo, 2009; Grover, Deakyne, Bajaj, & Roosevelt, 2012; Hampers & McNulty, 2002; Meischke et al., 2010; Weissman et al., 2005), palliative care (Kaufert, 1999; Roat, Kinderman, & Fernandez, 2011; Schenker, Fernandez, Kerr, O'Riordan, & Pantilat, 2012; Thornton, Pham, Engelberg, Jackson, & Curtis, 2009), inpatient care (Jimenez, Moreno, Leng, Buchwald, & Morales, 2012; Lindholm, Hargraves, Ferguson, & Reed, 2012; Schenker et al., 2011), and mental health (Bauer & Alegría, 2010; Flynn et al., 2013; Searight & Armock, 2013). Providers in different clinical settings often need to adopt different communicative strategies in response to specialty-specific demands. For example, a pediatrician who needs to communicate with child patients with attention deficit hyperactivity disorder and their parents is likely to have very different communicative patterns and priorities than a physician in emergency care who needs to communicate with an adult patient with internal bleeding. It is reasonable to expect that due to their specialty-specific, event-specific demands, they may have distinctive needs from healthcare interpreters. Rather than treating these clinical settings as generic background information, it is time to consider how and why these clinical settings may impose demands and constraints on interpreter-mediated interactions.

Third, despite different types of interpreters and interpreting modalities in healthcare settings, little is known about how providers decide which type of interpreter or interpreting modality to use in a given situation. Recent studies suggest that providers adopt different interactional styles, expectations, and assumptions when working with different types of interpreters. For example,

Rosenberg, Richard, Lussier, and Shuldiner (2011) found that providers are more likely to discuss emotions and psychological issues when using a professional interpreter rather than a family interpreter (42 percent versus 4 percent, $p = 0.001$). Rosenberg, Leanza, and Seller (2007, p. 290) concluded, "Most physicians use professional and family interpreters in distinct ways to successfully establish a relationship with the patient." Providers view professional interpreters as cultural brokers and adopt a conduit model of communication, treating interpreters as "translating machines." In contrast, they often assume family interpreters are also caregivers, relying on them to report symptoms that the patient does not mention and provide patient assistance beyond the appointment. If different types of interpreters entail unique characteristics, strengths, and weaknesses (Bond, Bateman, & Nassrally, 2012; Diamond, Tuot, & Karliner, 2012; Green, Free, Bhavnani, & Newman, 2005; Rosenberg et al., 2007; Rosenberg, Seller, & Leanza, 2008; Seeleman, Essink-Bot, Selleger, & Bonke, 2012), researchers should examine (a) how providers decide on their choice of interpreter, and (b) whether their choices for and interactional patterns with different types of interpreter are appropriate and effective.

In Chapter 5, I used statistical analysis to investigate the similarities and differences in providers' attitudes toward expected interpreter performances (see Chapter 5.A: Providers' Diversity, Expectations, and Agenda). Although providers across various specialties share specific expectations of interpreter functions (i.e., interpreters as health professionals and as provider proxies), we also found significant differences across clinical specialties in providers' expectations and needs for the interpreter's role as a patient ally, which centers on the interpreter's interpersonal functions in providing assistance and emotional support to patients.

Rather than conceptualizing professional interpreters and family interpreters as individuals with fixed levels of professionalism and interpreting skills, I propose to view them as individuals with distinct characteristics and skills that can be enhanced or compromised depending on the context, including interpersonal, clinical, organizational, and temporal contexts. In other words, family interpreters are not inherently less capable than professional interpreters of being a provider proxy or health professional. After all, a patient's family member can be particularly powerful and effective if s/he chooses to support the provider's agenda or encourages the patient to accept the provider's recommendation, as family members are often involved in patients' decision-making. Similarly, a family member can improve illness-related health literacy and knowledge during a patient's illness event. Although providers may be concerned about patient confidentiality, a patient may have more trust in a family member keeping his/her secret than a professional interpreter who also belongs to the same small ethnic community. As we continue the following investigation on providers' needs and expectations, I encourage readers to look beyond the immediate labeling of different types of interpreter. By identifying the wide variety of characteristics and traits that shape providers' needs and use of interpreters, I will demonstrate the specific skills and dimensions that an interpreter can develop to facilitate provider–patient interactions.

These skills and dimensions are not exclusive or unique properties of a particular type of interpreter. I argue that providers can accept and even appreciate any interpreter as long as the interpreter can demonstrate and perform these skills/dimensions effectively and appropriately. This approach also provides multiple intervention points for researchers and practitioners of bilingual health care because it does not reduce the complex clinical demands to a dichotomous choice of professional versus nonprofessional interpreter. Rather, it highlights the different areas in which an interpreter, any interpreter, can work on to achieve successful interpreter-mediated interactions.

In this chapter, I will:

- identify the various factors that shape providers' choice of interpreters
- examine providers' control over medical encounters
- explore the various dimensions that shape provider–interpreter trust
- discuss how these complex norms shape healthcare delivery.

A. Factors Shaping Providers' Choice of Interpreter

Based on grounded theory, I identified four themes that are influential in providers' choice of interpreters[1]: (a) time constraints, (b) alliances of care, (c) therapeutic objectives, and (d) organizational-level considerations.

A.1. Time Constraints

Providers in all five specialty areas (i.e., obstetrics-gynecology [ob/gyn], emergency department, oncology, mental health, and nursing) reported time as a major context influencing their decision-making process. Time constraints impose two primary limitations on providers' choices: (a) disruption to providers' schedule and priorities, and (b) increased responsibilities and competing demands.

Disruption to Providers' Schedule and Priorities

When discussing time constraints, providers' primary concerns centered on management of and disruption to their schedules. Ginger[OB/GYN] commented, "I prefer to have a professional but I feel silly calling them for a 20-second thing." Ed[EM] commented, "If we have a family member [... who] can adequately interpret, then we will utilize that just because it is the quickest way." Nora[NUR] explained:

> I would use [professional interpreters] SO MUCH MORE OFTEN if they were just right there where I could just say, 'hey, can you come here? I need

to ask you something real quick', instead of having to call and wait 25 minutes for them to get up here. [...] If we have a family member that speaks good English [...] we will utilize that just because it is the quickest way.

At times, on-site interpreters need to manage multiple demands from different departments within a hospital. As a result, tasks (e.g., a discharge from an ob/gyn inpatient unit) that are considered less time-sensitive may require a longer wait time. Nancy[NUR] explained her frustration when she had to explain to an interpreter, "You need to come. NOW! You don't understand. There are twenty people down in labor [...] and they've got more people delivering in the hallway. So we need them discharged." Having to wait for a professional interpreter can delay care to other scheduled patients and create a snowball effect of task delays for an entire clinic.

Although telephone interpreters may appear readily available, they may still impose significant disruption to providers' tasks. Ed[EM] argued, "It's just a very cumbersome process to have to speak to somebody on the phone, and then have to hand the phone to [the patient]. It's much more lengthy, especially if you are having a detailed conversation. It's VERY slow." Ginger[OB/GYN] explained, "We tried to do it on the speaker phone, but there's a lot of echo, so usually, I'll ask the question into the phone, and then hand the phone to the patient, who answers it, and then I get the phone back." Emily[EM] echoed, "Having someone in the room with you makes very much smoother conversation." Their frustration over the poor sound quality, awkward discursive style, and lack of immediacy through telephone interpreting was shared by many providers.

Due to concerns about disrupting their schedules and priorities, many providers advocated for in-clinic interpreters. Earl[EM] explained, "I wish we had an interpreter that lived in our department. I wish we had one around the clock." Others used family interpreters while recognizing their many flaws. Gloria[OB/GYN] explained, "We go to the family member not knowing what was really communicated. That is FAR from ideal, but it's usually time constraint." Eliot[EM] explained, "We need to know something right in there, and there's aunts and uncles, brothers and sisters there – that makes it easier."

Increased Responsibilities and Competing Demands

Several clinics managed the disruption to providers' schedules by hiring bilingual staff and/or bilingual physicians. Michael[MH] commented, "If there is a medical personnel, either on my team or right there in the unit, who speaks the language, we grab them." Earl[EM] explained that due to the need for an immediate diagnosis, they used a bilingual clerk from a different clinic. He explained, "Her role was to be a clerk, but she happened to be able to speak Spanish. And we needed someone at that point in time so we borrowed her." The terms used to explain how these personnel were solicited to do interpreting jobs (i.e., "grabbed" and "borrowed") are interesting because they implied a sense of imposition or indebtedness from the borrowers' perspectives.

When asked if other providers or nurses asked him to interpret for them, Eli[EM], a bilingual physician, said, "Oh, absolutely! All the time. I mean as soon as people knew I was pretty fluent in Spanish that's come up like a second job." On the other hand, Eric[EM] explained his refusal to use bilingual staff /providers as interpreters because "it is [an] unfair burden to carry on a regular patient load and then having to interpret for every family that needs it. [...The bilingual staff/provider who should be] making medical decisions or parting medical therapy [is] now tied up doing interpretation." Nacia[NUR] echoed, "I don't call [the bilingual coworkers] cause they've got their own patients to take care of."

Concerns for co-workers' increased workload and responsibilities may limit providers' choices. Norma[NUR] explained that to limit her impositions, she would only ask her bilingual co-worker to interpret "a couple of things" but not discharge teaching, which "takes about five to ten minutes." Michael[MH] expressed his frustration with having to wait for a professional interpreter but commented that bilingual nurses will not do because "they usually do not have [45 minutes for me] to go through a more thorough initial evaluation."

A.2. Alliances of Care

Alliances of care influence providers' decisions through: (a) management of patient empowerment and receptiveness and (b) facilitation of the provider's agenda.

Management of Patient Empowerment and Receptiveness

Many providers viewed interpreters as an essential resource in ensuring patients' empowered, informed, and active participation in medical encounters. Patient empowerment often centers on patients' informational needs and highlights a preference for accurate information relay and, thus, professional interpreters. For example, Nydia[NUR] explained, "If you're going to take the patient's baby away because [her] drug test was positive [...] I make sure I have an [professional] interpreter and make sure [the patient] understood everything." Eliot[EM] noted, "When we get detail history and we probably get the interpreter because sometimes family members they may ad lib for the patient or they may not ask exactly how we like it."

Several providers expressed concerns about male relatives from certain cultures (e.g., Saudi Arabian, Kuwaiti, or Hispanic cultures) serving as interpreters, as they are also in charge of the decision-making for all individuals of the household. Gloria[OB/GYN] noted, "He MIGHT be telling her, but he has decided that this is what she is going to do." Nacia[NUR] echoed, "The family gentleman was there, and I had to talk through him and that's very annoying. But [the patient] didn't want me advocating for her." Providers struggled between their desire to respect patients' cultural practices and patient empowerment. Some felt that male relatives may compromise patient autonomy; in contrast, others found the presence of male relatives comforting and reassuring to female patients, thus allowing the female patients to be more empowered and engaged in the provider–patient interactions.

Providers' concerns for patient receptiveness also motivate them to consider patients' emotional needs. Ed[EM] explained, "To have an interpreter that can not only interpret but can [also] assist in providing compassion and empathy is helpful." Garner[OB/GYN] praised an on-site interpreter because "he stepped out of the role of the interpreter and was there kind of as a support for her. And that was really important, I thought, for her." Many patients often come with trusted family members and friends who have served as their interpreters for years. Earl[EM] commented, "At least the interpreter was advocating for their family. There are probably some positives." Ed[EM] followed, "I will try to respect that unless I see that [the interpreter is] just totally inadequate." Several providers expressed concerns about telephone interpreters as a poor choice to meet patients' emotional needs. Norma[NUR] commented, "On-site interpreters make the patient feel better as opposed to [telephone interpreters, who are] just are more factual." Cecil[ONC] explained that when disclosing a poor prognosis, "I want somebody [who] stands in there WITH me. [...] I just couldn't use a telephone [interpreter]." As a result, there are situations in which a provider may prefer an untrained interpreter over a professional interpreter who is unable to provide the emotional support needed.

Facilitation of the Provider's Agenda

Providers evaluated their relationships with interpreters through alliances that allowed them to accomplish specific goals. Eric[EM] mentioned that he evaluates the success of a medical encounter based on whether the patient accepts his medical assessment; in addition, he relies "on the ability of the interpreter to repeat that salesmanship." Several providers mentioned incidents in which they filed a complaint when they suspected that the interpreter had failed to uphold their communicative agenda (e.g., supporting the patient's decision not to accept a lumbar puncture or epidural).

From this perspective, providers may prefer interpreters who are familiar with their procedures and who are willing to maintain their agenda. Ed[EM] commented, "[For interpreters that I have worked] with for a long time, I am very comfortable with them redirecting patients and stopping patients." Interpreters' familiarity with clinic-specific procedures and knowledge allows them to serve as a provider proxy. Mandy[MH] added, "I think the more we could get someone that's familiar with mental health the better." Gram[OB/GYN] echoed, "I [prefer] to work with an interpreter that is knowledgeable in the area where [I'm] working in." Cecil[ONC] noted that he allowed interpreters to convince the patient without interpreting back and forth, "The interpreter doesn't really say what they're saying. When I get through, the patient is relaxed about what I'm gonna do [and] says, 'okay, it's ok and I'll tolerate it.'" Cordell[ONC] agreed, "That's why I prefer for somebody who I have a relationship with because they will be trained over time."

A.3. Therapeutic Objectives

Whereas alliances of care highlight the interpersonal dimension of providers' choices, therapeutic objectives center on the clinical aspects of care. They influence providers' choices through: (a) clinical complexity, (b) clinical urgency, and (c) patient privacy.

Clinical Complexity

Providers' preferences for interpreters who are familiar with their procedures also include a preference for interpreters who are familiar with clinical complexities. Celia[ONC] explained, "We have some residents who are bilingual, and that can be very helpful sometimes, too. Cause they have a lot of medical knowledge." Michael[MH] also indicated a preference for medical staff, "I don't usually go for [bilingual] cleaning ladies or custodial workers. It's somebody's medical knowledge, so it's most typically a nurse." Eli[EM] echoed, "I would trust [bilingual nurses much more than professional interpreters]. Because they have more medical experience so they would know better how to explain exact procedures and diagnosis." While many providers commented that being bilingual does not mean bicultural, few providers questioned the competence of bilingual staff to serve as interpreters. Nevertheless, culture may be essential in assessing the patient's clinical conditions. For example, Mira[MH] explained, "We need to know the psychosocial details about the patients [...] whether the patients' complaint is typical or normal in that particular culture."

The provider's assessment of clinical complexity highlights the spectrum of tasks that may or may not require trained interpreters. For example, Norma[NUR] said, "For simple stuff, I might use [bilingual children as interpreters]." Nacia[NUR] also noted, "When I have little issues, my seventh grade Spanish can get me through." Ginger[OB/GYN] also explained, "When it's just something like 'roll on to your back,' I'm not going to call an interpreter up just for two sentences." Cecil[ONC] explained, "If all I need to do is put a needle in [...] I can get an okay from the patient and he understands what I'm gonna do, then I don't need an interpreter." Thus, providers made calculated decisions on what is considered minor (e.g., pain management) versus major (e.g., discharge instructions) and tried to weigh various options (e.g., wait for a professional interpreter versus provide some pain medication immediately). Natalie[NUR] noted, "It's one thing for me to use the family to see if they like to crochet [...] but it's another to ask if they are allergic to something [...which] could potentially be a life-threatening issue." Grace[OB/GYN] explained, "Dead babies. Cancer. You know, life altering situations, I will not do it without [professional] interpreters."

Clinical Urgency

Many providers also talked about how clinical urgency dictates their choice of interpreter. Mira[MH] noted, "Trust for our patient is such an important issue that I just don't think a telephone interpreter is a good solution unless it's an emergency." Natalie[NUR] noted, "I might use a six year old. Depending upon the immediacy of the need, like pain or something like that." Gloria[OB/GYN] also commented, "If you are in a fairly urgent situation, where you have to make a decision doing an emergency C-section or something like that, you go with what the family member says and you don't think about it." Ed[EM] explained,

> If somebody is critically ill, we will get whatever information we can whether that'll be a family member that speaks very little English, or even a younger child [...] I have a few phrases of Spanish [...] we will utilize what we can till we get an interpreter.

Differing from the impacts of clinical complexity through which providers make educated decisions for their best option in the given context, clinical urgency leaves providers with few choices in deciding the type of interpreter they'll work with.

Patient Privacy

Several providers noted that despite the availability of family interpreters, their presence may not always facilitate patient receptiveness or provider–patient communication. Michael[MH] explained that he generally avoids using family interpreters for sensitive topics; however, if "it's obvious that the patient is fully comfortable with or NEEDS the family member there to feel comfortable to get anything out of them, then I use them. So it's kind of a case-by-case judgment kind of call." Gloria[OB/GYN] said that refusing a family interpreter and requesting a professional interpreter is necessary if "the husband is controlling and manipulating and you are concerned about domestic abuse." Several providers also commented on situations where they needed to find a professional or same-gender interpreter for the patient due to a sensitive topic (e.g., sexual background and HIV diagnosis) or procedure (e.g., pap smear).

A.4. Organizational-level Constraints

Two issues emerged as organizational-level constraints: (a) resource limitations and (b) ethical guidelines.

Resource Limitations

Many providers expressed their desire to have a full-time professional interpreter stationed at their clinic. However, depending on patient demographics and clinical specialty, such a practice may not be feasible. By law, the cost of an interpreter cannot be transferred directly to the patient, so healthcare facilities often struggle to find sufficient funding through federal/state-level sources, insurance companies, and private funds (Youdelman, 2008). Gloria[OB/GYN] commented, "I agree that professional interpreters are our preference, but unfortunately, financially, it's nearly impossible to do that." As a result, healthcare organizations may purposefully recruit bilingual staff to meet the challenges of limited English proficiency (LEP) patients. For example, Cordell[ONC] explained, "We have hired specifically in our office and department some bilingual folks who have roles in our department as receptionist and data managers." Nevertheless, as we have discussed earlier, providers in our study also expressed reluctance to utilize their bilingual co-workers due to concerns about increasing others' workloads.

Ethical Guidelines

Whereas resource limitations restrict the options available to providers, ethical guidelines require providers to make certain choices to avoid potentially negative consequences. For example, Ed[EM] explained, "It's never okay to not to get consent out of a patient for a basic procedure just because we don't- can't communicate with them because of the language barrier." Eli[EM] echoed, "The university has guidelines. [...] I don't think you can get consent for going into the operating room without an official interpreter there." Many providers expressed concerns about the potential for lawsuits. Mira[MH] explained, "Everybody worries about malpractice. I think interpreters REDUCE my risks. Because you can communicate with patients more accurately and obtain better information." Cara[ONC] explained her preference for unbiased interpreters:

> You don't have to worry about somebody saying back later, "You never told me that. I was translating and you never said that." So, yeah, it's an extra level of protection to have a hospital hired [interpreter] as opposed to the family. The level of malpractice protection.

From this perspective, providers' concerns for ethical guidelines appear to center on protecting themselves in case of potential litigation.

B. Maintaining Control over Interpreter-Mediated Medical Encounters

It is not surprising that providers' preference for interpreters is influenced by their desired or prioritized goals. After all, interpreter as provider proxy is a shared

TABLE 7.1 Factors influencing providers' choice of interpreter

Factors	Corresponding dimensions	Sample narratives
Time constraints	Disruption to providers' schedule and priorities	I would use [professional interpreter] SO MUCH MORE OFTEN if they were just right there where I could just say, "Hey, can you come here? I need to ask you something real quick," instead of having to call and wait 25 minutes for them to get up here. (Nora[NUR])
	Increased responsibilities and competing demands	It is [an] unfair burden to carry on a regular patient load and then having to interpret for every family that needs it. [...The bilingual staff/provider who should be] making medical decisions or parting medical therapy [is] now tied up doing interpretation. (Eric[EM])
Alliances of care	Management of patient empowerment and patient receptiveness	[When disclosing poor prognosis,] I want somebody [who] stands in there WITH me. [...] I just couldn't use a telephone [interpreter]. (Cecil[ONC])
	Facilitation of the provider's agenda	PROFESSIONAL interpreter is supposed to be working for ME, as a go-between with the patient. Whereas the family member, may be working for themselves, or may be working for the patient, or who knows what. They are not THERE FOR ME. (Gloria[OB/GYN])
Therapeutic objectives	Clinical complexity	I would trust [bilingual nurses much more than professional interpreters]. Because they have more medical experience so they would know better how to explain exact procedures and diagnosis. (Eli[EM])
	Clinical urgency	If somebody is critically ill, we will get whatever information we can whether that'll be a family member that speaks very little English, or even a younger child [...] I have a few phrases of Spanish [...] we will utilize what we can till we get an interpreter. (Ed[EM])
	Patient privacy	[When working with family interpreters,] the obvious concern would be confidentiality issues. If the patient will not be forthcoming with the interpreter, then I cannot really ask [sensitive topics] I need to ask through a family interpreter. (Michael[MH])
Organizational-level considerations	Resource limitations	I agree that professional interpreters are our preference, but unfortunately, financially, it's nearly impossible to do that. (Gloria[OB/GYN])
	Ethical guidelines	You don't have to worry about somebody saying back later, "You never told me that. I was translating and you never said that." So, yeah, it's an extra level of protection to have a hospital hired [interpreter] as opposed to the family. The level of malpractice protection. (Cara[ONC])

* adapted from Hsieh (2015).

expectation across various clinical specialties (see Chapter 5.A). This expectation, however, is not consistent with another provider's common expectation: interpreters as neutral translating machines (Brämberg & Sandman, 2013; Fatahi, Hellstrom, Skott, & Mattsson, 2008; Rosenberg et al., 2007). The important question here is: How do providers reconcile these two competing, if not conflicting, expectations?

To answer this question, it may be useful to reconsider what providers had in mind when they said that they expect interpreters to assume a neutral, faithful, and passive role (i.e., the interpreter-as-conduit model) in provider–patient interactions (Fatahi et al., 2008; Rosenberg et al., 2007). Traditionally, the conduit model was envisioned as a way to limit interpreters' power and ensure other speakers' control over the communicative process (see Chapter 1.C). The primary concern for providers may not be about the interpreter's neutrality but about their ability to control the content and process of provider–patient interactions (Hsieh, 2010). By conceptualizing interpreters as word-for-word translating machines, providers adopt a *utilitarian view* of interpreters. In other words, interpreters are conceptualized as instruments in the process, providing utility without influencing the content or dynamics of provider–patient communication. Tension may result if a provider suspects an interpreter did not provide a word-for-word interpretation (Hsieh, 2010).

In this section, I will critically examine how providers construct a utilitarian view of interpreters' roles and functions. Some of the arguments presented here have been published in earlier publications (Hsieh, 2007; Hsieh & Hong, 2010; Hsieh & Kramer, 2012). However, I have reorganized my findings here to illustrate how they can be understood through the constructs of the BHC Model. In particular, I will examine providers' (a) exploitation of system norms, (b) expectation of others' submission of individual agency, and (b) objectification of interpreters and their emotion work.

B.1. Exploitation of System Norms

By adopting a utilitarian approach to interpreters, providers exploit the system norms in healthcare settings in which physicians are at the top of the institutional hierarchy. I recognize the fact that a healthcare team is, by nature, hierarchical. A utilitarian view of interpreters, however, suggests unidirectional communication (i.e., provider to interpreter). For example, Mindy[MH] said:

> I would prefer the interpreter give me *literally* what they understand the words are. And then, afterwards, I can ask the interpreter when the patient is gone, "Is that a code for so and so?" if I did not understand that.

In other words, she does not expect interpreters to interrupt the interaction but will ask the interpreter for clarification if she deems it necessary. This expectation, however, can be problematic. Although Mindy's comment recognizes the interpreter's cultural expertise, her comment suggests that she believes that only one meaning can be present in the appropriation of meanings in words. In addition, to an outsider, the literal meaning may still make sense and be meaningful even if it was not what the speaker meant. If the interpreter, as an insider, does not proactively provide the insider, culturally coded meaning, it may never come to the provider's mind to question the "literal meaning of the words."

Interpreters are trained to provide information about their roles, functions, and preferred communication styles for providers and interpreters (e.g., providers and patients should address each other directly and ignore the presence of the interpreter) at the beginning of each medical encounter. However, many interpreters complained about being under pressure to skip that introduction because providers do not have time to listen to them. For example, Cristie[1] explained, "There's no time for you to have the introduction, they just want to hurry up and finish all the interpreting job. [...] They don't have that patience to listen to you."

Because interpreters are viewed as tools, their opinions or perspectives are not expected, needed, or desired. Stella[1] noted that when she suggested that providers adopt communicative styles that are consistent with the conduit model (e.g., addressing the patient directly by using the first person and looking at the patient when talking), "Some of [the providers] just refuse to do it. They get mad at you, because they think you are telling them what to do. [...] They don't want to be told." Interpreters-as-tools are not expected or "allowed" to function if others are not there to utilize the tools. For example, Sherry[1] explained,

> I know what the prescription is, I'd come back and ask [the provider]. I do, and it's REALLY hard when you are an interpreter to do that. Because you can just pick up the prescription and say, "Oh, well, it says blah, blah, blah." But right now, if you are trained, you are thinking, "I'm liable. We go to court. It's me."

In contrast to the interpreter's sense of self-restraint in providing their opinions, knowledge, or suggestions to providers or patients, providers' narratives suggest a sense of hierarchy (and at times ownership) when discussing provider–interpreter relationships. For example, several providers noted that they prefer professional interpreters (as opposed to family interpreters) because they work for them. Gloria[OB/GYN] noted:

> I rely on the fact that the PROFESSIONAL interpreter is supposed to be working for ME, as a go-between with the patient. [...] The interpreter's ROLE is to be neutral and to communicate both sides. [...] Professional interpreters should not have a hidden agenda.

Nacia[NUR] commented, "I consider them colleagues, but ancillary services to mine. Ultimately [I am] in charge, so they're functioning underneath my umbrella." The hierarchical expectations of the provider–interpreter relationship, however, may make interpreters feel pressured into fulfilling the provider's (as opposed the patient's) expectations and needs.

B.2. Expectations of Others' Submission of Individual Agency

By exploiting the system norm of their institutional hierarchy, providers can exert control over others' performances. Medical sociology has produced rich literature on providers' exploitation and dominance in provider–patient interactions, which can lead to and be reinforced by an imbalance of power in provider–patient relationships (Ainsworth-Vaughn, 1998; Waitzkin, 1991). In other words, as providers dominate the provider–patient communication through the structure, duration, and content of talk, they claim power over patients; this further constructs and reinforces the patient's powerless position, allowing providers to silence patients' voices during provider–patient interactions.

In interprofessional healthcare teams, doctors continue to enjoy and exercise a broad pattern of power over other professionals (e.g., nurses, social workers, therapists) in various contexts, including decision-making, input into care delivery, the timing and topics of talk about care, and evaluation of care delivery (Nugus, Greenfield, Travaglia, Westbrook, & Braithwaite, 2010). Nugus et al. (2010, p. 898) argued, "Relationships among clinicians in various occupations are mediated by the expectation that doctors assume responsibility for patient management and coordinating roles in health care teams, and the degree of acuity of particular health care settings." Thus, providers' control over others in an interprofessional team can involve other team members' (voluntary) submission of their individual agency.

Interpreters' Loss of Individual Agency

Although the conduit role requires interpreters not to filter or change information, many interpreters noted that healthcare providers would give them specific instructions on how they would like to receive information and direct the information flow of the provider–patient interaction. For example, Vicky[1] said, "Sometimes, doctors say, 'Okay, I am going to ask a question, you give me the answer. *If it doesn't deal with my question, I don't want to hear it.*' I have that kind of doctors before." Eli[EM] noted, "The interpreter should at least have the capacity to be able to redirect the patient and kind of filter what they say, if the response is completely unrelated to the question." In interpreter-mediated interactions, providers rely on interpreters to cut off interactions that they would not have had even with English-speaking patients.

Providers' expectations, however, contradict interpreters' training in following the conduit model as the default role. Interpreters are frustrated about these situations. Recognizing that providers may not be familiar with their training or the conduit model of interpreting, Ulysses[1] explained, "You cannot dictate to the doctors. But I feel that providers should know some of the rules that we follow by." Some interpreters noted that they do not change their communicative behavior in spite of a provider's request. For example, Sara[1] noted, "I have doctors that go like, 'Please, tell him, I need the answer, I don't want all the other stuff. I am talking about this.' I have doctors like that. But I just said the same thing. Then, again, 'I'm interpreting exactly what they are saying.'" Other interpreters tried to accommodate the provider's expectations. For example, Rachel[1] explained:

> [I have a patient who] is a talker, you know. And every time, the doctor asked a question, he would ask yes or no question or just a short answer, and she answers it and then, after that, she tries to say different things. [...] What do I do? *I just control it.* I mean, I said, "Excuse me, please just answer the question." [...The doctor] was not interested in this, you know?

Interpreters are in a difficult situation because as a conduit, they should not screen or filter information. To refuse the provider's request is to challenge the provider's control over the information exchanged; similarly, to restrict the patient's comments is to silence their narratives when they may not feel comfortable in assessing the medical value of the comments. For example, Steve[1] explained:

> Sometimes, I get cut off when [the doctors] got the answers. I started interpreting what the patient says, and they would cut me off as soon as they hear their answers. Sometimes, the doctor or the provider would say, "Oh, yeah, yeah, I don't need to know all that." *I have to trust that the doctor has heard what they need to hear. I think that's about it. If I kept interpreting, they might not listen anyway.*

Such a utilitarian view of interpreters makes them feel powerless and may, in fact, put interpreters in positions in which they need to filter or even withhold "irrelevant" information.

Interpreters' Internalization of Providers' Goals

It is important to note that both interpreters and providers acknowledge the problems of interpreters bonding with patients or vice versa, arguing that such a situation patient-interpreter relationship may interfere with the provider's treatment objectives. For example, Sharon[1] noted, "There's consequences that kind of establishing some form of relationship would allow the patient to control the interpreter, because they are going to expect, they are going to want certain things from you." Mindy[MH] noted that interpreters may bond with a patient inappropriately by "stepping outside of their role, which is to be neutral." There may be a hidden tug-of-war between the provider and interpreter in competing for the patient's affection and trust. For example, Marcella[MH] noted, "Cause we need to be the ones [as opposed to interpreters] that bond with them. [The patients] would have to be able to trust us." In short, there is a general concern about how the interpreter's relationship with the patient may impact the provider's interpersonal, clinical, and therapeutic objectives. Both interpreters and providers cited incidents in which an interpreter was fired (or should be fired) because they acted as a patient advocate.

In contrast, providers and interpreters showed little concern about the impacts of interpreters siding with healthcare providers. Some providers explicitly stated their expectation of interpreter alliance. Camila[ONC] argued, "The translators should work with [providers] in a way that best meet their needs. I don't think patients are really thinking about the translator. I think they are thinking about their health care." Carmen[ONC] explained, "[Interpreters are] pursuing [my] agenda. Their bias is towards us."

At times, providers may expect interpreters to execute their objectives *without* their input. For example, Cecil[ONC] noted that as a pathologist, he cannot do his job without a sample of the patient's biopsy. Rather than having the interpreter interpret back and forth between him and the patient, he allows the interpreter to "push" the patient, convincing the patient independently to give consent to the procedure. He concluded:

> Usually the interpreter understands that this is really necessary. [...] *I don't know what they're saying. The interpreter doesn't really say what they're saying.* [...] The bottom line is [...] interpreter does whatever on their side, and the patient put their name to the permission [for the biopsy].

Although Cecil[ONC] is comfortable with the interpreter's independent conversation with the patient, his expectation is that the interpreter operates as an automated tool that executes his objectives (without his supervision or input). Many interpreters also talked about incidents in which a provider handed them a written consent form and asked them to go over the consent process with the patient. Here, the provider's utilitarian approach to the interpreter's role in fact supersedes their expectation of the conduit model, in which the interpreter is only the voice of others. One may argue that, in this particular situation, the interpreter actually adopts the provider's therapeutic objectives and thus assumes the (unspoken) voice of the provider.

Speakers use a variety of linguistic resources (i.e., communicative strategies) to fulfill their communicative goals (e.g., task, identity, and relationship goals). The distinction between communicative goals (i.e., the speaker's intended objectives) and communicative strategies (i.e., the speaker's linguistic practice) is particularly important for interpreters. An interpreter's non-conduit behavior may be motivated by their focus on the primary speaker's communicative goals.

With this strategy, the interpreter identifies and assumes the provider's communicative goals. The interpreter may evaluate whether the provider's communicative goals have been met and decide to independently accomplish the provider's goals. For example, an interpreter may determine that the patient's answer was not complete and initiate information re-seeking on behalf of the provider. In Extract 1, the interpreter (Christie[I]) helped the provider (Heather) seek information from the patient (Paula) about the newborn's feeding pattern.

Extract 1

101	H:	And she's giving how long and how frequent?
102	I:	那你每一次大概給她餵多久, 一天多少次?
103		(How long do you feed her each time and how many times
104		a day?)
105	P:	他因為我不知道是不是她不夠力, 虛。她都要40分鐘
106		(I am not sure if she does not have enough strength or [if
107		she is] weak, but she takes about 40 minutes.)
108		
109	I:	你說每次要40分鐘。然後一天大概要幾次?
110		(You said 40 minutes each time, and how many times a day?)
111	P:	我兩個小時就餵一次
112		(I feed her every two hours.)
113	I:	Okay. Every two hour, every time, probably around
114		40 minutes. And mom was concerned, maybe because
115		the baby's- I mean it's very difficult to suck
116		the milk or what, it takes 40 minutes
117		every time.

Paula only partially answered Heather's question (i.e., how long; line 105). Rather than interpreting the partial answer, Christie[I] re-initiated the provider's question in line 109 ("How many times a day?") so that the provider would obtain a complete answer for her question ("How long and how frequent?"; line 101). A conduit role expects the interpreter to provide the partial answer and defers to the provider to evaluate whether the information was sufficient, arguing that it is the provider's responsibility to manage the quality of information exchanged. However, Christie[I] adopted the provider's objectives, decided that the patient's answer was incomplete, and pursued the additional information by herself (i.e., Christie[I] took over the provider's responsibility in evaluating the quality of information).

Interpreters' persistence in obtaining information sought by the provider reflects their concern for the provider's communicative goals. In Extract 1, although the interpreter's linguistic strategy deviated from the conduit role, it maintained the provider's communicative goal. Several interpreters also commented that they would find a way to obtain the information needed by the provider independently. Silvia[1] explained, "I try to get an answer, unless the doctor says, 'What's going on?' Then, I said, 'The patient is not answering,' and I continue to ask the same question." Interpreters' adoption of providers' goals can be particularly important and valuable in contexts in which clinical urgency is a high priority (e.g., trauma patients).

B.3. Objectification of Interpreters and Their Emotion (work)

Equating the Presence of the Interpreter as Support for the Provider

Providers view interpreters as an extension of the Self, much like a prosthesis to a person with a lost limb or a mechanical arm necessary to execute their will. Eli[EM] noted, "The family sees the interpreter as an arm of the physician." Providers in our study were conscientious about the interpreter's role in relaying their identities. If the provider wants to be perceived as supportive to the patient, the interpreter needs to relay their attitudes to the patients. Grace[OB/GYN] explained:

> If I walk in and I like my patient's shoes, I'd say, "OH, I LOVE your shoes! They are so cute [high cheery tone]." [...] Some of [the interpreters] go like, "Yeah, haha." I'm like, "NO! Tell her! I like her shoes!!"

This means that providers may view interpreters' emotional support as a reenactment of their own supportive attitudes (as opposed to something that can only be initiated by the interpreter). Interpreters are there so that they can communicate with a patient like their real self. In other words, the language barrier has created a disability to communicate effectively and interpreters should act as they do (because the interpreter *is* the provider). As a result, the interpreter's function is not about what s/he can do to improve the quality of care but what providers can do through him/her to improve the quality of care.

For example, many providers emphasized that interpreters' emotional support is implied in their presence. A patient can be comforted by having an interpreter there. Ginger[OB/GYN] noted, "It's much easier to relate to someone who speaks your own language and maybe makes you feel more comfortable. And anytime you can have a patient feel more comfortable and more relaxed, I think it's a good thing." From this perspective, interpreters are not necessarily viewed by providers as active agents in providing support to the patient. This understanding of the interpreter's emotional support allows interpreters to remain as passive objects to be wielded by providers. Gemma[OB/GYN] explained, "[An interpreter is] a relayer of information. I think it's also a source of comfort. Having the patient to know that there's somebody there, literally understand them and can help and put them at ease." In other words, it is not what the interpreter can offer as a compassionate individual but the fact that their presence allows a patient to understand the situation and to communicate with the provider that constitutes emotional support.

If emotional support can be provided by having an interpreter to help the patient to communicate with the provider, then it would seem that both telephone and on-site interpreters can provide emotional support. However, providers viewed emotional support from these two types of interpreter very differently. Several providers contrasted telephone interpreters with on-site interpreters, illustrating why telephone interpreters could not offer emotional support the way that on-site interpreters could. Cara[NUR] commented, "It's a matter of eye contact, it's a matter of body habitus, [...] sometimes, the family NEEDS to be able to make eye contact, and feel like they are having some human CONNECTION." Norma[NUR] noted, "When [an interpreter] is on-site, one thing I have noticed is that [the patients] have a tendency to maybe ask one or two more questions. They do, versus being on the telephone." The ability of an on-site interpreter to provide nonverbal cues and emotional connection is particularly valued when the diagnosis is poor. Cecil[ONC] explained that when disclosing a poor prognosis, "I want somebody stands in there WITH me. To look me in the face, and let me know they understand and the patient understands. [...] For me, I just couldn't use a telephone [interpreter]." Several providers noted that when communicating with patients through telephone interpreters, information became succinct and focused on medical issues. In fact, no providers mentioned that they would use a telephone interpreter if they believed the situation might require emotional support.

Some providers, however, talked about the physical presence of an on-site interpreter as a form of the provider's emotional support to patients. Nacia[NUR] explained, "The translators are providing a service that a [telephone interpreter] can't give. And that's that personal: 'Your nurse is interested in you. [...] She's there FOR YOU. She'll contact [the interpreter] if you all are not communicating well.' So [the on-site interpreter] gives a personal touch to that." Nancy[NUR] also noted, "Personally I [prefer] on-site [interpreters] because I think it's more comfortable for the patient, you know it shows what you're caring and you brought somebody else in, for them to understand." On-site interpreters' physical presence is symbolic of the provider's emotional support to the patient, representing a caring gesture from the provider. As such, an on-site interpreter is better than a telephone interpreter because it implies the difficulties a provider had to go through to obtain one. Interpreters, thus, become "objects" to show providers' care and support for a patient.

Interpreters' Emotion Work Serves to Fulfill the Provider's Agenda

Interpreters often view emotional support as providing a human connection in healthcare settings. As a result, they are often conflicted about the appropriateness of providing emotional support (Hsieh & Hong, 2010), as it is not an expected or approved performance in the conduit model. However, interpreters also talked about providing support to patients so that they are more likely to accept the provider's suggestions. For example, Vicky[1] explained:

> Sometimes, to comfort the patient, you have to hold the patient's hand. [...] "Okay, these are difficult times. I know you are frustrated with your health. But you know, *this is what the doctor thinks. So, why don't we try.*" "Well, this doctor is not good enough. I am not going to take it." "Well, it's up to you. But *give yourself a try first.*"

Interpreters' emotional support and/or bonding can be a valuable resource in provider–patient interactions because of the natural tendency for patients to feel a connection with someone who shares the same language. For example, Mandy[MH] commented, "When [interpreters] get on one on one terms with the patient, with just the small talk, they can sometimes tell you WAY MORE than if you've had a formal communication with everybody in the room."

Providers' sense of effective communication, however, often centers on patients' willingness to accept their care. For example, Michael[MH] noted, "If [the patients] are connecting with the interpreter and the language gives them comfort, I want to connect myself with the interpreter if that's going to give us some kind of benefit to that patient that will improve their outcome." Ginger[OB/GYN] also said:

> The interpreter would tell me when it was not about their kids' soccer game and when it's something related to the medical care. So, they play sometimes a pretty big role of what information is important to relay and what is not.

Interpreters' emotional support allows them to enter into patients' private worlds, to which the providers may not be privy, which may provide additional treatment opportunities. Some providers also talked about how interpreters' emotional support allows the interpreter to become a trusted agent to the patient.

This expectation of emotional support views interpreters as active agents in pursuing providers' therapeutic objectives. Some non-conduit behaviors are thus considered acceptable, appropriate, and even valued. For example, interpreters' casual interactions with the patient may provide valuable information that may be medically relevant. Interpreters can communicate with the patient directly and independently to pursue the provider's agenda. Interpreters' emotional support is considered appropriate when interpreters utilize their relationship with the patient to promote the provider's therapeutic objectives. In other words, providers adopt a utilitarian view of the interpreter's relationship with the patient and see it as an opportunity and/or resource to achieve their own objectives.

C. Pathways to Stronger Provider–Interpreter Trust

An issue raised by analysis in the last section is providers' willingness to allow interpreters to act independently on their behalf, which may facilitate the physician's time management but also have other important consequences. This suggests that providers do not entirely expect interpreters to act as passive instruments even when they adopt a utilitarian approach. Instead, there may be specific conditions under which they are willing to share (and even hand over) their control of the provider–patient interaction. From this perspective, it is necessary to explore how provider–interpreter trust can be a factor in influencing how comfortable providers are in allowing interpreters to assume responsibilities that are typically beyond interpreters' cultural and linguistic expertise. This issue is directly tied to how medical interpreters' professional and ethical boundaries are shaped in healthcare settings.

Trust is an important element for interpersonal relationships in healthcare settings. Researchers have noted that healthcare providers' ability to demonstrate specific characteristics (e.g., competence and compassion) and to adopt certain communicative behaviors can be critical to the trust-building process in provider–patient relationships (Pearson & Raeke, 2000). In addition, researchers have argued that trust is a complicated, multidimensional concept that may be influenced both by social trust (e.g., trust in institutional regulations and normative expectations) and interpersonal trust (e.g., repeated interactions and existing identities) (Pearson & Raeke, 2000). Trust is not only important for provider–patient relationships but also for members of healthcare teams in providing quality care (Pullon, 2008). When professionals understand each other's roles and adopt communicative strategies appropriately and effectively, they are more likely to coordinate successfully with each other and provide quality care (Keenan, Cooke, & Hillis, 1998).

Trust is fundamental to provider–interpreter relationships and bilingual health care (Greenhalgh, Robb, & Scambler, 2006; Robb & Greenhalgh, 2006). A recent review identified the trust–control–power triangle as a major theme in interpreter-mediated medical encounters (Brisset, Leanza, & Laforest, 2013). The provider–interpreter relationship is distinct from other interprofessional relationships in healthcare settings; providers rely on interpreters to convey their voices, including their identities, emotions, and information to the patients. In other words, interpreters have control over the provider's identity and information management. Healthcare providers need to have faith that interpreters can provide services without distorting their voice or compromising the quality of care.

Trust is conceptualized and negotiated in the following four dimensions: (a) interpreter's competence, (b) shared goals, (c) professional boundaries, and (d) established pattern of collaboration.[2]

C.1. Ensuring Interpreters' Competence

The emphasis on the literal, neutral, faithful relay of information is often provided by providers as their *initial* response to what they expect from an interpreter. Only one provider (out of 39) explicitly stated that a literal interpretation is not preferred. Cara[ONC] stated, "[An interpreter is] a literal person who is impartial and unemotionally involved, who translates as much as possible, word-for-word of what you said." Providers' understanding of interpreters' competence often centered on their *linguistic ability* as opposed to their cultural competence or other skills. In particular, providers often emphasized the need to find equivalent medical terms and transfer the exact information across different languages. Interpreters are aware of such an expectation, emphasizing their efforts to stay within the conduit role. In fact, 21 of the 26 interpreters claimed various forms of a conduit role. Stella[I] explained: "I would try to use the same vocabulary that the doctor is using and use the same words to put that across. […I provide] as accurate as possible interpreting, word-for-word of what they are saying." Claire[I] stated: "When I went through the training, we have to interpret everything exactly as what the doctor said, even have to interpret exactly the same tone, and same expression, and the same use of words." Both the interpreters and providers considered that exact and literal interpreting builds the credibility of the interpreter's performance.

Providers have a dilemma because despite their desire for a neutral conduit, they do not have the language skills to evaluate the interpreter's performance. Candice[ONC] explained, "NOT knowing exactly what [interpreters] are saying is very frustrating [especially] if they are saying things that shouldn't be said. […] You are always worried." As a result, rather than directly evaluating the interpreter's linguistic skills, providers assess his/her competence through their *assumptions* about the interpreter's training, credentials, and official role. This is a type of social trust, as providers demonstrate a general confidence in the collective institutions that are based on shared interests and common norms and values (Pearson & Raeke, 2000). For example, Gram[OB/GYN] said, "I know that the ones hired by the hospital to work in women's clinic go through our HR people and so there's something about them in their background." Cordell[ONC] said that she prefers a paid interpreter because "for right or wrong somebody who works for the [hospital] is going to translate what I said word-for-word as opposed to family members who may tell their mother what they want to hear." The trust for the institutional control over the quality of interpreters is so strong that providers demonstrate trust for interpreters despite their lack of knowledge about their background, ability, or codes of ethics. For example:

> Nora[NUR]: I wouldn't have a clue what [the interpreters] were saying. So I have to trust them. I would *assume* that they also have certain policies. And that's where a lot of trust comes in too. It is because we see them as professionals and that they have guidelines and stuff.

Natelie[NUR]: I don't know anything about their training, but it would just make sense to me that you would have that kind of protocol, even policies in place that you only interpret what the nursing staff or what the doctor's saying.

Many providers believed that hospital interpreters are licensed or certified. However, although the medical interpreting industry has proposed some guidelines (Dysart-Gale, 2005), there is no official licensing or certification procedure for healthcare interpreters at the federal and state levels (in the states from which the participants were recruited). Many interpreters commented that the industry-standard 40-hour training is insufficient for the complexity of interpreting in medical contexts. In these cases, providers' trust for interpreters can be based on problematic assumptions, believing that professional interpreters have more credentials and training than they have in reality.

Providers' trust in interpreters' competence is also extended to their colleagues (e.g., physicians and nurses) who are bilingual. All providers said that they would fully trust their bilingual colleagues' interpreting and consider it just as good, if not better, than that of professional interpreters. Professional interpreters and bilingual medical professionals obtain the provider's trust for their competence differently. Whereas the provider's trust in professional interpreters centers on interpreters' linguistic competence, their trust in bilingual co-workers is based on their colleagues' knowledge of and familiarity with medical issues. As a result, several providers talked about how they have more confidence in interpreters stationed in their department than those who provide services intermittently (e.g., hospital or telephone interpreters). Some providers discussed how family interpreters can be problematic due to their lack of medical knowledge, even though the patients may have complete trust in them. From this perspective, interpreters' competence is understood through their medical expertise.

In fact, no provider questioned whether or not a bilingual colleague could be a competent interpreter. This assumption, however, is not without problems. Sherry[I] noted, "Just because you say you are bilingual, it does not mean that you are an interpreter." Sara[I] commented, "You are not only interpreting the words, you are also interpreting the culture. You have to be also bicultural, not only bilingual." In addition, Sharon[I], manager of an interpreting agency, noted that interpreters who have medical backgrounds often feel more liberty to modify the client's narrative, which can pose risks to the conduit role. In short, although some providers realized that being bilingual does not equate to cultural competence or language proficiency in medical contexts, their narratives reflect little concern for the interpreting competence of their colleagues.

An important aspect of providers' assessment of interpreters' competence is that providers often share stories about interpreters' problematic performances. One particular story that was mentioned repeatedly in different interviews involves an interpreter who failed to provide information neutrally. In a version of the story, Garner[OB/GYN] explained:

> One of my partners had an interpreter who was putting way too much of her personal views into things. But the aunt [of the patient] in the room spoke English and Spanish. And the aunt goes, "You know that she was saying things that you didn't say." Like when they said, "The baby had stage 4 cancer," the interpreter said, "Yes, stage 4 cancer. Say your prayers." That [interpreter] needed to be fired. That one was fired. [...] I mean the parents didn't know that doctor wasn't saying "say your prayers."

This is a story shared among providers in social settings and departmental meetings. In other versions of the story, the interpreter was reprimanded rather than fired or the providers of the same department were cautioned about the particular interpreter's tendency to add personal views. This story provides insights into an under-discussed counterforce to the social trust of interpreters' competence discussed earlier. Although a professional interpreter may be given trust automatically due to their official role, a failure in performance may lead to erosion of that trust. In addition, when the violation of expectations is significant, the loss of trust may be extended beyond the particular event and provider–interpreter pair to become an erosion of trust in the particular interpreter or even interpreters in general.

C.2. Identifying Shared Goals

As a dimension of trust, an interpreter's competence centers on the provider's evaluation and assessment of the interpreter. In contrast, the second dimension, shared goals of the healthcare team, highlights the partnership between the provider and the interpreter. Many providers said that they view interpreters as professional colleagues, who are members of the healthcare team. For example:

> **Cleo**[ONC]: I consider the translator part of our team. [...] The translator is absolutely VITAL to get the [medical] history. I mean, you have to be able to ask those questions in that language and get that answers back.
> **Gemma**[OB/GYN]: I hope [interpreters] don't feel like that they are on the lower totem pole because I can't do my job and take care of a patient without them. So, I value them as an equal colleague. Because despite the fact they don't have the MD behind their name, I couldn't be an MD without their assistance.

Interpreters also recognized the notion of teamwork and their important role in the treatment process. For example, Shirley[I] commented, "You are the person that the staff is depending on to provide that communication, to convey the same spirit that it is being given." Sandra[I] explained, "This is part of working as a team. Both of us are discovering what is going on."

The sense of team made some providers expect interpreters' alliance. Camila[ONC] argued, "The translators should work with [providers] in a way that best meet their needs. I don't think patients are really thinking about the translator. I think they are thinking about their health care." Carmen[ONC] explained, "[Interpreters are] pursuing [my] agenda. Their bias is towards us." Providers' expectation of alliance, along with the implied trust, is particularly strong for professional interpreters and bilingual co-workers. Gloria[OB/GYN] noted, "I rely on the fact that the PROFESSIONAL interpreter is supposed to be working for ME, as a go-between with the patient; whereas the family member may be working for themselves, or may be working for the patient, or who knows what. They are not THERE FOR ME." From this perspective, family members are distrusted due to their lack of relationship with the provider at both the organizational and interpersonal level. The notion of alliance is interesting because this expectation contradicts the neutral performance that is emphasized in interpreters' competence.

Many interpreters viewed themselves as members of the healthcare team. However, both providers and interpreters noted that because interpreters are often not stationed in the clinics they have a more peripheral membership and may feel like outsiders. For example, Steve[I] noted:

> Usually, [providers] don't see us as [professionals], a part of their team. […] Instead of seeing that we are providing a service for them, they see us more on the patient's side. They sometimes treat us like relatives of the patient. […] Like they are seeing me on the other side, like an outsider. Not part of the clinic.

The contrast between family members and professionals is important. Family members, regardless of their linguistic skills, are not subject to the control of the healthcare system; in contrast, providers and interpreters have a shared identity that grounds provider–interpreter trust in the shared goals of the team.

Providers also align themselves with interpreters, noting that they both share similar goals. One of the goals mentioned repeatedly is patient care. For example, Michael[MH] noted, "I want to connect myself with the interpreter if that's going to give us some kind of benefit to that patient to improve their outcome or their capacity to work with us." Monica[MH] noted, "We're all working as a team to make sure that person gets treated." Because patient care is viewed as a shared goal of the team, interpreters' active participation in provider–patient interactions is appreciated when their intervention facilitates the quality of care. Carmen[ONC] noted:

> I TRUST that [the interpreter in our department] is going to interpret what I say or at least maybe to *interpret it into a culturally appropriate discussion.* […] You know she's gonna empathize with the patient but it's not gonna become a relationship between she and the patient that could be a barrier to [what] I'm trying do.

It is important to note that with the second dimension of trust, interpreters are trusted for their ability to make active judgments to fulfill the goals of the team. Deviation from the conduit role is acceptable and even valued when it accomplishes the team's objectives. Providers commented that they hoped that interpreters would feel comfortable to interrupt them if the interpreters needed further clarification, believed that the provider's care was not culturally appropriate, or thought that the patient's care was compromised. Nacia[NUR] noted, "We're a team. If a translator said, 'What about this?' I'd go, 'Oh yeah, ask them anyway.' Or if it wasn't an issue, I'd say, 'Well, you don't need to worry about that.' I think that open dialogue is very important."

Many providers noted that they do not mind the interpreter developing rapport or providing emotional support to help the patient feel more comfortable. Others, like Carmen[ONC], agreed that it is okay for interpreters to change the information in a culturally appropriate way to facilitate provider–patient communication. In an earlier example, Cecil[ONC] allows the interpreter to "push" the patient, convincing the patient independently to give consent to the procedure. Hence, the interpreter's ability to actively identify and meet the needs of the healthcare team is critical to provider–interpreter trust.

Two issues emerged when contrasting providers' and interpreters' understanding of the shared goals of the team. First, interpreters seem to focus on the ever-present, umbrella goal of patient care, highlighting medically related issues. This focus may lead them to be less sensitive to the emergent, dynamic nature of provider–patient interactions. Various communicative goals may (a) emerge throughout various phases of a medical encounter and (b) be distinctive to the needs of the particular clinic/specialty. For example, ob/gyn providers noted that their rapport-building strategies are important to the therapeutic relationship. Providers in mental health also emphasized the importance of establishing the provider–patient relationship in the therapeutic processes. It is important for interpreters to recognize that some non-medical talk may still serve therapeutic purposes. On the other hand, the same behaviors may have different functions and consequences in different specialty areas. Oncologists noted that interpreters are greatly appreciated when they provide emotional support to their patients, who often experience emotional distress. In contrast, mental health professionals noted that interpreters are expected to refrain from chitchatting with their patients, let alone providing emotional support, because any talk with their patients may have serious clinical and therapeutic consequences. It is therefore important for interpreters to have a more fluid understanding of the shared goals of the healthcare team.

Second, interpreters may view providers' goals as the shared goal of the team due to the implicit hierarchy within the healthcare team. Past studies have found that interpreters often assume providers' communicative goals (Davidson, 2001; Hsieh, 2007) and are distressed when they believe that the provider's communicative practice may hinder the quality of care (Hsieh, 2006). Interpreters talked about how providers' time constraints may pose a threat to the quality of care. Rachel[I] explained, "What I feel is that sometimes like, the situation that you are between the doctor who is in a hurry, who wants to leave, and the patient who wants to talk, who needs time. You know, that's a really difficult situation." However, some providers differentiate their individual goals from the team goals. As discussed earlier, providers welcome interpreters' active intervention to ensure the quality of care, which may lengthen the time for or disrupt the flow of provider–patient interactions. Several providers argued that their personal agenda (e.g., time management) is secondary to the quality of care. They prioritized the shared team goals over their individual goals. Because providers' narratives are mediated through the interpreters, interpreters are faced with the tasks of differentiating and prioritizing the shared team goals and the provider's individual goals. However, the differences between team goals and providers' individual goals are not always clear due to the hierarchical nature of the healthcare team.

The first two dimensions of trust create an inherent tension, requiring interpreters to balance the neutrality that is valued in interpreters' competence with active interventions to protect and facilitate the shared goals of the team. The third dimension, professional boundaries, provides further insights into the delicate balance of the first two dimensions.

C.3. Maintaining Professional Boundaries

Interpreters often experience conflict as they contemplate the balance between quality care and their role boundaries. Interpreters noted the difficulties in challenging the provider's opinions, which often reflect their lower status in the institutional hierarchy and their concerns for the conduit role. For example, Sophia[I] explained, "When I am there, I cannot even tell the doctor, 'I don't think you are saying the truth.' Who is me? I am just there to be their voice and that's my role." Roland[I] echoed, "You don't want to overstep your duties. Nobody asks my opinion anyways. Doctors have their own opinions." These concerns may be unfounded as many of our providers noted that they welcome interpreters' inputs when they enhance the shared goals of the team. However, providers' willingness to accept interpreters' active role is not without limits.

Providers emphasized that interpreters should not overstep their role boundaries and take over the provider's control over the healthcare services. Several providers talked about the importance of interpreters maintaining their professional role. For example:

> **Norma**[NUR]: [The interpreter] was checking the arm bands with the mother and the baby. But see, that's not her responsibility. That's my responsibility. And I felt like she was overstepping her boundaries.

> **Mindy**[MH]: If [interpreters] chat [with patients], it should never be anything besides "How are you today?" [...] I mean, they are not friends. This is a boundary issue.

Role boundary, however, is not always a clear-cut issue in bilingual health care and is often intertwined with issues of institutional structure, professional expertise, and control over the medical encounter. First, interpreters' status in the institutional structure can be unclear. Because interpreters come from various sources and often move between clinics, providers may not always know the type of interpreter they are using. Some providers noted that interpreters sometimes claim to be the patient's relative or friend in an effort to advocate for the patient. One of our interpreters mentioned a similar strategy even though she is a professional interpreter. Stacey[1] noted, "When I assume the role of advocate, I let the doctor know that I am assuming the role. [...] I said, 'I am a *friend of the family*. And I know the situation. Let me explain to you the issues around this.' So, they understand." In later discussion, it was clear that she does not have any social interactions with her clients outside of healthcare settings and only claims the role for advocacy purposes. Part of the difficulties for interpreters in adopting an advocacy role is that their institutional role is often conceptualized as a neutral conduit, providing them little resources for other role alternatives within the institutional structure. By claiming roles outside of the institutional structure, interpreters are no longer subject to institutional control and may have more resources to mediate provider–patient conflicts. These strategies can be problematic because healthcare providers may become suspicious or uncertain about the role of the interpreters. Nacia[NUR] explained, "I don't know who you are. And I might ask and you might say that you're her aunty. I don't even believe that half the time."

Second, the boundaries of expertise in bilingual health care can be ambiguous. Ideally, regarding the management and control over a bilingual medical encounter, it is best to have the linguistically and culturally knowledgeable interpreter and the medically knowledgeable physician exercise their expertise in the corresponding area. However, the boundaries between what is medical, social, cultural, and linguistic are not always obvious. Interpreters are in a difficult position as any talk can be perceived as medically meaningful in a medical encounter. Mindy[MH], a mental health provider, explained that although the characteristics of a person's voice (e.g., volume, speech rate, and fluency) have diagnostic values, providers need to rely on interpreters to decipher the meanings of these signs. She explained, "If you hear people speaking Italian with their voice goes up or what if the interpersonal space is closer? To somebody who is only English dominant, it's 'Oh, they are going to have an argument.' But it's not. It's what's normal within the culture." Differences in sociolinguistic norms and their corresponding implicatures can have significant clinical consequences. For example, because American Sign Language uses facial expressions, body posture, and the space around the signer to communicate meanings, hearing physicians have been reported to misdiagnose "an expressive Deaf person as having tics, inappropriate affection, and personality and mood disorder" (Barnett, 1999, p. 19). From this perspective, interpreters are responsible for "diagnosing" the medical meanings of these nonverbal behaviors.

In addition, providers' understanding of what constitutes medically meaningful talk can vary dramatically during the discursive process and according to their area of specialty. Gloria[OB/GYN] talked about how she was frustrated about a patient who kept mentioning that her husband was going to be put on a ventilator that night. She concluded, "I got her into a psychiatrist after that too. *But that's not a pap smear.*" In this case, depression was considered medically irrelevant as it is not an ob/gyn issue. She added, "[the] [i]nterpreter needs to know how to keep the patient focused if the patient is not focusing so that the time management in the interaction is efficient as well." In contrast, Michael[MH], a psychologist, indicated that for his patients, even everyday casual interactions can have serious clinical consequences for his patients, some of whom may have paranoia or post-traumatic stress disorder. He explained:

> Cause I'm not there to participate in guiding that interaction. Should the family or the patient have a lot of angst or anxiety about seeing us, the interpreter won't be able to regulate that as well as if I was there. *So that may impact patient care* cause they are not gonna talk with us. Or they'll become too anxious and they'll kick us out or they're paranoid or afraid or angry.

Providers also welcomed interpreters taking a more active role because of their medical expertise. Nancy[NUR] explained, "If I feel that they've been a nurse or they've been a doctor or whatever, I'm little bit more comfortable to let them step over the boundary a little bit." Such an attitude was supported by some of our interpreters, who noted that, due to their medical background (e.g., being a nurse or a physician in their home country), providers had asked them to perform tasks that are typically not associated with interpreters. Thus, not all interpreters are endowed with the same set of professional boundaries. In short, interpreters' role boundaries can vary drastically depending on the tasks, the clinical specialty, and the provider's knowledge of their background.

Finally, having control over the medical encounter is critical to providers as they feel the need to be in charge of interpreter-mediated interactions. Some providers were adamant that they have to be in charge of the medical encounter. For example, Nacia[NUR] said, "I consider [interpreters] colleagues, but ancillary services to mine. I welcome [interpreters' input]. But I still get to CALL it. [laugh] I'm still the leader." Candice[ONC] also argued, "The [patients'] bonding and the feeling of OWNERSHIP is to be with the doctor. This is COMING from a doctor. [...] [Interpreters] are not the communicator. They are ASSISTING the communication." These comments reflect the provider's sense of hierarchy within the healthcare team. In addition, some providers noted that because interpreters are the voices of others, it is critical that they are clear about whose voice (e.g., the provider's, the patient's, or their own) they are representing and do not hide behind others' voices. Role boundary is an important issue because *all* voices are conveyed through the interpreter, which creates difficulties for a patient in differentiating between the opinions of the doctor and those of the interpreter. When an interpreter's opinion is blended into the provider's narrative, the provider loses control over his or her own voice yet may still be held responsible for the information that is provided to the patient. Several providers raised the issues of liability and legality. Nancy[NUR] explained:

> I can tell that [the interpreter] tells them the extra stuff. You can just tell. And I was thinking, "I didn't say that, I didn't say all that." [...She] forgets her boundaries and then she jumps into our boundaries. Then, what happens is LEGALLY we are responsible for that.

C.4. Establishing Successful Patterns of Collaboration

Providers noted that repeated interactions with a particular interpreter are desirable in the trust-building process. In particular, both providers and interpreters noted that repeated interactions build trust through established patterns of collaboration. An established pattern of collaboration is an emergent and evolving coordination between the provider–interpreter pair that is established over time. Candice[ONC] noted:

> I know [some interpreters] personally. Often, I've worked with them more than once or twice. So, I know their style and they know mine. They know the words I use and all that. I mean, it's just better to have someone you know and trust.

Different pairs will have different dynamics and each pair's pattern of collaboration may be different. In addition, the established pattern of collaboration allows the pair to work comfortably with each other even when they deviate from the normative expectations of the previous dimensions of trust.

Provider–interpreter trust is enhanced through their established pattern of collaboration in the following ways. First, both providers and interpreters can become more efficient at anticipating each other's communicative needs. For example, providers may become more sensitive to expressions that may be confusing when translated into different languages and cultures. Shirley[1] mentioned that providers are often not aware of how their talk may cause confusion. She once asked a provider to clarify the term "giddy," which may mean dizziness, lighthearted, or impulsive. Her questioning not only allowed her to interpret accurately but also made the provider more vigilant about possible confusions. Many providers said that they appreciate interpreters' suggestions to modify their narratives in a way that is culturally appropriate. For example, several oncologists talked about how using the concept of soup to discuss the components of blood (e.g., red and white cells) may not be appropriate for cultures that have only purée soup. Interpreters have valuable knowledge that can help providers to find the best metaphor in those situations. By learning each other's communicative needs and objectives, both providers and interpreters may help each other to become better communicators in future interactions.

Second, both providers and interpreters learn to adapt to and appreciate each other's communicative styles (see also Chapter 6.C). Interpreters are trained to adopt a specialized style of speech, including a first-person interpreting style (e.g., talk as the original speaker), simultaneous interpreting (i.e., interpreting while other speakers are talking), and specific nonverbal strategies (e.g., avoiding eye contact). For example, Stella[I] explained, "I detach myself emotionally from many things that are going on there, and I look at the floor, and I look at the ceiling or something. And I make sure that they talk to each other." Roger[I] echoed, "I look at the floor, I look down, and I just interpret immediately what he said, or what she said." Several interpreters talked about how they educate providers and patients to talk appropriately in interpreter-mediated interactions. For example, Sophia[I] said that when she met clients for the first time, she would say, "I am gonna be just your voice. [...] Don't look at me, you have to look at [each other] because the conversation is with [him or her]." Interpreters' specialized style of speech aims to reinforce the provider–patient relationship and minimize their intrusion into the medical encounter. Many providers, however, commented on how interpreters' style of speech can be confusing and counterintuitive. Cory[ONC] noted, "Before you finish your sentence, they are already speaking. That really bugs the tar out of me. [...] And not looking at the person and not looking at me. [...] *It is distracting to everybody in the room.*" As a result, some interpreters modified their interpreting style (e.g., changing from simultaneous to consecutive interpreting) to accommodate the provider's preference. Several providers also learned to adapt to and *appreciate* interpreters' strategies. For example, Candice[ONC] said, "[The interpreter] would be talking AS I was talking and there was NO emotional reaction. Once *I got used to that style*, I kind of like it. Because the parents are looking at ME and reading MY nonverbal and MY emotions." Other providers made an effort to address the patients directly, even when their intuition was to look at the interpreter. In short, interpreter-mediated interactions require individuals to adopt communicative styles that are different from the monolingual norms. As providers become more aware of interpreters' communicative styles, they gain insights into the functions and values of these strategies and learn to modify their communicative behaviors accordingly. Once providers and interpreters have established their pattern of collaboration, they do not question each other's awkward ways of speaking but learn to collaborate in a way that best meets their communicative goals.

Third, interpreters gain the opportunity to become more familiar with clinic-specific procedures. Many interpreters emphasized the importance of on-the-job training to complement their 40-hour training program. Some interpreters talked about their preferred clinics because they know the providers and the procedures of those clinics better. Many providers echoed the notion of having the *same* interpreter for their everyday tasks to ensure and improve the quality of interpreting. Providers emphasized that such a practice would increase the interpreter's familiarity with their routine talk, allowing them to provide better interpreting. In addition, providers argued that an interpreter who is familiar with their medical talk can be extremely valuable. For example, they can notice the variations across different patients, and be able to alert the provider if something warrants additional attention. Mindy[MH] explained, "It's like a baseline. If it's a skilled interpreter and they've seen many people coming with this problem, and this particular person is discussing it in a totally different way, then, I would want to know that." Several providers talked about incidents in which experienced interpreters reminded them about information that they forgot to ask or include in their routine procedure, arguing that the interpreter's active monitoring allows them to provide better care. Interpreters are thus trusted to have a certain level of medical expertise that is based on their familiarity with the clinic-specific procedures and medical dialogue.

It is important to note that it is not common practice to consistently send the same interpreter to the same clinic, provider, or patient. In fact, several managers commented that they intentionally avoid keeping the same patient–interpreter pair too long to avoid the development of patient–interpreter bonds. However, because the patient is likely to have the same provider throughout the course of their illness, changing the interpreter will also change the provider–interpreter pair. This practice may weaken the provider–interpreter trust because the new pair need to adapt to each other's communicative style again and develop new styles for collaboration.

C.5. A Caveat or Two

The four dimensions discussed above are interdependent, functioning simultaneously to construct provider–interpreter trust. Although interpreters' competence is mainly evaluated through their neutrality, other dimensions suggest that deviation from the conduit role is acceptable and even appreciated when certain requirements are met. Nevertheless, interpreters' active interventions may reinforce certain dimensions (e.g., shared goals) while posing risks to others (e.g., role boundaries). Trust building is therefore not a zero-sum game for each individual dimension but a delicate balance between all four dimensions. For example, if an interpreter is working with a provider for the first time, he or she can still gain trust through neutrality. When deviating from a conduit role, interpreters can still secure trust by emphasizing their efforts to maintain shared goals or explaining why their interventions are still within the bounds of their professional responsibilities. When significant trust is built through repeated interactions, an interpreter may even reshape their professional boundaries, being trusted with medically related responsibilities.

In addition, providers are not always consistent in their evaluation of interpreters' trustworthiness through these dimensions. During the interviews, several providers noticed how their expectations of interpreters contradict one another. Different providers may also have different criteria and expectations in evaluating an interpreter's trustworthiness. Because providers have different expectations, the same communicative behavior may be viewed as trust building by one provider and trust compromising by another. Finally, these dimensions of trust may vary significantly due to the history of the provider–interpreter pair. An interpreter may be trusted with medical responsibilities by one provider but not another. In short, these dimensions represent a set of multidimensional and situational expectations that are placed on interpreters, requiring them to be adaptive and responsive to providers' needs. They are best understood as situational and contextual guidelines, rather than fixed standards, to build trust.

D. Implications for Theory Development and Healthcare Delivery

By identifying the factors that shape providers' choice of interpreter and build provider–interpreter trust, I have demonstrated that providers' understanding of interpreter-mediated interactions is often shaped by multi-level factors, including clinical demands and organizational considerations. In addition, their choices are motivated by not only interpreters' ability to provide accurate information but also their ability to accomplish other goals, including forming alliances and facilitating the provider's therapeutic objectives.

In the following section, I will examine how our findings about providers' perspectives can guide us in theory development and healthcare delivery.

D.1. Problematizing Providers' Taken-for-granted Behaviors and Assumptions

Our findings suggest that providers have very specific criteria as they make decisions about the appropriateness of their choice of interpreters. These are also supported by other studies (Cohen, Moran-Ellis, & Smaje, 1999; Diamond et al., 2012; Maul, Regenstein, Andres, Wright, & Wynia, 2012). The different types of interpreter and interpreting modalities should be viewed as complementary, rather than competing or interchangeable, services. Depending on the tasks involved, a specific type of interpreter may be acceptable, preferred, or even required. For example, informed consent requires professional interpreters. When emotional support is needed, on-site interpreters, regardless of training, are often preferred over telephone interpreters. Depending on clinical urgency, a child interpreter can be better than a professional phone interpreter, who may have poor sound quality, is unable to observe nonverbal details, and requires significant coordination between all parties involved. When it is just a simple procedure, a provider may feel silly, if not time consuming, for calling in a professional interpreter. With only 10 weeks of medical Spanish, providers were found to reduce their use of interpreters but experienced an increase in patient satisfaction (Mazor, Hampers, Chande, & Krug, 2002). In short, the providers in our study made calculated decisions on the type of interpreter that was appropriate for the tasks and goals involved in the particular medical encounter.

At the surface level, providers' behaviors and decisions may appear reasonable and practical as they manage competing demands in patient care. However, it is important to identify and critically examine providers' normative rules and their corresponding impacts. After all, if the provider's assumptions or basis for assessment are problematic or unfounded, their decisions will inevitably be flawed.

For example, a provider's desire to control interpreter-mediated interactions can, in fact, compromise the quality of care. A study found that when there is poor mutual understanding, language-concordant patients are likely to continue to pursue their communicative agenda whereas language-discordant patients are likely to be silenced by the provider's increased control over the content and process of communication (Meeuwesen, Tromp, Schouten, & Harmsen, 2007). In fact, when compared to communicating with language-concordant patients, providers are likely to spend more time directly advising language-discordant patients and less time engaging them in the decision-making process (Butow, Bell, et al., 2011; Schouten, Meeuwesen, Tromp, & Harmsen, 2007). Increasing control over the communicative process when there is miscommunication can, in fact, further silence the patient's voice.

Providers may overestimate their linguistic skills or view communication as a means of gathering clinical information (as opposed to addressing patients' concerns) (Diamond et al., 2009, 2012). As a result, providers may feel satisfied because their informational needs have been met although they have failed to address their patient's informational and emotional needs. The increase in patient satisfaction (Mazor et al., 2002) may be a result of rapport building rather than patients' improved comprehension.

Providers' trust in interpreters may be misplaced if they are not reflective about their relationships with and assumptions about a particular interpreter. When providers assume that hospital interpreters (a) are certified when there is no federal or state certification available to these interpreters or (b) have more training than they actually do (i.e., 40 hours), they may underestimate the complexity of the tasks they impose on interpreters. Similarly, it can be problematic when they do not raise concerns about whether their bilingual colleagues have sufficient cultural competence when one in five dual-role staff interpreters had insufficient bilingual skills to serve as a medical interpreter (Moreno, Otero-Sabogal, & Newman, 2007). Providers' uncorroborated assumptions can pose potential threats to the quality of care.

Expecting interpreters to anticipate their communicative goals and (re)direct patients' narratives can reduce providers' control over the content and process of interpreter-mediated encounters. Our providers did not appear to be aware of their competing and often conflicting demands on interpreters. As such, interpreters may find it challenging to meet providers' needs and expectations, as fulfilling one may compromise the other.

In summary, a normative approach to bilingual health care does not simply accept providers' behaviors or attitudes. By identifying and critically examining providers' normative rules, both researchers and practitioners can generate a solid foundation to advance theory and improve practice by identifying potential intervention points. From this perspective, researchers and healthcare organizations need to (a) identify problematic assumptions held by providers and (b) develop appropriate guidelines and environmental resources to facilitate providers' decision-making.

D.2. Necessary Support from Organizational Resources and Policies

Policymakers and researchers are often at a loss when providers underutilize professional interpreters even though they are readily available. It is important to note that providers' behavioral norms are often shaped by organizational resources and guidelines. Our study found that providers do not have control over many factors (e.g., clinical urgency, patient receptiveness, or resource limitations) in their choice of medical interpreter. For example, organizational settings (e.g., managed care systems, teaching hospitals, medical research centers, independent clinics, or single-specialty medical groups) differ significantly in their utilization of interpreters (Gadon, Balch, & Jacobs, 2007; Rose et al., 2010). We found that a provider may need to use a family interpreter or a same-gender untrained interpreter to ensure patient receptiveness. Even though bilingual co-workers are available, they may choose to communicate with their LEP patient using their limited Spanish because their co-workers are already overwhelmed by their regular workload. A recent study found that bilingual residents spent a mean of 2.3 hours per week interpreting for other residents (O'Leary, Federico, & Hampers, 2003). Although many studies have noted the value of videoconferencing interpreting (Lion et al., in press; Locatis et al., 2010; Nápoles et al., 2010), providers do not always have access to such services due to organizational or environmental limitations. By not jumping to the conclusion that providers have failed the system, researchers and practitioners will be able to identify realistic policies and guidelines for flexible, effective, and ethical utilization of medical interpreters.

For factors that are beyond the provider's control, it critical for organizational structures and norms to respond to these issues. Organizational resources and guidelines need to be consistent with policy and desired professional norms. For example, one study found that providers in emergency medicine rarely use telephone interpreters because of "delays in contacting an interpreter in the required language and limited access to phones at the patient bedside" (Kazzi & Cooper, 2003, p. 262). To resolve the problem, the healthcare organization will need to modify the exam room to address the logistics of using a phone interpreter (e.g., good quality speaker phones that are easily accessible, secure conversations to respect patient privacy, and speed dial for interpreters of frequently requested languages). Availability of interpreters is meaningless without logistical and organizational support. Similarly, if organizations recruit bilingual staff with the intention of having them serve as a stationed interpreter for a specific clinic, it is essential to develop organizational policies to address the allocation and expectations of their responsibilities and workload. By doing so, other providers would feel more comfortable in requesting their assistance and thus decrease the likelihood of avoiding or minimizing communication when working with language-discordant patients. In short, our study highlights the important role of healthcare organizations in developing and supporting the appropriate and desirable use of interpreters (see also Chan et al., 2010; Karliner & Mutha, 2010).

D.3. Utilitarian Approach versus the Conduit Model

At the beginning of this section, I ask: How do providers reconcile the competing expectations of interpreter as provider proxy and interpreter as a conduit? Findings from my studies suggest that the conduit model is only one of the ways in which providers use interpreters as an instrument. The conduit model limits interpreters' power by objectifying them as language-transferring machines (Leanza, 2008), a restricted role that silences interpreters' voices. In contrast, a utilitarian approach is far more complicated and extensive in shaping interpreters' roles and functions: Interpreters as a whole, including their physical presence, emotions, and interpersonal relationships, are viewed as instruments to accomplish the provider's goals.

While the conduit model views all speakers' voices as equal (except the interpreter's voice), the utilitarian approach identified in our study privileges the provider's voice. Interpreters have been found to be biased toward providers' (as opposed to patients') perspectives, even when they are familiar with the conduit model (Bolden, 2000; Elderkin-Thompson, Silver, & Waitzkin, 2001; Kaufert & Koolage, 1984). We suspect that this is because the utilitarian approach has superseded the conduit model in guiding both providers' and interpreters' practices in bilingual health care. Despite healthcare communities' emphasis on a team approach and open communication (Dieleman et al., 2004), the utilitarian approach involves the presumption that the interpreter, while a part of the healthcare process and team, is also somewhat peripheral to the process, playing an auxiliary or supporting role. The interpreter's voice is silenced. More importantly, the patient's voice is marginalized as interpreters are expected to redirect patients and filter information when the discussion becomes irrelevant to the provider's agenda.

Our findings echo recent findings about differences between providers' communicative behaviors with language-concordant compared to language-discordant patients. In particular, when communicating with language-discordant patients, physicians are less likely to involve them in decision-making processes, less likely to check for their understanding, less likely to engage in rapport talk, less likely to respond to patients' emotional cues, and spend less time talking about cancer-related issues, but more time giving direct advice (Butow, Bell, et al., 2011; Schouten, Meeuwesen, & Harmsen, 2009; Seale, Rivas, & Kelly, 2013). These communicative patterns remained even when interpreters were present. Although researchers have observed these differences, little has been theorized about them.

I suspect that the utilitarian approach to interpreters and to bilingual health communication may have contributed to these patterns. For example, researchers have documented interpreters' tendency to overlook rapport talk and patients' emotional cues (Butow, Bell, et al., 2011), which may be a result of them acting as information-gatekeepers by screening out "non-medically relevant" information. A utilitarian approach to interpreters is likely to lead to a functional, pragmatic, one-sided view of provider–patient interactions, resulting in an emphasis on providers' (as opposed to other participants') needs and goals. In addition, the utilitarian approach can lead to divergent understanding about the success of a medical encounter (e.g., a provider may feel that all communicative goals have been met when the patient and/or the interpreter feels otherwise).

D.4. Conceptualizing the Interpreter as a Resourceful Utility

A humanistic, patient-centered approach requires providers to be attentive to patients' emotional needs (Bleakley & Bligh, 2009), which is echoed by our providers as they emphasize the interpreter's role in offering emotional support. Interpreters' ability to offer an emotional side of care is particularly salient as language-discordant patients often find them to be their primary, if not their only, link to a foreign world. Restrictions in suppressing interpreters' emotional support to patients may create tensions (Hsieh, 2008). Patients may place such tremendous trust in interpreters that they in fact become an "honorary family member" simply because of their "commonality in language, ethnicity and country of origin" (Robb & Greenhalgh, 2006, p. 441). As a result, interpreters may have substantial power in influencing the patient's attitudes and treatment decisions. Providers are keenly aware of interpreters' interpersonal functions and emotion work in healthcare settings. Our findings, however, suggest that they *rely* on it and strategically utilize it to their advantage (rather than addressing patients' emotional needs). This finding is disturbing considering that several studies have also found that interpreters are more likely to be biased toward providers' (as opposed to patients') perspectives (Bolden, 2000; Elderkin-Thompson et al., 2001; Kaufert & Koolage, 1984).

Our findings highlight the normative framework that providers have in their use of and relationships with interpreters. First, interpreters' interpersonal relationships and rapport with patients can be viewed as resources to providers. A utilitarian approach to interpreters' interpersonal functions may motivate providers to objectify interpreters' rapport with patients. Providers may consider family interpreters a valuable option when the family interpreter shows that they share the same goals and therapeutic objectives as the provider. In contrast, when a professional interpreter is unable to accomplish the provider's therapeutic objectives, the interpreter may be perceived to be incompetent or untrustworthy. This attitude is situated in the larger understanding that interpreters are subject to providers' control, as a supporting team member or even a tool that serves at the pleasure of the provider. This also highlights the goal-driven nature of providers' choices of interpreters and understanding of interpreter-mediated encounters.

Second, providers are flexible and accommodating when they can trust interpreters' ability and willingness to maintain therapeutic alliances by (a) honoring clear boundaries between the provider's and the interpreter's voice, *and* (b) recognizing provider's needs. Although therapeutic alliances with professional interpreters are presumed to be part of their organizational relationships and identities, our providers appear to have a broader understanding of alliances. For some providers, alliances are not dyadic between a provider and an interpreter, but triadic. To achieve optimal care, providers are willing to compromise on certain issues as they recognize gains in other areas. For example, an assertive male family interpreter who makes decisions for the female patient may not meet a provider's desire for patient autonomy, but many providers also recognize such practices as cultural norms. They argue that insisting on a professional interpreter and excluding the male family relative in the interpreter-mediated encounter may, in fact, create patient anxiety and distrustful relationships. When they recognize interpreters' familiarities in the clinical knowledge and procedures, they welcome interpreters' active involvement during the encounter (e.g., checking understanding or reminders of missed topics). In other words, our findings suggest that there are situations in which providers do not expect complete control over the process and content of the provider–patient interaction. When specific criteria are met, they are willing to accept and, in fact, welcome interpreters' active involvement in the communicative process. Again, it is important to examine providers' normative rules in determining the specific criteria and assess whether such rules and criteria are appropriate.

Finally, when interpreters are viewed as passive instruments, a utilitarian approach may compromise the quality of care by silencing patients' and interpreters' voices, objectifying interpreters' emotion work, and exploiting patients' needs. However, our providers demonstrate that they can incorporate interpreters in the communicative process in a different way. I propose that interpreters should be viewed as a form of smart technology rather than a passive instrument to be wielded by users. Whereas a hammer does not have control over its use or develop new skills over time, an intelligent program not only accommodates and learns from its users' needs but also sets clear parameters for its functionality. Because of the changing boundaries of medicine, culture, and language in bilingual medical encounters, providers and interpreters often need to negotiate their roles, responsibilities, and expertise (Hsieh, 2010). Although our findings suggest providers have used interpreters mostly as passive instruments, expecting interpreters to "not speak unless spoken to" fails to recognize the complex utility an interpreter can offer in culturally sensitive care (Hsieh & Hong, 2010; Tribe & Tunariu, 2009). When interpreters are viewed as smart technology, there will be a mutual learning process between the interpreter and the provider. For example, a provider may trust a particular interpreter to assume more responsibilities (e.g., filter information or obtain consent) over time when they are familiar with the interpreter's skills after long-term collaboration (Hsieh et al., 2010; MacPhail, 2014). Similarly, an interpreter may become better in his/her ability to anticipate a provider's needs and objectives and in his/her knowledge about illness-specific medical procedures and terminologies after working with a provider over a period of time.

A normative approach to providers' understanding of bilingual health care allows researchers and practitioners to identify meaningful intervention points. By examining providers' competing expectations about interpreters' roles and functions (e.g., interpreter as health professional versus interpreter as provider proxy; see Chapter 5.A), this line of research suggests that key predictors of providers' attitudes and behaviors are providers' communicative goals, their ability to maintain control over bilingual health communication, and the levels of provider–interpreter trust. By proposing a new way to conceptualize interpreter as utility (i.e., interpreter as smart technology), we create new possibilities for both providers and interpreters to accommodate, negotiate, and co-evolve with each other, allowing them to develop mutually agreeable and effective strategies to achieve their collaborative goal of optimal care (Kramer, 2011, 2013).

Notes

1   An earlier version of this section was published in the *Journal of General Internal Medicine* (Hsieh, 2015). Using the data set from the providers' interviews (see Chapter 3.C.2) and grounded theory, I examined the various factors that shape providers' choice of interpreter. For details about data analysis, please see Hsieh (2015).

2   Using interviews with providers and interpreters (see Chapter 3.B.3–4, and 3.C.2), my research team conducted constant comparative analysis to examine the dimensions and meanings of trust in the provider–interpreter relationship by exploring providers' evaluation of interpreters' trustworthiness and trust-building strategies. Findings in this section have been reported in an earlier publication (Hsieh, Ju, & Kong, 2010).

References

Abbe, M., Simon, C., Angiolillo, A., Ruccione, K., & Kodish, E. D. (2006). A survey of language barriers from the perspective of pediatric oncologists, interpreters, and parents. *Pediatric Blood & Cancer*, 47, 819–824.

Ainsworth-Vaughn, N. (1998). *Claiming power in doctor–patient talk*. New York: Oxford University Press.

Barnett, S. (1999). Clinical and cultural issues in caring for deaf people. *Family Medicine*, 31, 17–22.

Bauer, A. M., & Alegría, M. (2010). Impact of patient language proficiency and interpreter service use on the quality of psychiatric care: A systematic review. *Psychiatric Services*, 61, 765–773.

Bleakley, A., & Bligh, J. (2009). Who can resist Foucault? *Journal of Medicine and Philosophy*, 34, 368–383.

Bolden, G. B. (2000). Toward understanding practices of medical interpreting: Interpreters' involvement in history taking. *Discourse Studies*, 2, 387–419.

Bond, J., Bateman, J., & Nassrally, S. M. (2012). The role of ad-hoc interpreters in teaching communication skills with ethnic minorities. *Medical Teacher*, 34, 81.

Brämberg, E. B., & Sandman, L. (2013). Communication through in-person interpreters: A qualitative study of home care providers' and social workers' views. *Journal of Clinical Nursing*, 22, 159–167.

Brisset, C., Leanza, Y., & Laforest, K. (2013). Working with interpreters in health care: A systematic review and meta-ethnography of qualitative studies. *Patient Education and Counseling*, 91, 131–140.

Butow, P. N., Bell, M., Goldstein, D., Sze, M., Aldridge, L., Abdo, S., … Eisenbruch, M. (2011). Grappling with cultural differences; Communication between oncologists and immigrant cancer patients with and without interpreters. *Patient Education and Counseling*, 84, 398–405.

Butow, P. N., Goldstein, D., Bell, M. L., Sze, M., Aldridge, L. J., Abdo, S., … Eisenbruch, M. (2011). Interpretation in consultations with immigrant patients with cancer: How accurate is it? *Journal of Clinical Oncology*, 29, 2801–2807.

Butow, P. N., Lobb, E., Jefford, M., Goldstein, D., Eisenbruch, M., Girgis, A., … Schofield, P. (2012). A bridge between cultures: Interpreters' perspectives of consultations with migrant oncology patients. *Supportive Care in Cancer*, 20, 235–244.

Chan, Y.-F., Alagappan, K., Rella, J., Bentley, S., Soto-Greene, M., & Martin, M. (2010). Interpreter services in emergency medicine. *Journal of Emergency Medicine*, 38, 133–139.

Cohen, S., Moran-Ellis, J., & Smaje, C. (1999). Children as informal interpreters in GP consultations: Pragmatics and ideology. *Sociology of Health & Illness*, 21, 163–186.

Cunningham, H., Cushman, L. F., Akuete-Penn, C., & Meyer, D. D. (2008). Satisfaction with telephonic interpreters in pediatric care. *Journal of the National Medical Association*, 100, 429–434.

Davidson, B. (2001). Questions in cross-linguistic medical encounters: The role of the hospital interpreter. *Anthropological Quarterly*, 74, 170–178.

DeCamp, L. R., Kuo, D. Z., Flores, G., O'Connor, K., & Minkovitz, C. S. (2013). Changes in language services use by US pediatricians. *Pediatrics*, 132(2), e396–406.

Diamond, L. C., Schenker, Y., Curry, L., Bradley, E. H., & Fernandez, A. (2009). Getting by: Underuse of interpreters by resident physicians. *Journal of General Internal Medicine*, 24, 256–262.

Diamond, L. C., Tuot, D., & Karliner, L. (2012). The use of Spanish language skills by physicians and nurses: Policy implications for teaching and testing. *Journal of General Internal Medicine*, 27, 117–123.

Dieleman, S. L., Farris, K. B., Feeny, D., Johnson, J. A., Tsuyuki, R. T., & Brilliant, S. (2004). Primary health care teams: Team members' perceptions of the collaborative process. *Journal of Interprofessional Care*, 18, 75–78.

Dysart-Gale, D. (2005). Communication models, professionalization, and the work of medical interpreters. *Health Communication*, 17, 91–103.

Elderkin-Thompson, V., Silver, R. C., & Waitzkin, H. (2001). When nurses double as interpreters: A study of Spanish-speaking patients in a US primary care setting. *Social Science & Medicine*, 52, 1343–1358.

Fatahi, N., Hellstrom, M., Skott, C., & Mattsson, B. (2008). General practitioners' views on consultations with interpreters: A triad situation with complex issues. *Scandinavian Journal of Primary Health Care*, 26, 40–45.

Flores, G., Abreu, M., Barone, C. P., Bachur, R., & Lin, H. (2012). Errors of medical interpretation and their potential clinical consequences: A comparison of professional versus ad hoc versus no interpreters. *Annals of Emergency Medicine*, 60, 545–553.

Flores, G., Laws, M. B., Mayo, S. J., Zuckerman, B., Abreu, M., Medina, L., & Hardt, E. J. (2003). Errors in medical interpretation and their potential clinical consequences in pediatric encounters. *Pediatrics*, 111, 6–14.

Flores, G., Torres, S., Holmes, L. J., Salas-Lopez, D., Youdelman, M. K., & Tomany-Korman, S. C. (2008). Access to hospital interpreter services for limited English proficient patients in New Jersey: A statewide evaluation. *Journal of Health Care for the Poor and Underserved*, 19, 391–415.

Flynn, P. M., Ridgeway, J. L., Wieland, M. L., Williams, M. D., Haas, L. R., Kremers, W. K., & Breitkopf, C. R. (2013). Primary care utilization and mental health diagnoses among adult patients requiring interpreters: A retrospective cohort study. *Journal of General Internal Medicine*, 28, 386–391.

Gadon, M., Balch, G. I., & Jacobs, E. A. (2007). Caring for patients with limited English proficiency: The perspectives of small group practitioners. *Journal of General Internal Medicine*, 22, S341–346.

Ginde, A. A., Clark, S., & Camargo, C. A., Jr. (2009). Language barriers among patients in Boston emergency departments: Use of medical interpreters after passage of interpreter legislation. *Journal of Immigrant and Minority Health*, 11, 527–530.

Ginde, A. A., Sullivan, A. F., Corel, B., Caceres, J. A., & Camargo, C. A., Jr. (2010). Reevaluation of the effect of mandatory interpreter legislation on use of professional interpreters for ED patients with language barriers. *Patient Education and Counseling*, 81, 204–206.

Gray, B., Hilder, J., & Donaldson, H. (2011). Why do we not use trained interpreters for all patients with limited English proficiency? Is there a place for using family members? *Australian Journal of Primary Health*, 17, 240–249.

Green, J., Free, C., Bhavnani, V., & Newman, T. (2005). Translators and mediators: Bilingual young people's accounts of their interpreting work in health care. *Social Science & Medicine*, 60, 2097–2110.

Greenhalgh, T., Robb, N., & Scambler, G. (2006). Communicative and strategic action in interpreted consultations in primary health care: A Habermasian perspective. *Social Science & Medicine*, 63, 1170–1187.

Grover, A., Deakyne, S., Bajaj, L., & Roosevelt, G. E. (2012). Comparison of throughput times for limited English proficiency patient visits in the emergency department between different interpreter modalities. *Journal of Immigrant and Minority Health*, 14, 602–607.

Hampers, L. C., & McNulty, J. E. (2002). Professional interpreters and bilingual physicians in a pediatric emergency department: Effect on resource utilization. *Archives of Pediatrics and Adolescent Medicine*, 156, 1108–1113.

Hsieh, E. (2006). Conflicts in how interpreters manage their roles in provider–patient interactions. *Social Science & Medicine*, 62, 721–730.

Hsieh, E. (2007). Interpreters as co-diagnosticians: Overlapping roles and services between providers and interpreters. *Social Science & Medicine*, 64, 924–937.

Hsieh, E. (2008). "I am not a robot!" Interpreters' views of their roles in health care settings. *Qualitative Health Research*, 18, 1367–1383.

Hsieh, E. (2010). Provider–interpreter collaboration in bilingual health care: Competitions of control over interpreter-mediated interactions. *Patient Education and Counseling*, 78, 154–159.

Hsieh, E. (2015). Not just "getting by": Factors influencing providers' choice of interpreters. *Journal of General Internal Medicine*, 30, 75–82.

Hsieh, E., & Hong, S. J. (2010). Not all are desired: Providers' views on interpreters' emotional support for patients. *Patient Education and Counseling*, 81, 192–197.

Hsieh, E., Ju, H., & Kong, H. (2010). Dimensions of trust: The tensions and challenges in provider–interpreter trust. *Qualitative Health Research*, 20, 170–181.

Hsieh, E., & Kramer, E. M. (2012). Medical interpreters as tools: Dangers and challenges in the utilitarian approach to interpreters' roles and functions. *Patient Education and Counseling*, 89, 158–162.

Jimenez, N., Moreno, G., Leng, M., Buchwald, D., & Morales, L. S. (2012). Patient-reported quality of pain treatment and use of interpreters in Spanish-speaking patients hospitalized for obstetric and gynecological care. *Journal of General Internal Medicine*, 27, 1602–1608.

Karliner, L. S., & Mutha, S. (2010). Achieving quality in health care through language access services: Lessons from a California public hospital. *American Journal of Medical Quality*, 25, 51–59.

Kaufert, J. M. (1999). Cultural mediation in cancer diagnosis and end of life decision-making: The experience of Aboriginal patients in Canada. *Anthropology & Medicine*, 6, 405–421.

Kaufert, J. M., & Koolage, W. W. (1984). Role conflict among 'culture brokers': The experience of native Canadian medical interpreters. *Social Science & Medicine*, 18, 283–286.

Kazzi, G. B., & Cooper, C. (2003). Barriers to the use of interpreters in emergency room paediatric consultations. *Journal of Paediatrics and Child Health*, 39, 259–263.

Keenan, G. M., Cooke, R., & Hillis, S. L. (1998). Norms and nurse management of conflicts: Keys to understanding nurse-physician collaboration. *Research in Nursing and Health*, 21, 59–72.

Kramer, E. M. (2011). Preface. In S. Croucher & D. Cronn-Mills (Eds.), *Religious misperceptions: The case of Muslims and Christians in France and Britain*. New York: Hampton.

Kramer, E. M. (2013). Dimensional accrual and dissociation: An introduction. In J. Grace & E. M. Kramer (Eds.), *Communication, comparative cultures, and civilizations* (Vol. 3, pp. 123–184). New York: Hampton.

Kuo, D. Z., O'Connor, K. G., Flores, G., & Minkovitz, C. S. (2007). Pediatricians' use of language services for families with limited English proficiency. *Pediatrics*, 119, e920–927.

Leanza, Y. (2008). Community interpreter's power: The hazards of a disturbing attribute. *Journal of Medical Anthropology*, 31, 211–220.

Lindholm, M., Hargraves, J. L., Ferguson, W. J., & Reed, G. (2012). Professional language interpretation and inpatient length of stay and readmission rates. *Journal of General Internal Medicine, 27,* 1294–1299.

Lion, K. C., Brown, J. C., Ebel, B. E., Klein, E. J., Strelitz, B., Gutman, C. K., . . . Mangione-Smith, R. (in press). Effect of telephone vs video interpretation on parent comprehension, communication, and utilization in the pediatric emergency department: A randomized clinical trial. *JAMA Pediatrics.*

Locatis, C., Williamson, D., Gould-Kabler, C., Zone-Smith, L., Detzler, I., Roberson, J., . . . Ackerman, M. (2010). Comparing in-person, video, and telephonic medical interpretation. *Journal of General Internal Medicine, 25,* 345–350.

Lubrano di Ciccone, B., Brown, R. F., Gueguen, J. A., Bylund, C. L., & Kissane, D. W. (2010). Interviewing patients using interpreters in an oncology setting: Initial evaluation of a communication skills module. *Annals of Oncology, 21,* 27–32.

MacPhail, S. L. (2014, July 2). Expanding interpreter role to include advocacy and care coordination improves efficiency and leads to high patient and provider satisfaction. Retrieved March 14, 2015, from https://innovations.ahrq.gov/profiles/expanding-interpreter-role-include-advocacy-and-care-coordination-improves-efficiency-and

Maul, L., Regenstein, M., Andres, E., Wright, R., & Wynia, M. K. (2012). Using a risk assessment approach to determine which factors influence whether partially bilingual physicians rely on their non-English language skills or call an interpreter. *Joint Commission Journal on Quality & Patient Safety, 38,* 328–336.

Mazor, S. S., Hampers, L. C., Chande, V. T., & Krug, S. E. (2002). Teaching Spanish to pediatric emergency physicians: Effects on patient satisfaction. *Archives of Pediatrics & Adolescent Medicine, 156,* 693–695.

Meeuwesen, L., Tromp, F., Schouten, B. C., & Harmsen, J. A. M. (2007). Cultural differences in managing information during medical interaction: How does the physician get a clue? *Patient Education and Counseling, 67,* 183–190.

Meischke, H., Chavez, D., Bradley, S., Rea, T., & Eisenberg, M. (2010). Emergency communications with limited-English-proficiency populations. *Prehospital Emergency Care, 14,* 265–271.

Moreno, M. R., Otero-Sabogal, R., & Newman, J. (2007). Assessing dual-role staff-interpreter linguistic competency in an integrated healthcare system. *Journal of General Internal Medicine, 22,* S331–335.

Nápoles, A. M., Santoyo-Olsson, J., Karliner, L. S., O'Brien, H., Gregorich, S. E., & Pérez-Stable, E. J. (2010). Clinician ratings of interpreter mediated visits in underserved primary care settings with ad hoc, in-person professional, and video conferencing modes. *Journal of Health Care for the Poor and Underserved, 21,* 301–317.

Nugus, P., Greenfield, D., Travaglia, J., Westbrook, J., & Braithwaite, J. (2010). How and where clinicians exercise power: Interprofessional relations in health care. *Social Science & Medicine, 71,* 898–909.

O'Leary, S. C. B., Federico, S., & Hampers, L. C. (2003). The truth about language barriers: One residency program's experience. *Pediatrics, 111,* e569–573.

Papic, O., Malak, Z., & Rosenberg, E. (2012). Survey of family physicians' perspectives on management of immigrant patients: Attitudes, barriers, strategies, and training needs. *Patient Education and Counseling, 86,* 205–209.

Pearson, S. D., & Raeke, L. H. (2000). Patients' trust in physicians: Many theories, few measures, and little data. *Journal of General Internal Medicine, 15,* 509–513.

Pullon, S. (2008). Competence, respect and trust: Key features of successful interprofessional nurse-doctor relationships. *Journal of Interprofessional Care, 22,* 133–147.

Roat, C. E., Kinderman, A., & Fernandez, A. (2011). Interpreting in Palliative Care. Retrieved March 14, 2015, from http://www.chcf.org/publications/2011/11/interpreting-palliative-care-curriculum

Robb, N., & Greenhalgh, T. (2006). "You have to cover up the words of the doctor": The mediation of trust in interpreted consultations in primary care. *Journal of Health Organization & Management, 20*, 434–455.

Rose, D. E., Tisnado, D. M., Malin, J. L., Tao, M. L., Maggard, M. A., Adams, J., … Kahn, K. L. (2010). Use of interpreters by physicians treating limited English proficient women with breast cancer: Results from the provider survey of the Los Angeles Women's Health Study. *Health Services Research, 45*, 172–194.

Rosenberg, E., Leanza, Y., & Seller, R. (2007). Doctor-patient communication in primary care with an interpreter: Physician perceptions of professional and family interpreters. *Patient Education and Counseling, 67*, 286–292.

Rosenberg, E., Richard, C., Lussier, M.-T., & Shuldiner, T. (2011). The content of talk about health conditions and medications during appointments involving interpreters. *Family Practice, 28*, 317–322.

Rosenberg, E., Seller, R., & Leanza, Y. (2008). Through interpreters' eyes: Comparing roles of professional and family interpreters. *Patient Education and Counseling, 70*, 87–93.

Schenker, Y., Fernandez, A., Kerr, K., O'Riordan, D., & Pantilat, S. Z. (2012). Interpretation for discussions about end-of-life issues: Results from a national survey of health care interpreters. *Journal of Palliative Medicine, 15*, 1019–1026.

Schenker, Y., Pérez-Stable, E. J., Nickleach, D., & Karliner, L. S. (2011). Patterns of interpreter use for hospitalized patients with limited English proficiency. *Journal of General Internal Medicine, 26*, 712–717.

Schenker, Y., Wang, F., Selig, S. J., Ng, R., & Fernandez, A. (2007). The impact of language barriers on documentation of informed consent at a hospital with on-site interpreter services. *Journal of General Internal Medicine, 22*, 294–299.

Schouten, B. C., Meeuwesen, L., & Harmsen, H. A. M. (2009). GPs' interactional styles in consultations with Dutch and ethnic minority patients. *Journal of Immigrant and Minority Health, 11*, 468–475.

Schouten, B. C., Meeuwesen, L., Tromp, F., & Harmsen, H. A. M. (2007). Cultural diversity in patient participation: The influence of patients' characteristics and doctors' communicative behaviour. *Patient Education and Counseling, 67*, 214–223.

Seale, C., Rivas, C., & Kelly, M. (2013). The challenge of communication in interpreted consultations in diabetes care: A mixed methods study. *British Journal of General Practice, 63*, e125–e133.

Searight, H. R., & Armock, J. A. (2013). Foreign language interpreters in mental health: A literature review and research agenda. *North American Journal of Psychology, 15*, 17–38.

Seeleman, C., Essink-Bot, M.-L., Selleger, V., & Bonke, B. (2012). Authors' response to letter from Bond et al. – The role of ad-hoc interpreters in teaching communication skills with ethnic minorities. *Medical Teacher, 34*, 81–82.

Thornton, J. D., Pham, K., Engelberg, R. A., Jackson, J. C., & Curtis, J. R. (2009). Families with limited English proficiency receive less information and support in interpreted intensive care unit family conferences. *Critical Care Medicine, 37*, 89–95.

Tribe, R., & Tunariu, A. (2009). Mind your language: Working with interpreters in healthcare settings and therapeutic encounters. *Sexual and Relationship Therapy, 24*, 74–84.

VanderWielen, L. M., Enurah, A. S., Rho, H. Y., Nagarkatti-Gude, D. R., Michelsen-King, P., Crossman, S. H., & Vanderbilt, A. A. (2014). Medical interpreters: Improvements to address access, equity, and quality of care for limited-English-proficient patients. *Academic Medicine*, 89, 1324–1327.

Waitzkin, H. (1991). *The politics of medical encounters: How patients and doctors deal with social problems.* New Haven, CT: Yale University Press.

Weissman, J. S., Betancourt, J., Campbell, E. G., Park, E. R., Kim, M., Clarridge, B., ... Maina, A. W. (2005). Resident physicians' preparedness to provide cross-cultural care. *Journal of the American Medical Association*, 294, 1058–1067.

Youdelman, M. K. (2008). The medical tongue: US laws and policies on language access. *Health Affairs*, 27, 424–433.

8

INTERPRETER-MEDIATED ENCOUNTERS AS GOAL-ORIENTED COMMUNICATIVE ACTIVITY

Healthcare interpreting is a unique form of interpreting (see also Chapter 2.D) because it is ancillary to a larger communicative event, cross-cultural care, which often entails specific goals (e.g., achieving optimal care). Providing a neutral performance while contributing to compromised care cannot be considered an appropriate or acceptable performance. When a young resident fails to contain his excitement when seeing a severely ill patient and shouts with a big smile, "That's the worst case I've ever seen!", interpreting the same comment with equal enthusiasm does not help the quality of care nor improve the patient's experience of disparities or inequalities. When examining interpreter-mediated medical encounters, researchers found that interpreters actively mediated in the moral arena of provider–patient discourse by not interpreting nurses' potentially stigmatizing information that might reveal ignorance or rudeness (Seale, Rivas, Al-Sarraj, Webb, & Kelly, 2013). Raymond (2014) found that when there is a problematic interaction, interpreters assume the role of epistemic brokers and "valorize patients' experiences as relevant aspects of the medical encounter, as well as provide opportunities for providers to do the same." These examples highlight the fact that there is a higher value (i.e., Quality and Equality of Care; see Chapter 5.C.1) in healthcare interpreting beyond interpreter neutrality or faithfulness.

In this chapter, I will critically examine how the meaning of Quality and Equality of Care (QEC) is understood and enacted through individuals' management of communicative goals in interpreter-mediated encounters. In particular, I will examine how patient empowerment and patient autonomy are constructed and understood by interpreters and providers. Then, I will present two case studies, using (a) interpreters as co-diagnosticians and (b) interpreters' emotion work as examples, to explore the various normative tensions in QEC that make certain behaviors more or less effective and/or appropriate than others. By recognizing the diverging normative values, I will explore how a normative approach can predict or explain interpreters' strategies and the corresponding impacts on bilingual health care.

In this chapter, I will:

- discuss the meanings and social constructions of patient autonomy
- propose meaningful ways for interpreters to support patient empowerment
- examine the performance of interpreters as co-diagnosticians through a normative approach
- examine interpreters' emotion work through a normative approach.

A. Patient Autonomy and Patient Empowerment

Moving away from the traditional emphasis on the importance of and the necessity for interpreters to act as conduits (i.e., to transfer information neutrally without editorializing information) as the only way to ensure quality care, many researchers have now demonstrated that interpreters are active participants who systematically adopt purposeful strategies to improve a patient's health literacy (e.g., ability to seek, provide, and process information when communicating with providers), to protect institutional resources (Davidson, 2000), to reduce the cultural gap between the provider and the patient, to reconcile provider–patient conflicts, and to ensure the quality of provider–patient interactions (Hsieh, 2006). As researchers have noticed interpreters' active involvement in the communicative process, they have also questioned their ethics and raised concerns about how some of their communicative strategies may infringe on providers' authority or patients' autonomy (Hsieh, 2010; Leanza, 2008; Rosenberg, Seller, & Leanza, 2008).

In the following section, I will critically examine interpreters' influence on patient health literacy and patient empowerment, exploring its clinical, interpersonal, and ethical implications.[1]

A.1. Interpreters' Discursive Strategies for Patient Empowerment

Extending from previous studies that noted interpreters' active involvement in provider–patient interactions, the interpreters in my study adopt a variety of strategies aiming to improve patients' health literacy. English-speaking patients also struggle with health literacy (Kutner, Greenberg, Jin, & Paulsen, 2006). However, researchers have found that patients' active participation (e.g., asking questions, providing information) in provider–patient interactions can lead to an increase in providers' patient-centered communication (Cegala & Post, 2009) and better coordination between providers' and patients' goals (Cegala, Street, & Clinch, 2007). In this section, I will highlight two distinctive strategies employed by interpreters to facilitate provider–patient communication: (a) making inexplicit information explicit, and (b) providing means of self-efficacy for the patient.

Making Inexplicit Information Explicit

In everyday talk, people do not apprehend the meaning of an utterance just through what is said (i.e., the words uttered) but also make inferences of the speaker's intended meaning based on their understanding of the conventional norms and other relevant contexts (Grice, 1975). Inexplicit language requires the hearer to rely on contexts to understand the intended meaning (J. Lee, 2009). Because providers and patients do not share the same conventional norms or contexts in bilingual/cross-cultural health care, they are likely to experience miscommunication or confusion if an interpreter provides little assistance in helping them to be aware of the relevant contexts.

Interpreters can elaborate on a speaker's comment to improve a patient's ability to request services, to understand medical procedures, and to engage in effective provider–patient interactions. In Extract 1, Claire[1] elaborated the provider's comment to improve the patient's understanding.

> Extract 2[2]
> 201   H: Has she ever heard of Equal?
> 202   I: 你有沒有聽過Equal?英文叫Equal的這個糖,代糖,他們叫代
> 203   糖, 不是真正自然生產的糖,他們叫代糖,老美叫代糖。名
> 204   牌叫
> 205   Equal。
> 206   (Have you heard of Equal? The English term for this
> 207   sugar, Equal, they call it substitute sugar, it's not a naturally
> 208   produced sugar.
> 209   They call it substitute sugar. Americans call it substitute sugar;
> 210   the brand name is Equal.)
> 211   P: 不知道
> 212   (No.)
> 213   I: No.

Claire's elaboration of the term Equal helps the patient to better understand the provider's information by giving background information about what substitute sugar is and that Equal is just a brand name. When communicating with one another, people often make culture-specific inferences and assumptions that are embedded in their language practices. These inferences and assumptions, however, may not be transferable to another language and culture (also see J. Lee, 2009). Interpreters' familiarity with the social norms and cultural knowledge can be valuable in ensuring accurate and effective exchange of information between providers and patients.

It is important to note that these cultural differences are not always transparent; as a result, an interpreter's ability to detect and clarify the divergent understanding between the provider and the patient can be critical in ensuring quality of care. The following interaction took place during an education session in which a dietician was educating a patient with gestational diabetes about portion size.

Extract 3

301	H:	One-third of a cup of rice is a serving.
302	I:	三分之一杯的煮熟的米飯就是,一個分量。
303		(One-third of a cup of cooked rice is a serving.)
304	H:	Does she have measuring cups at home?
305	I:	家裡有沒有量杯?
306		(Do you have a measuring cup at home?)
307		P: 就是米飯的那個杯子。
308		(Just the cup for rice.)
309	I:	Is it the same measuring cup for rice?
310	H:	hmhm, yes.
311	P:	都是一樣的。
312		(It's the same.)
313	I:	Is it the same?
314	H:	The-
315	I:	Are they?
316	H:	I don't know what she is referring to. I'll show her what
317		I have.
318	I:	她有一個。
319		(She has one.)
320		(H took out a glass measuring cup from the drawer.)
321	P:	這麼大阿!
322		(That's big!)

Claire[I] adopted several strategies here that are critical to the patient's health literacy. First, she used "cooked rice" (line 302) rather than the term "rice" (line 301) used by the provider. Recognizing that there are significant portion size differences between cooked versus uncooked rice (i.e., one cup of uncooked rice makes about three cups of cooked rice), Claire[I] preemptively changed the provider's term, while keeping the provider's comment accurate, to ensure that the patient did not misunderstand the provider's comments.

Second, when the patient made statements (i.e., "just the cup for rice" [line 307] and "it's the same" [line 311]), Claire[I] modified the statements into direct information-seeking questions. Previous studies in provider–patient communication have found that due to the power differences between providers and patients, patients often (a) do not ask questions even when they desire more information, and (b) when they do, they avoid using direct questions when seeking information from their providers (Cegala, 1997). Instead of treating the patient's assertion (which may be a form of embedded question) as a statement, Claire[1] changed it to a direct question to seek and clarify information ("Is it the same measuring cup for rice?" [line 309]). Similarly, when the patient acknowledged the provider's confirmation (line 310) by restating the implications ("It's the same." [line 311]), Claire[1] treated the patient's utterance as an active information-seeking question (line 313). In fact, Claire[1]'s persistence in seeking and verifying the information exposed a miscommunication that would have been originally ignored by the provider. Claire[1]'s direct question ("is it the same?" [line 313]) and its restatement ("Are they?" [line 315]) forced the provider to admit potential misunderstanding ("I don't know what she's referring to.") and to resolve the problem ("I'll show her what I have."). The patient's comment on line 321 ("That's big!") showed that there was a real difference in the size of measuring cups that the provider and the patient had in mind and that there could have been significant clinical consequences had Claire[1] not insisted on pursuing accurate information.

Third, an important feature in this interaction is how closely Claire[1] followed the patient's narrative, but at the same time changed its nature. Claire[1]'s strategies could not be categorized as neutral or faithful; yet, these strategies are essential in facilitating provider–patient communication. By explicitly stating the inexplicit information (e.g., "cooked rice" as opposed to "rice"), Claire[1] also improved the patient's ability to understand the information accurately and effectively. Because of the power differences, a patient may not feel comfortable to ask the provider a direct question. For example, a patient may say, "I feel tired all the time," instead of asking "Is fatigue a side effect of the medication?"

Recent studies have highlighted that the quality of provider–patient communication is co-constructed through both the provider's and the patient's communicative behaviors. For example, providers are more likely to offer more information when patients adopt direct information-seeking strategies (e.g., direct questions) as opposed to indirect information-seeking strategies (e.g., assertions as embedded questions; Cegala, Post, & McClure, 2001). However, minority and marginalized populations are more likely to have lower health literacy (Osborn et al., 2011; Shaw, Huebner, Armin, Orzech, & Vivian, 2009) and to adopt a submissive communicative style even when they experience poor understanding (Butow, Bell, et al., 2011; Schouten & Meeuwesen, 2006). In the excerpts above, a passive, word-by-word interpreting style would have ended up reinforcing the problematic information exchanges. By reformulating the patient's narratives into active information-seeking strategies, Claire[1] significantly increased the patient's ability to seek information.

Providing Means of Self-advocacy

In addition to modifying others' utterances to enhance patients' health literacy, interpreters may enhance a patient's quality of care through providing means of self-advocacy. By providing means of self-advocacy, interpreters provide patients with access to resources available in various areas (e.g., medical knowledge and relevant information). This is different from the advocate role defined by interpreters' training, which involves "any action an interpreter takes on *behalf of the patient outside* [italics added] the bounds of an interpreted interview" (Roat, Putsch, & Lucero, 1997, pp. 17–18) to rectify problematic situations (e.g., inequality or injustice of healthcare services). Interpreters in the advocate role require patients to accept other-advocacy; in contrast, by providing means of self-advocacy to patients, interpreters empower patients to act as self-advocates.

Interpreters' familiarity with topic transitions and information flow allows patients to communicate in a way that is consistent with providers' expectations and management of the medical encounter. In Extract 4, in an earlier conversation with the interpreter, the patient had indicated her concerns that her baby was losing weight. After the provider asked the mother about her feeding pattern, Christine[I] initiated the following information exchange sequence.

Extract 4
401   I: 你是不是要問醫生她今天量的體重比出生的時候還要少?
402   (Didn't you want to ask the doctor why she is weighing less today
403   than when she was born?)
404   P: 對啊。
405   (Yes.)
406   I: Another question, before, the nurse weighed her, and she
407   was born 7 pounds 11 oz., then today, the weight is only- It lost
408   about 6 oz.
409   H: 6 oz. It's normal.
410   I: 她說這是正常的。
411   (She said it's normal.)

The interaction between Christine[I] and the provider in lines 406–409 is consistent with the earlier discussion in which the interpreter issued a direct question while making inexplicit information explicit. Christine[I] not only provided the baby's original birth weight but also highlighted the amount of weight loss. The information had been obtained in a previous conversation with a nurse but not with the current provider. Christine's[I] use of meta-communication (i.e., "another question") and inclusion of the exact amount of weight loss (i.e., 6 oz.) allows the provider to respond to and evaluate the patient's concerns more effectively.

What is particularly interesting in this interaction, however, is that when Christine[I] first initiated the question (line 401), it was directed to the patient. Christine[I] might have felt that the patient's concern was appropriate as the next topic after the information exchanged about the baby's feeding patterns. Such a judgment requires an ability to understand the norm of information exchange patterns in provider–patient interactions, which an interpreter may have more experience with than a patient. In the interviews, several interpreters noted that they often remind and prompt patients about topics to discuss with the provider. By directing the question to the patient first (as opposed to directing the question to the provider), the patient is empowered to have control over the provider–patient interaction and socialized into the norms of topic transitions. In the future, the patient may be able to initiate a question without the interpreter's assistance. In other words, the interpreter's strategy in Extract 4 not only allowed the patient to have control over the topics discussed in the current interaction but also educated her about the norms of future provider–patient interactions.

An interpreter may also coach a patient about *how* to request proper services or information. In Extract 5, the patient complained that the hospital provided water with ice for her to drink after her delivery, a practice that contradicts a Chinese custom which specifies that women should only drink hot water after delivery.

Extract 5

501 P: Yeah, 我這天-我兩天在醫院都是喝冰水。

502   (Yeah, these days- I drank chilled water in the hospital.)

503 I: 其實醫院它有熱開水,你跟護士講, 她就會給你熱開水。

504   (Actually, they have hot water in the hospital. If you tell the

505   nurse, she'd give you hot water.)

506 P: 我說-我說給她聽, 我不要ice,它都不是凍的, 她就沒有放

507   ice。

508   (I said- I told her that I don't want ice. So, it's not icy. She

509   didn't put ice in it).

510 I: 沒有放冰,對對。 你應該跟她說hot water。

511   (No ice. Right. Right. You should tell her, "hot water.")

512 P: Hot water.

This interaction happened when the patient and Christine[l] were alone in the exam room, waiting for the provider. Christine[l] informed the patient about services available in the hospital (line 503) and the proper way to ask for the services (line 510). Christine[l] used the English term "hot water" (line 510) instead of saying its equivalent Chinese term, showing that Christine[l] was providing the patient with the tool to obtain the services. The patient's verification of the information and repetition of the English term in line 512 shows that she understood Christine's[l] communicative goal of empowering the patient.

Patients who are from a different culture and/or society may not be familiar with the kinds of services available, their rights as patients, or the appropriate norms of provider–patient interaction. Because interpreters are familiar with the typical exchanges in medical encounters and have observed successful and problematic provider–patient interactions, they can be extremely helpful and valuable in assisting patients to navigate the healthcare system. Stacy[1] explained:

> Because [patients] might be worried, but they don't know what they are worried about. So, I ask them, 'Would you like to ask if taking that medication has side effects?' So, I help them to understand some of the procedures and foresee something so that they would not worry about later on.

Sara[1], another interpreter, talked about a situation in which a Spanish-speaking father explicitly told her that he did not know what questions to ask; in response, she coached him to ask the physician to provide clarification of the diagnosis, to discuss alternative treatments, and to explain long-term consequences of the disease. In another case, after witnessing a provider's prejudicial attitude, Colin[1] informed the patient that if he wished to file a complaint, he would be able to take him to the complaint office and interpret for him. In such situations, by providing access to illness-related information and healthcare facilities, interpreters significantly enhance the patient's abilities to obtain quality care.

A.2. Patient Empowerment and Patient Autonomy in Bilingual Health Care

It is important to recognize that interpreters' involvement and intervention is not without limits (Hsieh, 2010). A few interpreters in our study raised concerns that their active involvement might infringe on patient autonomy (i.e., the patient's right to make decisions without the influence of providers and/or other health professionals). Shirley[1], manager of the interpreter office of a major hospital and a trainer of an interpreting program, explained, "By NOT empowering, by giving your opinion, going immediately into an advocacy role as a medical interpreter, I feel that you keep [that patient], that parent or that guardian, or primary caretaker, from becoming empowered." Sharon[1], the director of an interpreting agency, echoed, "They do more harm than good when you try to be more than an interpreter, when you try to be an advocate for the patient." Although acting as direct advocates (e.g., acting on behalf of the patient without the patient's or provider's explicit consent) may be efficient in meeting the patient's needs (Hsieh, 2008; Messias, McDowell, & Estrada, 2009; Rosenberg et al., 2008), such strategies may blur the lines between the patient's and the interpreter's agendas and communicative goals (Hsieh & Kramer, 2012; Leanza, Boivin, & Rosenberg, 2010; Rosenberg et al., 2008).

Although patient empowerment is often perceived as the communicative goal of the advocate role (Hsieh, 2008), some interpreters argued that advocating for patients or acting on a patient's behalf can be problematic because it compromises patient empowerment. From this perspective, the best form of patient empowerment is to allow patients to have full control over the medical encounter without the influence of the interpreter (see Hsieh, 2008). The emphasis on patient autonomy echoes the traditional emphasis of the conduit as the interpreter's default role, in which they are only the voices of others (Hsieh, 2009; Kaufert & Putsch, 1997; Messias et al., 2009). In the United States, patient autonomy emerged in the 1960s in the overall atmosphere of anti-paternalism and redefined beneficence as medical paternalism (Rothman, 2001). As a result, an ideal patient is an informed patient who is capable and willing to assume all responsibilities in their illness events (Kapp, 2007).

Fundamental to the debates about whether interpreters should intervene in problematic provider–patient interactions is the meaning of Quality of Care. Can quality of care be achieved when patients' voices are infringed by interpreters?

Conceptualizing interpreters' non-interference as respect to patient autonomy, however, is based on problematic assumptions. The interpreter-as-conduit model assumes that: (a) all participants are competent speakers who can communicate effectively and appropriately, (b) it is desirable to maintain the existing structure of relationships and patterns of communication, and (c) there are minimal differences between speakers' cultural knowledge and social practices. However, medical interpreters do not operate on a level playing field in which providers and patients are equal participants (Kaufert & Putsch, 1997). Literature on provider–patient communication has long documented that the differences in power and medical knowledge often compromise patients' full participation in provider–patient interactions (Elderkin-Thompson, Silver, & Waitzkin, 2001; Waitzkin, 1991). Compared to their English-speaking counterparts, patients in interpreter-mediated interactions often make fewer comments and receive less information, response, and social support from their provider (Rivadeneyra, Elderkin-Thompson, Silver, & Waitzkin, 2000; Thornton, Pham, Engelberg, Jackson, & Curtis, 2009). Language-discordant patients often experience prejudicial attitudes and cultural differences, which can lead to reduced patient satisfaction and compromised care (Dohan & Levintova, 2007; Hicks, Tovar, Orav, & Johnson, 2008). Finally, patients from different cultures desire different degrees of patient autonomy in their illness events (Back & Huak, 2005; Blackhall, Murphy, Frank, Michel, & Azen, 1995).

In bilingual health communication, patients and providers are not on equal footing and neither do they share cultural, social, or communicative norms. A patient may not know how to voice their concerns. Stacey[1] said that she often asks her patients to "give [her] a word or something that they don't understand" so she can "ask different questions to the doctor on their behalf." In other cultures, it may not be appropriate to disclose one's illness (see the example from Yetta[1] in Chapter 6.B.1). In these situations, if interpreters maintain neutrality by avoiding active intervention (e.g., encouraging patients to voice their concerns, to seek information, or to assert their rights), they ignore their important functions in addressing the social inequality embedded in bilingual health communication (Messias et al., 2009).

A.3. Benevolence, Social Justice, and Health Literacy

Interpreters' beneficent actions (i.e., behaviors to help prevent or remove harm or to simply improve the situation of others; Pantilat, 2008) should not be viewed as medical paternalism. They may serve as interventions aiming to ensure patient autonomy and communicative competence in bilingual health care. Patient autonomy is not simply about allowing the patient to make their own decisions; rather, providers are obligated to create the conditions necessary for autonomous choice in others (Pantilat, 2008; Quill & Brody, 1996). If patients do not know what information to seek, what services are available, or what rights they have, they are not in a position to make autonomous decisions. To ensure patient autonomy in bilingual health care, it is essential that medical interpreters (and providers) actively respond to the situational and contextual demands to ensure that a patient is informed and empowered to make autonomous decisions.

Providers rely on interpreters to offer culturally sensitive care. Interpreters are extremely valuable to providers in understanding a patient's distress. Gemma[OB/GYN] noted, "If [interpreters] can be more than just the verbal communication, if they can help bridge the culture, it's HUGE."

Gram [OB/GYN] explained:

> If your interpreter is comfortable and has been doing this for a while, they can be very helpful and pick up on, "She wants to know something else." Or they can look at you [...] and you can tell there's something that is not being said here. And you can just stop and say, "What is it? What is it? What is it that I need to know that I'm not hearing or that I'm not asking about?" And, they'll talk and all of a sudden, maybe it will come out that here's a whole other issue.

Because of the cultural, power, and socioeconomic differences between providers and language-discordant patients, it is likely that patients may not actively express all of their concerns. Providers also may face challenges in interpreting patients' subtle nonverbal cues, which are often culture specific. As a result, an interpreter who not only relays all information but also actively monitors (and intervenes in) the communicative process is essential in protecting patient autonomy.

It is important to note that some of the communicative strategies used by interpreters may appear to facilitate provider–patient communication to seek or give "accurate" information but do not necessarily empower patients or enhance other speakers' communicative competence. For example, Ulysses[1] talked about modifying providers' utterances when they may be considered problematic in his culture (i.e., Muslim). He explained:

[The doctors] ask about sexual contacts outside of the marriage, which is a really really very bad question. It is very offensive. For Muslim ladies in particular. [...] I said, "Does *your husband* go to other women?" [...] Even though they might be practicing [adultery], they do not talk. But there is a way to make it soft, just ask another way.

Ulysses[1] intervened in the diagnostic process by changing the provider's actual question (e.g., "Do *you* have other sexual partners?") to what he considered a more culturally appropriate one. He argued that Muslim women would recognize that the doctor was intending to evaluate sex-related health risks and would provide an accurate answer to their situation, even if the husband is faithful. Although Ulysses[1] was able to avoid a potential provider–patient conflict, his intervention denied the opportunity for the provider to become more culturally sensitive or for the patient to become familiar with the medical dialogue in the United States.

When interviewing providers, I used Ulysses' scenario to solicit their reflection on his strategies. While recognizing the potential cultural differences and conflicts, providers often emphasize their desire to be informed about the cultural differences. Gloria[OB/GYN] explained:

If we don't understand the cultural aspect, then we need to know: That's offensive. Well, you can preface it with "I understand that this might be something that would not be asked in your home country. This is why I need to ask this question." [...] I absolutely want to know. Because we want the patient to understand, in order to have choices, in order to feel right about it, because it's what her decision is. We want her to feel good about it.

Gloria[OB/GYN] viewed it as her responsibility to know the cultural differences, as such knowledge empowers her to honor patient autonomy. Several providers also voiced concerns about interpreters' strategies in modifying their narratives without out consulting with them first, believing that such strategies infringe their control over the medical dialogue (see Hsieh, 2010). In addition, they argued that cultural knowledge is essential in helping them to interact with future patients appropriately and effectively.

A.4. Quality and Equality of Care in Interpreter-mediated Medical Encounters

Individuals' understanding about whether interpreters should intervene in problematic medical encounters is often shaped by their understanding of the specific values (e.g., patient autonomy, informed decision-making, and patient empowerment) that are central to QEC in Western medicine. In other words, when individuals are faced with conflicting normative beliefs (between their own competing goals or with others' competing value systems), QEC can provide the guiding principles to sort through these intrapersonal or interpersonal conflicts (see Chapter 5.C).

By recognizing the guiding principles, researchers can reconcile competing theoretical arguments in the literature and offer solutions to interactional dilemmas in bilingual health care. For example, rather than focusing on the theoretical discussion about whether interpreter visibility infringes patient agency, I ask: In what ways can interpreter visibility enhance or compromise QEC? In other words, how can QEC be achieved (and the corresponding values protected) in interpreter-mediated medical encounters? Are some ways of achieving QEC better than others?

It appears that our providers and interpreters both recognize that their individual goals and their normative values are secondary to QEC. When patients lack agency to seek information or are not aware of system norms in healthcare settings, providers welcome interpreters' efforts (and intervention) to empower patients to engage in the medical discourse appropriately and effectively. One can argue that because QEC in Western medicine involves an active, engaged, informed patient, interpreters' interventions to encourage such patient performances are valued. In other words, despite the repeated findings of interpreters' dissonance about maintaining neutrality during problematic medical encounters (Brua, 2008; Hsieh, 2008; Messias et al., 2009), it seems that their frustration can be alleviated by focusing on interventions that enhance QEC.

However, our providers and interpreters also expressed concern about how some communicative strategies, while they may appear to empower patients, can compromise other participants' agency, including self-efficacy, and thus affect QEC in the long run. For example, when interpreters advocate for patients without educating them about potential cultural differences or modify the medical discourse without informing providers about their lack of cultural competence, other participants remain unaware of the miscommunication and are likely to make the same mistakes in the future. Based on our data, it seems that *transparency* in the discursive process is necessary for all participants to actively manage and negotiate the meanings of QEC. As interpreters make their interventions transparent, other participants gain the opportunity to develop the skills necessary for individual agency or to become familiar with alternative system norms.

Transparency can be particularly important in situations where different parties hold divergent understandings of QEC. For example, not all cultures expect patients to be active participants in provider–patient interactions (Meeuwesen, van den Brink-Muinen, & Hofstede, 2009; Schouten & Meeuwesen, 2006). For interpreters who work with patients from those cultures, patient empowerment may mean that they actively inform and educate providers about what the patient needs and expect in a medical encounter rather than forcing an uncomfortable patient to actively engage in decision-making. Nevertheless, these should be joint decisions, actively managed between the provider, the patient, and the interpreter. After all, a patient's desires and expectations of provider–patient interactions are shaped not only by cultural norms but also by their acculturation level and personal characteristics (Schouten, Meeuwesen, Tromp, & Harmsen, 2007; Su, Li, & Pagán, 2008; Thomson & Hoffman-Goetz, 2009). Transparency in interpreters' understanding and management of their own and others' communicative goals is therefore critical to generating shared understanding and open discussion about QEC.

QEC is not an abstract concept. Rather, it represents a specific set of values and principles that guide individuals' understanding, practices, and evaluations in healthcare settings. QEC is the guiding principle for the BHC Model. In the next two sections, I will use (a) interpreters as co-diagnosticians and (b) interpreters' emotion work as examples to explore how a normative approach can provide insight into our understanding and evaluation of the appropriateness and effectiveness of interpreters' communicative strategies.

B. Case Study I: A Normative Approach to Interpreters as Co-diagnosticians

B.1. What is Interpreter as Co-diagnostician?

In bilingual health care, interpreters and providers inevitably share overlapping roles and services due to the blurred boundaries between language, culture, and medicine (Hsieh & Kramer, 2012; Zimányi, 2013). At times, interpreters will assume a specific role that enables them to provide services typically associated with providers (Angelelli, 2004; Bolden, 2000). For example, Angelelli (2004) noted instances in which interpreters gave advice that was not given by the physician and assumed the provider's role in obtaining medical history and giving medically related instructions. Angelelli argued that these behaviors were necessary for successful provider–patient interactions. I use *co-diagnostician* to describe this role, highlighting (a) interpreters' active involvement in patients' diagnostic and treatment processes and (b) the overlapping roles and services between providers and interpreters. One can argue that the co-diagnostician role highlights that interpreters can be guided by the principles of QEC and, to a certain degree, system norms, with or without the explicit consent of or supervision from the provider.

Interpreters' co-diagnostic performances are not simply a mistake of interpreters playing doctors; rather, these behaviors reflect interpreters' attempts and struggles to maintain the quality of care. By examining the overlapping roles and services between providers and interpreters, I identified five strategies that interpreters adopt to assume the role of co-diagnosticians: (a) assuming the provider's communicative goals (see also Chapter 7.B.3), (b) editorializing information for medical emphases, (c) initiating information-seeking behaviors, (d) participating in diagnostic tasks, and (e) volunteering medical information to the patients (for more details, see Hsieh, 2007). In that article, I also critically examined the potential impacts of these strategies, noting that many of them would be considered interpreting errors.

In the following discussion, rather than repeating the categorical findings, I aim to demonstrate how a normative approach can provide insights into why interpreters would be motivated to adopt these co-diagnostician strategies and explore how such behaviors may be evaluated.

B.2. Interpreters' Co-diagnostic Strategies

I will focus my discussion on two of the co-diagnostic strategies mentioned above: editorializing information for medical emphases and initiating information seeking for health information. First, I want to share with readers possible performances of these two strategies.

Editorializing Information for Medical Emphases

Editorializing information for medical emphases is categorized as a co-diagnostician behavior because the interpreter, rather than the provider, decides whether certain information has medical value or not. Interpreters who adopt this strategy may ignore or downplay the provider's actual communicative goals and focus solely on medically related information.

Interpreters talked about how they explicitly inform patients about what information is appropriate in a medical encounter. For example, Vicky[I] mentioned that patients from her culture (i.e., Vietnam) are often not knowledgeable about the appropriate content and sequence of a medical encounter. Vicky[I] explained:

> If [the patients] feel comfortable with you, they will tell you, "Please tell the doctor this, this, this." [I would tell them,] "Okay. Slow down. Let's talk about today's symptoms. Not the symptoms we have a week ago, a month ago. […] *Don't bother him with too much information.*"

Vicky[I] managed the patient's narrative by informing them about what information should be given to the provider. This suggests that interpreters may not only editorialize the speakers' narratives during a medical encounter but also exert control over the speakers' communicative behaviors (i.e., informing the patient about what to say and what *not* to say). Vicky[I] acted as a co-diagnostician by controlling the communicative process of the medical encounter.

Interpreters were observed to editorialize the *provider's* utterances for medical emphases as well. In Extract 6, the provider (Hannah) tried to educate the patient (Pam) about diabetes. The provider's identity has been changed significantly by the interpreter's (Claire[I]) editorialized message:

Extract 6

601	H:	[in an animated and caring tone] When you have diabetes, it's
602		very important for you- because you are not just this baby's
603		mother, you are this baby's nurse, doctor. Because when you do
604		the right thing, your sugar is controlled. It's very important
605		for you to eat right diet, take care of, you know, your sugar. If
606		you don't, you know, you can affect your baby. It's very
607		important; you are not just a mother. You are the nurse of this
608		baby. And you are the doctor for the- The doctor cannot do
609		anything. The nurse cannot do anything.
610	I:	你現在懷孕, 你就是胎兒的醫生和護士, 所以你要遵從
611		醫生告訴你怎麼做, 飲食要注意。 要好好控制飲食。
612		(You are now pregnant and you are the baby's doctor and
613		nurse. You need to follow doctor's instructions. Pay attention
614		to your diet.
615		Control your diet.)

Although the literal meaning (i.e., the content) of the provider's message (lines 601–609) and the interpreter's message (lines 610–611) appear to be similar, the interactional meaning (i.e., the meaning in context) of the messages are quite different (Tracy, 2013). The provider's tone was animated and caring. The repetition of the message (e.g., "It's very important ..." was repeated three times) is *not* redundant but serves a prosodic function. Essentially, this is a role performance that highlights the provider's warm personality and relationship with the patient. In contrast, the interpreter's message was much more concise. The provider's prosodic performance (e.g., "It's very important for you to eat right diet, take care of, you know, your sugar. If you don't, you know, you can affect your baby.") was changed into directives ("Pay attention to your diet. Control your diet."). The interpreter focused on the medical (as opposed to interpersonal) aspects of the provider's narrative, creating a more professional, authoritative identity for the provider.

Interpreters' focus on medical information may cause them to ignore the provider's other communicative goals (e.g., interpersonal goals). In Extract 7, a nutritionist (Hilda) educates Pam about diabetes and Claire[1] is the interpreter.

Extract 7

701	H:	Oh, oh. Has she ever heard of carbohydrate?
702	I:	你有沒有聽過碳水化合物?
703		(Have you heard of carbohydrate?)
704	P:	(laugh)喔, 我知道。 (笑氣音)
705		[laugh] (Oh.hhh. I know. hhh.)
706	I:	yes.

707	→ H:	Okay. Good, cause sometimes people don't know what it
708		is. That's why I asked. (laugh)
709		(.5)
710	H:	Okay. These are the groups- Carbohydrate is what
711		raises blood sugar.
712	I:	這一類, 就是全都是碳水化合物,提高糖分的。
713		(This group. It's all carbohydrates and raises blood sugar.)

The patient's laughter and tone of voice (line 704) indicates that she considers the provider's question awkward, funny, different, or face-threatening (Haakana, 2002; Jefferson, 1984). The provider's response (lines 707–708) was a strategy to reduce the face-threat by explaining the reason for her question (Jefferson, 1984). The silence after the provider's comment (line 709) suggests that the provider may be waiting for the interpretation, which was not provided. The interpreter ignored the provider's effort to reduce the face-threat that was meaningful to the provider–patient relationship but not to the diagnostic purpose.

An interpreter's active evaluation of other speakers' communicative goals also may be reflected in their emphases in the communicative process. For example, an interpreter may assume a provider's diagnostic goals and evaluate the types of information to be interpreted in the medical encounter. In Extract 8, the medical encounter involves a newborn baby's first follow-up. The mother is Paula. The provider (Heather) is seeking information about the baby's sleeping patterns. The interpreter's (Christie[1]) strategies suggest that she focused on medically related information.

Extract 8

801	H:	Okay, where's baby's sleeping?
802	I:	小孩子在哪裡睡?
803		(Where does the baby sleep?)
804	P:	在baby床。
805		(The baby bed)
806	I:	The baby bed.
807	→ H:	Bes- okay, Bassinet. All right. How's baby sleeping?
808	→ I:	小孩子睡得情形怎麼樣?
809		(How's baby sleeping?)
810	H:	Overnight?
811	I:	晚上的時候?
812		(At night?)
813	H:	When the baby awakes for feeding, how many hours she's
814		(awake)?
815	I:	如果說他半夜起來要喝奶的時候, 起來大概多久?

816		(If she wakes up at night for feeding, how long is she
817		awake?)
818	P:	一個小時。
819		(One hour.)
820	I:	那一次-半夜裡面會起來幾次?
821		(Once every- How many times is she awake?)
822	P:	一次。
823		(Once.)
824	I:	One time in one night.
825	H:	One time awakes.
826	I:	Yeah.
827	H:	That's good.
828	I:	And then, probably one hour once she wakes up.
829	H:	For one hour.
830	I:	Hmm.

The interpreter disregarded the provider's information verification comment in line 807 (i.e., editorializing information for medical emphases). When the provider verified that the baby sleeps in a bassinet and continued the next question (i.e., How's baby sleeping?), the interpreter's next turn focused on the diagnostic-related information seeking (line 808; "How's baby sleeping?"). An interpreter who focuses on diagnostic-related goals may disregard information that is not diagnostic-related (e.g., comments that do not require the patient's response [e.g., lines 825, 827, and 829] or comments that serve other goals, such as building rapport).

In all these examples, the interpreters editorialized the provider's utterances for medical emphases. Consistent with past studies, the interpreters in this study focused on information that is relevant to the patient's understanding of medical information but ignored information that does not appear to have clinical consequences. Interpreters' editorialization of providers' utterances also influenced the provider–patient relationship and the primary speakers' identity management.

Initiating Information Seeking for Health Information

Whereas (a) assuming providers' communicative goals requires interpreters to identify and adopt the provider's objectives (see Chapter 7.B.3), and (b) editorializing information shows that interpreters actively evaluate and prioritize the primary speakers' narratives, initiating information seeking reflects interpreters' personal judgment about the necessary information in a medical encounter. Interpreters in this study initiated information seeking about illness-related information when the providers were present. In Extract 8, the interpreter *initiated* a question to obtain more detailed information for diagnostic purposes.

In lines 813–814, the provider asked, "How many *hours* is she awake?" The patient answered, "one hour" (line 818). The sequence for the provider's question should have ended after the patient's comment; however, the interpreter then initiated further information seeking (line 820; "How many times is she awake?") without another speaker's prompting. Later, the interpreter provided information about the length of time *and* the frequency that the baby is awake (lines 824 and 828), which was more than the provider had originally requested (i.e., the length of time). This strategy is different from assuming the provider's communicative goals, which requires the interpreter to maintain the *provider's* conversational content and sequences. Initiating information seeking is about the interpreter pursuing information that he or she deems necessary. This is about the *interpreter's* evaluation of the communicative needs (e.g., the necessary content and sequence) of the medical encounter.

Interpreters were also observed to initiate information seeking without the presence of the provider. In Extract 9, a patient who is pregnant (Paula) asked the provider (Hilary) about stem cells, because they may be helpful to her first son's genetic illness. At this point, Paula only briefly mentioned her son's illness but didn't provide any details. The provider left the room to find more information, leaving the interpreter (Christie[l]) and Paula in the same room. Christie[l] then initiated the conversation with Paula.

Extract 9

901	→ I:	那他現在生活上面有什麼不方便嗎?
902		(Does he experience any inconvenience in daily activities?)
903	P:	他現在每年都去醫院照這個大腦
904		(He goes to the hospital to examine his brain every
905		year now.)
906	I:	照大腦。
907		(Examining his brain.)
908	P:	還有這個腎臟, 還有這個眼。
909		(And his kidney and his eyes.)
910	→ I:	他會有什麼明顯的, 比如說-
911		(Are there obvious- such as-)
912	P:	他皮膚全部都一粒粒。
913		(His skin is granular everywhere.)
914	I:	硬硬的啊?
915		(Is it hard?)
916	P:	很像這個小瘤。
917		(Like the little wart.)

Later in the interaction, Christie[l] asked for the official diagnosis and looked it up in a medical dictionary. The interaction between Christie[l] and Paula is very similar to what would have happened in a medical history-taking session between a provider and a patient. One could argue that Christie[1] asked for the information out of curiosity. However, Christie's[1] later behavior (e.g., asking for the official diagnosis and looking it up in the dictionary) suggested that these were purposeful behaviors to facilitate later interpretation.

Several interpreters talked about the difficulties of their tasks because, unlike providers and patients, who have access to the patient's medical history, an interpreter may interpret for cases without prior knowledge of the speakers. Many interpreters commented that working with a new patient is challenging. Sandra[1] talked about her strategy to resolve the challenges:

> [When I am alone with the patients,] I also ask them what are the reasons they are there? Do they have any problems? Because I know that all these are going to come up when I get into the office and it is going to be easier for me when I say, "Well, the patient is here for this reason." […] *I think this is going to make it faster, the appointment.*

Actively seeking information from the patient allows Sandra[1] to accomplish the communicative goals of (a) having more background knowledge about the medical encounter and (b) better control of the interpreting sessions. Other interpreters talked about how they request information about case history so that they can feel that they are included in the illness event, working as a team. Interpreters do not see these behaviors as encroaching on the role of the provider; rather, they argue that the "chitchatting" allows them to prepare better for later interactions.

B.3. A Normative Approach to Interpreters as Co-diagnosticians

A normative approach asks "How do different participants coordinate with each other during the communicative event of provider–patient interactions?" (see also Chapter 5.B). If QEC is the guiding principle for interpreter-mediated medical encounters, how can we understand and evaluate interpreters' choices in adopting co-diagnostician behaviors?

First, we find that interpreters' co-diagnostic behaviors can be motivated by their desire to achieve optimal care by fulfilling providers' expectations and conserving institutional resources (e.g., providers' time). It is unrealistic to expect interpreters to conserve the providers' time and workload without allowing them to actively evaluate and manage the content and the process of provider–patient interactions and to take initiatives to ensure the quality of care. In fact, in earlier chapters (Chapters 6.A.1 and 7.A.2), providers expressed their desire for interpreters to actively control patients' narratives. As a result, we expect providers to be appreciative of interpreters' efforts in anticipating their needs, conserving their time, and fulfilling their agenda.

However, the interpreter's preconception of providers' expected roles, rather than their assessment of the emergent interaction, may have a significant influence on their co-diagnostician role. Our findings also suggest that rather than assuming providers' communicative goals, interpreters appear to adopt a generic and rigid understanding of healthcare contexts. Interpreter-mediated interactions imply that the provider's identities and roles are mediated by the interpreter. Interpreters in this study situated the providers in a traditional, biomedical, and authoritarian role. The finding of interpreters' emphasis on providers' goals (see also Chapter 7, Extract 1) and medical information (Extract 6) is also supported by past literature (Bolden, 2000; Davidson, 2000). In addition, interpreters were found to ignore the provider's effort to reduce face-threats (Extract 7) and to impose an authoritative identity on the provider (Extract 6). These behaviors were independent of the provider's actual communicative goals during the interaction and reinforced the hierarchy in healthcare settings (i.e., giving the physicians a higher status). Similarly, a recent study found that 4.9 percent of interpreters' alterations to providers' speech conveyed a harder, more paternalistic/authoritarian tone and 3 percent conveyed more certainty than the provider had intended (Butow, Goldstein, et al., 2011). Together, these findings suggest that interpreters do not necessarily respond to providers' emergent management of communicative goals.

As a result, the BHC Model would predict that providers would hold negative views of interpreters' co-diagnostician behaviors when providers do not adopt a traditional, biomedical, and/or authoritarian role in medical encounters. The BHC Model would also predict that the higher the match between the provider's desired communicative goals and the interpreter's performed communicative goals, the more satisfied the provider would be. The emergence of patient-centered care means that interpreters' failure to reflect providers' efforts to develop an equal, collaborative relationship with patients may pose a significant challenge to the quality of bilingual health care.

From this perspective, it is important to train interpreters to identify providers' goals by paying close attention to the dynamic, emergent interactions, and to educate providers in monitoring interpreters' ability to respond to their emergent goals. For example, depending on the therapeutic objectives, a physician may adopt different communicative strategies. In a study about interpreting in mental health settings, Zimányi (2013, p. 106) found that although some interpreters may control the patients' narratives through interruptions and editorialization, others may choose to avoid interrupting the patients' talk even when it becomes unintelligible because "mental health professionals do not necessarily find it problematic if they do not fully understand what the client is saying as long as the client, who is very often traumatized, has an opportunity to voice his or her pain." To maintain the quality of care, an interpreter may need to interrupt a patient's incoherent talk in emergency care but allow another patient to continue his/her incomprehensible narrative in a mental health clinic. A mental health provider may allow a patient to express his/her thoughts uninterrupted in the first few sessions but become more aggressive in controlling the medical discourse in later sessions. In other words, the key to maintaining QEC is not based on a behavioral guideline (e.g., interpreters should or should not interrupt a patient's talk); rather, it is about how the meanings of QEC are understood and co-constructed by all participants in the medical encounter. Interpreters' co-diagnostician behaviors can be helpful when they fulfill providers' goals or ensure the quality of care.

From an institutional perspective, researchers should examine the institutional expectations and available resources for medical interpreters. For example, to consider the possibilities for interpreters to adopt co-diagnostician behaviors, researchers need to (a) examine the ethical guidelines for these behaviors, (b) explore the training required for the interpreter's expected roles, and (c) investigate the institutional resources and barriers that may facilitate or hinder the interpreter's performance.

From an interpersonal perspective, researchers need to examine the collaboration between the provider and the interpreter in managing the communicative process. For example, a provider may have different role expectations for the interpreter depending on the communicative needs of the context. This means that researchers should examine (a) the variables that influence providers' role expectations for interpreters, (b) the contextual cues that motivate interpreters' choice of strategies, and (c) the strategies that are effective in signaling the providers' communicative goals and role expectations.

C. Case Study II: A Normative Approach to Interpreters' Emotion Work

Health professionals' emotional management (i.e., the management of feeling to create a publicly observable emotional display) and emotion work (i.e., emotional management takes *work*) in clinical settings have a significant impact on patients' quality of care, well-being, and health outcomes, including patient satisfaction and treatment adherence (Annuziata & Muzzatti, 2013; De Maesschalck, Deveugele, & Willems, 2011; Street, 2013). Many researchers have highlighted the importance of providing emotional support in healthcare services (Brunson & Lawrence, 2002; Morse, Bottorff, Anderson, O'Brien & Solberg, 2006; Norris et al., 2005). Burleson (2003) noted that (a) the receipt of sensitive emotional support is associated with diverse indices of well-being, and (b) the appropriate and effective provision of emotional support is situated in cultural contexts. However, interpreters' emotional support is a complicated issue that requires closer examination.

Throughout this book, interpreters' emotion work has not gone unnoticed by interpreters or providers. Interpreters reported that they feel frustrated when they are unable to establish normal, friendly relationships with patients (see Chapter 6.B.1). Providers also referred to their appreciation and even reliance on interpreters' rapport with patients (see Chapter 7.B).

In this section, I aim to problematize interpreters' emotion work. First, I will provide some examples of interpreters' emotion work, including their management and performance of others' emotions. I will then discuss providers' normative attitudes, focusing on their reservations about interpreters' emotion work. Finally, I will discuss how a normative approach can explain and predict interpreters' emotion work and the corresponding evaluations.

C.1. Examples of Interpreters' Emotion Work

In their professional training, interpreters are encouraged to maintain an affective neutral professional performance, and this is central to their ability to maintain a neutral conduit role. However, in the participant observation data, it is not uncommon to find patients discussing their emotional and social stress with the interpreter (outside the presence of providers). It is not surprising that a patient would want to seek comfort from a person who shares the same language and culture. However, not all patients' help-seeking or support-seeking efforts were adequately addressed by interpreters. For example, in Extract 10, Claire[I] failed to respond to Pam's concerns despite Pam's repeated effort to bring up the topic.

Extract 10
1001	P:	我見到四個醫生了, 每個都說我的肚子特別小。所以
1002		我擔心死了!
1003		(I've seen four doctors. Everyone said my belly is extremely
1004		small. I'm worried to death!)
1005	I:	你見了四個醫生?
1006		(You've seen four doctors?)
1007	P:	我以前的醫生, 他休假去了。就另外有人幫他, 就說我
1008		肚子特別小。 有一次他的學生幫我看, 也說我的肚子
1009		特別小。
1010		(My former doctor went on vacation. So someone
1011		helped him out. He told me that my belly is
1012		extremely small. Another time, his student gave
1013		me an exam and he also said that my belly is super
1014		small.)
1015	I:	四個都是在這裡的嗎?都是這醫院的?
1016		(Four from here? All from this hospital?)
1017	P:	對, 都是在這醫院。
1018		(Yes, they are all from this hospital.)

In line 1001, even though Pam indicated that her concern (i.e., an extremely small belly) was supported by many physicians and ended her comment highlighting the extent of her worries ("worried to death!"), Claire's[I] follow-up question focused on the number of physicians that she has visited. Then, in lines 1007–1009, Pam repeated her concerns twice ("my belly is extremely small"; "my belly is super small"), noting that two other physicians had supported the assessment. Rather than responding to Pam's concern, Claire[1] continued to keep the discussion on fact-checking the identities of the physicians. Pam eventually gave up on her support-seeking talk (line 1017). It is unclear whether Claire[1] meant to used distraction as a supportive strategy or if she failed to notice Pam's support-seeking efforts. Nevertheless, we can guess that Pam is unlikely to walk away from this interaction feeling comforted.

Interpreters are valuable in providing emotional support to patients. At times, interpreters may provide empathy, counseling, and comfort to the patients. For example, a pregnant mother (Paula) talked to the interpreter (Christie[1]) about her concerns about the condition of her first child, who suffered from a genetic disease that was deteriorating fast.

Extract 11

1101	P:	他驗這個血, 說是遺傳。不過現在我有了這個baby我
1102		和我的先生, 和這個baby-baby驗這個羊水,
1103		我和我先生驗這個血, 都沒有這個情況。我都不
1104		知道到我兒子他為什麼會有這個情況。 還有我
1105		的家屬, 所有的人, 也都沒有。
1106		(They tested the blood and said it was a
1107		genetic disease. But now, when I had this
1108		baby, we test the amniotic fluid; my husband
1109		and I tested our blood, and there was no
1110		such condition. I don't know why my
1111		son had this problem. All my family
1112		members, everybody, none had this
1113		condition.)
1114	I:	也都沒有。
1115		(Don't have this condition.)
1116		(2 sec)
1117 →	I:	不用擔心啦。
1118		(Don't worry about it.)
1119	P:	不是啦, 這個都是很擔心的問題。因為他這個都很麻
1120		煩, 他裡面有一粒粒。 這個東西勒,
1121		他會生出來, 不是固定的。
1122		(No. This is really a worrisome problem. Because
1123		his situation was very difficult,
1124		he has granulation everywhere. The
1125		granulation just happens without any patterns.)
1126 →	I:	我知道, 我知道你的意思。
1127		(I understand. I know what you mean.)
1128		(5 sec)

1129 → I: 不過你要放寬心去面對它。

1130 (But you have to face the problem with ease.)

Researchers have indicated that how individuals respond to others' support-seeking behaviors can have an important impact on individuals' understanding of their identities and relationships (Goldsmith, 2004; Goldsmith & Brashers, 2008; Goldsmith, Lindholm, & Bute, 2006). In addition, some forms of supportive strategy are more effective than others. For example, in line 1117, Christie's[1] supportive comment ("Don't worry about it") fails to validate Paula's worries as legitimate and, in fact, challenges the appropriateness of her current emotions (Burleson, 2009; Goldsmith, 1992, 1994). When Paula responds to Christie's problematic support effort by providing more details about the genetic illness (lines 1119–1121), Christie, recognizing the failure of her earlier support effort, shifts her strategy by validating Paula's feelings (line 1126; "I understand. I know what you mean") and encouraging perspective taking (line 1129; "But you have to face the problem with ease"). Both strategies were found to be effective in validating support-seekers' concerns about identity, relationships, and emotion needs (Burleson, 2009; Burleson & MacGeorge, 2002).

Such an interaction can be quite normal in everyday life as individuals serve as supportive others in social interactions. The comforting communicative behaviors that interpreters adopted may have significant impact in clinical care. However, few researchers have talked about how the patient–interpreter relationship, including the interpreter's success or failure in providing emotional support to the patient, may influence a patient's perception of quality of health care (e.g., patient satisfaction and provider–patient relationships) as well as the actual interaction between a provider and a patient.

Interpreters' expression of emotions can be a complicated issue because in interpreter-mediated medical encounters, providers' and interpreters' identities and performances are intertwined. As a result, it may not be immediately clear whether the interpreter is reenacting others' emotions or expressing his/her own emotions (see also Chapters 6.A.2 and 7.B.3). The following example (Extract 12) took place when the patient (Paula) brought her newborn back to the hospital for the first time after the delivery.

Extract 12

1201 H: Can you say congratulations in China- Chinese.
1202 A BEAUTIFUL BABY, SHE MUST BE VERY
1203 HAPPY, VERY PROUD, EVERYBODY IN THE
1204 BLOCK MUST BE JEALOUS OF HER!! [in a dramatic
1205 tone and loud volume]
1206 I: 他說喔, 恭喜你有這麼漂亮的小孩子, 你們街頭上面的
1207 人一定都會對你很羨慕的!!

1208		He sai:d, CONGRATULATION FOR SUCH
1209		A BEAUTIFUL BABY. People in your neighborhood
1210		must be very jealous of you!! [in a dramatic tone
1211		and loud volume].)
1212	P:	Thank you!!

Some readers may notice that the literal message of the interpreter's (Christie[1]) interpretation is somewhat different from what the provider (Hank) said. Nevertheless, the communicative goal of the provider was to create a congratulatory message with a dramatic flair, which was successfully emulated by the interpreter.

On the other hand, an interpreter may intentionally downplay others' emotions. For example, in Extract 13, the interpreter (Christie[1]) modified the provider's (Hester) comment to the patient (Pearl), who was concerned that her unborn child had a large head for the age of the fetus. The following interaction took place during the patient's follow-up ultrasound examination.

Extract 13

1301	H:	The baby is growing fine and everything looks
1302		normal. It's measuring normal.
1303	I:	他說小孩子成長的很好, 那所有的尺寸都很正常。
1304		(She said that the baby is growing well. All
1305		measurements are very normal.)
1306	P:	那上一次說那個-
1307		(Then, last time she said that-)
1308	I:	How about last time that you mentioned that the-
1309	→ H:	It's measuring normal. That's what I'm saying [in an
1310		abrupt and mildly irritated tone]. (Everything's)
1311		measuring normal.
1312	→ I:	他現在檢查是正常的。
1313		(It is measuring normal now.) [in a calm tone]

The provider's response in lines 1309–1310 seemed inappropriate because of her tone and impatient attitude. The interpreter, however, removed the negative emotion of the provider's comment but kept the medical information (line 1312).

C.2. Tensions in Normative Attitudes

Because the literature shows that the benefits of providing emotional support in healthcare settings are clear, I will focus on some of the reservations that interpreters and providers have toward interpreters' emotional support.

Affective Neutral Professionals versus Compassionate Human Beings

The conduit model embraces the presentation of an affective neutral professional, which is rooted in the Western understanding of professionalism (see also Chapter 1.C). Interpreters often struggle to find a balance between being a professional and being a human being (Hsieh, 2006). Interpreters used a robot metaphor to highlight the dissonance between the affective neutral conduit role and their own emotional reaction in medical encounters. For example:

> **Rachel**: Sometimes, we learned that we don't have to talk to patients. We learned that. We are not allowed, right? I don't like that. I can tell you it's not right. We are not robots. We have training; I know why we are here. But I say that because it's not true, I am not a robot.
>
> **Selena**: I don't know if it's the nurse in me or just the human being in me. That you need to reach out to that person. You cannot be a robot. Because a machine will interpret everything but it expresses no emotion. And I don't think it's real, to us people, to just be a machine. You can't.
>
> **Silvia**: Interpreting is very robotic. You know, you are a human being. You are a person. And you are not supposed to show emotions? And you go into this room, you see this beautiful 9-year-old boy who is dying of cancer and he's their only son, and the parents have been fighting this disease for years. And all of a sudden, even the doctor is crying and you are not supposed to cry. You are supposed to hold your feelings?!

In fact, many providers also noted their concerns about the conduit model, which may come across as emotionless or uncaring. Carmen[ONC] explained, "It makes everybody in the room uncomfortable when a human being is acting like a computer. You know, without any emotions. I think it would make both the doctor and patient a little uncomfortable if there's NO body language, there's NO emotions." Cara[ONC] said, "Because the translator is a PERSON, for better or worse there, a person. And for them to act like they are not. It just doesn't work." These comments suggest that providers were aware of the interpreters' practice in showing little emotion but viewed such performances as failing to accomplish the human side of care.

This is an important departure from the interpreter-as-conduit model because the providers recognize that, aside from their institutional roles, interpreters are also human beings. Candice[ONC] noted, "It's okay to put their hands on the patient to show support. I don't want them to be a non-human being in the room." Some providers also noted interpreters' ability to offer emotional support both inside and outside of medical encounters. For example, Curtis[ONC] mentioned a case where both the mother and the child were diagnosed with cancer. He explained, "The translator has become very attached and would visit the patient before I go into the room and she'd visit them afterwards. I've seen her visiting when I don't need her." Both Curtis[ONC] and Claudia[ONC] found the interpreter's volunteer visits helpful to the mother.

Interpreters' emotions and emotional support, however, are not without limits. Ed[EM] commented, "I like the interpreters that are compassionate and empathetic in the appropriate situations." Many mental health providers noted the importance of the interpreter concealing emotions during the treatment process even though it is human nature to be shocked or emotional at some of the stories or behaviors of their patients (e.g., war-crime victims). The challenge faced by interpreters is to find a balance between these two roles (e.g., human being vs. professional). Carmen[ONC] commented:

> Is there an in-between? I guess that's what we are saying. You don't want [the interpreters] to be the person's friend and you don't want [them] to hold their hands and give them hugs but you want them to still be a human and act like they care.

The interpreter's human emotion is bounded by their institutional obligations.

Risks to Provider–patient Bonding

The triadic relationship in interpreter-mediated medical encounters implies an inherent tension: The growth of one relationship may threaten other relationships. Several providers appeared ambivalent about the interpreter's emotional support. For example, Mira[MH] explained, "I'm not sure about [emotional support]. It is important for our patients to build trust with physicians to share information with them. I would imagine that the patients need to trust the interpreters too." Cordell[ONC] noted, "I think that we in oncology provide emotional support all the time. You have to support your patient through difficult decisions. I think it's an important part. That's why I'm uncomfortable having the third party do that." Candice[ONC] explained that she likes the conduit model of interpreting because "the parents are looking at ME and reading MY nonverbal and MY emotions. And they are bonded to me, not the interpreter. [...] I'm the one that has the child's back." In short, providers in our study viewed interpreter–patient relationships as a potential threat to provider–patient relationships. As a result, interpreters' emotional support is not desired if it threatens the provider–patient relationship, which they believe to be the primary relationship in bilingual health care.

Providers in our study also showed strong concerns about interpreters' emotional support if they suspect that it may hinder the therapeutic process. Mira[MH] noted:

> You don't want interpreters to interact with that patient so much that the patient begin to TRUST the interpreter more than the physician. The triangulation can be damaging to the therapeutic relationship between the provider and the patient. [...] If the patient opens up so much to the

interpreter that they become so emotional or have an emotional break-down that can interfere with the treatment process tremendously.

Several mental health providers shared similar attitudes, noting that the provider–patient relationship is not just about bonding but serves therapeutic functions. As a result, they were particularly concerned about how the interpret-er's relationship with the patient may impact the therapeutic process.

Risks to Therapeutic Objectives

Providers also noted that interpreters' seemingly supportive behaviors may contra-dict their therapeutic objectives. For example, Earl[EM] noted a case in which he believed that giving a baby a lumbar puncture was essential for diagnostic purposes; however, the family was reluctant to have the procedure and the interpreter's sup-port for the family's decision did not help the situation. Earl[EM] eventually resorted to the threat of court order to convince the family to accept the treatment.

The type of interpreter may have a different impact as well. For example, several providers argued that family interpreters would interfere with the inter-action by interjecting their own opinions or making decisions for the patient even though they are a convenient source of support to the patient. Mira[MH] com-mented that a telephone interpreter is not acceptable because her patients "can be paranoid, and the presence of a voice without knowing who the person is can make them even more paranoid and unwilling to open up."

It is important to note that the providers' concerns about the risks to provider–patient relationships and therapeutic objectives are conceptually dis-tinct. These two categories, however, are not mutually exclusive. For example, for mental health providers, the provider–patient relationship is fundamental to their therapeutic processes. However, providers from other specialties often viewed provider–patient relationships as good-natured interpersonal interactions that are not necessarily related to their therapeutic objectives.

Risk of Malpractice Litigation

Curtis[ONC] commented, "With the medical malpractice climate in the United States, it's probably something in the back of every physician's mind somewhere, almost all the time." It is important to note that all providers, regardless of the spe-cialty, felt strongly about interpreters not offering medical opinions in the guise of emotional support. For example, Ginger[OB/GYN] explained:

> I don't like it when we are in the middle of trying to explain how epi-dural works and they are like, "Well, when I have my baby. Let me tell you about it." [...] If they want to add any of their personal thing, make a DISTINCTION between when we are done talking and the medical

translation part is finished and when it's just a conversation between the two people.

Gloria[OB/GYN] also noted, "It is [the interpreter's] role to help both sides understand, be it cultural or language. But it is not their role to make a medical decision or to offer medical treatment options." Because interpreters may speak for the providers or speak as themselves, providers emphasized the importance of separating the interpreter's emotional support and the provider's medical opinions. Mira[MH] commented, "Interpreters should never be therapeutic. But they should be supportive and trusting to our patients." Ginger [OB/GYN] said that she does not mind if the interpreter chitchats with the patient when she is conducting a physical exam. However, she also said, "When I am not talking to the patient, I would hope the patient would know that none of it is coming from me." Providers often cited malpractice litigation as a potential risk when discussing their concerns about situations in which a patient might be uncertain about whether the specific information came from the provider or the interpreter.

C.3. A Normative Approach to Interpreters' Emotion Work

Goldsmith (2001, p. 515) explained, "One important goal of a normative theory is to provide a basis for recommendations about how communicators can achieve desirable outcomes." Rather than presenting prescriptive behavioral guidelines (e.g., specific behavioral strategies) to regulate interpreters' behavior, I appeal to QEC as the guiding principle for interpreters' decision-making about their emotion work (see also Hsieh & Nicodemus, 2015). For example, most people may feel that it is appropriate and effective for interpreters to reenact other speakers' exaggerated performance of positive emotions because it facilitates QEC. In Extract 12, Christie[I] successfully portrayed Hank as a supportive, loving, and fun-loving provider. Such a portrayal of Hank's identity contributes to a strong provider–patient relationship. As a result, the BHC Model would predict that interpreters are likely to relay positive emotions, and this would also be evaluated positively by other participants.

The BHC Model would predict that when one believes that failure to provide comfort compromises the quality of care or that success in providing comfort helps alleviate the patient's stress, one is likely to support interpreters' strategies in offering emotional support. This is why we cannot help but cringe at Claire's[I] repeated failures to respond to Pam's attempts at support-seeking or be relieved when Christie[I] changed her support strategy to validate Paula's experience of anxiety and encourage new perspective taking. Our understanding of what constitutes QEC shapes our evaluation of the appropriateness of interpreters' behaviors.

Then what about Extract 13, when the interpreter downplayed the provider's negative emotions? Would that be appropriate? After all, the patient misses the opportunity to learn that her provider may not be as friendly as she thought. How would the BHC Model explain concerns related to interpreters' management and relay of others' negative emotions?

I argue that the conflicts arise from competing components of QEC. In addition to "do no harm" (i.e., beneficence), patient autonomy and informed decision-making are also important components of QEC (Campbell, Roland, & Buetow, 2000; Nicodemus, Swabey, & Witter-Merithew, 2011). Whereas not disclosing a provider's prejudicial attitude may satisfy the values of beneficence, it also deprives a patient from making an informed, autonomous decision about the quality of their provider. Similarly, an interpreter may feel reluctant to relay a provider's negative attitude to avoid future repercussions (e.g., risks to a supportive provider–patient relationship) that might compromise QEC. As a result, interpreters are faced with competing values within a healthcare system.

So, whether and how should an interpreter relay a provider's negative emotions? A normative approach does not offer a predetermined answer. Rather, it encourages participants to identify and prioritize the various sociocultural norms that are relevant to the specific communicative event. Although QEC is a guiding principle for all healthcare deliveries, we argue that its meaning is not fixed or predetermined but is socially constructed at particular points in time and place. The challenge faced by interpreters, then, is to identify and prioritize the various components that may constitute the definition of QEC in that particular interaction.

In other words, the BHC Model would predict that an interpreter's choice of strategy is dependent on his/her understanding of the priorities of these values. If an interpreter believes that the patient's right to informed decision-making and autonomy is more important, the interpreter is more likely to relay the provider's emotional tone. On the other hand, if an interpreter puts priority on beneficence, then s/he is more likely to downplay or even mask a provider's problematic behavior. In addition, even when the goal is to achieve QEC by protecting patient autonomy, an interpreter's response can be shaped by the extent of a normative violation (Burgoon, 1993). For example, an interpreter may choose to embed a mildly irritated tone in his/her interpretation but openly refuse to relay prejudicial comments (while informing the patient about the provider's problematic behaviors). An interpreter thus actively evaluates the best strategy to achieve QEC by prioritizing and balancing other important values relevant to the medical encounter (e.g., beneficence, provider–patient trust, speakers' control over the communicative event).

In summary, my research and the literature have highlighted several common tensions in individuals' normative attitudes about interpreters' emotion work. First, providing emotional support contradicts the prevalent ideology of interpreter-as-conduit and may create tensions with the provider's expectation, which is often that interpreters should maintain neutrality in healthcare settings (Fatahi, Hellstrom, Skott, & Mattsson, 2008; Leanza, 2008; Rosenberg, Leanza,

& Seller, 2007). Second, because providers' expectations tend to focus on their own therapeutic objectives, they may react negatively to an interpreter's emotional support to a patient when it reinforces that patient's disagreement with the provider's agenda. Third, providing emotional support may blur the differences between the roles of interpreter and patient advocate, creating role conflicts for interpreters (Hsieh, 2006). Fourth, interpreters' emotional support may encroach on providers' responsibilities or service or blur the identities between the provider and the interpreter, which may entail (both positive and negative) clinical consequences (Hsieh, 2007; Leanza, 2008). Finally, our data suggest that differences in providers' specialty (e.g., nursing vs. emergency medicine) may lead to different expectations of and preferences for interpreters' emotional support. These normative tensions can result in diverging understanding, practices, and evaluations about what constitutes QEC.

Although the providers in our study valued interpreters' emotional support, this is not without limits. For example, interpreters need to recognize that although emotional support is natural in ordinary interpersonal interactions, it carries clinical consequences and therapeutic implications in healthcare settings. Whether an interpreter's emotional support will be positively evaluated or not is dependent on its impact on QEC (as opposed to normative expectations in everyday life). As a result, interpreters need to be conscious of the impact of their emotional support on the provider–patient relationship and the provider's therapeutic objectives.

Providers' and interpreters' emotional support are intertwined with one another and may be difficult to separate. Thus, interpreters need to recognize that providers rely on them to provide emotional support to the patient. This highlights the importance of interpreters giving medical talk and rapport-building talk equal attention in medical encounters. Although the providers in our study believed interpreters should not interact with patients in such a way that the provider's and interpreter's voices are blended together, they also viewed interpreters' emotional support as the reproduction of their emotional support to the patient (see Chapter 7.B). For example, an interpreter's physical presence was symbolic of their attentive care to the patient. They expected an interpreter's emotional expression to reflect their own emotional tone. In addition, interpreters' cultural information allows them to provide emotional support to the patient more effectively. Because (a) providers' and interpreters' voices are presented as one through the interpreter's performance (Hsieh & Kramer, 2012) and (b) patients do not necessarily separate the provider's and interpreter's voices (Brunson & Lawrence, 2002), providers' expectation of drawing a clear line between their and the interpreter's voices/attitude/emotional support may not be realistic. Instead, a more realistic and effective way of conceptualizing emotional support in bilingual health care is to consider providers and interpreters as allies, complementing each other to support the patient's emotional needs. Rather than competing with each other to establish bonding/a relationship with the patient, providers and interpreters should share the same goal of providing QEC to language-discordant patients.

D. Implications for Theory Development and Healthcare Delivery

In this chapter, we have examined how the guiding principles of QEC can shape the content and process of interpreter-mediated medical encounters. It is important to note that while these guiding principles may appear as individuals' communicative goals during the medical encounter, these goals are, in fact, driven by individuals' understanding of QEC. These goals may be inherent in the medical discourse in Western medicine (e.g., patient autonomy) or may emerge dynamically during problematic medical encounters (e.g., low communicative competence). In addition, not all participants share the same understanding of what constitutes QEC and how it can be achieved.

Our studies have demonstrated that medical encounters involve a fluid co-construction of meanings and goals between multiple parties; nevertheless, a major problem identified in our studies is that interpreters do not appear to be vigilant about the dynamic, emergent shifts in provider–patient interaction. Various studies have consistently demonstrated that interpreters often adopt a physician-centered approach in managing provider–patient interactions (Baraldi, 2009; Bolden, 2000), favoring providers' biomedical perspectives and ignoring patients' non-medical talk. In addition, some early evidence suggests that interpreters are likely to reinforce physicians' authoritative roles/voices with minimal regard to the emergent dynamics of provider–patient interactions or the provider's intended performance (Butow, Goldstein, et al., 2011; Hsieh, 2007; Hsieh, Ju, & Kong, 2010). This is likely due to interpreters' (a) assumption of providers' authoritative expert identity and (b) failure to recognize and/or respond to the emergent shifts in providers' multilayered identities and multiple goals. If we continue to develop prescriptive behavioral guidelines (e.g., specific behavioral strategies) to train interpreters and providers, we are likely to encourage and foster a rigid understanding about interpreter-mediated interactions.

From this perspective, processual guidelines (i.e., underlying principles/values to guide practices) which recognize the complexity and multivocality of human interactions (W. S. Lee, Wang, Chung, & Hertel, 1995) may be much more meaningful and beneficial to interpreter and provider training. In other words, by recognizing interpreter-mediated medical encounters as goal-oriented communicative activities, we argue that we should avoid looking for one-size-fits-all answers. This is particularly true when providers and interpreters need to negotiate their control, management, and understanding of QEC (Hsieh, 2010; Hsieh & Kramer, 2012; Zimányi, 2013).

After examining dual-role interpreters' interpreting strategies, Mueller et al. (2011, p. 88) concluded:

> Each [interpreting style] has advantages in a medical setting, and [interpreters' choice of] style is influenced by healthcare provider preference,

interpreter–provider trust and familiarity, and medical knowledge of the interpreter. In addition to style, interpreters are challenged by the patients' dialects, educational level, provider personalities, gender issues, and out of clinic relationships with the patients.

The best interpreters are those who have multiple strategies and solutions to a given situation, allowing them to be flexible and adaptive to the corresponding contexts (Bischoff, Kurth, & Henley, 2012; Greenhalgh, Robb, & Scambler, 2006; Penn & Watermeyer, 2012). This is what ultimately separates interpreters from machines. Interpreters see the fear of an angry father fighting for his child's life and hear the sorrow in a physician's assertive voice, noticing that meanings are being emergently negotiated. They respond to the subtle shifts with the resources available to them. Maybe it's a softer tone of voice. Maybe it's to downplay emotions when discussing end-of-life care. Maybe it's to ask the doctor to discuss the issue in a different way. There are no correct answers.

The best providers are no different. As a provider develops different strategies and repertoires to work with patients from different cultures or with different types of interpreters, QEC is not defined by whether the provider performs in exactly the same way or says exactly the same thing across all settings. Rather, a good provider is one who is able to recognize the various contexts, anticipate patients' concerns, and be adaptive in his/her strategies in negotiating and meeting the needs of the particular provider–patient interactions.

Rather than presenting a formulaic solution of "If this, do that," I argue that a better approach is "If this, here are the options. Knowing that one should be concerned about these principles and values, pick one that best fits your situation." This approach requires interpreters and providers to be critical thinkers and problem-solvers, making judgments about what constitutes the best solution.

Notes

1 Four data sets are presented in this section (see Chapter 3 B.2–4, C.2).
2 The numbering of the extracts is based on the sequential order in the book, rather than the book chapter. As a result, the first extract within this particular chapter begins with 2.

References

Angelelli, C. V. (2004). *Medical interpreting and cross-cultural communication*. Cambridge, UK: Cambridge University Press.

Annuziata, M. A., & Muzzatti, B. (2013). Improving communication effectiveness in oncology: The role of emotions. In A. Surbone, M. Zwitter, M. Rajer, & R. Stiefel (Eds.), *New challenges in communication with cancer patients* (pp. 235–246). New York: Springer.

Back, M. F., & Huak, C. Y. (2005). Family centred decision making and non-disclosure of diagnosis in a South East Asian oncology practice. *Psycho-Oncology*, 14, 1052–1059.

Baraldi, C. (2009). Forms of mediation: The case of interpreter-mediated interactions in medical systems. *Language and Intercultural Communication*, 9, 120–137.

Bischoff, A., Kurth, E., & Henley, A. (2012). Staying in the middle: A qualitative study of health care interpreters perceptions of their work. *Interpreting*, 14, 1–22.

Blackhall, L. J., Murphy, S. T., Frank, G., Michel, V., & Azen, S. (1995). Ethnicity and attitudes toward patient autonomy. *Journal of the American Medical Association*, 274, 820–825.

Bolden, G. B. (2000). Toward understanding practices of medical interpreting: Interpreters' involvement in history taking. *Discourse Studies*, 2, 387–419.

Brua, C. (2008). Role-blurring and ethical grey zones associated with lay interpreters: Three case studies. *Communication & Medicine*, 5, 73–79.

Brunson, J. G., & Lawrence, P. S. (2002). Impact of sign language interpreter and therapist moods on deaf recipient mood. *Professional Psychology: Research and Practice*, 33, 576–580.

Burgoon, J. K. (1993). Interpersonal expectations, expectancy violations, and emotional communication. *Journal of Language and Social Psychology*, 12, 30–48.

Burleson, B. R. (2003). The experience and effects of emotional support: What the study of cultural and gender differences can tell us about close relationships, emotion and interpersonal communication. *Personal Relationships*, 10, 1–23.

Burleson, B. R. (2009). Understanding the outcomes of supportive communication: A dual-process approach. *Journal of Social and Personal Relationships*, 26, 21–38.

Burleson, B. R., & MacGeorge, E. L. (2002). Supportive communication. In M. L. Knapp & J. A. Daly (Eds.), *Handbook of interpersonal communication* (3rd ed., pp. 374–424). Thousand Oaks, CA: Sage.

Butow, P. N., Bell, M., Goldstein, D., Sze, M., Aldridge, L., Abdo, S., … Eisenbruch, M. (2011). Grappling with cultural differences; Communication between oncologists and immigrant cancer patients with and without interpreters. *Patient Education and Counseling*, 84, 398–405.

Butow, P. N., Goldstein, D., Bell, M. L., Sze, M., Aldridge, L. J., Abdo, S., … Eisenbruch, M. (2011). Interpretation in consultations with immigrant patients with cancer: How accurate is it? *Journal of Clinical Oncology*, 29, 2801–2807.

Campbell, S. M., Roland, M. O., & Buetow, S. A. (2000). Defining quality of care. *Social Science & Medicine*, 51, 1611–1625.

Cegala, D. J. (1997). A study of doctors' and patients' communication during a primary care consultation: Implications for communication training. *Journal of Health Communication*, 2, 169–194.

Cegala, D. J., & Post, D. M. (2009). The impact of patients' participation on physicians' patient-centered communication. *Patient Education and Counseling*, 77, 202–208.

Cegala, D. J., Post, D. M., & McClure, L. (2001). The effects of patient communication skills training on the discourse of older patients during a primary care interview. *Journal of the American Geriatrics Society*, 49, 1505.

Cegala, D. J., Street, R. L., Jr., & Clinch, C. (2007). The impact of patient participation on physicians' information provision during a primary care medical interview. *Health Communication*, 21, 177–185.

Davidson, B. (2000). The interpreter as institutional gatekeeper: The social-linguistic role of interpreters in Spanish–English medical discourse. *Journal of Sociolinguistics*, 4, 379–405.

De Maesschalck, S., Deveugele, M., & Willems, S. (2011). Language, culture and emotions: Exploring ethnic minority patients' emotional expressions in primary healthcare consultations. *Patient Education and Counseling*, 84, 406–412.

Dohan, D., & Levintova, M. (2007). Barriers beyond words: Cancer, culture, and translation in a community of Russian speakers. *Journal of General Internal Medicine*, 22, S300–305.

Elderkin-Thompson, V., Silver, R. C., & Waitzkin, H. (2001). When nurses double as interpreters: A study of Spanish-speaking patients in a US primary care setting. *Social Science & Medicine*, 52, 1343–1358.

Fatahi, N., Hellstrom, M., Skott, C., & Mattsson, B. (2008). General practitioners' views on consultations with interpreters: A triad situation with complex issues. *Scandinavian Journal of Primary Health Care*, 26, 40–45.

Goldsmith, D. J. (1992). Managing conflicting goals in supportive interaction: An integrative theoretical framework. *Communication Research*, 19, 264–286.

Goldsmith, D. J. (1994). The role of facework in supportive communication. In B. R. Burleson (Ed.), *Communication of social support: Messages, interactions, relationships, and community* (pp. 29–49). Thousand Oaks, CA: Sage.

Goldsmith, D. J. (2001). A normative approach to the study of uncertainty and communication. *Journal of Communication*, 51, 514–533.

Goldsmith, D. J. (2004). *Communicating social support*. New York: Cambridge University Press.

Goldsmith, D. J., & Brashers, D. E. (2008). Communication matters: Developing and testing social support interventions. *Communication Monographs*, 75, 320–329.

Goldsmith, D. J., Lindholm, K. A., & Bute, J. J. (2006). Dilemmas of talking about lifestyle changes among couples coping with a cardiac event. *Social Science & Medicine*, 63, 2079–2090.

Greenhalgh, T., Robb, N., & Scambler, G. (2006). Communicative and strategic action in interpreted consultations in primary health care: A Habermasian perspective. *Social Science & Medicine*, 63, 1170–1187.

Grice, H. P. (1975). Logic and conversation. In P. Cole & J. L. Morgan (Eds.), *Syntax and semantics: Speech acts* (Vol. 3, pp. 41–58). Cambridge, MA: Harvard University.

Haakana, M. (2002). Laughter in medical interaction: From quantification to analysis, and back. *Journal of Sociolinguistics*, 6, 207–235.

Hicks, L. S., Tovar, D. A., Orav, E., & Johnson, P. A. (2008). Experiences with hospital care: Perspectives of Black and Hispanic patients. *Journal of General Internal Medicine*, 23, 1234–1240.

Hsieh, E. (2006). Conflicts in how interpreters manage their roles in provider–patient interactions. *Social Science & Medicine*, 62, 721–730.

Hsieh, E. (2007). Interpreters as co-diagnosticians: Overlapping roles and services between providers and interpreters. *Social Science & Medicine*, 64, 924–937.

Hsieh, E. (2008). "I am not a robot!" Interpreters' views of their roles in health care settings. *Qualitative Health Research*, 18, 1367–1383.

Hsieh, E. (2009). Bilingual health communication: Medical interpreters' construction of a mediator role. In D. E. Brashers & D. J. Goldsmith (Eds.), *Communicating to manage health and illness* (pp. 121–146). New York: Routledge.

Hsieh, E. (2010). Provider–interpreter collaboration in bilingual health care: Competitions of control over interpreter-mediated interactions. *Patient Education and Counseling*, 78, 154–159.

Hsieh, E., Ju, H., & Kong, H. (2010). Dimensions of trust: The tensions and challenges in provider–interpreter trust. *Qualitative Health Research*, 20, 170–181.

Hsieh, E., & Kramer, E. M. (2012). The clashes of expert and layman talk: Constructing meanings of interpreter-mediated medical encounters. In C. Callahan (Ed.), *Communication, comparative cultures and civilizations* (Vol. 2, pp. 19–44). New York: Hampton.

Hsieh, E. & Nicodemus, B. (2015). Conceptualizing emotion in healthcare interpreting: A normative approach to interpreters' emotion work. *Patient Education and Counseling*, 98, 1474-1481.

Jefferson, G. (1984). On the organization of laughter in talk about troubles. In J. M. Atkinson & J. Heritage (Eds.), *Structures of social action: Studies in conversation analysis* (pp. 346–369). Cambridge, UK: Cambridge University Press.

Kapp, M. B. (2007). Patient autonomy in the age of consumer-driven health care: Informed consent and informed choice. *Journal of Legal Medicine*, 28, 91–117.

Kaufert, J. M., & Putsch, R. W., III. (1997). Communication through interpreters in healthcare: Ethical dilemmas arising from differences in class, culture, language, and power. *The Journal of Clinical Ethics*, 8, 71–87.

Kutner, M., Greenberg, E., Jin, Y., & Paulsen, C. (2006). The health literacy of America's adults: Results from the 2003 National Assessment of Adult Literacy. Retrieved March 14, 2015, from http://nces.ed.gov/pubs2006/2006483.pdf.

Leanza, Y. (2008). Community interpreter's power: The hazards of a disturbing attribute. *Journal of Medical Anthropology*, 31, 211–220.

Leanza, Y., Boivin, I., & Rosenberg, E. (2010). Interruptions and resistance: A comparison of medical consultations with family and trained interpreters. *Social Science & Medicine*, 70, 1888–1895.

Lee, J. (2009). Interpreting inexplicit language during courtroom examination. *Applied Linguistics*, 30, 93–114.

Lee, W. S., Wang, J., Chung, J., & Hertel, E. (1995). A sociohistorical approach to intercultural communication. *Howard Journal of Communications*, 6, 262–291.

Meeuwesen, L., van den Brink-Muinen, A., & Hofstede, G. (2009). Can dimensions of national culture predict cross-national differences in medical communication? *Patient Education and Counseling*, 75, 58–66.

Messias, D. K. H., McDowell, L., & Estrada, R. D. (2009). Language interpreting as social justice work: Perspectives of formal and informal healthcare interpreters. *Advances in Nursing Science*, 32, 128–143.

Morse, J. M., Bottorff, J., Anderson, G., O'Brien, B., & Solberg, S. (2006). Beyond empathy: Expanding expressions of caring. *Journal of Advanced Nursing*, 53, 75–87.

Mueller, M.-R., Roussos, S., Hill, L., Salas, N., Villarreal, V., Baird, N., & Hovell, M. (2011). Medical interpreting by bilingual staff whose primary role is not interpreting: Contingencies influencing communication for dual-role interpreters. In J. J. Kronenfeld (Ed.), *Access to care and factors that impact access, patients as partners in care and changing roles of health providers* (pp. 77–91). Bingley, UK: Emerald.

Nicodemus, B., Swabey, L., & Witter-Merithew, A. (2011). Establishing presence and role transparency in healthcare interpreting: A pedagogical approach for developing effective practice. *Rivista di Psicolinguistica Applicata*, 11, 69–83.

Norris, W. M., Wenrich, M. D., Nielsen, E. L., Treece, P. D., Jackson, J. C., & Curtis, J. R. (2005). Communication about end-of-life care between language-discordant patients and clinicians: Insights from medical interpreters. *Journal of Palliative Medicine*, 8, 1016–1024.

Osborn, C. Y., Cavanaugh, K., Wallston, K. A., Kripalani, S., Elasy, T. A., Rothman, R. L., & White, R. O. (2011). Health literacy explains racial disparities in diabetes medication adherence. *Journal of Health Communication*, 16, 268–278.

Pantilat, S. (2008). Ethics fast fact: Autonomy vs. beneficence. Retrieved March 14, 2015, from http://missinglink.ucsf.edu/lm/ethics/Content%20Pages/fast_fact_auton_bene.htm.

Penn, C., & Watermeyer, J. (2012). When asides become central: Small talk and big talk in interpreted health interactions. *Patient Education and Counseling*, 88, 391–398.

Quill,T. E., & Brody, H. (1996). Physician recommendations and patient autonomy: Finding a balance between physician power and patient choice. *Annals of Internal Medicine*, 125, 763–769.

Raymond, C. W. (2014). Conveying information in the interpreter-mediated medical visit: The case of epistemic brokering. *Patient Education and Counseling*, 97, 38–46.

Rivadeneyra, R., Elderkin-Thompson, V., Silver, R. C., & Waitzkin, H. (2000). Patient centeredness in medical encounters requiring an interpreter. *American Journal of Medicine*, 108, 470–474.

Roat, C. E., Putsch, R. W., III, & Lucero, C. (1997). *Bridging the gap over the phone: A basic training for telephone interpreters serving medical settings*. Seattle, WA: Cross Cultural Health Care Program.

Rosenberg, E., Leanza, Y., & Seller, R. (2007). Doctor-patient communication in primary care with an interpreter: Physician perceptions of professional and family interpreters. *Patient Education and Counseling*, 67, 286–292.

Rosenberg, E., Seller, R., & Leanza, Y. (2008). Through interpreters' eyes: Comparing roles of professional and family interpreters. *Patient Education and Counseling*, 70, 87–93.

Rothman, D. J. (2001). The origins and consequences of patient autonomy: A 25-year retrospective. *Health Care Analysis*, 9, 255–264.

Schouten, B. C., & Meeuwesen, L. (2006). Cultural differences in medical communication: A review of the literature. *Patient Education and Counseling*, 64, 21–34.

Schouten, B. C., Meeuwesen, L., Tromp, F., & Harmsen, H. A. M. (2007). Cultural diversity in patient participation: The influence of patients' characteristics and doctors' communicative behaviour. *Patient Education and Counseling*, 67, 214–223.

Seale, C., Rivas, C., Al-Sarraj, H., Webb, S., & Kelly, M. (2013). Moral mediation in interpreted health care consultations. *Social Science & Medicine*, 98, 141–148.

Shaw, S. J., Huebner, C., Armin, J., Orzech, K., & Vivian, J. (2009). The role of culture in health literacy and chronic disease screening and management. *Journal of Immigrant and Minority Health*, 11, 460–467.

Street, R. L., Jr. (2013). How clinician–patient communication contributes to health improvement: Modeling pathways from talk to outcome. *Patient Education and Counseling*, 92, 286–291.

Su, D., Li, L., & Pagán, J. A. (2008). Acculturation and the use of complementary and alternative medicine. *Social Science & Medicine*, 66, 439–453.

Thomson, M. D., & Hoffman-Goetz, L. (2009). Defining and measuring acculturation: A systematic review of public health studies with Hispanic populations in the United States. *Social Science & Medicine*, 69, 983–991.

Thornton, J. D., Pham, K., Engelberg, R. A., Jackson, J. C., & Curtis, J. R. (2009). Families with limited English proficiency receive less information and support in interpreted intensive care unit family conferences. *Critical Care Medicine*, 37, 89–95.

Tracy, K. (2013). *Everyday talk: Building and reflecting identities* (2nd ed.). New York: Guilford.

Waitzkin, H. (1991). *The politics of medical encounters: How patients and doctors deal with social problems*. New Haven, CT: Yale University Press.

Zimányi, K. (2013). Somebody has to be in charge of a session: On the control of communication in interpreter-mediated mental health encounters. *Translation and Interpreting Studies*, 8, 94–111.

9

MOVING FORWARD: THEORY DEVELOPMENT AND PRACTICE RECOMMENDATIONS

The field of bilingual health care has provided much momentum to theory development for translation and interpreting studies and practical implications for healthcare delivery. Overall, the field is maturing, which is reflected in the recent emergence of large-scale reviews (e.g., Brisset, Leanza, & Laforest, 2013; Flores, 2005; Karliner, Jacobs, Chen, & Mutha, 2007; Ramirez, Engel, & Tang, 2008; Sleptsova, Hofer, Morina, & Langewitz, 2014). At the same time, researchers and clinicians are slow in moving away from the old, text-oriented paradigm that often emphasizes interpreters' passive, neutral role and focuses on interpreters' linguistic performances. The diversity of researchers in the field has contributed to an emergence of different perspectives. More importantly, it has become clear that there are many different ways and perspectives to consider and evaluate the effectiveness and appropriateness of interpreter-mediated medical encounters that do not necessarily center on interpreters' linguistic performances.

A. Tensions in Normative Attitudes and Implications for Practice

Readers may have noticed tensions in the normative perspectives and/or practices examined throughout this book. There are also tensions between evidence-based research and these normative attitudes. Nevertheless, despite the counterarguments made in this book, some of the prevalent attitudes remain quite robust in and are essential to healthcare practices. In the following sections, I will reexamine these common, normative perspectives, highlighting the specific ways in which they can be incorporated into practice.

A.1. Professional Interpreters versus Normative Practices

There are significant tensions in the ideology for and normative practices of providers' choice of interpreters. An argument that is pervasive in journal articles and among practitioners is the necessity for professional interpreters. I agree with the argument that professional interpreters are extremely valuable in healthcare settings, as several reviews have also found valid support for the benefits of professional interpreting (Flores, 2005; Karliner et al., 2007). However, this is different from promoting the exclusive use of professional interpreters in healthcare settings.

My studies have highlighted that providers have complex understandings about bilingual health care. Their concerns are not limited to interpreters' professionalism, ethical standards, or litigation risks. Even though telephone interpreters are professional interpreters, providers may be concerned about the lack of immediacy and emotional connection with their patients when using such interpreters. The geographic location, hours of service, patient language, clinical complexity, and clinical urgency can all influence the availability/accessibility of the different types of interpreters and interpreting modalities (see also Andres, Wynia, Regenstein, & Maul, 2013; Diamond, Schenker, Curry, Bradley, & Fernandez, 2009; Ramirez et al., 2008). As a result, arguing for the exclusive use of professional interpreters, including on-site and remote interpreting, can be unrealistic.

The reality is that providers underutilize interpreters even when interpreters are readily available, when they perceive the benefits of professional interpreters, and where there is longstanding state legislation requiring access to professional interpreters (Diamond et al., 2009; Ginde, Sullivan, Corel, Caceres, & Camargo, 2010). We need to understand why these behaviors take place. Identifying the facilitators and barriers to the use of professional interpreters, instituting organizational guidelines on the appropriate use of interpreters, and empowering providers to make strategic, meaningful, and appropriate use of interpreters are essential in ensuring the quality of bilingual health care. Portraying nonprofessional interpreters as substandard and inappropriate simply prohibits a healthy discussion on interpreter utilization.

In recent years, researchers have examined the strengths and weaknesses of different types of interpreter, including family interpreters (Leanza, Boivin, & Rosenberg, 2013; Meeuwesen, Twilt, ten Thije, & Harmsen, 2010), technology-based interpreters (Carroll, Calhoun, Subido, Painter, & Meischke, 2013; Phillips, 2013; Price, Pérez-stable, Nickleach, Lopez, & Karliner, 2012), and bilingual medical professionals (Elderkin-Thompson, Silver, & Waitzkin, 2001; Moreno, Otero-Sabogal, & Newman, 2007; Wros, 2009). By recognizing the interdependent nature of participants' performances in interpreter-mediated interactions, our attention should shift to identifying the facilitators and barriers to Quality and Equality of Care (QEC) when working with different types of interpreters. For example, by recognizing that patients are less likely to express emotional cues when working with family interpreters (Schouten & Schinkel, 2014), providers can adopt strategies to actively solicit emotion-related talk when working with family interpreters. On the other hand, because providers are more likely to interrupt patients' Lifeworld talk (e.g. illness-related concerns or anxiety) when working with professional interpreters (Leanza, Boivin, & Rosenberg, 2010), they should be encouraged to avoid interrupting patients' contextualized narrative when working with professional interpreters. In other words, by identifying the facilitators and barriers to bilingual health communication, providers can have better control over QEC.

Finally, it is important to recognize that these facilitators and barriers can exist at individual (e.g., health literacy and self-efficacy), interpersonal (e.g., interpersonal trust), organizational (e.g., organizational culture and policies), and sociocultural/sociopolitical (e.g., structural racism against immigrants and public funding for interpreting services) levels.

A.2. Interpreter Type versus Interpreter Competence

A major concern for incorporating different types of interpreters in healthcare settings is the lack of institutional control over interpreter competence and thus the quality of interpreting and quality of care. How can we reconcile the tensions between interpreter type and interpreter competence?

It is important to note that interpreters' linguistic competence is a prerequisite for successful bilingual health communication. For our providers, interpreters simply are not trustworthy if they do not have the necessary linguistic competence (see Chapter 7.C.1). In addition, providers appear to be much more concerned about interpreters' linguistic competence than they are about their cultural competence. Such an attitude can become problematic when providers become less sensitive to bilingual medical professionals' potential lack of cultural competence, resulting in compromised care. In this section, however, I want to address the issue of interpreters' linguistic competence more directly.

Because linguistic competence is a prerequisite for quality interpreting, it is essential for health organizations to develop meaningful training and assessment to ensure interpreters' linguistic proficiency and to provide guidelines for interpreter utilization. Assessment of linguistic proficiency and interpreting skills is important not only for hospital interpreters but also for bilingual medical professionals and even family interpreters.

Assessment for bilingual medical professionals is important and necessary because providers are strategic in their interpreter utilization: Depending on the contexts and tasks involved, they may prefer or accept different types of interpreters and modalities of interpreting (see Chapter 7). For example, providers who self-reported high Spanish skills were likely to carry out all conversations themselves, whereas providers with a self-reported medium level of Spanish skills were likely to use their own Spanish for information-based activities but rely on professional interpreters for difficult conversations (Diamond, Tuot, & Karliner, 2012). However, one study found that one in five dual-role bilingual medical professionals does not have sufficient skill to serve as a healthcare interpreter (Moreno et al., 2007). Researchers have emphasized the importance of institutional assessments for medical professionals because providers' self-reported language proficiency does not necessarily match their actual language skills (Diamond, Luft, Chung, & Jacobs, 2012; Diamond, Tuot, et al., 2012; Lion et al., 2013). This is especially true for providers who report to have a mid-range proficiency (Diamond et al., 2014). Together, these findings highlight the importance for providers to accurately assess their Spanish-speaking level *and* the variety and complexity of the tasks involved (i.e., providers may not have an accurate assessment of their language proficiency or the complexity of the tasks involved).

In recent years, researchers have noted that bilingual family members, including children, can be valuable resources in healthcare settings (Green, Free, Bhavnani, & Newman, 2005). I recognize the common concerns about bilingual children serving as healthcare interpreters, including potential threats to the quality of care (e.g., the child may lack necessary knowledge), the child's well-being (e.g., imposition of responsibilities and increased anxiety), and family dynamics (e.g., disruption to social roles; Cohen, Moran-Ellis, & Smaje, 1999; Levine, 2006). However, it is equally important to recognize that these bilingual children often adopt the role of interpreter, helping family members navigate public services/spaces in the host society (J. Green et al., 2005; Reynolds & Orellana, 2009; Valdés, 2003). For these children, interpreting in healthcare settings is not a sudden imposition or unexpected request but an expected social function that they take pride in providing for their family (Angelelli, 2010; J. Green et al., 2005).

It is from this perspective that I believe providing institutional training and assessment for family members who serve as healthcare interpreters would allow providers and health institutions to make informed decisions about the appropriateness and effectiveness of a particular family interpreter. This would also allow providers and institutions to set clear boundaries about the specific contexts and situations that make use of family interpreters acceptable. In situations where a patient has a chronic illness (e.g., diabetes) or requires long-term treatment (e.g., cancer), a qualified, certified family interpreter can be a valuable member of the healthcare team as s/he would have the time to develop the necessary medical knowledge and could provide important background information about the patient's illness management. On the other hand, such an assessment could also assist these bilingual youngsters and family members to gain additional power/ resource in the host society (Valdés, 2003).

By allowing family interpreters to participate in the organizational assessment of interpreting skills, health organizations can have formal control over their quality, training, and practices. Health organizations could have guidelines requiring certain tasks to be performed only by institutionally certified interpreters, including certified family interpreters. Researchers have also recommended that physician training include communicative skills when working with family interpreters (Bond, Bateman, & Nassrally, 2012; Seeleman, Essink-Bot, Selleger, & Bonke, 2012). This allows motivated family members to be actively engaged in the patient-centered care. In addition, through the required training and assessment, family interpreters can learn to anticipate and appreciate providers' different needs and perspectives, allowing them to better meet the clinical demands of healthcare interpreting.

Assessments could include required training as well as certification in multiple levels and/or different clinical specialties. In other words, individuals who pass a certain level of assessment are deemed appropriate to perform specific interpreting tasks (e.g., medical history taking, patient education, procedural consent, or difficult conversations). For example, researchers have argued that interpreters who work in mental health settings require additional training for specialty-specific knowledge and procedures so that they do not normalize a patient's thought processes or affective expression to "make sense" of a patient's incoherent talk (Marcos, 1979), or alternatively, so that they do not make a patient appear more psychiatrically ill through inappropriate use of cultural references (Kilian, Swartz, Dowling, Dlali, & Chiliza, 2014). Other researchers have suggested that interpreters may benefit from specific training to ensure the patient's quality of care and the interpreter's well-being in palliative care (Schenker, Fernandez, Kerr, O'Riordan, & Pantilat, 2012) and oncology settings (Butow et al., 2012). The National Consortium of Interpreter Education Centers has also offered a series of specialty-specific webinars and training for ASL/English healthcare interpreters (The CATIE Center at St. Catherine University, 2014). Finally, interpreters may also need training in self-care to avoid vicarious traumatization (Green, Sperlinger, & Carswell, 2012; Splevins, Cohen, Joseph, Murray, & Bowley, 2010).

Health organizations can impose specific guidelines for certain tasks. For example, family interpreters could be acceptable for routine follow-up appointments for chronic illnesses but if specific clinical concerns are identified, a professional interpreter needs to be scheduled for the next appointment (or requested immediately), or, for surgical consents, only professional interpreters are acceptable except in highly urgent situations. With proper training and assessment, providers, patients, and their interpreters, including bilingual medical professionals and family interpreters, can be much more confident in the appropriateness of their choices. There will also be more institutional control over the quality of bilingual health communication. In addition, the different levels of assessment allow interpreters, including bilingual medical professionals and family interpreters, to easily decline tasks that they are not prepared for or comfortable about (which has been reported as a source of interpreter distress; see J. Green et al., 2005; Splevins et al., 2010; Yang & Gray, 2008).

Finally, with clear institutional guidelines, both providers and interpreters will be empowered to accept or decline certain types of interpreter. Without guidelines, healthcare providers are left with their own judgment, which may be inconsistent or inaccurate. Bilingual medical professionals may feel pressured into performing interpreting tasks that they are not comfortable with because they do not wish to be disagreeable to their colleagues. Quality of healthcare delivery is ensured when providers and interpreters understand their boundaries. For example, an interpreter can feel confident and comfortable to explain that they can perform certain types of interpreting (e.g., patient education) but not others (e.g., surgical consent) based on organizational standards. My findings suggest that providers are willing to follow organizational guidelines when adequate and appropriate resources are provided.

A.3. Interpreters as Passive Conduits versus Active Agents

For providers in our study, the dilemma of viewing interpreters as passive conduits as opposed to active agents is salient. The conduit model of interpreting remains influential in shaping providers' expectations. Providers across five specialty areas share a common expectation of *interpreter as health professional* (Professional), which includes the following dimensions: ability to not take sides, ability to remain emotionally detached, ability to offer literal translation, and medical knowledge and medical terminology (see Chapter 5.A). By viewing interpreters' physical presence as providers' support and as objects that can be offered as a gift (e.g., a caring gesture; see Chapter 7.B.3), providers in our study echoed the prevalent ideology of viewing interpreters as conduits (Dysart-Gale, 2007). However, providers in our study also expected interpreters to be more than conduits: to be human and compassionate and to be proactive in offering culturally sensitive care by noting issues (e.g., nonverbal or emotional cues) that providers may fail to notice. In fact, in addition to the common expectation of the conduit role, researchers have also found providers to expect interpreters to assume a wide variety of roles, including active agents in providing culturally appropriate and sensitive care (Brisset et al., 2014; Greenhalgh, Robb, & Scambler, 2006). In short, the literature has demonstrated that providers experience competing, if not conflicting, expectations of interpreter performances (Bischoff, Kurth, & Henley, 2012; Brisset et al., 2014; Hsieh, 2006; Leanza, 2005). However, rather than simply categorizing these expectations as unrealistic or incompatible, it may be helpful to investigate (a) the various factors and contexts that shape providers' expectations and impact the corresponding interpreter-mediated interactions, and (b) how these expectations are incorporated into providers' normative beliefs and practices.

For example, an earlier study found that inexperienced interpreters are more likely to adopt a conduit role, whereas experienced interpreters actively influence the dynamics and process of medical encounters (Hatton & Webb, 1993). In contrast, my study suggests that when providers become more experienced with interpreter-mediated interactions, they value the Professional dimension more. Providers and interpreters thus appear to diverge on the Professional dimension, which can result in challenges to provider–interpreter collaboration.

In addition, our study suggests that this may be a universal expectation across all specialties, even when providers recognize the value of interpreters' active roles in bilingual health care. As a result, rather than proposing a rejection of the conduit model, a more realistic approach to this phenomenon is to explore how Professional as a theoretical dimension shapes providers' expectations of and collaboration with interpreters. For example, interpreters need to demonstrate mastery of medical knowledge and terminology to be perceived as competent and trustworthy by providers (Flores et al., 2003; Hsieh, Ju, & Kong, 2010). Failure to maintain this Professional dimension may lead to provider–interpreter conflicts even when interpreters view their active intervention as legitimate (Butow et al., 2012; Hsieh, 2006). On the other hand, when relationship bonding takes priority in providers' therapeutic objectives, an interpreter may be expected to adopt an interpreting style that is affectionate and actively protects the patient's Lifeworld. The mixed findings and the apparent tensions of these normative attitudes may be a result of failing to recognize providers' emergent shifts in communicative needs and goals during medical encounters. It is not that providers have conflicting demands but that they expect interpreters to assume different performances depending on moment-by-moment communicative needs.

By taking this approach, we may be able to address many of the conflicting findings in the literature. Rather than identifying *one* ideal form of interpreting style, interpreter type, or interpreting modality that leads to positive outcomes, my findings highlight the importance of being adaptive and responsive to communicative contexts. In other words, the best interpreting style or modality depends on the sociocultural, interpersonal, organizational, temporal, and/or clinical context. A utilitarian approach to interpreters can be valuable and necessary in certain situations, while interpreters-as-co-diagnosticians can be essential in others. A professional interpreter may be necessary when obtaining surgical consent, but a family interpreter can be valuable when taking medical history. An individual's ability to identify the relevant contexts, negotiate their perspectives and objectives, and anticipate others' needs is critical to a successful interpreter-mediated interaction.

B. Advancing the Literature: The Model of Bilingual Health Communication

By presenting the Model of Bilingual Health Communication and synthesizing findings of my decade-long research, my goal is to build on the momentum of current research and to demonstrate the tremendous potential a normative approach holds for providing insights into interpreter-mediated medical encounters (see also Chapter 5.B). Rather than focusing only on interpreters' behaviors or clinical outcomes, I aim to connect these two. In other words, as a normative model for bilingual health care, the Model aims to "provide a basis for recommendations about how communicators can achieve desirable outcomes"

(Goldsmith, 2001, p. 515). From this perspective, the Model is applied with the aim of resolving problems in real healthcare settings. In language-concordant provider–patient interactions, desirable outcomes are not necessarily fixed target variables to be achieved. Rather, desirable outcomes are emergently negotiated and continually (re)evaluated during the evolving, dynamic, and emergent process of a patient's illness event (Dy & Purnell, 2012; Politi & Street, 2011). Similarly, in interpreter-mediated medical encounters, desirable outcomes are not fixed targets to be achieved but are socially constructed through meaningful interactions among all participants.

Finally, because the Model is significantly different from previous theories and perspectives that have been used to examine interpreter-mediated medical encounters, it also has tremendous potential to advance the current literature by highlighting the goal-oriented, interpersonally coordinated, and temporally situated nature of bilingual health care.

B.1. A Multi-party Model of Interpreting

I use the term multi-party (rather than triadic) model of interpreting to highlight that not all interpreter-mediated medical encounters involve (only) three participants (see also Chapter 2.D). All participants (e.g., the provider, the interpreter, the patient, family members, and other health professionals) in interpreter-mediated medical encounters can influence the process and quality of bilingual health communication (Hsieh, 2006, 2010), a finding also supported by recent studies (Fryer, Mackintosh, Stanley, & Crichton, 2013; Leanza et al., 2013; Smith, Swartz, Kilian, & Chiliza, 2013; Zimányi, 2013). In addition, participant dynamics are constantly changing. A meaningful, practical and theoretical model of healthcare interpreting should recognize the possibility of family members (and other participants) influencing the process and content of interpreter-mediated interaction. This approach allows researchers to explore issues that they have observed but largely ignored in the literature.

For example, what happens when a language-discordant patient insists on communicating directly with the provider, or vice versa, despite the presence of an interpreter? Is this a dyadic or triadic interaction? Is this case relevant to the study of interpreter-mediated interaction? How should the role of interpreter be understood and conceptualized here?

A patient's desire to establish direct communication and bonding certainly is not without merit. To insist that whenever an interpreter is available, all communication should be channeled through him/her is to simplify provider–patient communication into "accurate" exchanges of information. However, when we communicate, what is exchanged is not just the information, but also our identities and relationships. This is why our providers insist on maintaining rapport talk with their patients (e.g., "I like her shoes!!" "Tell HER I LOVE HER BABY!"). When a physician with limited language skills communicates with the patient directly even though an interpreter may be readily available, the motivating reason may not just be that the physician is "lazy" or "getting by." As when a request for an on-site interpreter shows more effort than using a telephone interpreter (and thus becomes a show of support by the provider; see Chapter 7.B.3), physicians may believe that the benefits of direct communication outweigh the necessity of having accurate information for the task involved. All of us can appreciate it when our providers make the effort to learn our language to communicate with us. When a provider utters, "你好!," "¡Hola!," or "こんにちは," it means much more than "Hello!" It says, "I care. I respect your uniqueness and cultural identity."

A multi-party model of healthcare interpreting also allows researchers not to become unduly concerned with the number of participants involved. Rather, I ask how are the communicative goals best identified, prioritized, negotiated, and maintained by the parties involved? In other words, if the communicative goal to establish provider–patient bonding is more important than the goal to obtain accurate information (or avoid litigation risks), then direct communication between the provider and the patient should be acceptable, if not welcomed. Providers can establish secondary measures to protect other goals, such as asking an interpreter to stay in the encounter to monitor the effectiveness and appropriateness of the interaction and to intervene as necessary (Watermeyer, 2011).

Another example of a commonly observed but rarely discussed phenomenon is when a family member accompanying a patient to a medical encounter initiates direct communication with the provider in English. Should the hospital interpreter interpret for the patient? Why? Is this relevant to interpreter-mediated medical encounters? How do we conceptualize this change of dynamics in the BHC Model?

Again, neither the dyadic nor the triadic model of interpreting would be sufficient to explain the interaction or provide guidelines for practice. However, a multi-party, normative model of interpreting argues that the appropriate interpreter response is dependent on the normative expectations. If the patient appears curious but remains quiet, the interpreter could move closer to the patient and begin whisper interpreting (i.e., providing simultaneous interpreting at a low volume – whispering in the client's ears). This allows the patient to stay engaged without disrupting the provider–family member interactions. If the patient does not appear to be interested in the conversation or trusts the family member to explain the discussion later, then an interpreter may choose not to provide interpreting at all. On the other hand, if the family member intentionally communicates in English to exclude the patient from the conversation, an interpreter may choose to confront the issue by asserting the interpreter's function of patient empowerment (e.g., "I'm sorry, but I am obligated to keep the patient informed about all interactions that take place during the medical encounter"), challenge other participants' practice through indirect communication (e.g., "Should I interpret what you say?"), or request the provider's guidance (e.g., "Doctor, should I interpret what was just said to the patient?"). The most appropriate answer is context dependent, requiring each individual to identify and negotiate the relevant tasks, identities, and relationships involved to achieve optimal care.

Patient communicative competence (e.g., the ability to seek and provide information) is positively correlated with the quality of information provided by the provider (Cegala & Post, 2009). In bilingual health care, interpreters can play a significant role in this process by overtly and covertly enhancing others' communicative competence. For example, to ensure effective and appropriate provider–interpreter interactions, interpreters may conceal a provider's stigmatizing attitudes (Seale, Rivas, Al-Sarraj, Webb, & Kelly, 2013) or ask questions on behalf of the patient (Hsieh, 2008). Interpreters actively provide emotional support by noting the need to bridge cultural differences and to ensure quality care (Hsieh, 2006, 2008; Hsieh & Hong, 2010; Leanza, 2008; Smith et al., 2013). Conversely, interpreters' behaviors may compromise other speakers' communicative competence. For example, when an interpreter focuses on medical information and ignores the provider's rapport-building talk, providers may appear emotionally detached (Aranguri, Davidson, & Ramirez, 2006).

In short, by taking a multi-party view of interpreting, researchers can expand our investigation beyond the linguistic transformation in interpreter-mediated interactions. When all parties are viewed as active participants in the medical encounter, a new world is opened to researchers of bilingual health care. A wide variety of contextual factors (e.g., communicative goals, interpersonal trust, ongoing relationships, and identity management) become relevant to the process of interpreter-mediated interactions (Hsieh & Hong, 2010; Hsieh et al., 2010; Hsieh, Pitaloka, & Johnson, 2013; Johnson, Thompson, & Downs, 2009). By recognizing the variety of interpreters (e.g., on-site vs. telephone vs. family interpreters) available in healthcare settings, researchers have explored the impacts of different types of interpreter on patient satisfaction, provider expectations, patient–interpreter relationships, institutional costs, discursive processes, and clinical consequences (MacFarlane et al., 2009; Messias, McDowell, & Estrada, 2009; Price et al., 2012). Interpreters, along with their interpersonal relationships, diverse functions, emotions, and job-related hazards, become legitimate issues to be explored (Doherty, MacIntyre, & Wyne, 2010; Splevins et al., 2010). This not only marks a new milestone in the investigation of healthcare interpreting but also expands the field of investigation by recognizing the true complexity of the multilingual, multicultural healthcare process.

B.2. Healthcare Settings as a System-level Structure

While expanding the theoretical frame from a dyadic (i.e., the conduit model) to a multi-party view of healthcare interpreting enables researchers to expand their horizons, it is also important to recognize that the multi-party view has its limits. In particular, the multi-party view of interpreting does not account for structural and/or system-level influences on the process and content of interpreting.

Throughout this book, I have highlighted the many system-level influences that shape providers' expectations and choices of interpreters. For example, I have demonstrated that providers' choices are not necessarily shaped by their desire to cut corners but by factors and variables that are truly beyond their individual control. One major contribution of this book is to highlight the system-level influences on the process and content of interpreter-mediated interactions. If researchers are to treat healthcare interpreting as a particular genre of interpreting, we must not stop at investigating and evaluating technical knowledge or processes of interpreter-mediated interactions in general. In other words, I want to urge researchers to investigate the particular challenges and contexts of healthcare settings.

For example, a healthcare setting is constructed for a specific purpose, to treat ill people. A medical encounter is considered unsuccessful when a patient does not receive quality care, does not experience better health outcomes (e.g., patient satisfaction and/or other biological indicators), and/or experiences health disparities at any stage of their illness experiences (e.g., disparities in diagnosis, treatment, or recovery). In this applied context, interpreting serves a greater purpose than fulfilling patients' or providers' individual communicative goals. Interpreting, as well as provider–patient interaction, is a goal-oriented activity. The goal is to ensure that the patient receives quality and equality in care, with improved health outcomes and minimal health disparities.

From this perspective, healthcare interpreters' roles and functions are distinct from those of all other types of interpreter. Optimal care, rather than neutrality, should be the basis for evaluating interpreters' roles and performances (Solomon, 1997). In other words, there are system-level structures and considerations that may supersede individual communicative goals. For example, although there is a general emphasis on patient autonomy, researchers have argued that if patients do not have the skills to make autonomous decisions (e.g., low health literacy, inadequate communicative competence, lacking relevant knowledge or understanding of social norms), providers are obligated to create the conditions necessary for them to make autonomous decisions (Pantilat, 2008; Quill & Brody, 1996). In bilingual health care, interpreters should serve as system agents, working to achieve the necessary conditions for patients to be empowered in the multi-party, processual model of communication (Hsieh, 2013).

This model recognizes and highlights the reality that interpreters do not simply serve the provider or the patient but have a higher responsibility and obligation in healthcare settings. This attitude is reflected in healthcare providers' willingness to accept interpreters' interventions to ensure quality care despite possible conflicting personal desires and communicative goals (Hsieh, 2010). Similarly, despite their low ranking in the hierarchical healthcare system, an interpreter may feel obligated and justified to resist a provider's prejudicial attitudes or challenge unethical behaviors. In other words, system-level influences become the shared values and constraints that consolidate the diverging views and perspectives of all parties involved in interpreter-mediated interactions. Researchers therefore should (a) identify the system-level influences that condition providers', patients', and interpreters' behaviors in medical encounters, (b) examine the impacts of these system-level influences in enhancing/compromising quality care, and (c) explore the system-level structures that best promote successful bilingual health care.

B.3. Temporal Dimensions of Bilingual Health Care

Reconceptualizing the Meanings of "Time"

One of the undertheorized system-level factors in the literature is time. The literature on interpreter-mediated medical encounters traditionally has conceptualized time as an inescapable constraint. Provider time is a limited resource that is protected through interpreters' non-conduit performances (Davidson, 2000; Hsieh, 2008). Time constraints and the lack of interpreter availability/accessibility are often cited as major reasons for providers' underutilization of professional interpreters (K. C. Lee et al., 2006; Ramirez et al., 2008).

However, by focusing on time as a system constraint, researchers have confounded a wide variety of facilitators and barriers to bilingual health care. For example, providing available/accessible professional interpreters does not necessarily address providers' concerns about disruption to their schedules and priorities (i.e., lack of time). Providers with patients who are unable to concentrate for a coherent conversation for a long period of time, are too weak to move the phone back and forth for an extended period of time, or require immediate interventions due to a clinical crisis, may prefer to rely on an on-site interpreter, regardless of training, as opposed to a professional telephone interpreter. To argue that providers' underutilization of professional interpreters is caused by time constraints or time pressure is to confound the influences of patients' illness symptoms, illness severity, and clinical urgency.

Rather than conceptualizing time as a quantifiable, prized resource to be protected or depleted, it may be more useful to identify and examine the functions and impacts of time (pressure) on individuals' perceptions and decision-making in healthcare settings. For example, providers may make specific decisions based on their perception of time (e.g., using untrained interpreters due to their desire to save time). Studies have found that providers do not in fact spend more time with language-discordant patients (as opposed to language-concordant patients) when they use professional, on-site interpreters (Fagan, Diaz, Reinert, Sciamanna, & Fagan, 2003; Schouten & Schinkel, 2014; Seale, Rivas, & Kelly, 2013; Tocher & Larson, 1999; Wallbrecht, Hodes-Villamar, Weiss, & Ernst, 2014). Nevertheless, providers believe that they do (Tocher & Larson, 1999). Fagan et al. (2003) found that patients with telephone or family interpreters spend significantly more time with their providers and in clinic. In contrast, Locatis et al. (2010) found that patients with telephone interpreters spend significantly less interview time with their provider than patients using in-person or videoconferencing interpreters. Grover, Deakyne, Bajaj, and Roosevelt (2012) found that in-person interpreters significantly reduced the total throughput time for emergency care visits compared to telephone interpreters or bilingual providers.

The important question here is not which mode of interpreting is most time saving but what is happening with the time saved or extended. The fact that professional interpreters do not extend the duration of medical encounters is intriguing. After all, if providers communicate exactly the same way with patients with limited English proficiency as they would with English-speaking patients, the interpreter should increase the length of time. Recent studies identified some intriguing communicative patterns in interpreter-mediated medical encounters. For example, two studies found that patients with interpreters speak significantly less than language-concordant patients; however, providers appear to maintain the same amount of speaking time in both groups (Schouten & Schinkel, 2014; Seale, Rivas, & Kelly, 2013). Seale et al. (2013) found that compared to English-speaking encounters, providers in interpreted encounters are less likely to use humor or discuss patients' feelings or personal circumstances. In fact, Aranguri et al. (2006) found that compared to Spanish-speaking medical encounters, interpreter-mediated medical encounters had virtually no rapport-building talk, a speech genre that is particularly important to Hispanic patients who value interpersonal bonding. These findings suggest that patients with interpreters experience different care, particularly in the area of provider–patient relationships.

In our study, providers talked about the value of interpreters redirecting patients and guiding patients in their communicative process to save time. As such, it would be interesting to examine whether such practices facilitate patient empowerment (e.g., helping patients to seek and provide information) or suppress patients' voices. In other words, rather than focusing on the length of time, a discursive/observational approach to the qualitative differences in provider–patient interactions between types of interpreters or between language-concordant provider-patient pairs versus language-disconcordant pairs would provide significant insights into the content and process of interpreter-mediated medical encounters.

The Temporal Dimension of Illness Management

Another way to consider the impact of time is to examine interpreters' performance and its *long-term* influence on participant communicative competence and quality of care. Most studies in bilingual health care do not consider previous interactions or interpersonal history/relationships between participants. This is consistent with the traditional emphasis on the conduit model, in which interpreters are viewed as language machines (Leanza, 2005). If interpreters perform properly like good machines do, there should be minimal differences from one interpreter to another or from one session to another. After all, a machine either works or it does not. A computer should work today the same way it worked yesterday and the day before yesterday. There is no learning, no memory, and no history or prior relationship between the user and the computer that may influence their future interactions. In other words, if interpreters were treated simply as a functional tool, a sort of dumb terminal – a pure conduit, to facilitate communication, their performance and impact would be limited to the specific interaction. Such an attitude is reflected in researchers' approach to interpreter-mediated interactions, which traditionally has been limited to the immediate, turn-by-turn talk. Few studies explore how interpreters' strategies may influence the quality of communication, quality of care, or interpersonal relationships over time. Instead, it is uncritically presumed that good quality means machine-like in-the-moment translation and that only that approach to interpreting yields good quality health care.

However, researchers have argued that the temporal aspect of illness management requires individuals to learn to coordinate with others efficiently and appropriately (Brashers, Goldsmith, & Hsieh, 2002). Learning is a longitudinal process. It involves evolution over time and the accumulation of experience. As participants learn about each other's communicative needs and styles, there may be important changes in their communicative behaviors. For example, a family interpreter may act on behalf of the patient because they are also caregivers and are aware of the patient's concerns (Rosenberg, Seller, & Leanza, 2008). Professional interpreters have reported that a prior relationship with a patient makes the interpreting task less challenging, as they learn to anticipate the patient's concerns and become familiar with the patient's communicative style (Hsieh, 2006). Providers also noted that familiarity with an interpreter's communicative styles allows them to work more efficiently with the interpreter (Fatahi, Hellstrom, Skott, & Mattsson, 2008; Hsieh et al., 2010). The history between the provider–patient–interpreter triad influences how they interact with each other.

Medical interpreters, thus, need to be mindful about the complexity of their roles, functions, and relationships in healthcare settings. Their performance in bilingual health care and its corresponding influences entail both immediate and long-term consequences. Interpreters adopt various strategies to meet the multiple, emergent, and often conflicting demands in provider–patient interactions (Hsieh, 2006, 2009; White & Laws, 2009). During provider–patient interactions, interpreters need to anticipate providers' and patients' communicative expectations and needs and actively address potential issues of social inequality and cultural difference. For example, when an interpreter makes a speaker's implied meaning explicit in their interpreted text, they draw little attention to the nuances of the potential misunderstanding while ensuring the communication continues smoothly. When an interpreter changes an indirect information-seeking statement into a direct information-seeking question, they improve the provider's ability to hear and to respond to the patient's information needs. Although these strategies were often treated as interpreting errors with negative consequences (e.g., Flores et al., 2003), researchers have noted that some of these strategies can enhance provider–patient communication and relationships (Pham, Thornton, Engelberg, Jackson, & Curtis, 2008). The success of these strategies, however, relies on the interpreter's ability to anticipate and understand the speaker's communicative goals. This can be enhanced over time. If an interpreter misunderstands a speaker's intended meaning, the misinterpreted texts may lead to confusion if not conflict, or even constitute unethical intervention (J. Lee, 2009). From this perspective, developing effective communication practices (e.g., taking the time for meta-communication about the speakers' objectives prior to the medical encounter) to help interpreters learn and to accurately anticipate speakers' intended meanings is critical in ensuring the quality of interpreter-mediated interactions.

On the other hand, interpreters need to recognize that their communicative strategies can influence how patients and providers interact with each other *in the future* (e.g., their health literacy, cultural sensitivity, and communication competence). When interpreters take the time to provide means of self-efficacy to patients, patients not only are empowered to participate in the immediate interaction but also have the opportunity to extend their new skills and knowledge with other providers in future interactions. In contrast, when interpreters actively change a speaker's utterances without informing the speaker about the changes, they deprive the speaker of the opportunity to develop communicative competence. Interpreters thus need to further evaluate the appropriateness of their involvement and intervention in provider–patient interactions. Some strategies may be efficient in the immediate context but do not empower speakers for future interactions.

For example, previous studies have suggested that due to pressure to maintain a neutral performance, interpreters often "hide" their intervention (a) outside of the medical encounter (e.g., coaching patients about their rights or questions to ask when providers are not around; Hsieh, 2006; Smith et al., 2013) or (b) in the voices of others (e.g., imposing their own agenda while appear to be interpreting for others; Leanza et al., 2010; Rosenberg et al., 2008). These strategies allow interpreters to appear neutral while manipulating the process and content of provider–patient communication. Although these strategies may be well intended (as in the case of Ulysses' modification to the provider's question in Chapter 8.A.3), they also limit other speakers' abilities to understand the complexity of bilingual health care. As the providers in our study indicated, they are interested to learn more about the cultural expectations and social norms of their patients (Fatahi et al., 2008; Rosenberg, Leanza, & Seller, 2007).

Such learning of knowledge and communicative skills over time will enable individuals to provide better quality health care and outcomes in the future. A healthcare team with years of experience working with Hispanic patients is different from a healthcare team with little or no experience when they encounter a Hispanic patient. This illustrates the larger principle that familiarity and cultural proximity impacts communicative competence generally and within healthcare settings specifically. Interpreting involves cultural literacy as well as linguistic competence. Such literacy takes time and experience to acquire.

In summary, time as a unit of temporal measurement or an abstract concept fails to appreciate the lived phenomenon of time as duration in relationships and thus fails to encompass the complexity of its influences on provider–patient interactions. By critically examining the functions and impacts of time on provider–patient interactions, we can significantly advance the theoretical development of bilingual health communication.

C. Bilingual Health Communication as Coordinated Achievement

A successful interpreter-mediated medical encounter is a coordinated achievement between all participants involved. By recognizing that the communicative process, the meaning of an illness event, and even the quality of care are socially constructed, the Model of Bilingual Health Communication provides multiple opportunities and entry points for theory development and practice implications.

C.1. The Interdependent Nature of Bilingual Health Communication

Interpreters do not simply transfer information from one language to another. As they provide their linguistic services, they are also in a position to inform, educate, and empower other speakers for future interactions. It is important for providers and healthcare organizations to recognize this central aspect of the interpreter's functions. Some recent studies have highlighted that healthcare providers continue to emphasize interpreters' conduit role (Fatahi et al., 2008; Leanza, 2005). Such attitudes, however, put pressure on interpreters (a) to avoid intervening in the provider–patient communication even when they perceive problematic interactions (Hsieh, 2006, 2009) or (b) to conceal or disguise their intervention to avoid others' scrutiny (Keselman, Cederborg, & Linell, 2010; Leanza et al., 2010). As researchers highlight that successful interpreter-mediated interaction requires providers, patients, and interpreters to coordinate and negotiate their communicative goals (Hsieh, 2010; Leanza et al., 2010), it is important to incorporate these aspects of interpreters' functions into the communicative practices and organizational cultures in healthcare settings. For example, developing organizational cultures that support and value interpreters' clarification and/or elaboration of cultural issues (as opposed to viewing these behaviors as an intrusion on the provider's time) will allow both providers and patients to have better communicative competence in future interactions. Providing training for interpreters to develop interpreting styles that are adaptive and responsive to emergent challenges during medical encounters will improve interpreters' agency in managing problematic encounters (Raymond, 2014; Seale, Rivas, Al-Sarraj, et al., 2013; Watermeyer, 2011).

Examining providers' attitudes and communicative behaviors in interpreter-mediated medical encounters will also be critical to advance theories and practices of bilingual health care. Many researchers have examined providers' impact on interpreter-mediated encounters through their choice of interpreter utilization, including potential barriers and facilitators that may influence their choices (DeCamp, Kuo, Flores, O'Connor, & Minkovitz, 2013; Diamond, Tuot, et al., 2012; Papic, Malak, & Rosenberg, 2012). However, providers' influences over the quality of interpreter-mediated encounters extend far beyond these pre-encounter decisions. Successful interpreter-mediated medical encounters also rely on their abilities to monitor the communicative process, communicate their priorities, negotiate their therapeutic goals with others' communicative needs, and be responsive and adaptive to emergent shifts in the changing boundaries of language, culture, and medicine (Hsieh, 2010; Zimányi, 2013). We know little about whether certain strategies to achieve these objectives are better than others and how providers can best develop these skills.

By examining and comparing monolingual and bilingual provider–patient interactions, researchers can explore best practices for providers to communicate and negotiate their communicative goals during the emergent interactions, maintain control over the quality of care, and develop strategies and skills to work with different types of interpreter. Recent evidence-based studies have demonstrated that providers adopt different communicative behaviors when working with patients who are immigrants or from marginalized populations (Aranguri et al., 2006; Seale et al., 2013). It is important to investigate the causes, processes, and impacts of such practices.

Many scholars have recommended setting up provider–interpreter meetings before provider–patient interactions to identify and prioritize communicative goals (Norris et al., 2005) and after the encounter to debrief potential miscommunication or concerns (Schenker, Smith, Arnold, & Fernandez, 2012). While these are valuable strategies to ensure providers and interpreters can generate shared goals and understandings, they fail to address two issues. First, they are inadequate in helping participants to manage and address communicative challenges during emergent interactions. Communicative goals and needs shift constantly during a medical encounter. For example, a physician may assert an authoritative identity to convince a patient to accept his/her treatment recommendation but shift to a caring, egalitarian identity once the patient has agreed to accept the treatment. Not all communicative goals and needs can be planned ahead through pre-meetings. The interdependent nature of participant behaviors highlights that when one participant experiences poor understanding or miscommunication, other participants can address these challenges immediately *during* the medical encounter. To do so, each individual needs to develop skills and strategies to respond to interactional dilemmas as they emerge. These skills are essential to individual communicative competence and the quality of bilingual health care.

In addition, the focus on provider–interpreter collaboration overlooks patients' voices and goals in the medical discourse. In other words, while provider–interpreter collaborations are essential to successful medical encounters, they are not sufficient in addressing the communicative needs of all participants. Concerns about interpreter–patient bonding and the natural tendency to prioritize the provider's agenda over others' goals in healthcare settings have contributed to the lack of attention to interpreter–patient collaboration. The literature on provider–patient communication has demonstrated that when patients have high communicative competence, providers are also better at meeting their communicative needs and providing better information (Cegala & Post, 2009). Throughout this book, I have discussed interpreters' communicative strategies that allow patients to be empowered and informed and to engage in medical encounters. I have also discussed how providers' communicative strategies may have unintended meanings and consequences in intercultural contexts. The literature on minority and language-discordant populations has noted that these patients are often marginalized in both the host society and healthcare settings. Researchers may further contribute to these disparities if they overlook strategies and practices that could best incorporate these patients' voices in interpreter-mediated encounters.

Possible solutions to incorporating patients' voices include a pre/post-consultation meeting with the interpreter, which would allow the patient to coordinate with the interpreter to best communicate and negotiate their communicative goals and illness-related needs. Providing training, assessment, and guidelines for family interpreters who wish to provide a meaningful contribution to their family member's illness experiences would also help protect the patient's voice and agenda. For example, when a family interpreter recognizes that s/he does not have adequate ability to perform interpreting services in a particular situation through his/her training, s/he will be empowered to make an educated decision to decline the task and thus help the provider and health institution to ensure quality of care. Another possible way to include patients' voices in medical discourse is to provide information to educate patients about their rights to professional interpreter services and to arrange patient training to develop communicative competence in interpreter-mediated medical encounters.

In summary, recognizing the interdependent nature of the communicative process allows researchers to consider a wide variety of interventions that are not limited to interpreters' language performances. The literature has just begun to recognize and investigate the provider's role in contributing to the quality of bilingual health communication. However, the patient's role in bilingual health care remains one of the underinvestigated areas in the current literature. It is important for researchers and practitioners to consider how best to include and protect the patient's voice and agenda in bilingual health communication, which will lead to a significant contribution to theory development and practice implications.

C.2. Bilingual Health Communication as Cross-cultural Care

In Chapter 1, I examined the various disciplines that share common interests in interpreter-mediated medical encounters, noting the emergence of complex research designs and evidence-based approaches in recent years. Bilingual health care, as an interdisciplinary area of study, can benefit greatly by integrating insights from many areas of study (e.g., minority health, health communication, cross-cultural care, health disparities, health literacy, and provider–patient communication) that have long been investigated by different disciplines.

Recognizing that interpreter-mediated medical encounters are communicative activities specific to healthcare settings, I have proposed a paradigm shift: Move away from the text-oriented, interpreter-centered approach by recognizing bilingual health care as a goal-oriented, context-situated communicative activity that requires coordination between multiple parties. Throughout this book, I have demonstrated how a normative approach can generate new research directions for bilingual health care to advance theories and improve practices. Providing practice recommendations grounded in evidence-based, theory-oriented research has always been one of the most fulfilling aspects of my scholarship. In this final section, I want to highlight a few issues that I have implied but have yet to address directly in this book.

Cross-cultural Applicability of the BHC Model

As a normative model of communication, the BHC Model views bilingual health care as a socially constructed, goal-driven communicative activity that requires multi-party coordination on the meanings and processes of healthcare delivery. In other words, while the theoretical constructs of the Model remain consistent in different contexts (e.g., clinical, cultural, and sociopolitical contexts), how these constructs are understood, interpreted, and enacted by participants from different cultures (and systems) may differ.

Some of my discussions about QEC as the transcending value/principle for the BHC Model may have privileged a Western perspective as my data and participants are based in the United States. However, as I explained in Chapter 5, the meanings of QEC are culturally and socially constructed. When a provider believes that respecting family values compromises a patient's autonomy and as such is the equivalent of destroying the provider's "moral compass" (Solomon, 1997), cultural differences in communicative behaviors take on additional meanings as they represent the seemingly irreconcilable cultural and value differences between the provider and the patient.

Arguing that QEC is defined by the universal values of (Western) medicine does not necessarily circumvent the cultural and value differences embedded in system norms. For example, Parsons et al. (2007) identified significant differences between US and Japanese providers' communicative patterns about children's cancer diagnosis although both practice Western-style medicine. Whereas 65 percent of US physicians reported that they always tell children about their cancer diagnoses, only 9.5 percent of Japanese physicians reported the same. In fact, less than 1 percent of US physicians reported rarely or never telling children about their cancer diagnoses, but 34.5 percent of Japanese physicians reported doing so. It is important to note that these communicative patterns are culturally situated and are driven by system norms, reflecting corresponding beliefs, ethics, and values. For example, whereas 92.8 percent of US physicians believe that informing a child of a cancer diagnosis would not increase parental burden, 43.5 percent of Japanese physicians believe that it would. Parsons et al. (2007, p. 64) noted:

> US physicians endorsed the belief (completely agreed or generally agreed) that it is their responsibility to tell the child the cancer diagnosis (98%), that the child's knowledge enhances their participation in their care (99.1%), and that knowledge of the cancer diagnosis within the community would enhance the child's psychosocial support (98.3%). [...] The pattern of response was significantly different (by χ^2 p-value) for Japanese physicians for each of these variables.

It is also important to remember that parents and physicians in the United States do not always subscribe to such disclosure practices. Prior to 1960, both parents and physicians in the United States believed that children should not be informed about their cancer diagnoses (Chesler, Paris, & Barbarin, 1986). The shift in US physicians' and parents' attitudes further highlights the socially constructed nature of provider–patient interactions. In other words, what appears to be a universal value within Western medicine (e.g., patients' right to information) is, in fact, a recently emerged social construct of US culture.

Because all participants' communicative behaviors are driven by their system norms and the corresponding beliefs, ethics, and values, provider–patient conflicts over system norms can be particularly difficult. By proposing that QEC should serve as the guiding principle in conflicting system norms *and* acknowledging that QEC is still a social construct, the BHC Model recognizes that best practices for interpreter-mediated medical encounters in the United States may not be appropriate in other countries or cultures due to differences in cultural expectations of provider–patient–interpreter relationships and hierarchy, family members' roles and responsibilities, and patients' right to autonomous and informed decisions (see Chapter 5.C). An English–Japanese healthcare interpreter who provides services to a Japanese parent of a child with cancer in the United States will face very different challenges from another interpreter who works for an American parent with a child with cancer in Japan, and so their effective communicative practices and appropriate performances may differ significantly.

For example, because once a cancer disclosure has been made to a child it cannot be taken back, an interpreter may need to address this issue *immediately* if a US physician made the disclosure unexpectedly without the Japanese parents' knowledge or consent (e.g., by stopping the interpreting to check for parental consent or to educate the physician about Japanese cultural norms). On the other hand, when a Japanese physician does not share cancer information even when the US child asks for it, an interpreter may choose to discuss this issue *later* in post-consultation meetings (e.g., explaining to the physician about US cultural norms for patients' informed decision-making) to minimize challenges to the physician's authority, an important cultural value for Japanese culture, which has high power differences. In both cases, providers and patients share different cultural norms about cancer disclosure, which emerge as interactional dilemmas during the discursive process. However, best practices for interpreters' solutions are different due to the nature of the communication (i.e., a disclosure cannot be unheard) and the cultural expectation of provider identity (e.g., egalitarian versus hierarchical). Successful bilingual health communication requires interpreters to have individual agency to make these on-line decisions and perform the necessary tasks as these interactional challenges emerge during the discursive process.

Finally, because individuals may still differ in their individual agency and communicative goals, each interpreter-mediated medical encounter may entail different communicative strategies that are effective and/or appropriate. In short, the BHC Model aims to accommodate and provide guidelines not just for differences across cultures but also between individuals, and for emergent shifts in communicative goals.

Addressing Social Injustice/Inequality

One may argue that QEC is likely to be determined by the dominant values and norms of the host society. For example, physicians in the United States may request court custody to take a child patient away from Hmong parents who are unable to give accurate medications (Fadiman, 1997). As a result, patients are likely to be subjected to the system norms of power and hierarchy in the host society and its healthcare system. For example, an analysis of cancer surgeons suggested that the surgeons had "a predictable cancer philosophy" that they applied to all patients *irrespective* of individual differences between patients (Taylor, 1988). In other words, as far as truth-telling of prognosis is concerned, as the less-dominant person in the physician–patient communication as well as the person who is more likely to be influenced by the result of telling (or not telling) the diagnosis, a patient is often at the mercy of his or her physician (Miyaji, 1993).

A challenge faced by a normative model is that it is often regulated by sociocultural norms. As such, it can be vulnerable to the social injustice and inequality that are embedded in the social norms of a particular community, time, or place.

Nevertheless, a unique aspect of the BHC Model is its recognition of interpreters' agency and responsibility in addressing social injustice and protecting patients' voices and perspectives. Such an attitude has been reflected in current literature, which recognizes the needs and values for interpreters to serve as patient advocates and system agents (Leanza, 2005; Messias et al., 2009; Roat, 1996). In other words, interpreters are expected *not* to blindly reinforce the existing unbalanced or unjust processes of communication/relationship in bilingual health communication. The BHC Model expects a skillful interpreter to have high individual agency in providing all participants with equal access to and effectiveness of clinical and interpersonal care. This is necessary to ensure QEC (i.e., individuals' understanding of their well-being and having comparable access and effectiveness of care).

In other words, an interpreter is obligated to help protect all participants' voices and perspectives. A truly marginalized individual may not have the knowledge, skill, or agency to voice their opinions or needs. From this perspective, if a patient does not have sufficient health literacy to ask questions, an interpreter should feel empowered to help the patient address potential concerns. When Stacey [1] asked her patients with low communicative competence to "give [her] a word or something that they don't understand" so she could "ask different questions to the doctor on their behalf" (see Chapter 8), she gave the patient access to the medical discourse and allowed the patient's perspectives to be heard. This is not an infringement of the patient's voice; rather, this approach recognizes interpreters' critical role in ensuring QEC by protecting individuals' access to and effectiveness of care during the communicative process.

I recognize that conceptualizing interpreters as social agents who are obligated to protect individuals' equal access to and effectiveness of bilingual health communication may appear to be a Western value, as not all cultures believe that all individuals should have equal footing in a communicative event. In this regard, I view interpreters instrumental in ensuring one of the fundamental human rights delineated in The Universal Declaration of Human Rights (The United Nations, 1948): "Article 19: Everyone has the right to freedom of opinion and expression; this right includes freedom to hold opinions without interference and to seek, receive and impart information and ideas through any media and regardless of frontiers." This obligation to human rights transcends any cultural/system norms and is essential to the communicative process in healthcare settings. The common denominator is our shared humanity.

In summary, while QEC is a social construct, individuals in interpreter-mediated encounters should work to generate an integrated value that serves as the guiding principle to resolve conflicts between system norms. Recognizing that not all systems and participants are of equal footing, the BHC Model argues that interpreters are obligated to protect all participants' voices, allowing their perspectives and needs to be heard during the communicative process.

Transparency in the Communicative Process

It is important to note that interpreters' obligation within the BHC Model is to the *process* rather than the outcome of communication. After all, an interpreter cannot and should not dictate the definition of quality of care. This is particularly important as interpreters' understandings can be flawed as well (e.g., providing emotional support that interferes with the mental health provider's therapeutic goals). It is from this perspective that I argued earlier in this book that *transparency* in the discursive process is necessary for all participants to actively manage and negotiate the meanings of QEC.

Previous studies have suggested that providers may be open to interpreters' intervention but expect transparency in the process (e.g., informing providers about their alterations; Hsieh, 2010). However, there may be situations in which an interpreter may find maintaining transparency difficult. For example, because interpreters are sensitive to others' communicative goals as they manage the discursive process, they may find providers' management of multiple goals problematic. A study about actual provider–patient interactions concluded that although providers often advocated shared decision-making as a central value of patient-centered care, treatment decisions "tended to be unilaterally made, using a variety of persuasive approaches to ensure agreement with the physician's recommendation" (Karnieli-Miller & Eisikovits, 2009, p. 6). As interpreters become aware of providers' competing values and goals, they may find the providers' manipulation of information giving and withholding (along with other persuasive approaches) problematic if not unethical. Although interpreters' training has provided them with more active roles, such as patient advocate or system agent (Brisset et al., 2013), interpreters may find it difficult to challenge providers' (deceptive) manipulation of information due to the organizational hierarchy, provider–patient relationship, clinical complexity, and even lack of job security.

When and how interpreters can best provide their intervention, including pragmatic alterations and physician education, may be dependent on various contexts (e.g., clinical, interpersonal, organizational, sociocultural, and ethical). In addition, many of the contextual issues are beyond what can be addressed through interpreter training. What works for a senior on-site hospital interpreter who has a supportive organizational culture and shares strong provider–interpreter trust may not work for a telephone interpreter who randomly works with a nationwide pool of professionals. An interpreter for mental health care may need a different approach than an interpreter in an emergency department (see also Hsieh & Hong, 2010; Hsieh et al., 2013). As a result, interpreter training cannot offer standardized solutions to interpreter interventions. Rather, we can only educate interpreters about the variety of issues they need to consider as they contemplate *whether*, *when*, and *how* they should intervene in provider–patient interactions.

Assessing Quality of Care in Cross-cultural Contexts

Bilingual health communication is a complicated communicative activity as it is situated in provider–patient interactions in intercultural contexts. Traditionally, researchers have examined interpreters' ability to provide accurate, faithful, and neutral interpreting as indicators of quality of care. Throughout this book, I have provided numerous examples about how such understanding fails to recognize the complexity of bilingual health care.

As researchers continue to assess quality of care in interpreter-mediated medical encounters, a major challenge will be how the theoretical component is measured. To accurately compare the differences between language-concordant and language-discordant medical encounters and to derive meaningful interpretations and interventions, we need to remember that patients from different cultures often have different expectations of and preferences for provider–patient interactions (Schouten & Meeuwesen, 2006). In other words, differences in communicative patterns between language-concordant interactions versus interpreted interactions do not necessarily mean one group of patients receives inferior care. It could be a result of providers or interpreters accommodating the needs and expectations of language-discordant patients. For example, researchers noted that compared to English-speaking medical encounters, providers rarely use medical jargon when communicating with Spanish-speaking patients, regardless of the presence or type of interpreters (Simon et al., 2013). Considering that low health literacy disproportionally affects individuals from ethnic minorities and marginalized groups in the United States, providers' avoidance of using medical jargon may improve Spanish-speaking patients' quality of care. Although the use of humor in medical encounters is common in the United States to promote the provider–patient relationship and patient satisfaction (Scholl, 2007; Scholl & Ragan, 2003), providers' joking or teasing in healthcare settings can be perceived to be insensitive or patronizing in Japanese culture (Hsieh & Terui, 2015; Ishikawa, Takayama, Yamazaki, Seki, & Katsumata, 2002). As a result, if we observe reduced use of humor or an interpreter omitting humorous talk for Japanese-speaking patients in the United States, the phenomenon should be recognized as culturally sensitive care rather than coded as "lack of rapport talk."

Similarly, researchers will need to be more critical and vigilant about their research designs. There are several issues that should foreground their understanding and their planning of research design. First, language-concordant encounters in different languages/cultures may differ significantly from one another due to differences in cultural norms and social expectations (Schouten & Meeuwesen, 2006). In addition, language concordance may include various combinations. For example, both the provider and the patient may be native speakers of the language. Alternatively, it may be that one of them speaks in their second language, with varying fluency level (e.g., a physician who has had a 10-week training course in medical Spanish or a patient who speaks English after living in the United States for 10 years). Second, successful communication for language-discordant patients may look very different due to differences in contexts (e.g., clinical, sociocultural, or sociopolitical contexts). For example, effective communicative practices for providers working with family interpreters may not be appropriate when working with professional interpreters. Appropriate interpreter behaviors for a Japanese patient may be problematic for a Russian patient. Interpreter interventions in the

United States, where social equality is prevalent, may not work in another culture where social hierarchy is embraced.

From this perspective, researchers should avoid oversimplifying the differences between language-concordant and language-discordant medical encounters. I recognize the difficulties faced when conducting studies in bilingual healthcare settings due to the limited number of interpreter-mediated interactions for meaningful comparisons across various conditions. By clearly identifying participant characteristics as well as the conditions and presumptions of the comparisons, researchers and readers will be in a better position to derive meaningful interpretations and valuable interventions. In short, as we critically examine the dynamics and impacts of interpreter-mediated interactions in intercultural contexts, it is important for researchers to be sensitive to the complex contexts that shape the meanings of our findings.

References

Andres, E., Wynia, M., Regenstein, M., & Maul, L. (2013). Should I call an interpreter? How do physicians with second language skills decide? *Journal of Health Care for the Poor and Underserved*, 24, 525–539.

Angelelli, C. V. (2010). A professional ideology in the making: Bilingual youngsters interpreting for their communities and the notion of (no) choice. *Translation and Interpretation Studies*, 5, 94–108.

Aranguri, C., Davidson, B., & Ramirez, R. (2006). Patterns of communication through interpreters: A detailed sociolinguistic analysis. *Journal of General Internal Medicine*, 21, 623–629.

Bischoff, A., Kurth, E., & Henley, A. (2012). Staying in the middle: A qualitative study of health care interpreters' perceptions of their work. *Interpreting*, 14, 1–22.

Bond, J., Bateman, J., & Nassrally, S. M. (2012). The role of ad-hoc interpreters in teaching communication skills with ethnic minorities. *Medical Teacher*, 34, 81.

Brashers, D. E., Goldsmith, D. J., & Hsieh, E. (2002). Information seeking and avoiding in health contexts. *Human Communication Research*, 28, 258–271.

Brisset, C., Leanza, Y., & Laforest, K. (2013). Working with interpreters in health care: A systematic review and meta-ethnography of qualitative studies. *Patient Education and Counseling*, 91, 131–140.

Brisset, C., Leanza, Y., Rosenberg, E., Vissandjée, B., Kirmayer, L., Muckle, G., ... Laforce, H. (2014). Language barriers in mental health care: A survey of primary care practitioners. *Journal of Immigrant and Minority Health*, 16, 1238–1246.

Butow, P. N., Lobb, E., Jefford, M., Goldstein, D., Eisenbruch, M., Girgis, A., ... Schofield, P. (2012). A bridge between cultures: Interpreters' perspectives of consultations with migrant oncology patients. *Supportive Care in Cancer*, 20, 235–244.

Carroll, L. N., Calhoun, R. E., Subido, C. C., Painter, I. S., & Meischke, H. W. (2013). Serving limited English proficient callers: A survey of 9-1-1 police telecommunicators. *Prehospital and Disaster Medicine*, 28, 286–291.

The CATIE Center at St. Catherine University. (2014). Interpreting in healthcare settings. Retrieved March 14, 2015, from www.healthcareinterpreting.org/.

Cegala, D. J., & Post, D. M. (2009). The impact of patients' participation on physicians' patient-centered communication. *Patient Education and Counseling*, 77, 202–208.

Chesler, M. A., Paris, J., & Barbarin, O. A. (1986). "Telling" the child with cancer: Parental choices to share information with ill children. *Journal of Pediatric Psychology*, 11, 497–516.

Cohen, S., Moran-Ellis, J., & Smaje, C. (1999). Children as informal interpreters in GP consultations: Pragmatics and ideology. *Sociology of Health & Illness*, 21, 163–186.

Davidson, B. (2000). The interpreter as institutional gatekeeper: The social-linguistic role of interpreters in Spanish–English medical discourse. *Journal of Sociolinguistics*, 4, 379–405.

DeCamp, L. R., Kuo, D. Z., Flores, G., O'Connor, K., & Minkovitz, C. S. (2013). Changes in language services use by US pediatricians. *Pediatrics*, 132(2), e396–406.

Diamond, L. C., Chung, S., Ferguson, W., Gonzalez, J., Jacobs, E. A., & Gany, F. (2014). Relationship between self-assessed and tested non–English-language proficiency among primary care providers. *Medical Care*, 52, 435–438.

Diamond, L. C., Luft, H. S., Chung, S., & Jacobs, E. A. (2012). "Does this doctor speak my language?" Improving the characterization of physician non-English language skills. *Health Services Research*, 47, 556–569.

Diamond, L. C., Schenker, Y., Curry, L., Bradley, E. H., & Fernandez, A. (2009). Getting by: Underuse of interpreters by resident physicians. *Journal of General Internal Medicine*, 24, 256–262.

Diamond, L. C., Tuot, D., & Karliner, L. (2012). The use of Spanish language skills by physicians and nurses: Policy implications for teaching and testing. *Journal of General Internal Medicine*, 27, 117–123.

Doherty, S. M., MacIntyre, A. M., & Wyne, T. (2010). How does it feel for you? The emotional impact and specific challenges of mental health interpreting. *Mental Health Review Journal*, 15, 31–44.

Dy, S. M., & Purnell, T. S. (2012). Key concepts relevant to quality of complex and shared decision-making in health care: A literature review. *Social Science & Medicine*, 74, 582–587.

Dysart-Gale, D. (2007). Clinicians and medical interpreters: Negotiating culturally appropriate care for patients with limited English ability. *Family & Community Health*, 30, 237–246.

Elderkin-Thompson, V., Silver, R. C., & Waitzkin, H. (2001). When nurses double as interpreters: A study of Spanish-speaking patients in a US primary care setting. *Social Science & Medicine*, 52, 1343–1358.

Fadiman, A. (1997). *The spirit catches you and you fall down: A Hmong child, her American doctors, and the collision of two cultures*. New York: Farrar, Straus and Giroux.

Fagan, M. J., Diaz, J. A., Reinert, S. E., Sciamanna, C. N., & Fagan, D. M. (2003). Impact of interpretation method on clinic visit length. *Journal of General Internal Medicine*, 18, 634–638.

Fatahi, N., Hellstrom, M., Skott, C., & Mattsson, B. (2008). General practitioners' views on consultations with interpreters: A triad situation with complex issues. *Scandinavian Journal of Primary Health Care*, 26, 40–45.

Flores, G. (2005). The impact of medical interpreter services on the quality of health care: A systematic review. *Medical Care Research & Review*, 62, 255–299.

Flores, G., Laws, M. B., Mayo, S. J., Zuckerman, B., Abreu, M., Medina, L., & Hardt, E. J. (2003). Errors in medical interpretation and their potential clinical consequences in pediatric encounters. *Pediatrics*, 111, 6–14.

Fryer, C. E., Mackintosh, S. F., Stanley, M. J., & Crichton, J. (2013). 'I understand all the major things': How older people with limited English proficiency decide their need for a professional interpreter during health care after stroke. *Ethnicity & Health*, 18, 610–625.

Ginde, A. A., Sullivan, A. F., Corel, B., Caceres, J. A., & Camargo, C. A., Jr. (2010). Reevaluation of the effect of mandatory interpreter legislation on use of professional interpreters for ED patients with language barriers. *Patient Education and Counseling*, 81, 204–206.

Goldsmith, D. J. (2001). A normative approach to the study of uncertainty and communication. *Journal of Communication*, 51, 514–533.

Green, H., Sperlinger, D., & Carswell, K. (2012). Too close to home? Experiences of Kurdish refugee interpreters working in UK mental health services. *Journal of Mental Health*, 21, 227–235.

Green, J., Free, C., Bhavnani, V., & Newman, T. (2005). Translators and mediators: Bilingual young people's accounts of their interpreting work in health care. *Social Science & Medicine*, 60, 2097–2110.

Greenhalgh, T., Robb, N., & Scambler, G. (2006). Communicative and strategic action in interpreted consultations in primary health care: A Habermasian perspective. *Social Science & Medicine*, 63, 1170–1187.

Grover, A., Deakyne, S., Bajaj, L., & Roosevelt, G. E. (2012). Comparison of throughput times for limited English proficiency patient visits in the emergency department between different interpreter modalities. *Journal of Immigrant and Minority Health*, 14, 602–607.

Hatton, D. C., & Webb, T. (1993). Information transmission in bilingual, bicultural contexts: A field study of community health nurses and interpreters. *Journal of Community Health Nursing*, 10, 137–147.

Hsieh, E. (2006). Conflicts in how interpreters manage their roles in provider–patient interactions. *Social Science & Medicine*, 62, 721–730.

Hsieh, E. (2008). "I am not a robot!" Interpreters' views of their roles in health care settings. *Qualitative Health Research*, 18, 1367–1383.

Hsieh, E. (2009). Bilingual health communication: Medical interpreters' construction of a mediator role. In D. E. Brashers & D. J. Goldsmith (Eds.), *Communicating to manage health and illness* (pp. 135–160). New York: Routledge.

Hsieh, E. (2010). Provider–interpreter collaboration in bilingual health care: Competitions of control over interpreter-mediated interactions. *Patient Education and Counseling*, 78, 154–159.

Hsieh, E. (2013). Health literacy and patient empowerment: The role of medical interpreters in bilingual health communication. In M. J. Dutta & G. L. Kreps (Eds.), *Reducing health disparities: Communication intervention* (pp. 41–66). New York: Peter Lang.

Hsieh, E., & Hong, S. J. (2010). Not all are desired: Providers' views on interpreters' emotional support for patients. *Patient Education and Counseling*, 81, 192–197.

Hsieh, E., Ju, H., & Kong, H. (2010). Dimensions of trust: The tensions and challenges in provider–interpreter trust. *Qualitative Health Research*, 20, 170–181.

Hsieh, E., Pitaloka, D., & Johnson, A. J. (2013). Bilingual health communication: Distinctive needs of providers from five specialties. *Health Communication*, 28, 557–567.

Hsieh, E., & Terui, S. (2015). Inherent tensions and challenges of oncologist–patient communication: Implications for interpreter training in health-care settings. *Journal of Applied Communication Research*, 43, 141–162.

Ishikawa, H., Takayama, T., Yamazaki, Y., Seki, Y., & Katsumata, N. (2002). Physician–patient communication and patient satisfaction in Japanese cancer consultations. *Social Science & Medicine*, 55, 301–311.

Johnson, H., Thompson, A., & Downs, M. (2009). Non-Western interpreters' experiences of trauma: The protective role of culture following exposure to oppression. *Ethnicity & Health*, 14, 407–418.

Karliner, L. S., Jacobs, E. A., Chen, A. H., & Mutha, S. (2007). Do professional interpreters improve clinical care for patients with limited English proficiency? A systematic review of the literature. *Health Services Research*, 42, 727–754.

Karnieli-Miller, O., & Eisikovits, Z. (2009). Physician as partner or salesman? Shared decision-making in real-time encounters. *Social Science & Medicine*, 69, 1–8.

Keselman, O., Cederborg, A.-C., & Linell, P. (2010). "That is not necessary for you to know!" Negotiation of participation status of unaccompanied children in interpreter-mediated asylum hearings. *Interpreting*, 12, 83–104.

Kilian, S., Swartz, L., Dowling, T., Dlali, M., & Chiliza, B. (2014). The potential consequences of informal interpreting practices for assessment of patients in a South African psychiatric hospital. *Social Science & Medicine*, 106, 159–167.

Leanza, Y. (2005). Roles of community interpreters in pediatrics as seen by interpreters, physicians and researchers. *Interpreting*, 7, 167–192.

Leanza, Y. (2008). Community interpreter's power: The hazards of a disturbing attribute. *Journal of Medical Anthropology*, 31, 211–220.

Leanza, Y., Boivin, I., & Rosenberg, E. (2010). Interruptions and resistance: A comparison of medical consultations with family and trained interpreters. *Social Science & Medicine*, 70, 1888–1895.

Leanza, Y., Boivin, I., & Rosenberg, E. (2013). The patient's Lifeworld: Building meaningful clinical encounters between patients, physicians and interpreters. *Communication & Medicine*, 10, 13–25.

Lee, J. (2009). Interpreting inexplicit language during courtroom examination. *Applied Linguistics*, 30, 93–114.

Lee, K. C., Winickoff, J. P., Kim, M. K., Campbell, E. G., Betancourt, J. R., Park, E. R., … Weissman, J. S. (2006). Resident physicians' use of professional and nonprofessional interpreters: A national survey. *Journal of the American Medical Association*, 296, 1050–1053.

Levine, C. (2006). Use of children as interpreters. *Journal of the American Medical Association*, 296, 2802.

Lion, K. C., Thompson, D. A., Cowden, J. D., Michel, E., Rafton, S. A., Hamdy, R. F., … Ebel, B. E. (2013). Clinical Spanish use and language proficiency testing among pediatric residents. *Academic Medicine*, 88, 1478–1484.

Locatis, C., Williamson, D., Gould-Kabler, C., Zone-Smith, L., Detzler, I., Roberson, J., … Ackerman, M. (2010). Comparing in-person, video, and telephonic medical interpretation. *Journal of General Internal Medicine*, 25, 345–350.

MacFarlane, A., Dzebisova, Z., Karapish, D., Kovacevic, B., Ogbebor, F., & Okonkwo, E. (2009). Arranging and negotiating the use of informal interpreters in general practice consultations: Experiences of refugees and asylum seekers in the west of Ireland. *Social Science & Medicine*, 69, 210–214.

Marcos, L. R. (1979). Effects of interpreters on the evaluation of psychopathology in non-English-speaking patients. *American Journal of Psychiatry*, 136, 171–174.

Meeuwesen, L., Twilt, S., ten Thije, J. D., & Harmsen, H. (2010). "Ne diyor?" (What does she say?): Informal interpreting in general practice. *Patient Education and Counseling*, 81, 198–203.

Messias, D. K. H., McDowell, L., & Estrada, R. D. (2009). Language interpreting as social justice work: Perspectives of formal and informal healthcare interpreters. *Advances in Nursing Science*, 32, 128–143.

Miyaji, N. T. (1993). The power of compassion: Truth-telling among American doctors in the care of dying patients. *Social Science & Medicine*, 36, 249–264.

Moreno, M. R., Otero-Sabogal, R., & Newman, J. (2007). Assessing dual-role staff-interpreter linguistic competency in an integrated healthcare system. *Journal of General Internal Medicine*, 22, S331–335.

Norris, W. M., Wenrich, M. D., Nielsen, E. L., Treece, P. D., Jackson, J. C., & Curtis, J. R. (2005). Communication about end-of-life care between language-discordant patients and clinicians: Insights from medical interpreters. *Journal of Palliative Medicine*, 8, 1016–1024.

Pantilat, S. (2008). Ethics fast fact: Autonomy vs. beneficence. Retrieved March 14, 2015, from http://missinglink.ucsf.edu/lm/ethics/Content%20Pages/fast_fact_auton_bene.htm.

Papic, O., Malak, Z., & Rosenberg, E. (2012). Survey of family physicians' perspectives on management of immigrant patients: Attitudes, barriers, strategies, and training needs. *Patient Education and Counseling*, 86, 205–209.

Parsons, S. K., Saiki-Craighill, S., Mayer, D. K., Sullivan, A. M., Jeruss, S., Terrin, N., … Block, S. (2007). Telling children and adolescents about their cancer diagnosis: Cross-cultural comparisons between pediatric oncologists in the US and Japan. *Psycho-Oncology*, 16, 60–68.

Pham, K., Thornton, J. D., Engelberg, R. A., Jackson, J. C., & Curtis, J. R. (2008). Alterations during medical interpretation of ICU family conferences that interfere with or enhance communication. *Chest*, 134, 109–116.

Phillips, C. (2013). Remote telephone interpretation in medical consultations with refugees: Meta-communications about care, survival and selfhood. *Journal of Refugee Studies*, 5, 505–523.

Politi, M. C., & Street, R. L. (2011). The importance of communication in collaborative decision making: Facilitating shared mind and the management of uncertainty. *Journal of Evaluation in Clinical Practice*, 17, 579–584.

Price, E. L., Pérez-stable, E. J., Nickleach, D., Lopez, M., & Karliner, L. S. (2012). Interpreter perspectives of in-person, telephonic, and videoconferencing medical interpretation in clinical encounters. *Patient Education and Counseling*, 87, 226–232.

Quill, T. E., & Brody, H. (1996). Physician recommendations and patient autonomy: Finding a balance between physician power and patient choice. *Annals of Internal Medicine*, 125, 763–769.

Ramirez, D., Engel, K. G., & Tang, T. S. (2008). Language interpreter utilization in the emergency department setting: A clinical review. *Journal of Health Care for the Poor and Underserved*, 19, 352–362.

Raymond, C. W. (2014). Conveying information in the interpreter-mediated medical visit: The case of epistemic brokering. *Patient Education and Counseling*, 97, 38–46.

Reynolds, J. F., & Orellana, M. F. (2009). New immigrant youth interpreting in White public space. *American Anthropologist*, 111, 211–223.

Roat, C. E. (1996). *Bridging the gap: A basic training for medical interpreters*. Seattle, WA: Cross Cultural Health Care Program.

Rosenberg, E., Leanza, Y., & Seller, R. (2007). Doctor-patient communication in primary care with an interpreter: Physician perceptions of professional and family interpreters. *Patient Education and Counseling*, 67, 286–292.

Rosenberg, E., Seller, R., & Leanza, Y. (2008). Through interpreters' eyes: Comparing roles of professional and family interpreters. *Patient Education and Counseling*, 70, 87–93.

Schenker, Y., Fernandez, A., Kerr, K., O'Riordan, D., & Pantilat, S. Z. (2012). Interpretation for discussions about end-of-life issues: Results from a national survey of health care interpreters. *Journal of Palliative Medicine*, 15, 1019–1026.

Schenker, Y., Smith, A. K., Arnold, R. M., & Fernandez, A. (2012). "Her husband doesn't speak much English": Conducting a family meeting with an interpreter. *Journal of Palliative Medicine*, 15, 494–498.

Scholl, J. C. (2007). The use of humor to promote patient-centered care. *Journal of Applied Communication Research*, 35, 156–176.

Scholl, J. C., & Ragan, S. L. (2003). The use of humor in promoting positive provider–patient interactions in a hospital rehabilitation unit. *Health Communication*, 15, 319–330.

Schouten, B. C., & Meeuwesen, L. (2006). Cultural differences in medical communication: A review of the literature. *Patient Education and Counseling*, 64, 21–34.

Schouten, B. C., & Schinkel, S. (2014). Turkish migrant GP patients' expression of emotional cues and concerns in encounters with and without informal interpreters. *Patient Education and Counseling*, 97, 23–29.

Seale, C., Rivas, C., Al-Sarraj, H., Webb, S., & Kelly, M. (2013). Moral mediation in interpreted health care consultations. *Social Science & Medicine*, 98, 141–148.

Seale, C., Rivas, C., & Kelly, M. (2013). The challenge of communication in interpreted consultations in diabetes care: A mixed methods study. *British Journal of General Practice*, 63, e125–e133.

Seeleman, C., Essink-Bot, M.-L., Selleger, V., & Bonke, B. (2012). Authors' response to letter from Bond et al. – The role of ad-hoc interpreters in teaching communication skills with ethnic minorities. *Medical Teacher*, 34, 81–82.

Simon, M. A., Ragas, D. M., Nonzee, N. J., Phisuthikul, A. M., Luu, T. H., & Dong, X. (2013). Perceptions of patient-provider communication in breast and cervical cancer-related care: A qualitative study of low-income English- and Spanish-speaking women. *Journal of Community Health*, 38, 707–715.

Sleptsova, M., Hofer, G., Morina, N., & Langewitz, W. (2014). The role of the health care interpreter in a clinical setting: A narrative review. *Journal of Community Health Nursing*, 31, 167–184.

Smith, J., Swartz, L., Kilian, S., & Chiliza, B. (2013). Mediating words, mediating worlds: Interpreting as hidden care work in a South African psychiatric institution. *Transcultural Psychiatry*, 50, 493–514.

Solomon, M. Z. (1997). From what's neutral to what's meaningful: Reflections on a study of medical interpreters. *The Journal of Clinical Ethics*, 8, 88–93.

Splevins, K. A., Cohen, K., Joseph, S., Murray, C., & Bowley, J. (2010). Vicarious posttraumatic growth among interpreters. *Qualitative Health Research*, 20, 1705–1716.

Taylor, K. M. (1988). "Telling bad news": Physicians and the disclosure of undesirable information. *Sociology of Health & Illness*, 10, 109–132.

Tocher, T. M., & Larson, E. B. (1999). Do physicians spend more time with non-English-speaking patients? *Journal of General Internal Medicine*, 14, 303–309.

The United Nations. (1948). The Universal Declaration of Human Rights. Retrieved March 14, 2015, from www.un.org/en/documents/udhr/.

Valdés, G. (2003). *Expanding definitions of giftedness: The case of young interpreters from immigrant communities.* Mahwah, NJ: Erlbaum.

Wallbrecht, J., Hodes-Villamar, L., Weiss, S. J., & Ernst, A. A. (2014). No difference in emergency department length of stay for patients with limited proficiency in English. *Southern Medical Journal*, 107, 1–5.

Watermeyer, J. (2011). "She will hear me": How a flexible interpreting style enables patients to manage the inclusion of interpreters in mediated pharmacy interactions. *Health Communication*, 26, 71–81.

White, K., & Laws, M. (2009). Role exchange in medical interpretation. *Journal of Immigrant and Minority Health*, 11, 482–493.

Wros, P. (2009). Giving voice: Incorporating the wisdom of Hispanic RNs into practice. *Journal of Cultural Diversity*, 16, 151–157.

Yang, C.-F., & Gray, B. (2008). Bilingual medical students as interpreters: What are the benefits and risks? *New Zealand Medical Journal*, 121, 15–28.

Zimányi, K. (2013). Somebody has to be in charge of a session: On the control of communication in interpreter-mediated mental health encounters. *Translation and Interpreting Studies*, 8, 94–111.

GLOSSARY

Terms	Description	Subordinate to	See also
acculturation	Acculturation explains the process through which individuals adapt to a new culture through familiarizing, learning, and eventually internalizing the new cultural norms and values. Increasingly, researchers argue that acculturation is a form of cultural fusion in which individuals develop additional cultural repertoires that allow them to transition between cultures as they manage multiple goals to achieve desirable outcomes (Kramer, 2000).		cultural fusion medical pluralism
advocate	When assuming the role of advocate, an interpreter is concerned about advocacy and patient education for patients' language rights, access to health care, and interventions in compromised quality of care (Arocha, 2015). While some researchers argued that the advocate role should not be performed during an interpreting task, others noted that interactional dynamics and problems related to quality of care can emerge during the process of care, requiring interpreters' immediate, active intervention (Hsieh, 2008).	interpreter role	
agency	Agency is an important concept rooted in philosophy, elaborated in sociology, and has now been widely incorporated in the social sciences (Archer, 2000). It is a product of modernity and involves properties of individualism, presuming that individuals can make independent judgments, choices, and acts that are not dictated by social structures (i.e., free will). I view interpreter agency as a type of problem-solving capacity which requires interpreters to actively evaluate a communicative event, identify potential problems and solutions, and coordinate with other participants to achieve desirable outcomes.		

Terms	Description	Subordinate to	See also
alliances	Alliance refers to the therapeutic alliance an individual develops with others with the goal of assisting a patient to achieve optimal health. The term was first proposed in mental health to describe the provider–patient relationship as a therapeutic or working relationship. However, in recent years, health professionals have used the term to refer to interprofessional collaborations and a team approach to healthcare delivery. For example, a provider may form therapeutic alliances with a patient's family member, a nurse, and/or an interpreter to facilitate a patient's illness management.		
ambiguity	Ambiguity is common in everyday talk as multiple meanings often co-exist in natural languages (Nordentoft & Fredsted, 1998). Language users generally reply on sociocultural norms and sociolinguistic conventions to interpret and derive meanings in social interactions. For example, "Can you open the door?" is heard as a request whereas "Do you have the physical ability to open the door?" is under-stood as a yes/no question. It is important to note that language users may also strategically and intentionally create ambiguity in their narratives to manage communicative challenges and interactional dilemmas (Eisenberg, 1984).		
appropriateness	Appropriateness involves adherence to social rules and norms as expected in the particular time and place of a communicative activity.	communica-tive competence	
bilingual health care	I use the term bilingual health care to refer to healthcare services and delivery that involve two or more languages.		bilingual health communication

interpreter role

bilingual health communication
Bilingual health communication refers to communicative activities that involve users of different languages. It can involve situations that require more than one interpreter. For example, a deaf pediatric patient with a Spanish-speaking parent in the USA may require a signed language interpreter and a Spanish interpreter to ensure a successful medical encounter. While this can be perceived as trilingual health communication, I have decided to use the term bilingual health communication as most interpreting activities in healthcare settings are likely to be limited to two languages.

clarifier
Clarifier as an interpreter role refers to situations in which an interpreter departs from a conduit role and provides linguistic clarification in situations where there are no linguistic equivalences between two languages (Dysart-Gale, 2005).

code-switching
Code-switching was first used to explain situations in which a speaker shifts between different languages. However, by recognizing that different speech communities have different speech codes, researchers have argued that different codes can allow users to claim or access different resources (Bernstein, 1964). For example, a physician may choose to greet a Spanish-speaking patient directly in Spanish to develop rapport but rely on an interpreter when making a diagnosis and giving informed consent to ensure the quality of care. Code-switching allows language users to manage and define the meanings and interpersonal dynamics in social interactions (Auer, 2013).

Terms	Description	Subordinate to	See also
co-diagnostician	Davidson (2001) first coined the term co-diagnostician as an interpreter role; however, he did not further elaborate on how and why an interpreter might perform such a role. Based on participant observation and interviews, I identified five strategies for the co-diagnostician role: Assuming the provider's communicative goals; editorializing information for medical emphasis; initiating information-seeking behaviors; participating in diagnostic tasks; and volunteering medical information to the patient (Hsieh, 2007).	interpreter role	
communicative competence	Communicative competence is a product of both effectiveness and appropriateness, both of which are socially and culturally situated (Westmyer, DiCioccio, & Rubin, 1998). It is possible that not all participants share the same perceptions of the appropriateness and effectiveness of a communicative event. For example, in cross-cultural care, an American oncologist may try to use jokes and teasing to develop rapport but such communicative practices may be perceived to be insensitive by a Japanese patient who shares different cultural expectations and norms about appropriate provider–patient interactions in a medical consultation about cancer.		appropriateness; effectiveness

communicative frame	The communicative frame imposes expected behaviors and obligations on participants of a communicative activity (Goffman, 1959). For example, when a person asks a question, the other person is expected to provide an answer. The communicative frame involves (a) frames of interpretation that allow individuals to derive the meanings of the particular interaction, and (b) knowledge structure (i.e., schema) of the expected interactional sequences within the frame (Tannen & Wallat, 1987). In cross-cultural care, because of differences in sociocultural and sociolinguistic norms, it is possible that individuals do not share the same understanding about the specific or dominant frame that is in play during a social interaction. For example, a patient may mistake history taking by a nurse as a time to offer primary complaints about the medical encounter, which is typically done with a physician. In addition, frames are co-constructed and negotiated between participants of a communicative event, rather than solely dictated by a single person (Goffman, 1959, 1974). For example, when a person makes abusive comments toward a provider, an interpreter can ask, "Are you sure you want me to say that to your doctor who just saved your life?"
communicative goal	In interpersonal interactions, individuals often hold various task, identity, and relational goals as their communicative goals (Tracy, 2013). It is important to note that these goals may or may not be compatible with one another. For example, a provider may want to appear supportive but also want to deny an elderly patient's desire for aggressive treatment for his/her end-stage cancer.
communicative pattern	Communicative pattern refers to the patterned behaviors an individual (or a group) adopts in a communicative activity. For example, a physician may systematically exert dominance and control by adopting specific communicative strategies (e.g., interrupting a patient's talk or talking for longer).
communicative practice	Communicative practice refers to the routine, discursive behaviors that are culturally situated in everyday life.
speech community	

Terms	Description	Subordinate to	See also
communicative strategy	Communicative strategy involves interactional tactics that an individual adopts to achieve specific communicative goals or desired outcomes. Such behaviors can either be planned (e.g., a patient asks a family member to go to a medical appointment with them and ask questions that s/he may fail to ask) or spontaneous (e.g., an interpreter claims to be a patient's family member in order to assume the role of patient advocate). In addition, communicative strategies can be utilized purposefully and systematically (e.g., an interpreter speaks in first-person style to minimize their presence in a medical encounter) but can also be employed subconsciously or intuitively without a user's awareness (e.g., a provider subconsciously uses more medical jargon to claim medical expertise).		
conduit	Conduit has long been used as a metaphor to describe a communicative process in which individuals send and receive meanings through encoding and decoding messages that are transmitted through a medium (e.g., languages) (Grady; 1998).	interpreter role	
constant comparative method	The constant comparative method is a core component of grounded theory, a qualitative analytic method. The constant comparative method was first proposed by Glaser and Strauss (1967). It is generally understood as the process of data analysis in grounded theory (Bryant & Charmaz, 2010b). Within grounded theory, the constant comparative method is an analytical process that generates successively essential concepts and theories through the abductive processes of comparing data with data, data with category, category with category, and category to concepts.	grounded theory	
construct	A construct is a theoretical concept that may not be directly observable but can help explain how and why certain phenomena behave the way they do.		

Term	Definition	Related terms
context	Context is a key concept in the field of pragmatics and in ethnography of communication. By raising the issue of context, researchers argued that "the focal event cannot be properly understood, interpreted appropriately, or described in a relevant fashion, unless one looks beyond the event itself to other phenomena (for example cultural setting, speech situation, shared background assumptions) within which the event is embedded, or alternatively that features of the talk itself invoke particular background assumptions relevant to the organization of subsequent interaction" (Goodwin & Duranti, 1992, p. 3).	
cross-cultural care	Rather than conceptualizing health and illness from a biological or biomedical perspective, medical anthropologists and sociologists have emphasized that culture is essential to individuals' understanding and experiences of health and illnesses (Kleinman, Eisenberg, & Good, 1978). As such, when interacting with patients from different cultures, providers are cautioned against imposing Western values or norms on people who do not share those values and norms.	cross-cultural communication; intercultural communication
cross-cultural communication	According to Gudykunst (2003, p. vii), cross-cultural communication grew out of cultural anthropological studies of communicative processes in different cultures, with a particular emphasis in comparative studies between cultures. Cross-cultural communication is a major research area within the larger field of intercultural communication. From this perspective, interpreter-mediated medical encounters should be termed intercultural care rather than cross-cultural care. However, because cross-cultural care is a term that has been widely used in the field of medicine, I have decided not to challenge the use of the term "cross-cultural care."	communication
cultural broker	Cultural broker as an interpreter role refers to situations in which an interpreter departs from the conduit role and provides the necessary cultural framework to assist others to understand and interpret the meanings of a social interaction (Dysart-Gale, 2005).	interpreter role

Terms	Description	Subordinate to	See also
cultural fusion	Cultural fusion refers to the accrual and association of different cultures as one encounters values, norms, and practices of different cultures. It is important to note that cultural fusion does not take place universally and uniformly within a person or a group (Kramer, 2002). Rather, individuals (and groups) may have increased levels of cultural fusion in some areas but remain unassimilated in other areas. In addition, unlike assimilation, which may imply that individuals abandon their prior cultural selves as they join the host culture, researchers have found that cultural fusion tends to be the norm, in which individuals develop additional cultural views and repertories and transition between cultures to best meet their needs.		
culture	Depending on the discipline, culture has been conceptualized and defined differently. In this book, I primarily conceptualize culture in the traditions of ethnography of communication: Culture involves values, expectations, and norms that are enacted through the social practices/interactions of a particular speech community. Culture guides individual behaviors of the community and provides an interpretive frame to evaluate the effectiveness and appropriateness of individuals' intentions and behaviors.		speech community
dialectics	Dialectics refers to a critical approach toward the conceptualization of the nature of social interaction (Montgomery, 1993). By conceptualizing interpreter-mediated medical encounters through dialectics, I acknowledge that multiple meanings and goals can co-exist during interpersonal interactions, resulting in diverging interpretations that may or may not be consistent or compatible with one another. The interplay of conflicting and interconnected meanings is shaped by and reflected through participants' behavioral patterns, interpersonal dynamics, and the corresponding contextual factors.		

Term	Definition	Related terms
discursive strategies	Discursive strategies refer to individuals' strategic and resourceful use of discourse in constructing and negotiating their goals in social interactions. Discourse is both a product and resource for participants in a speech community as they perform and negotiate meanings in everyday interactions. For example, by using technical terms and medical acronyms, healthcare providers can claim medical expert identities in medical encounters; in contrast, a physician may intentionally use folk language and avoid medical jargon to generate rapport with a patient.	speech community; communicative strategies
effectiveness	Effectiveness involves accomplishing or achieving the specific goals set for the communicative activity. Researchers have argued that communicative competence requires consideration of others' perspectives (i.e., appropriateness) and a temporal dimension as some communicative strategies can be highly effective (e.g., deception) within a specific interaction but compromise long-term goals and relationships.	communicative competence
emotion work	Emotion work highlights that individuals' expressions of emotions are not necessarily limited to their felt emotions but also include their understanding of their professional and organizational roles (Hochschild, 1979). For example, health professionals' emotion management (e.g., expressing empathy or withholding grief) may be dependent on organizational values or therapeutic objectives.	
equality of care	By noting that good health is a necessary condition for an individual to flourish as a human being and that access to medical care is part of fundamental human rights (The United Nations, 1948), researchers have proposed that equality of care should be "conditional upon a respect for personal preferences (or, in medical ethics, the principle of 'autonomy') and upon a prohibition on reductions in current health" (Culyer & Wagstaff, 1993, pp. 454–455). From this perspective, equality of care is particularly important for marginalized and underserved populations as it aims to achieve an equal distribution of health in the larger society.	quality of care

Terms	Description	Subordinate to	See also
equivalence	In translation and interpreting studies, the notion of equivalence is a constant concern. However, researchers debate about the different ways that equivalence can be conceptualized, applied, and operationalized in interpreting. For example, different cultures and languages may have different linguistic structures and forms. An interpreter who tries to achieve equivalence in linguistic structure may result in producing socially awkward or incomprehensible target texts. As a result, researchers and theorists have suggested using functional equivalence (i.e., evaluating utterances on the basis of the functions they are designed to perform) as a criterion to evaluate the quality of interpreting (Wadensjö, 1998).		
expert power	Expert power refers to the extent of the knowledge that one is believed to hold in a given area. For example, due to their medical training, providers hold expert power in healthcare settings.	power	
factor	Factor and variable are used interchangeably in this book.		variable
faithfulness	Faithfulness, like equivalence, has been often cited as a criterion for evaluating the quality of interpreting. By conceptualizing faithfulness as fidelity to the source text, interpreters are often instructed not to modify the text in any way, including its structure, content, or meaning (Clifford, 2004). However, Gile (1995) found that users of interpreting services are poor judges of fidelity. Kurz (2001) argued that quality of interpreting services is evaluated by users in terms of what they actually received in relation to what they expected rather than by an objective evaluation of fidelity to the source text.		equivalence
footing	Footing is the interpersonal relationships that are constructed in conversational frames (Goffman, 1979). For example, a provider may choose to say, "How are we feeling today?" as opposed to "How are you feeling today?" to signal that the provider and the patient are together as a team to manage the illness event.		

grounded theory Grounded theory is a qualitative research method that aims to generate theoretical frameworks that are grounded in data (Glaser & Strauss, 1967). By following the principles of abduction, "it combines the rational and the imaginative aspects of research; the former by defining a logical form of inference, and the latter by acknowledging the role played by insight and insinuation" (Bryant & Charmaz, 2010a, p. 16). While grounded theorists have diverged in their approaches, assumptions, and epistemologies, grounded theory as a research method is committed to generating theories through rigorous procedures for data analysis. I follow the principles and procedures of a constructionist approach to grounded theory as proposed by Charmaz (2006). By doing so, I recognize the continuous interplay between the processes of data collection, data analysis, and researcher as I developed the various components of the Model of Bilingual Health Communication.

health literacy The Institute of Medicine defines health literacy as "the degree to which individuals have the capacity to obtain, process, and understand basic health information and services needed to make appropriate health decisions." In addition, health literacy is "a shared function of cultural, social, and individual factors. Both the causes and the remedies for limited health literacy rest with our cultural and social framework, the health and education systems that serve it, and the interactions between these factors" (Institute of Medicine, 2004, p. 32). Language barriers have been identified as a major contributor to patients' low health literacy. However, because language-discordant patients often experience challenges in other social determinants of health (e.g., marginalization and cultural differences), the causes of their low health literacy can involve complex and interconnected issues in healthcare settings and in their everyday life.

Terms	Description	Subordinate to	See also
health outcomes	Different disciplines may share diverse understanding and definitions of health outcomes (McDowell, 2006). Health outcomes include biomedical indicators of health status (e.g., condition-specific measures, including mortality and physiological measures), cost/process measures (e.g., duration of hospital stay), patient-specific measures (e.g., patient satisfaction), behavioral outcomes (e.g., treatment adherence and communicative competence), cognitive measures (e.g., medical knowledge and health literacy), and context-specific measures (e.g., resource utilization).		
illness ideology	Illness ideology refers to the explanatory model individuals (or cultural groups) hold about the causes, processes, treatments, and/or outcomes of health and illness and of specific health conditions. For example, for Hmong people, epilepsy is a gift from God and is caused by spirits, whereas for Western biomedical physicians, epilepsy is an uncontrolled electrical storm in the brain (Fadiman, 1997). In cross-cultural care, differences in illness ideology can lead to challenges to provider–patient communication and treatment adherence.		
individual agency	In sociology, individual agency and social structure are conceptualized as the forces that shape human behaviors. Whereas social structure refers to the patterned, structural forces within the larger sociocultural, sociopolitical, socioeconomic, and environmental contexts that may limit individuals' opportunities and choices, individual agency refers to individuals' ability to exercise their free will and act independently.		agency
interactional dilemma	Interactional dilemma refers to a situation in which a participant of a social interaction experiences structural, interpersonal, or situational challenges that make it difficult to manage his/her task, identity, or relational goals. For example, an interpreter may find it difficult to relay a patient's abusive behavior or a physician's discriminating comments due to concerns about the provider–patient relationship.		

Term	Definition	See also
intercultural communication	According to Gudykunst (2003, p. vii), intercultural communication "generally involves face-to-face communication between people from different national cultures." In this sense, interpreter-mediated medical encounters are intercultural communication. The term is also used frequently to include all aspects of the study of culture and communication.	communication cross-cultural communication
interpreter accessibility	It is possible that interpreters may be available but not accessible. For example, although a hospital may have contracted services with telephone interpreters or video-based interpreters 24/7 (i.e., high availability), interpreter accessibility may still be low if access to these interpreters requires specialized equipment (e.g., speaker phone or video cart) that may not be available or accessible at the time of provider–patient interaction.	
interpreter availability	Interpreter availability has traditionally been limited by geographic locations, clinic hours, cost concerns, and language combinations. In recent years, the increased availability and cost-effectiveness of technology-based interpreting (e.g., telephone interpreting and video-based interpreting) have significantly reduced the challenges to interpreter availability (Kelly, 2007). Nevertheless, researchers continue to observe providers' underutilization of interpreters in medical encounters.	interpreter accessibility
interpreter role	Interpreters' role performances have been influential in the theoretical development of interpreting studies. By conceptualizing interpreters' communicative strategies and practices as guided by roles, researchers have highlighted issues related to interpreters' agency and influence in mediating and managing interpersonal interactions.	
interpreter visibility	Interpreter visibility is often conceptualized as the extent of interpreters' intrusiveness in the primary interaction. Angelelli (2004, p. 67) defined visibility as "the interpreter's role extends beyond the role of language switcher." By demonstrating the spectrum of interpreter visibility (e.g., minor visibility versus major visibility), Angelelli argued that interpreters strategically manage their visibility level to control the process and content of provider–patient interactions.	

Terms	Description	Subordinate to	See also
interpreting	Interpretation or interpreting is the communication in which one transfers oral or signed information from one language to another. Interpreting can be performed in consecutive mode (i.e., an interpreter relays the information after a speaker has finished a turn of talk) or simultaneous mode (i.e., an interpreter and a speaker communicate simultaneously). An interpreter can transfer between speech and speech (e.g., from Chinese to English) or from sign to speech (from American Sign Language to English).		bilingual health communication
interpreting studies	Interpreting studies as a field of research has traditionally been influenced by translation studies. However, with the increasing recognition of interpreting as an oral performance and an interpersonal communicative activity that is distinct from translation as a communicative activity, interpreting studies is becoming increasingly interdisciplinary, attracting researchers from a wide variety of disciplines, including linguistics, sociology, anthropology, neurosciences, communication, ethics, medicine, education, law, among others (Pöchhacker, 2013).		
language barriers	Language barriers can impact the access, process, and outcome of care. At a structural level, language-discordant patients may have limited access to care, including preventive care, due to a lack of social policies to ensure quality and equality of care. Language barriers can also impact the process of care due to compromised provider–patient communication and relationships. Because of concerns about potential discrimination and sociocultural differences, language-discordant patients may adopt avoidance behaviors that delay their care. In summary, language barriers have been found to be a major predictor of compromised quality of care and health outcomes.		

		power
legitimate power	Legitimate power is embodied through social structures which grant a person a legitimate right to influence others and mean that others internalize such expectations and feel obligated to accept such influence. Cultural values, acceptance of the social structure, and designation by a legitimizing agent can all serve as the bases of legitimate power (French & Raven, 1959). For example, in healthcare settings, because physicians have passed medical board exams and are situated at the top of the hierarchy of a healthcare team, they can claim legitimate power over other members of a healthcare team.	expert power, referent power
medical paternalism	Medical paternalism stands in contrast to the valued principles of self-determinism and patient autonomy. Rather than arguing that patients have the right to make informed health decisions, medical paternalism is rooted in the traditions of beneficence (i.e., do no harm). Medical paternalism implies an asymmetrical provider–patient relationship as the provider is granted unlimited medical authority over the patient and the patient is obligated to submit to the provider's wishes (Beisecker & Beisecker, 1993). Nevertheless, both parties assume that the provider has the patient's best interests and well-being in mind.	
medical pluralism	Medical pluralism is the adaptation of more than one medical system in one's healthcare practices. Researchers found that individuals often develop complex understanding and management of their health and illness as they strategically combine various medical systems (Gardiner et al., 2013), including Western biomedicine, folk medicine (e.g., honey for sore throats), and ethnic medicine (e.g., traditional Chinese medicine), to achieve desirable outcomes for their health and other normative values (e.g., cultural identity) (Kong & Hsieh, 2012).	cultural fusion

Terms	Description	Subordinate to	See also
neutrality	Field-based observational studies have provided ample evidence that interpreter neutrality (i.e., interpreter as neutral conduit) is an unrealistic and impractical ideology that cannot be realized in reality (Forman, 2002; Metzger, 1999). Nevertheless, interpreters develop specific discursive strategies that allow them to appear neutral and unbiased as they relay information from one language to another and mediate sociocultural differences in intercultural interactions (Atkinson, 1992; Jacobs, 2002).		
nocebo effect	Nocebo effect is the opposite of the placebo effect. One can experience negative impacts or effects on one's health when one believes that the inert substance, therapy, or procedure can cause harm.		
normative approach	By recognizing that individuals' behaviors, values, and expectations are guided by the norms of a social system, researchers can explain and predict the effectiveness and appropriateness of individuals' behaviors by identifying the norms that provide the interpretive framework for such behaviors (Goldsmith, 2001). A normative approach attends to the distinctive and variable meanings that emerge through social interactions.		
normative framework	A normative framework is the interpretive frame that individuals use to construct and interpret the meanings of a given social interaction. The framework is established and maintained through norms, including normative values, expectations, and behaviors, or through a social system.		
normative theory	According to Goldsmith (2001, p. 518), "A normative theory includes description of the expectations that structure a speech event, a range of ways in which individuals may respond to these expectations, and the normative principles against which performances may be judged to be better or worse."		
normative values	Normative values are values that are culturally situated and contextually dependent within a given social system.		

	interpreter role	advocate
patient advocate	See advocate.	
patient autonomy	The principle of patient autonomy argues that patients have the right to make informed decisions about their medical care. Bioethicists (e.g., Fan, 1997) have argued that in Western cultures, patient autonomy is rooted in the values and beliefs of self-sovereignty (i.e., a person has a privilege to make decisions about his/her own body) and self-determinism (i.e., a patient has the final authority to decide his medical care). However, in Eastern cultures, patient autonomy holds the principle of family-determinism, which argues that (a) a person should make his/her decisions and actions harmoniously in cooperation with other relevant people and (b) the family has the final say in clinical decisions (i.e., family-sovereignty).	
patient empowerment	A review of the medical literature found that patient empowerment is guided by the principle of self-determination and may be facilitated by healthcare providers if they adopt a patient-centered approach to care. Patient empowerment involves providing patients with the necessary support and resources to reflect on their experiences and values to make self-directed, informed decisions that best meet their health and life goals (Anderson & Funnell, 2010). As patients become empowered, they may develop a greater sense of self-efficacy toward their health behaviors, resulting in better health and life outcomes (Aujoulat, d'Hoore, & Deccache, 2007).	

Terms	Description	Subordinate to	See also
performance	I follow the traditions of ethnography of communication, noting that individuals' communicative practices are situated in the larger sociocultural contexts and norms of their speech community. Performance refers to individuals' use of language and communicative practices as cultural performances (of their speech community). Such performances can serve both as a product and a resource for their everyday life as they assert, maintain, and negotiate their tasks, identities, and relationships. For example, a male interpreter is trained to interpret in first-person style (i.e., speak as the original speaker) even when his client is a pregnant woman in a prenatal care clinic. For people who are unfamiliar with interpreters' speech practices, it may seem awkward for a male interpreter to say, "I am concerned about my vaginal bleeding." However, this performance allows the interpreter to maintain an invisible presence while reinforcing the provider–patient relationship.		
power	Power in interpersonal relationships has been conceptualized as the probability that individuals within a social relationship will be able to carry out their will despite resistance, influence others in the way they desire, and resist influences from others to modify their behaviors against their will. In healthcare settings, provider–patient relationships often entail asymmetry of power, with providers having high legitimate, referent, and expert power (Haug, 1997).		legitimate power, referent power, expert power
quality of care	Campbell, Roland, and Buetow (2000, p. 1614) defined quality of care for individual patients as: "whether individuals can access the health structures and processes of care which they need and whether the care received is effective." From this perspective, quality of care can be improved by ensuring accessibility and effectiveness of individual patients' access to the healthcare structure, process of care, and health outcomes.		

		power	expert power, legitimate power
			health literacy
referent power	Referent power is the power of an individual over others due to others' high level of identification with, admiration of, or respect for the person. A person may not be consciously aware of the referent power others have over him/her. Nevertheless, because a person with referent power is often held in high regard, others are motivated to identify and conform to his/her will as a gesture of demonstrating alliances. Rodin and Janis (1979) argued that providers' referent power can be critical to patients' treatment adherence. In interpreter-mediated medical encounters, interpreters can have high referent power over a patient due to their shared language and successful adaptation to the host society.		
self-advocacy	Self-advocacy in healthcare settings is enacted health literacy. Self-advocacy requires one to have (a) knowledge of what one wants, (b) knowledge of what one is entitled to, and (c) the ability to achieve one's goal (Brinckerhoff, 1994). Patients with high self-advocacy are likely to have increased illness education, assertiveness, and mindful non-adherence (Brashers, Haas, & Neidig, 1999). Because greater speaking and listening skills are critical to patient advocacy (Martin et al., 2011), patients with language barriers can be particularly at risk of low self-advocacy.		
self-efficacy	Self-efficacy is an individual's perceived ability to accomplish a specific task or to succeed in a specific situation. Bandura (1997) argued that self-efficacy is influenced by enactive mastery experience (e.g., preexisting self-knowledge structures and task difficulty), vicarious experience (e.g., performance similarities), verbal persuasion (e.g., others' supportive messages that promote self-affirming beliefs), and physiological and affective states (e.g., mood).		
social system	A social system entails patterned behaviors of a group of people who share similar characteristics, behaviors, rules, and/or values that involve specific responsibilities and obligations toward others in the system. A social system can be a family unit, an organization, a clinical specialty, a professional field (e.g., medical or legal system), a culture, or a government/country/society as a whole.		

Terms	Description	Subordinate to	See also
speech community	Speech community refers to a group of people who share a set of norms, expectations, and patterned behaviors that are reflected through their communicative practices (Gumperz, 2009). Such practices allow the group to establish, assert, and reinforce their cultural/group identities. In healthcare settings, one can argue that physicians and nurses are two speech communities as each group have different speech practices that allow them to claim different identities and relationships with patients and with other health professionals.		
speech event	The speech event is a specific communicative frame which participants engage in to accomplish distinctive task, identity, and/or relational goals. Dell Hymes (1972) proposed the "S-P-E-A-K-I-N-G" model, arguing that a speech event entails its unique set of setting, participants, ends, act sequences, key, instrumentalities, and genre. For example, medical history taking is a speech event in which providers ask questions to elicit comprehensive information from a patient to ensure accurate diagnosis; in contrast, informed consent is a speech event in which providers actively provide a patient with the necessary and meaningful information to assist him/her to make appropriate decisions about his/her healthcare services.		
system agent	Leanza (2005, p. 186) proposed the system agent as one of the community interpreter roles in which "the interpreter transmits the dominant discourse, norms, and values to the patient. Cultural differences are denied in favor of the dominant culture. Cultural differences tend to be elided or assimilated." In this role, an interpreter is concerned about maintaining the norms and values of the dominant social system.	interpreter role	
system norm	The system norm refers to the normative rules, values, and expectations of a social system. Individuals within a social system are oriented to the system norms to guide and evaluate the appropriateness and effectiveness of their own and others' behaviors in any given interaction.	social system	
translation	Translation is the communication in which one transfers written texts from one language to another language.		interpreting

transparency | Transparency is recognized as a required and essential component of all qualitative research. Through transparency, researchers are expected to provide clear and thorough information so that readers can independently evaluate the quality of all phases of a study (Hiles, 2008). In a healthcare setting, the National Council on Interpreting in Health Care defines transparency as "The principle that during the encounter the interpreter informs all parties of any action he or she takes, including speaking for him – or herself, outside of direct interpreting" (2005, p. 12). Strategies to maintain transparency can involve both verbal and nonverbal cues. It is important to note that I do not view transparency as the interpreter's obligation to relay everything verbatim as said by other participants. Rather, I conceptualize transparency as an interpreter's responsibility in providing clarity in their interpreting or communicative strategies, including their decision to editorialize information or to pursue information on behalf of the provider, so that all other participants are able to understand, evaluate, and negotiate the appropriateness and effectiveness of interpreter-mediated provider–patient interactions.

variable | Variables are operationalized measures that allow researchers to assess the level/extent of a particular construct.

construct |

Glossary References

Anderson, R. M., & Funnell, M. M. (2010). Patient empowerment: Myths and misconceptions. *Patient Education and Counseling, 79*(3), 277–282.

Angelelli, C. V. (2004). *Medical interpreting and cross-cultural communication.* Cambridge, UK: Cambridge University Press.

Archer, M. S. (2000). *Being human: The problem of agency.* Cambridge, UK: Cambridge University Press.

Arocha, I. (2015). Medical interpretation. In S. Loue & M. Sajatovic (Eds.), *Encyclopedia of immigrant health* (pp. 1062–1066). New York: Springer.

Atkinson, J. M. (1992). Displaying neutrality: Formal aspects of informal court proceedings. In P. Drew & J. Heritage (Eds.), *Talk at work: Interaction in institutional settings* (pp. 199–211). Cambridge, UK: Cambridge University Press.

Auer, P. (Ed.). (2013). *Code-switching in conversation: Language, interaction and identity.* New York: Routledge.

Aujoulat, I., d'Hoore, W., & Deccache, A. (2007). Patient empowerment in theory and practice: Polysemy or cacophony? *Patient Education and Counseling, 66*(1), 13–20.

Bandura, A. (1997). *Self-efficacy: The exercise of control.* New York: Freeman.

Beisecker, A. E., & Beisecker, T. D. (1993). Using metaphors to characterize doctor-patient relationships: Paternalism versus consumerism. *Health Communication, 5,* 41–58.

Bernstein, B. (1964). Elaborated and restricted codes: Their social origins and some consequences. *American Anthropologist, 66*(6Pt. 2), 55–69.

Brashers, D. E., Haas, S. M., & Neidig, J. L. (1999). The patient self-advocacy scale: Measuring patient involvement in health care decision-making interactions. *Health Communication, 11*(2), 97–122.

Brinckerhoff, L. C. (1994). Developing effective self-advocacy skills in college-bound students with learning disabilities. *Intervention in School and Clinic, 29*(4), 229–237.

Bryant, A., & Charmaz, K. (2010a). Introduction: Grounded theory research: Methods and practices. In A. Bryant & K. Charmaz (Eds.), *The SAGE handbook of grounded theory* (pp. 1–28). Thousand Oaks, CA: Sage.

Bryant, A., & Charmaz, K. (2010b). *The SAGE handbook of grounded theory.* Thousand Oaks, CA: Sage.

Campbell, S. M., Roland, M. O., & Buetow, S. A. (2000). Defining quality of care. *Social Science & Medicine, 51*(11), 1611–1625.

Charmaz, K. (2006). *Constructing grounded theory: A practical guide through qualitative analysis.* Thousand Oaks, CA: Sage.

Clifford, A. (2004). Is fidelity ethical? The social role of the healthcare interpreter. *TTR: Traduction, Terminologie, Rédaction: Etudes sur le Texte et Ses Transformations, 17*(2), 89–114.

Culyer, A. J., & Wagstaff, A. (1993). Equity and equality in health and health care. *Journal of Health Economics, 12*(4), 431–457.

Davidson, B. (2001). Questions in cross-linguistic medical encounters: The role of the hospital interpreter. *Anthropological Quarterly, 74*(4), 170–178.

Dysart-Gale, D. (2005). Communication models, professionalization, and the work of medical interpreters. *Health Communication, 17*(1), 91–103.

Eisenberg, E. M. (1984). Ambiguity as strategy in organizational communication. *Communication Monographs, 51*(3), 227–242.

Fadiman, A. (1997). *The spirit catches you and you fall down: A Hmong child, her American doctors, and the collision of two cultures.* New York: Farrar, Straus and Giroux.

Fan, R. (1997). Self-determination vs. family-determination: Two incommensurable principles of autonomy. *Bioethics*, 11(3–4), 309–322.

Forman, W. (2002). The bias of neutrality: The role of interpreters in health care settings. *Vision*, 8(14), 20–22.

French, J. R. P., Jr., & Raven, B. (1959). The bases of social power. In D. Cartwright (Ed.), *Studies in social power* (pp. 150–167). Ann Arbor, MI: Institute for Social Research.

Gardiner, P., Whelan, J., White, L., Filippelli, A., Bharmal, N., & Kaptchuk, T. (2013). A systematic review of the prevalence of herb usage among racial/ethnic minorities in the United States. *Journal of Immigrant and Minority Health*, 15(4), 817–828.

Gile, D. (1995). Fidelity assessment in consecutive interpretation: An experiment. *Target*, 7(1), 151–164.

Glaser, B. G., & Strauss, A. L. (1967). *The discovery of grounded theory: Strategies for qualitative research*. Hawthorne, NY: Aldine de Gruyter.

Goffman, E. (1959). *The presentation of self in everyday life*. Garden City, NY: Doubleday.

Goffman, E. (1974). *Frame analysis: An essay on the organization of experience*. Cambridge, MA: Harvard University Press.

Goffman, E. (1979). Footing. *Semiotica*, 25, 1–29.

Goldsmith, D. J. (2001). A normative approach to the study of uncertainty and communication. *Journal of Communication*, 51(3), 514–533.

Goodwin, C., & Duranti, A. (1992). Rethinking context: An introduction. In A. Duranti & C. Goodwin (Eds.), *Rethinking context: Language as an interactive phenomenon* (pp. 1–42). Cambridge, UK: Cambridge University Press.

Grady, J. (1998). The conduit metaphor revisited: A reassessment of metaphors for communication. In J.-P. Koenig (Ed.), *Discourse and cognition: Bridging the gap* (pp. 205–218). Stanford, CA: CSLI Publications.

Gudykunst, W. D. (Ed.). (2003). *Cross-cultural and intercultural communication*. Thousand Oaks, CA: Sage.

Gumperz, J. J. (2009). The speech community. In A. Duranti (Ed.), *Linguistic anthropology: A reader* (2nd ed., pp. 66–73). Malden, MA: Blackwell.

Haug, M. R. (1997). Physician power and patients' health behavior. In D. S. Gochman (Ed.), *Handbook of health behavior research: Provider determinants* (Vol. 2, pp. 49–62). New York: Plenum Press.

Hiles, D. R. (2008). Transparency. In L. Given (Ed.), *The SAGE encyclopedia of qualitative research methods* (pp. 891–893). Thousand Oaks, CA: Sage.

Hochschild, A. R. (1979). Emotion work, feeling rules, and social structure. *American Journal of Sociology*, 85(3), 551–575.

Hsieh, E. (2007). Interpreters as co-diagnosticians: Overlapping roles and services between providers and interpreters. *Social Science & Medicine*, 64(4), 924–937.

Hsieh, E. (2008). "I am not a robot!" Interpreters' views of their roles in health care settings. *Qualitative Health Research*, 18(10), 1367–1383.

Hymes, D. (1972). Models of the interaction of language and social life. In J. J. Gumperz & D. Hymes (Eds.), *Directions in sociolinguistics: Ethnography of communication* (pp. 35–71). New York: Holt, Rinehart, & Winston.

Institute of Medicine. (2004). *Health literacy: A prescription to end confusion*. Washington, DC: National Academics.

Jacobs, S. (2002). Maintaining neutrality in dispute mediation: Managing disagreement while managing not to disagree. *Journal of Pragmatics*, 34(10–11), 1403–1426.

Kelly, N. (2007). *Telephone interpreting: A comprehensive guide to the profession*. Victoria, BC: Trafford.

Kleinman, A., Eisenberg, L., & Good, B. (1978). Culture, illness, and care: Clinical lessons from anthropologic and cross-cultural research. *Annals of Internal Medicine*, 88, 251–258.

Kong, H., & Hsieh, E. (2012). The social meanings of traditional Chinese medicine: Elderly Chinese immigrants' health practice in the United States. *Journal of Immigrant and Minority Health*, 14(5), 841–849.

Kramer, E. M. (2000). Cultural fusion and the defense of difference. In M. K. Asante & J. E. Min (Eds.), *Socio-cultural conflict between African and Korean Americans* (pp. 182–223). New York: University Press of America.

Kramer, E. M. (2002). Cosmopoly and cultural fusion: Cultural homogenization in the face of neo-globalism. In M. Isa & M. Masazumi (Eds.), *Intercultural communication: A reader* (pp. 88–106). Thousand Oaks, CA: Sage.

Kurz, I. (2001). Conference interpreting: Quality in the ears of the user. *Meta: Journal des Traducteurs / Translators' Journal*, 46(2), 394–409.

Leanza, Y. (2005). Roles of community interpreters in pediatrics as seen by interpreters, physicians and researchers. *Interpreting*, 7(2), 167–192.

McDowell, I. (2006). *Measuring health: A guide to rating scales and questionnaires* (3rd ed.). Oxford, UK: Oxford University Press.

Martin, L. T., Schonlau, M., Haas, A., Derose, K. P., Rosenfeld, L., Buka, S. L., & Rudd, R. (2011). Patient activation and advocacy: Which literacy skills matter most? *Journal of Health Communication*, 16(sup3), 177–190.

Metzger, M. (1999). *Sign language interpreting: Deconstructing the myth of neutrality*. Washington, DC: Gallaudet University Press.

Montgomery, B. M. (1993). Relationship maintenance versus relationship change: A dialectical dilemma. *Journal of Social and Personal Relationships*, 10(2), 205–223.

National Council on Interpreting in Health Care. (2005). National standards of practices for interpreters in health care. Retrieved November 5, 2015, from: www.asli.com/NCIHC_National_Standards_of_Practice.pdf.

Nordentoft, K., & Fredsted, E. (1998). On semantic and pragmatic ambiguity. *Journal of Pragmatics*, 30(5), 527–541.

Pöchhacker, F. (2013). *Introducing interpreting studies*. New York: Routledge.

Rodin, J., & Janis, I. L. (1979). The social power of health-care practitioners as agents of change. *Journal of Social Issues*, 35(1), 60–81.

Tannen, D., & Wallat, C. (1987). Interactive frames and knowledge schemas in interaction: Examples from a medical examination/interview. *Social Psychology Quarterly*, 50(2), 205–216.

Tracy, K. (2013). *Everyday talk: Building and reflecting identities* (2nd ed.). New York: Guilford.

The United Nations. (1948). The Universal Declaration of Human Rights. Retrieved March 14, 2015, from www.un.org/en/documents/udhr/.

Wadensjö, C. (1998). *Interpreting as interaction*. London: Longman.

Westmyer, S. A., DiCioccio, R. L., & Rubin, R. B. (1998). Appropriateness and effectiveness of communication channels in competent interpersonal communication. *Journal of Communication*, 48(3), 27–48.

REFERENCES

Abbe, M., Simon, C., Angiolillo, A., Ruccione, K., & Kodish, E. D. (2006). A survey of language barriers from the perspective of pediatric oncologists, interpreters, and parents. *Pediatric Blood & Cancer*, 47, 819–824.

Adler, P. A., & Adler, P. (1994). Observational techniques. In N. K. Denzin & Y. S. Lincoln (Eds.), *Handbook of qualitative research* (pp. 377–392). Thousand Oaks, CA: Sage.

Agich, G. J. (1980). Professionalism and ethics in health care. *Journal of Medicine and Philosophy*, 5, 186–199.

Ainsworth-Vaughn, N. (1998). *Claiming power in doctor–patient talk*. New York: Oxford University Press.

Alderete, J. F. (1967). The induction of hypnosis through an interpreter. *American Journal of Clinical Hypnosis*, 10, 138–140.

Aligning Forces for Quality. (2010). Quality & equality in US health care: A message handbook. Retrieved March 14, 2015, from www.rwjf.org/content/dam/farm/reports/reports/2010/rwjf69340.

Allen, B. (Writer). (2011). Signing on: A documentary about Deaf breast cancer survivors [Motion picture]. United States: Screen Porch Films.

American Medical Association. (2007). Official guide to communicating with limited English proficient patients. (2nd ed). Retrieved March 30, 2008, from www.ama-assn.org/ama1/pub/upload/mm/433/lep_booklet.pdf.

Andersen, M. R., Sweet, E., Zhou, M., & Standish, L. J. (2015). Complementary and alternative medicine use by breast cancer patients at time of surgery which increases the potential for excessive bleeding. *Integrative Cancer Therapies*, 14, 119–124.

Anderson, L. M., Scrimshaw, S. C., Fullilove, M. T., Fielding, J. E., Normand, J., & Task Force on Community Preventive Services. (2003). Culturally competent healthcare systems: A systematic review. *American Journal of Preventive Medicine*, 24, 68–79.

Anderson, R. M., & Funnell, M. M. (2010). Patient empowerment: Myths and misconceptions. *Patient Education and Counseling*, 79(3), 277–282.

Andres, E., Wynia, M., Regenstein, M., & Maul, L. (2013). Should I call an interpreter? How do physicians with second language skills decide? *Journal of Health Care for the Poor and Underserved*, 24, 525–539.

Andrulis, D., Goodman, N., & Pryor, C. (2002). What a difference an interpreter can make: Health care experiences of uninsured with limited English proficiency. Retrieved March 14, 2015, from www.accessproject.org/downloads/c_LEPreportENG.pdf.

Angelelli, C. V. (2002). *Deconstructing the invisible interpreter: A critical study of the interpersonal role of the interpreter in a cross-cultural linguistic communicative event.* University of Michigan, Ann Arbor. ProQuest database. (UMI No. AAT 302676).

Angelelli, C. V. (2003). The visible co-participant: The interpreter's role in doctor-patient encounters. In M. Metzger, S. Collins, V. Dively, & R. Shaw (Eds.), *From topic boundaries to omission: New research on interpretation* (pp. 3–26). Washington, DC: Gallaudet University Press.

Angelelli, C. V. (2004). *Medical interpreting and cross-cultural communication.* Cambridge, UK: Cambridge University Press.

Angelelli, C. V. (2004). *Revisiting the interpreters' roles: A study of conference, court, and medical interpreters in Canada, Mexico, and the United States.* Amsterdam, The Netherlands: John Benjamins.

Angelelli, C. V. (2010). A professional ideology in the making: Bilingual youngsters interpreting for their communities and the notion of (no) choice. *Translation and Interpretation Studies,* 5, 94–108.

Angelos, P., DaRosa, D. A., Bentram, D., & Sherman, H. (2002). Residents seeking informed consent: Are they adequately knowledgeable? *Current Surgery,* 59, 115–118.

Annuziata, M. A., & Muzzatti, B. (2013). Improving communication effectiveness in oncology: The role of emotions. In A. Surbone, M. Zwitter, M. Rajer, & R. Stiefel (Eds.), *New challenges in communication with cancer patients* (pp. 235–246). New York: Springer.

Aranguri, C., Davidson, B., & Ramirez, R. (2006). Patterns of communication through interpreters: A detailed sociolinguistic analysis. *Journal of General Internal Medicine,* 21, 623–629.

Archer, M. S. (2000). *Being human: The problem of agency.* Cambridge, UK: Cambridge University Press.

Arocha, I. (2015). Medical interpretation. In S. Loue & M. Sajatovic (Eds.), *Encyclopedia of immigrant health* (pp. 1062–1066). New York: Springer.

Atkinson, J. M. (1992). Displaying neutrality: Formal aspects of informal court proceedings. In P. Drew & J. Heritage (Eds.), *Talk at work: Interaction in institutional settings* (pp. 199–211). Cambridge, UK: Cambridge University Press.

Auer, P. (Ed.). (2013). *Code-switching in conversation: Language, interaction and identity.* New York: Routledge.

Aujoulat, I., d'Hoore, W., & Deccache, A. (2007). Patient empowerment in theory and practice: Polysemy or cacophony? *Patient Education and Counseling,* 66(1), 13–20.

Avery, M.-P. B. (2001). The role of the health care interpreter: An evolving dialogue. Retrieved March 14, 2015, from www.ncihc.org/mc/page.do?sitePageId=57022&orgId=ncihc.

Back, M. F., & Huak, C. Y. (2005). Family centred decision making and non-disclosure of diagnosis in a South East Asian oncology practice. *Psycho-Oncology,* 14, 1052–1059.

Bagchi, A. D., Dale, S., Verbitsky-Savitz, N., Andrecheck, S., Zavotsky, K., & Eisenstein, R. (2011). Examining effectiveness of medical interpreters in emergency departments for Spanish-speaking patients with limited English proficiency: Results of a randomized controlled trial. *Annals of Emergency Medicine,* 57, 248–256.

Baker, D. W., & Hayes, R. (1997). The effect of communicating through an interpreter on satisfaction with interpersonal aspects of care. *Journal of General Internal Medicine,* 12, 117.

Baker, D. W., Hayes, R., & Fortier, J. P. (1998). Interpreter use and satisfaction with interpersonal aspects of care for Spanish-speaking patients. *Medical Care*, 36, 1461–1470.

Baker, D. W., Parker, R. M., Williams, M. V., Coates, W. C., & Pitkin, K. M. (1996). Use and effectiveness of interpreters in an emergency department. *Journal of the American Medical Association*, 275, 783–788.

Bakhtin, M. M. (1981). *The dialogic imagination: Four essays by M. M. Bakhtin* (M. Holquist & C. Emerson, Trans.). Austin, TX: University of Texas Press.

Bancroft, M. (2005). The interpreter's world tour: An environmental scan of standards of practice for interpreters. Retrieved March 14, 2015, from www.hablamosjuntos.org/resources/pdf/The_Interpreter's_World_Tour.pdf.

Bandura, A. (1997). *Self-efficacy: The exercise of control.* New York: Freeman.

Bandura, A. (2001). Social cognitive theory: An agentic perspective. *Annual Review of Psychology*, 52, 1–26.

Baraldi, C. (2009). Forms of mediation: The case of interpreter-mediated interactions in medical systems. *Language and Intercultural Communication*, 9, 120–137.

Barbour, R. S. (1995). Using focus groups in general practice research. *Family Practice*, 12, 328–334.

Barnett, S. (1999). Clinical and cultural issues in caring for deaf people. *Family Medicine*, 31, 17–22.

Bauer, A. M., & Alegría, M. (2010). Impact of patient language proficiency and interpreter service use on the quality of psychiatric care: A systematic review. *Psychiatric Services*, 61, 765–773.

Baumslag, D. (1998). Choosing scientific goals: The need for a normative approach. *Studies in History and Philosophy of Science*, 29, 81–96.

Bavelas, J. B., Black, A., Chovil, N., & Mullett, J. (1990). *Equivocal communication.* Thousand Oaks, CA: Sage.

Baxter, L. A., & Montgomery, B. M. (1996). *Relating: Dialogues and dialectics.* New York: Guilford Press.

Beauchamp, T. L. (2004). Does ethical theory have a future in bioethics? *Journal of Law, Medicine & Ethics*, 32, 209–217.

Beisecker, A. E. (1990). Patient power in doctor–patient communication: What do we know? *Health Communication*, 2, 105–122.

Beisecker, A. E., & Beisecker, T. D. (1993). Using metaphors to characterize doctor-patient relationships: Paternalism versus consumerism. *Health Communication*, 5(1), 41–58.

Berkman, N. D., Sheridan, S. L., Donahue, K. E., Halpern, D. J., & Crotty, K. (2011). Low health literacy and health outcomes: An updated systematic review. *Annals of Internal Medicine*, 155, 97–107.

Berkman, N. D., Sheridan, S. L., Donahue, K. E., Halpern, D. J., Viera, A., Crotty, K., ... Viswanathan, M. (2011). Health literacy interventions and outcomes: An updated systematic review. Retrieved March 14, 2015, from http://www.ncbi.nlm.nih.gov/books/NBK82434/

Bernstein, B. (1964). Elaborated and restricted codes: Their social origins and some consequences. *American Anthropologist*, 66(6Pt. 2), 55–69.

Bernstein, J., Bernstein, E., Dave, A., Hardt, E., James, T., Linden, J., ... Safi, C. (2002). Trained medical interpreters in the emergency department: Effects on services, subsequent charges, and follow-up. *Journal of Immigrant Health*, 4, 171–176.

Bischoff, A. (2012). Do language barriers increase inequalities? Do interpreters decrease inequalities? In D. Ingleby, A. Chiarenza, W. Devillé, & I. Kotsioni (Eds.), *COST series on health and diversity. Volume 2: Inequalities in health care for migrants and ethnic minorities* (pp. 128–143). Philadelphia, PA: Garant.

Bischoff, A., & Hudelson, P. (2010a). Access to healthcare interpreter services: Where are we and where do we need to go? *International Journal of Environmental Research & Public Health, 7*, 2838–2844.

Bischoff, A., & Hudelson, P. (2010b). Communicating with foreign language-speaking patients: Is access to professional interpreters enough? *Journal of Travel Medicine, 17*, 15–20.

Bischoff, A., Hudelson, P., & Bovier, P. A. (2008). Doctor–patient gender concordance and patient satisfaction in interpreter-mediated consultations: An exploratory study. *Journal of Travel Medicine, 15*, 1–5.

Bischoff, A., Kurth, E., & Henley, A. (2012). Staying in the middle: A qualitative study of health care interpreters perceptions of their work. *Interpreting, 14*, 1–22.

Blackhall, L. J., Frank, G., Murphy, S., & Michel, V. (2001). Bioethics in a different tongue: The case of truth-telling. *Journal of Urban Health, 78*, 59–71.

Blackhall, L. J., Murphy, S. T., Frank, G., Michel, V., & Azen, S. (1995). Ethnicity and attitudes toward patient autonomy. *Journal of the American Medical Association, 274*, 820–825.

Bleakley, A., & Bligh, J. (2009). Who can resist Foucault? *Journal of Medicine and Philosophy, 34*, 368–383.

Bloom, M., Hanson, H., Frires, G., & South, V. (1966). The use of interpreters in interviewing. *Mental Hygiene, 50*, 214–217.

Bogdewic, S. P. (1992). Participant observation. In B. F. Crabtree & W. L. Miller (Eds.), *Doing qualitative research* (pp. 45–69). Thousand Oaks, CA: Sage.

Bolden, G. B. (2000). Toward understanding practices of medical interpreting: Interpreters' involvement in history taking. *Discourse Studies, 2*, 387–419.

Bond, J., Bateman, J., & Nassrally, S. M. (2012). The role of ad-hoc interpreters in teaching communication skills with ethnic minorities. *Medical Teacher, 34*, 81.

Bot, H. (2005). Dialogue interpreting as a specific case of reported speech. *Interpreting, 7*, 237–261.

Bowling, A. (1997). *Research methods in health: Investigating health and health services*. Bristol, PA: Open University Press.

Brämberg, E. B., & Sandman, L. (2013). Communication through in-person interpreters: A qualitative study of home care providers' and social workers' views. *Journal of Clinical Nursing, 22*, 159–167.

Brashers, D. E., Goldsmith, D. J., & Hsieh, E. (2002). Information seeking and avoiding in health contexts. *Human Communication Research, 28*, 258–271.

Brashers, D. E., Haas, S. M., & Neidig, J. L. (1999). The patient self-advocacy scale: Measuring patient involvement in health care decision-making interactions. *Health Communication, 11*(2), 97–122.

Bridges, S., Drew, P., Zayts, O., McGrath, C., Yiu, C. K. Y., Wong, H. M., & Au, T. K. F. (2015). Interpreter-mediated dentistry. *Social Science & Medicine, 132*, 197–207.

Brinckerhoff, L. C. (1994). Developing effective self-advocacy skills in college-bound students with learning disabilities. *Intervention in School and Clinic, 29*(4), 229–237.

Brisset, C., Leanza, Y., & Laforest, K. (2013). Working with interpreters in health care: A systematic review and meta-ethnography of qualitative studies. *Patient Education and Counseling, 91*, 131–140.

Brisset, C., Leanza, Y., Rosenberg, E., Vissandjée, B., Kirmayer, L., Muckle, G., … Laforce, H. (2014). Language barriers in mental health care: A survey of primary care practitioners. *Journal of Immigrant and Minority Health, 16*, 1238–1246.

Brown, J. B. (1999). The use of focus groups in clinical research. In B. F. Crabtree & W. L. Miller (Eds.), *Doing qualitative research* (2nd ed., pp. 109–124). Thousand Oaks, CA: Sage.

Brown, P. L. (2009, September 20). A doctor for disease, a shaman for the soul. *The New York Times*, p. A20. Retrieved September 16, 2015, from www.nytimes.com/2009/09/20/us/20shaman.html.

Brua, C. (2008). Role-blurring and ethical grey zones associated with lay interpreters: Three case studies. *Communication & Medicine*, 5, 73–79.

Bruce, W., & Anderson, R. (1976). Perspectives on the role of interpreter. In R. W. Brislin (Ed.), *Translation: Applications and research* (pp. 208–228). New York: Gardner.

Brunson, J. G., & Lawrence, P. S. (2002). Impact of sign language interpreter and therapist moods on deaf recipient mood. *Professional Psychology: Research and Practice*, 33, 576–580.

Bryant, A., & Charmaz, K. (2010a). Introduction: Grounded theory research: Methods and practices. In A. Bryant & K. Charmaz (Eds.), *The SAGE handbook of grounded theory* (pp. 1–28). Thousand Oaks, CA: Sage.

Bryant, A., & Charmaz, K. (2010b). *The SAGE handbook of grounded theory*. Thousand Oaks, CA: Sage.

Bureau of Labor Statistics. (2014). Occupational outlook handbook, 2014–15 edition. Retrieved March 14, 2015, from www.bls.gov/ooh/media-and-communication/interpreters-and-translators.htm.

Burgoon, J. K. (1993). Interpersonal expectations, expectancy violations, and emotional communication. *Journal of Language and Social Psychology*, 12, 30–48.

Burleson, B. R. (2003). The experience and effects of emotional support: What the study of cultural and gender differences can tell us about close relationships, emotion and interpersonal communication. *Personal Relationships*, 10, 1–23.

Burleson, B. R. (2009). Understanding the outcomes of supportive communication: A dual-process approach. *Journal of Social and Personal Relationships*, 26, 21–38.

Burleson, B. R., & MacGeorge, E. L. (2002). Supportive communication. In M. L. Knapp & J. A. Daly (Eds.), *Handbook of interpersonal communication* (3rd ed., pp. 374–424). Thousand Oaks, CA: Sage.

Butow, P. N., Bell, M., Goldstein, D., Sze, M., Aldridge, L., Abdo, S., … Eisenbruch, M. (2011). Grappling with cultural differences; Communication between oncologists and immigrant cancer patients with and without interpreters. *Patient Education and Counseling*, 84, 398–405.

Butow, P. N., Goldstein, D., Bell, M. L., Sze, M., Aldridge, L. J., Abdo, S., … Eisenbruch, M. (2011). Interpretation in consultations with immigrant patients with cancer: How accurate is it? *Journal of Clinical Oncology*, 29, 2801–2807.

Butow, P. N., Lobb, E., Jefford, M., Goldstein, D., Eisenbruch, M., Girgis, A., … Schofield, P. (2012). A bridge between cultures: Interpreters' perspectives of consultations with migrant oncology patients. *Supportive Care in Cancer*, 20, 235–244.

Cambridge, J. (1999). Information loss in bilingual medical interviews through an untrained interpreter. *Translator*, 5, 201–219.

Campbell, S. M., Roland, M. O., & Buetow, S. A. (2000). Defining quality of care. *Social Science & Medicine*, 51, 1611–1625.

Carrasquillo, O., Orav, E. J., Brennan, T. A., & Burstin, H. R. (1999). Impact of language barriers on patient satisfaction in an emergency department. *Journal of General Internal Medicine*, 14, 82–87.

Carroll, L. N., Calhoun, R. E., Subido, C. C., Painter, I. S., & Meischke, H. W. (2013). Serving limited English proficient callers: A survey of 9-1-1 police telecommunicators. *Prehospital and Disaster Medicine*, 28, 286–291.

Castillo, R. J. (1997). *Culture & mental illness: A client-centered approach.* Belmont, CA: Brooks/ Cole Publishing.

The CATIE Center at St. Catherine University. (2014). Interpreting in healthcare settings. Retrieved March 14, 2015, from www.healthcareinterpreting.org/.

Cegala, D. J. (1997). A study of doctors' and patients' communication during a primary care consultation: Implications for communication training. *Journal of Health Communication, 2,* 169–194.

Cegala, D. J., & Broz, S. L. (2002). Physician communication skills training: A review of theoretical backgrounds, objectives and skills. *Medical Education, 36,* 1004–1016.

Cegala, D. J., Gade, C., Broz, S. L., & McClure, L. (2004). Physicians' and patients' perceptions of patients' communication competence in a primary care medical interview. *Health Communication, 16,* 289–304.

Cegala, D. J., & Post, D. M. (2009). The impact of patients' participation on physicians' patient-centered communication. *Patient Education and Counseling, 77,* 202–208.

Cegala, D. J., Post, D. M., & McClure, L. (2001). The effects of patient communication skills training on the discourse of older patients during a primary care interview. *Journal of the American Geriatrics Society, 49,* 1505.

Cegala, D. J., Street, R. L., Jr., & Clinch, C. (2007). The impact of patient participation on physicians' information provision during a primary care medical interview. *Health Communication, 21,* 177–185.

Chan, Y.-F., Alagappan, K., Rella, J., Bentley, S., Soto-Greene, M., & Martin, M. (2010). Interpreter services in emergency medicine. *Journal of Emergency Medicine, 38,* 133–139.

Charmaz, K. (1991). *Good days, bad days: The self in chronic illness and time.* New Brunswick, NJ: Rutgers University Press.

Charmaz, K. (2006). *Constructing grounded theory: A practical guide through qualitative analysis.* Thousand Oaks, CA: Sage.

Chen, A. H., Youdelman, M. K., & Brooks, J. (2007). The legal framework for language access in healthcare settings: Title VI and beyond. *Journal of General Internal Medicine, 22,* S362–367.

Chesler, M. A., Paris, J., & Barbarin, O. A. (1986). "Telling" the child with cancer: Parental choices to share information with ill children. *Journal of Pediatric Psychology, 11,* 497–516.

Chun, M. B. J., Jackson, D. S., Lin, S. Y., & Park, E. R. (2010). A comparison of surgery and family medicine residents' perceptions of cross-cultural care training. *Hawaii Medical Journal, 69,* 289–293.

Chung, V. C. H., Ma, P. H. X., Lau, C. H., Wong, S. Y. S., Yeoh, E. K., & Griffiths, S. M. (2012). Views on traditional Chinese medicine amongst Chinese population: A systematic review of qualitative and quantitative studies. *Health Expectations, 17*(5), 622–636.

Clifford, A. (2004). Is fidelity ethical? The social role of the healthcare interpreter. *TTR: Traduction, Terminologie, Rédaction: Etudes sur le Texte et Ses Transformations, 17*(2), 89–114.

Cohen, A. L., Rivara, F., Marcuse, E. K., McPhillips, H., & Davis, R. (2005). Are language barriers associated with serious medical events in hospitalized pediatric patients? *Pediatrics, 116,* 575–579.

Cohen, S., Moran-Ellis, J., & Smaje, C. (1999). Children as informal interpreters in GP consultations: Pragmatics and ideology. *Sociology of Health & Illness, 21,* 163–186.

Crossman, K. L., Wiener, E., Roosevelt, G., Bajaj, L., & Hampers, L. C. (2010). Interpreters: Telephonic, in-person interpretation and bilingual providers. *Pediatrics, 125,* e631–638.

Culyer, A. J., & Wagstaff, A. (1993). Equity and equality in health and health care. *Journal of Health Economics*, 12, 431–457.

Cunningham, H., Cushman, L. F., Akuete-Penn, C., & Meyer, D. D. (2008). Satisfaction with telephonic interpreters in pediatric care. *Journal of the National Medical Association*, 100, 429–434.

d'Ardenne, P., & Farmer, E. (2009). Using interpreters in trauma therapy. In N. Grey (Ed.), *A casebook of cognitive therapy for traumatic stress reactions* (pp. 283–300). New York: Routledge.

David, R. A., & Rhee, M. (1998). The impact of language as a barrier to effective health care in an underserved urban Hispanic community. *Mount Sinai Journal of Medicine*, 65, 393–397.

Davidson, B. (2000). The interpreter as institutional gatekeeper: The social-linguistic role of interpreters in Spanish–English medical discourse. *Journal of Sociolinguistics*, 4, 379–405.

Davidson, B. (2001). Questions in cross-linguistic medical encounters: The role of the hospital interpreter. *Anthropological Quarterly*, 74, 170–178.

Davis, J. M., Anderson, M. C., Stankevitz, K. A., & Manley, A. R. (2013). Providing pre-medical students with quality clinical and research experience: The Tobacco Science Scholars Program. *Wisconsin Medical Journal*, 112, 195–198.

De Jaegher, H., & Froese, T. (2009). On the role of social interaction in individual agency. *Adaptive Behavior*, 17, 444–460.

De Maesschalck, S., Deveugele, M., & Willems, S. (2011). Language, culture and emotions: Exploring ethnic minority patients' emotional expressions in primary healthcare consultations. *Patient Education and Counseling*, 84, 406–412.

Dean, R. K. (2014). Condemned to repetition? An analysis of problem-setting and problem-solving in sign language interpreting ethics. *Translation & Interpreting*, 6, 60–75.

Dean, R. K., & Pollard, R. Q. (2011). Context-based ethical reasoning in interpreting. *The Interpreter and Translator Trainer*, 5, 155–182.

DeCamp, L. R., Kuo, D. Z., Flores, G., O'Connor, K., & Minkovitz, C. S. (2013). Changes in language services use by US pediatricians. *Pediatrics*, 132, e396–406.

Derose, K. P., Hays, R. D., McCaffrey, D. F., & Baker, D. W. (2001). Does physician gender affect satisfaction of men and women visiting the emergency department? *Journal of General Internal Medicine*, 16, 218–226.

Diamond, L. C., Chung, S., Ferguson, W., Gonzalez, J., Jacobs, E. A., & Gany, F. (2014). Relationship between self-assessed and tested non–English-language proficiency among primary care providers. *Medical Care*, 52, 435–438.

Diamond, L. C., & Jacobs, E. A. (2010). Let's not contribute to disparities: The best methods for teaching clinicians how to overcome language barriers to health care. *Journal of General Internal Medicine*, 25, S189–193.

Diamond, L. C., Luft, H. S., Chung, S., & Jacobs, E. A. (2012). "Does this doctor speak my language?" Improving the characterization of physician non-English language skills. *Health Services Research*, 47, 556–569.

Diamond, L. C., & Reuland, D. S. (2009). Describing physician language fluency: Deconstructing medical Spanish. *Journal of the American Medical Association*, 301, 426–428.

Diamond, L. C., Schenker, Y., Curry, L., Bradley, E. H., & Fernandez, A. (2009). Getting by: Underuse of interpreters by resident physicians. *Journal of General Internal Medicine*, 24, 256–262.

Diamond, L. C., Tuot, D., & Karliner, L. (2012). The use of Spanish language skills by physicians and nurses: Policy implications for teaching and testing. *Journal of General Internal Medicine, 27,* 117–123.

Dieleman, S. L., Farris, K. B., Feeny, D., Johnson, J. A., Tsuyuki, R. T., & Brilliant, S. (2004). Primary health care teams: Team members' perceptions of the collaborative process. *Journal of Interprofessional Care,* 18, 75–78.

Dohan, D., & Levintova, M. (2007). Barriers beyond words: Cancer, culture, and translation in a community of Russian speakers. *Journal of General Internal Medicine,* 22, S300–305.

Doherty, S. M., MacIntyre, A. M., & Wyne, T. (2010). How does it feel for you? The emotional impact and specific challenges of mental health interpreting. *Mental Health Review Journal,* 15, 31–44.

Donabedian, A. (1980). *The definition of quality and approaches to its assessment.* Michigan, MI: Health Administration Press.

Drennan, G., & Swartz, L. (2002). The paradoxical use of interpreting in psychiatry. *Social Science & Medicine,* 54, 1853–1866.

Dutta, M. J. (2007). Communicating about culture and health: Theorizing culture-centered and cultural sensitivity approaches. *Communication Theory,* 17, 304–328.

Dutta, M. J., & Basu, A. (2007). Health among men in rural Bengal: Exploring meanings through a culture-centered approach. *Qualitative Health Research,* 17, 38–48.

Dy, S. M., & Purnell, T. S. (2012). Key concepts relevant to quality of complex and shared decision-making in health care: A literature review. *Social Science & Medicine,* 74, 582–587.

Dysart-Gale, D. (2005). Communication models, professionalization, and the work of medical interpreters. *Health Communication,* 17, 91–103.

Dysart-Gale, D. (2007). Clinicians and medical interpreters: Negotiating culturally appropriate care for patients with limited English ability. *Family & Community Health,* 30, 237–246.

Eamranond, P. P., Davis, R. B., Phillips, R. S., & Wee, C. C. (2009). Patient–physician language concordance and lifestyle counseling among Spanish-speaking patients. *Journal of Immigrant and Minority Health,* 11, 494–498.

Ebden, P., Bhatt, A., Carey, O., & Harrison, B. (1988). The bilingual medical consultation. *The Lancet,* 331, 347.

Edwards, R., Temple, B., & Alexander, C. (2005). Users' experiences of interpreters: The critical role of trust. *Interpreting,* 7, 77–95.

Eisenberg, E. M. (1984). Ambiguity as strategy in organizational communication. *Communication Monographs,* 51(3), 227–242.

Elderkin-Thompson, V., Silver, R. C., & Waitzkin, H. (2001). When nurses double as interpreters: A study of Spanish-speaking patients in a US primary care setting. *Social Science & Medicine,* 52, 1343–1358.

Ellerby, J. H., McKenzie, J., McKay, S., Gariepy, G. J., & Kaufert, J. M. (2000). Bioethics for clinicians: 18. Aboriginal cultures. *Canadian Medical Association Journal,* 163, 845–850.

Emerson, R. M., Fretz, R. I., & Shaw, L. L. (1995). *Writing ethnographic fieldnotes.* Chicago, IL: University of Chicago Press.

Engstrom, D. W., Piedra, L. M., & Min, J. W. (2009). Bilingual social workers: Language and service complexities. *Administration in Social Work,* 33, 167–185.

Fadiman, A. (1997). *The spirit catches you and you fall down: A Hmong child, her American doctors, and the collision of two cultures.* New York: Farrar, Straus and Giroux.

Fagan, M. J., Diaz, J. A., Reinert, S. E., Sciamanna, C. N., & Fagan, D. M. (2003). Impact of interpretation method on clinic visit length. *Journal of General Internal Medicine*, 18, 634–638.

Fan, R. (1997). Self-determination vs. family-determination: Two incommensurable principles of autonomy. *Bioethics*, 11(3–4), 309–322.

Farnill, D., Todisco, J., Hayes, S. C., & Bartlett, D. (1997). Videotaped interviewing of non-English speakers: Training for medical students with volunteer clients. *Medical Education*, 31, 87–93.

Fatahi, N., Hellstrom, M., Skott, C., & Mattsson, B. (2008). General practitioners' views on consultations with interpreters: A triad situation with complex issues. *Scandinavian Journal of Primary Health Care*, 26, 40–45.

Feldman, M. D., Zhang, J., & Cummings, S. R. (1999). Chinese and US internists adhere to different ethical standards. *Journal of General Internal Medicine*, 14, 469–473.

Fenton, S. (1997). The role of the interpreter in the adversarial courtroom. In S. E. Carr, R. P. Roberts, A. Dufour, & D. Steyn (Eds.), *The critical link: Interpreters in the community* (pp. 29–34). Amsterdam, The Netherlands: John Benjamins.

Fernandez, A., Schillinger, D., Warton, E. M., Adler, N., Moffet, H. H., Schenker, Y., ... Karter, A. J. (2011). Language barriers, physician-patient language concordance, and glycemic control among insured Latinos with diabetes: The Diabetes Study of Northern California (DISTANCE). *Journal of General Internal Medicine*, 26, 170–176.

Flores, G. (2005). The impact of medical interpreter services on the quality of health care: A systematic review. *Medical Care Research & Review*, 62, 255–299.

Flores, G., Abreu, M., Barone, C. P., Bachur, R., & Lin, H. (2012). Errors of medical interpretation and their potential clinical consequences: A comparison of professional versus ad hoc versus no interpreters. *Annals of Emergency Medicine*, 60, 545–553.

Flores, G., Abreu, M., & Tomany-Korman, S. C. (2005). Limited English proficiency, primary language at home, and disparities in children's health care: How language barriers are measured matters. *Public Health Reports*, 120, 418–430.

Flores, G., Laws, M. B., Mayo, S. J., Zuckerman, B., Abreu, M., Medina, L., & Hardt, E. J. (2003). Errors in medical interpretation and their potential clinical consequences in pediatric encounters. *Pediatrics*, 111, 6–14.

Flores, G., Torres, S., Holmes, L. J., Salas-Lopez, D., Youdelman, M. K., & Tomany-Korman, S. C. (2008). Access to hospital interpreter services for limited English proficient patients in New Jersey: A statewide evaluation. *Journal of Health Care for the Poor and Underserved*, 19, 391–415.

Flynn, P. M., Ridgeway, J. L., Wieland, M. L., Williams, M. D., Haas, L. R., Kremers, W. K., & Breitkopf, C. R. (2013). Primary care utilization and mental health diagnoses among adult patients requiring interpreters: A retrospective cohort study. *Journal of General Internal Medicine*, 28, 386–391.

Fontana, A., & Frey, J. H. (1994). Interviewing: The art of science. In N. K. Denzin & Y. S. Lincoln (Eds.), *Handbook of qualitative research* (pp. 361–376). Thousand Oaks, CA: Sage.

Forman, W. (2002). The bias of neutrality: The role of interpreters in health care settings. *Vision*, 8(14), 20–22.

French, J. R. P., Jr., & Raven, B. (1959). The bases of social power. In D. Cartwright (Ed.), *Studies in social power* (pp. 150–167). Ann Arbor, MI: Institute for Social Research.

Fryer, C. E., Mackintosh, S. F., Stanley, M. J., & Crichton, J. (2013). "I understand all the major things": How older people with limited English proficiency decide their need for a professional interpreter during health care after stroke. *Ethnicity & Health*, 18, 610–625.

Gadon, M., Balch, G. I., & Jacobs, E. A. (2007). Caring for patients with limited English proficiency: The perspectives of small group practitioners. *Journal of General Internal Medicine*, 22, S341–346.

Gaiba, F. (1998). *The origins of simultaneous interpretation: The Nuremberg Trial*. Ottawa, Canada: University of Ottawa Press.

Gany, F., Kapelusznik, L., Prakash, K., Gonzalez, J., Orta, L. Y., Tseng, C.-H., & Changrani, J. (2007). The impact of medical interpretation method on time and errors. *Journal of General Internal Medicine*, 22, 319–323.

Gany, F., Leng, J., Shapiro, E., Abramson, D., Motola, I., Shield, D. C., & Changrani, J. (2007). Patient satisfaction with different interpreting methods: A randomized controlled trial. *Journal of General Internal Medicine*, 22, S312–318.

Gao, G., Burke, N., Somkin, C. P., & Pasick, R. (2009). Considering culture in physician–patient communication during colorectal cancer screening. *Qualitative Health Research*, 19, 778–789.

Gardiner, P., Whelan, J., White, L., Filippelli, A., Bharmal, N., & Kaptchuk, T. (2013). A systematic review of the prevalence of herb usage among racial/ethnic minorities in the United States. *Journal of Immigrant and Minority Health*, 15(4), 817–828.

Gattellari, M., Voigt, K. J., Butow, P. N., & Tattersall, M. H. N. (2002). When the treatment goal is not cure: Are cancer patients equipped to make informed decisions? *Journal of Clinical Oncology*, 20, 503–513.

Gavioli, L., & Baraldi, C. (2011). Interpreter-mediated interaction in healthcare and legal settings: Talk organization, context and the achievement of intercultural communication. *Interpreting*, 13, 205–233.

Gawande, A. (2002). *Complications: A surgeon's notes on an imperfect science*. New York: Metropolitan Books.

Gentile, A., Ozolins, U., & Vsilakakos, M. (1996). *Liaison interpreting: A handbook*. Victoria, Australia: Melbourne University Press.

Gilchrist, V. J., & Williams, R. L. (1999). Key informant interviews. In B. F. Crabtree & W. L. Miller (Eds.), *Doing qualitative research* (2nd ed., pp. 71–88). Thousand Oaks, CA: Sage.

Gile, D. (1995). Fidelity assessment in consecutive interpretation: An experiment. *Target*, 7, 151–164.

Gill, P. S., Beavan, J., Calvert, M., & Freemantle, N. (2011). The unmet need for interpreting provision in UK primary care. *PLoS One*, 6, 1–6.

Ginde, A. A., Clark, S., & Camargo, C. A., Jr. (2009). Language barriers among patients in Boston emergency departments: Use of medical interpreters after passage of interpreter legislation. *Journal of Immigrant and Minority Health*, 11, 527–530.

Ginde, A. A., Sullivan, A. F., Corel, B., Caceres, J. A., & Camargo, C. A., Jr. (2010). Reevaluation of the effect of mandatory interpreter legislation on use of professional interpreters for ED patients with language barriers. *Patient Education and Counseling*, 81, 204–206.

Glaser, B. G., & Strauss, A. L. (1967). *The discovery of grounded theory: Strategies for qualitative research*. Hawthorne, NY: Aldine de Gruyter.

Goffman, E. (1959). *The presentation of self in everyday life*. Garden City, NY: Doubleday.

Goffman, E. (1974). *Frame analysis: An essay on the organization of experience*. Cambridge, MA: Harvard University Press.

Goffman, E. (1979). Footing. *Semiotica: Journal of the International Association for Semiotic Studies/Revue de l'Association Internationale de Sémiotique*, 25, 1–29.

Goffman, E. (1983). The interaction order. *American Sociological Review*, 48, 1–17.

Goldsmith, D. J. (1992). Managing conflicting goals in supportive interaction: An integrative theoretical framework. *Communication Research*, 19, 264–286.

Goldsmith, D. J. (1994). The role of facework in supportive communication. In B. R. Burleson (Ed.), *Communication of social support: Messages, interactions, relationships, and community* (pp. 29–49). Thousand Oaks, CA: Sage.

Goldsmith, D. J. (2001). A normative approach to the study of uncertainty and communication. *Journal of Communication*, 51, 514–533.

Goldsmith, D. J. (2004). *Communicating social support*. New York: Cambridge University Press.

Goldsmith, D. J., & Brashers, D. E. (2008). Communication matters: Developing and testing social support interventions. *Communication Monographs*, 75, 320–329.

Goldsmith, D. J., & Fitch, K. (1997). The normative context of advice as social support. *Human Communication Research*, 23, 454–476.

Goldsmith, D. J., Lindholm, K. A., & Bute, J. J. (2006). Dilemmas of talking about lifestyle changes among couples coping with a cardiac event. *Social Science & Medicine*, 63, 2079–2090.

Goodwin, C. (2007). Interactive footing. In E. Holt & R. Clift (Eds.), *Reporting talk: Reported speech in interaction* (pp. 16–46). Cambridge: Cambridge University Press.

Goodwin, C., & Duranti, A. (1992). Rethinking context: An introduction. In A. Duranti & C. Goodwin (Eds.), *Rethinking context: Language as an interactive phenomenon* (pp. 1–42). Cambridge, UK: Cambridge University Press.

Gostin, L. O. (1995). Informed consent, cultural sensitivity, and respect for persons. *Journal of the American Medical Association*, 274, 844–845.

Grady, J. (1998). The conduit metaphor revisited: A reassessment of metaphors for communication. In J.-P. Koenig (Ed.), *Discourse and cognition: Bridging the gap* (pp. 205–218). Stanford, CA: CSLI Publications.

Gray, B., Hilder, J., & Donaldson, H. (2011). Why do we not use trained interpreters for all patients with limited English proficiency? Is there a place for using family members? *Australian Journal of Primary Health*, 17, 240–249.

Green, A. R., Ngo-Metzger, Q., Legedza, A. T. R., Massagli, M. P., Phillips, R. S., & Iezzoni, L. I. (2005). Interpreter services, language concordance, and health care quality: Experiences of Asian Americans with limited English proficiency. *Journal of General Internal Medicine*, 20, 1050–1056.

Green, H., Sperlinger, D., & Carswell, K. (2012). Too close to home? Experiences of Kurdish refugee interpreters working in UK mental health services. *Journal of Mental Health*, 21, 227–235.

Green, J., Free, C., Bhavnani, V., & Newman, T. (2005). Translators and mediators: Bilingual young people's accounts of their interpreting work in health care. *Social Science & Medicine*, 60, 2097–2110.

Greenbaum, M., & Flores, G. (2004). Lost in translation: Professional interpreters needed to help hospitals treat immigrant patients. *Modern Healthcare*, 34, 21.

Greenhalgh, T., Robb, N., & Scambler, G. (2006). Communicative and strategic action in interpreted consultations in primary health care: A Habermasian perspective. *Social Science & Medicine*, 63, 1170–1187.

Gregg, J., & Saha, S. (2007). Communicative competence: A framework for understanding language barriers in health care. *Journal of General Internal Medicine*, 22, S368–370.

Grice, H. P. (1975). Logic and conversation. In P. Cole & J. L. Morgan (Eds.), *Syntax and semantics: Speech acts* (Vol. 3, pp. 41–58). Cambridge, MA: Harvard University Press.

Grover, A., Deakyne, S., Bajaj, L., & Roosevelt, G. E. (2012). Comparison of through-put times for limited English proficiency patient visits in the emergency department between different interpreter modalities. *Journal of Immigrant and Minority Health*, 14, 602–607.

Gubrium, J. F., & Holstein, J. A. (1995). Individual agency, the ordinary, and postmodern life. *Sociological Quarterly*, 36, 555–570.

Gudykunst, W. D. (Ed.). (2003). *Cross-cultural and intercultural communication*. Thousand Oaks, CA: Sage.

Gudykunst, W. B. (2003). Foreword. In W. B. Gudykunst (Ed.), *Cross-cultural and intercultural communication* (pp. vii–ix). Thousand Oaks, CA: Sage.

Guercio, L. R. M. D. (1960). *The multilingual manual for medical interpreting*. New York: Pacific Print.

Gumperz, J. J. (2009). The speech community. In A. Duranti (Ed.), *Linguistic anthropology: A reader* (2nd ed., pp. 66–73). Malden, MA: Blackwell.

Gutmann, E. J. (2003). Pathologists and patients: Can we talk? *Modern Pathology*, 16, 515–518.

Haakana, M. (2002). Laughter in medical interaction: From quantification to analysis, and back. *Journal of Sociolinguistics*, 6, 207–235.

Hadziabdic, E., Albin, B., Heikkilä, K., & Hjelm, K. (2010). Healthcare staffs perceptions of using interpreters: A qualitative study. *Primary Health Care Research and Development*, 11, 260–270.

Hadziabdic, E., Albin, B., Heikkilä, K., & Hjelm, K. (2014). Family members' experiences of the use of interpreters in healthcare. *Primary Health Care Research and Development*, 15, 156–169.

Hale, S. B. (2004). *The discourse of court interpreting: Discourse practices of the law, the witness, and the interpreter*. Amsterdam, The Netherlands: John Benjamins.

Hale, S. B. (2007). *Community interpreting*. London, UK: Palgrave Macmillan.

Hall, S. (1983). Train-gone-sorry: The etiquette of social conversations in American Sign Language. *Sign Language Studies*, 41, 291–309.

Hampers, L. C., & McNulty, J. E. (2002). Professional interpreters and bilingual physicians in a pediatric emergency department: Effect on resource utilization. *Archives of Pediatrics and Adolescent Medicine*, 156, 1108–1113.

Hardacre, H. (1997). *Marketing the menacing fetus in Japan*. Berkeley, CA: University of California Press.

Harmsen, H., Meeuwesen, L., van Wieringen, J., Bernsen, R., & Bruijnzeels, M. (2003). When cultures meet in general practice: Intercultural differences between GPs and parents of child patients. *Patient Education and Counseling*, 51, 99–106.

Harmsen, J. A. M., Bernsen, R. M. D., Bruijnzeels, M. A., & Meeuwesen, L. (2008). Patients' evaluation of quality of care in general practice: What are the cultural and linguistic barriers? *Patient Education and Counseling*, 72, 155–162.

Harris, B. (1997). Foreword: A landmark in the evolution of interpreting. In S. E. Carr, R. P. Roberts, A. Dufour, & D. Steyn (Eds.), *The critical link: Interpreters in the community* (pp. 1–3). Amsterdam, The Netherlands: John Benjamins.

Harrison, B., Bhatt, A., Carey, J., & Ebden, P. (1988). The language of the bilingual medical consultation. In P. Grunwell (Ed.), *Applied linguistics in society: Papers from the annual meeting of the British Association for Applied Linguistics (20th, Nottingham, United Kingdom, September 1987)* (pp. 67–73). London: Centre for Information on Language Teaching and Research.

Harshman, P. (1984). A misinterpreted word worth $71 million. *Medical Economics*, 61, 298–292.

Hasbún Avalos, O., Pennington, K., & Osterberg, L. (2013). Revolutionizing volunteer interpreter services: An evaluation of an innovative medical interpreter education program. *Journal of General Internal Medicine*, 28, 1589–1595.

Hatim, B., & Mason, I. (1990). *Discourse and the translator*. New York: Longman.

Hatton, D. C., & Webb, T. (1993). Information transmission in bilingual, bicultural contexts: A field study of community health nurses and interpreters. *Journal of Community Health Nursing*, 10, 137–147.

Haug, M. R. (1997). Physician power and patients' health behavior. In D. S. Gochman (Ed.), *Handbook of health behavior research: Provider determinants* (Vol. 2, pp. 49–62). New York: Plenum Press.

Hernandez, R. G., Cowden, J. D., Moon, M., Brands, C. K., Sisson, S. D., & Thompson, D. A. (2014). Predictors of resident satisfaction in caring for limited English proficient families: A multisite study. *Academic Pediatrics*, 14, 173–180.

Hicks, L. S., Tovar, D. A., Orav, E., & Johnson, P. A. (2008). Experiences with hospital care: Perspectives of Black and Hispanic patients. *Journal of General Internal Medicine*, 23, 1234–1240.

Hiles, D. R. (2008). Transparency. In L. Given (Ed.), *The SAGE encyclopedia of qualitative research methods* (pp. 891–893). Thousand Oaks, CA: Sage.

Hilliard, R. (2013). Using interpreters in healthcare settings. Retrieved March 14, 2015, from www.kidsnewtocanada.ca/care/interpreters.

Hinton, D. E., Nguyen, L., Tran, M., & Quinn, S. (2005). Weak kidney and panic attacks in a traumatized Vietnamese male. *Culture, Medicine and Psychiatry*, 29, 125–135.

Ho, A. (2008). Using family members as interpreters in the clinical setting. *The Journal of Clinical Ethics*, 19, 223–233.

Hochschild, A. R. (1979). Emotion work, feeling rules, and social structure. *American Journal of Sociology*, 85(3), 551–575.

Hogue, C. J. R., Hargraves, M. A., Collins, K. S., & Fund, C. (2000). *Minority health in America: Findings and policy implications from the Commonwealth Fund Minority Health Survey*. Baltimore, MD: Johns Hopkins University Press.

Houtlosser, P., & van Rees, A. (Eds.). (2006). *Considering pragma-dialectics*. Mahwah, NJ: Erlbaum.

Hsieh, E. (2002). Necessary changes in translation ideology. 翻譯學研究集刊 *Fan I Hsueh Yen Chiu Chi K'an [Studies of Translation and Interpretation]*, 7, 399–435.

Hsieh, E. (2006). Conflicts in how interpreters manage their roles in provider–patient interactions. *Social Science & Medicine*, 62, 721–730.

Hsieh, E. (2006). Understanding medical interpreters: Reconceptualizing bilingual health communication. *Health Communication*, 20, 177–186.

Hsieh, E. (2007). Interpreters as co-diagnosticians: Overlapping roles and services between providers and interpreters. *Social Science & Medicine*, 64, 924–937.

Hsieh, E. (2008). "I am not a robot!" Interpreters' views of their roles in health care settings. *Qualitative Health Research*, 18, 1367–1383.

Hsieh, E. (2009). Bilingual health communication: Medical interpreters' construction of a mediator role. In D. E. Brashers & D. J. Goldsmith (Eds.), *Communicating to manage health and illness* (pp. 135–160). New York: Routledge.

Hsieh, E. (2010). Provider–interpreter collaboration in bilingual health care: Competitions of control over interpreter-mediated interactions. *Patient Education and Counseling*, 78, 154–159.

Hsieh, E. (2013). Health literacy and patient empowerment: The role of medical interpreters in bilingual health communication. In M. J. Dutta & G. L. Kreps (Eds.), *Reducing health disparities: Communication intervention* (pp. 41–66). New York: Peter Lang.

Hsieh, E. (2014). Emerging trends and the corresponding challenges in bilingual health communication. In B. Nicodemus & M. Metzger (Eds.), *Investigations in healthcare interpreting* (pp. 70–103). Washington, DC: Gallaudet University Press.

Hsieh, E. (2015). Not just "getting by": Factors influencing providers' choice of interpreters. *Journal of General Internal Medicine, 30*, 75–82.

Hsieh, E. (in press). The Model of Bilingual Health Communication: Theorizing interpreter-mediated medical encounters. In E. A. Jacobs & L. C. Diamond (Eds.), *Providing health care in the context of language barriers: International perspectives*. Bristol, UK: Multilingual Matters.

Hsieh, E., Bruscella, J., Zanin, A., & Kramer, E. M. (in press). "It's not like you need to live 10 or 20 years": Challenges to patient-centered care in gynecologic oncologist-patient interactions. *Qualitative Health Research*.

Hsieh, E., & Hong, S. J. (2010). Not all are desired: Providers' views on interpreters' emotional support for patients. *Patient Education and Counseling, 81*, 192–197.

Hsieh, E., Ju, H., & Kong, H. (2010). Dimensions of trust: The tensions and challenges in provider–interpreter trust. *Qualitative Health Research, 20*, 170–181.

Hsieh, E., & Kramer, E. M. (2012). The clashes of expert and layman talk: Constructing meanings of interpreter-mediated medical encounters. In C. Callahan (Ed.), *Communication, comparative cultures and civilizations* (Vol. 2, pp. 19–44). New York: Hampton.

Hsieh, E., & Kramer, E. M. (2012). Medical interpreters as tools: Dangers and challenges in the utilitarian approach to interpreters' roles and functions. *Patient Education and Counseling, 89*, 158–162.

Hsieh, E. & Nicodemus, B. (2015). Conceptualizing emotion in healthcare interpreting: A normative approach to interpreters' emotion work. *Patient Education and Counseling, 98*, 1474–1481.

Hsieh, E., Pitaloka, D., & Johnson, A. J. (2013). Bilingual health communication: Distinctive needs of providers from five specialties. *Health Communication, 28*, 557–567.

Hsieh, E., & Terui, S. (2015). Inherent tensions and challenges of oncologist–patient communication: Implications for interpreter training in health-care settings. *Journal of Applied Communication Research, 43*, 141–162.

Hymes, D. (1972). Models of the interaction of language and social life. In J. J. Gumperz & D. Hymes (Eds.), *Directions in sociolinguistics: Ethnography of communication* (pp. 35–71). New York: Holt, Rinehart, & Winston.

Institute for Innovation in Health and Human Services. (2014). Blue Ridge Area Health Education Center. Retrieved March 14, 2015, from www.brahec.jmu.edu/index.html.

Institute of Medicine. (2004). *Health literacy: A prescription to end confusion*. Washington, DC: National Academics.

International Medical Interpreters Association. (2014). National certification. Retrieved March 14, 2015, from www.imiaweb.org/advocacy/nationalcertificatereport.asp.

IQ Solutions. (2001). *National standards for culturally and linguistically appropriate services*. Washington, DC: US Department of Health and Human Services. Retrieved September 16, 2015, from http://minorityhealth.hhs.gov/assets/pdf/checked/finalreport.pdf.

Ishikawa, H., Takayama, T., Yamazaki, Y., Seki, Y., & Katsumata, N. (2002). Physician–patient communication and patient satisfaction in Japanese cancer consultations. *Social Science & Medicine, 55*, 301–311.

Jackson, J. C., Nguyen, D., Hu, N., Harris, R., & Terasaki, G. S. (2011). Alterations in medical interpretation during routine primary care. *Journal of General Internal Medicine*, 26, 259–264.

Jackson, J. C., Zatzick, D., Harris, R., & Gardiner, L. (2008). Loss in translation: Considering the critical role of interpreters and language in the psychiatric evaluation of non-English-speaking patients. In S. Loue & M. Sajatovic (Eds.), *Diversity issues in the diagnosis, treatment, and research of mood disorders* (pp. 135–163). New York: Oxford University Press.

Jacobs, B., Kroll, L., Green, J., & David, T. J. (1995). The hazards of using a child as an interpreter. *Journal of the Royal Society of Medicine*, 88, 474P–475P.

Jacobs, E. A., Chen, A. H., Karliner, L. S., Agger-Gupta, N., & Mutha, S. (2006). The need for more research on language barriers in health care: A proposed research agenda. *Milbank Quarterly*, 84, 111–133.

Jacobs, E. A., Diamond, L. C., & Stevak, L. (2010). The importance of teaching clinicians when and how to work with interpreters. *Patient Education and Counseling*, 78, 149–153.

Jacobs, E. A., Fu, P. C., Jr., & Rathouz, P. J. (2012). Does a video-interpreting network improve delivery of care in the emergency department? *Health Services Research*, 47, 509–522.

Jacobs, E. A., Lauderdale, D. S., Meltzer, D., Shorey, J. M., Levinson, W., & Thisted, R. A. (2001). Impact of interpreter services on delivery of health care to limited-English-proficient patients. *Journal of General Internal Medicine*, 16, 468–474.

Jacobs, S. (2002). Maintaining neutrality in dispute mediation: Managing disagreement while managing not to disagree. *Journal of Pragmatics*, 34, 1403–1426.

Jacobs, S., & Aakhus, M. (2002). What mediators do with words: Implementing three models of rational discussion in dispute mediation. *Conflict Resolution Quarterly*, 20, 177–203.

Jefferson, G. (1984). On the organization of laughter in talk about troubles. In J. M. Atkinson & J. Heritage (Eds.), *Structures of social action: Studies in conversation analysis* (pp. 346–369). Cambridge, UK: Cambridge University Press.

Jiang, S., & Quave, C. (2013). A comparison of traditional food and health strategies among Taiwanese and Chinese immigrants in Atlanta, Georgia, USA. *Journal of Ethnobiology and Ethnomedicine*, 9, 1–14.

Jimenez, N., Moreno, G., Leng, M., Buchwald, D., & Morales, L. S. (2012). Patient-reported quality of pain treatment and use of interpreters in Spanish-speaking patients hospitalized for obstetric and gynecological care. *Journal of General Internal Medicine*, 27, 1602–1608.

Joffe, S., Cook, E. F., Cleary, P. D., Clark, J. W., & Weeks, J. C. (2001). Quality of informed consent in cancer clinical trials: A cross-sectional survey. *The Lancet*, 358, 1772–1777.

Johnson, H., Thompson, A., & Downs, M. (2009). Non-Western interpreters' experiences of trauma: The protective role of culture following exposure to oppression. *Ethnicity & Health*, 14, 407–418.

Jorgensen, D. L. (1989). *Participant observation: A methodology for human studies.* Newbury Park, CA: Sage.

Kapp, M. B. (2007). Patient autonomy in the age of consumer-driven health care: Informed consent and informed choice. *Journal of Legal Medicine*, 28, 91–117.

Karliner, L. S., Hwang, E. S., Nickleach, D., & Kaplan, C. P. (2011). Language barriers and patient-centered breast cancer care. *Patient Education and Counseling*, 84, 223–228.

Karliner, L. S., Jacobs, E. A., Chen, A. H., & Mutha, S. (2007). Do professional interpreters improve clinical care for patients with limited English proficiency? A systematic review of the literature. *Health Services Research*, 42, 727–754.

Karliner, L. S., & Mutha, S. (2010). Achieving quality in health care through language access services: Lessons from a California public hospital. *American Journal of Medical Quality*, 25, 51–59.

Karnieli-Miller, O., & Eisikovits, Z. (2009). Physician as partner or salesman? Shared decision-making in real-time encounters. *Social Science & Medicine*, 69, 1–8.

Kaufert, J. M. (1999). Cultural mediation in cancer diagnosis and end of life decision-making: The experience of Aboriginal patients in Canada. *Anthropology & Medicine*, 6, 405–421.

Kaufert, J. M., & Koolage, W. W. (1984). Role conflict among "culture brokers": The experience of native Canadian medical interpreters. *Social Science & Medicine*, 18, 283–286.

Kaufert, J. M., & Putsch, R. W., III. (1997). Communication through interpreters in healthcare: Ethical dilemmas arising from differences in class, culture, language, and power. *The Journal of Clinical Ethics*, 8, 71–87.

Kaufert, J. M., Putsch, R. W., III, & Lavallée, M. (1999). End-of-life decision making among Aboriginal Canadians: Interpretation, mediation, and discord in the communication of "bad news". *Journal of Palliative Care*, 15, 31–38.

Kazzi, G. B., & Cooper, C. (2003). Barriers to the use of interpreters in emergency room paediatric consultations. *Journal of Paediatrics and Child Health*, 39, 259–263.

Keenan, G. M., Cooke, R., & Hillis, S. L. (1998). Norms and nurse management of conflicts: Keys to understanding nurse-physician collaboration. *Research in Nursing and Health*, 21, 59–72.

Kelly, L. G. (1979). *The true interpreter: A history of translation theory and practice in the West.* New York: St. Martin's Press.

Kelly, N. (2007). *Telephone interpreting: A comprehensive guide to the profession.* Victoria, BC: Trafford.

Keselman, O., Cederborg, A.-C., & Linell, P. (2010). "That is not necessary for you to know!" Negotiation of participation status of unaccompanied children in interpreter-mediated asylum hearings. *Interpreting*, 12, 83–104.

Kilian, S., Swartz, L., Dowling, T., Dlali, M., & Chiliza, B. (2014). The potential consequences of informal interpreting practices for assessment of patients in a South African psychiatric hospital. *Social Science & Medicine*, 106, 159–167.

Kleinman, A., Eisenberg, L., & Good, B. (1978). Culture, illness, and care: Clinical lessons from anthropologic and cross-cultural research. *Annals of Internal Medicine*, 88, 251–258.

Knapp, M. L., & Hall, J. A. (2006). *Nonverbal communication in human interaction* (6th ed.). New York: Wadsworth.

Kong, H., & Hsieh, E. (2012). The social meanings of traditional Chinese medicine: Elderly Chinese immigrants' health practice in the United States. *Journal of Immigrant and Minority Health*, 14, 841–849.

Kosny, A., MacEachen, E., Lifshen, M., & Smith, P. (2014). Another person in the room: Using interpreters during interviews with immigrant workers. *Qualitative Health Research*, 24(6), 837–845.

Kramer, E. M. (2000). Cultural fusion and the defense of difference. In M. K. Asante & J. E. Min (Eds.), *Socio-cultural conflict between African and Korean Americans* (pp. 182–223). New York: University Press of America.

Kramer, E. M. (2002). Cosmopoly and cultural fusion: Cultural homogenization in the face of neo-globalism. In M. Isa & M. Masazumi (Eds.), *Intercultural communication: A reader* (pp. 88–106). Thousand Oaks, CA: Sage.

Kramer, E. M. (2011). Preface. In S. Croucher & D. Cronn-Mills (Eds.), *Religious misperceptions: The case of Muslims and Christians in France and Britain*. New York: Hampton.

Kramer, E. M. (2013). Dimensional accrual and dissociation: An introduction. In J. Grace & E. M. Kramer (Eds.), *Communication, comparative cultures, and civilizations* (Vol. 3, pp. 123–184). New York: Hampton.

Kulick, D. (1992). *Language shift and cultural reproduction: Socialization, self, and syncretism in a Papua New Guinea village*. New York: Cambridge University Press.

Kuo, D., & Fagan, M. J. (1999). Satisfaction with methods of Spanish interpretation in an ambulatory care clinic. *Journal of General Internal Medicine*, 14, 547–550.

Kuo, D. Z., O'Connor, K. G., Flores, G., & Minkovitz, C. S. (2007). Pediatricians' use of language services for families with limited English proficiency. *Pediatrics*, 119, e920–927.

Kurz, I. (2001). Conference interpreting: Quality in the ears of the user. *Meta: Journal des Traducteurs/Translators' Journal*, 46(2), 394–409.

Kutner, M., Greenberg, E., Jin, Y., & Paulsen, C. (2006). The health literacy of America's adults: Results from the 2003 National Assessment of Adult Literacy. Retrieved March 14, 2015, from http://nces.ed.gov/pubs2006/2006483.pdf.

Laidsaar-Powell, R. C., Butow, P. N., Bu, S., Charles, C., Gafni, A., Lam, W. W. T., … Juraskova, I. (2013). Physician–patient–companion communication and decision-making: A systematic review of triadic medical consultations. *Patient Education and Counseling*, 91, 3–13.

Lang, R. (1976). Orderlies as interpreters in Papua New Guinea. *Papua New Guinea Medical Journal*, 18, 172–177.

LanguageLine Solutions. (2014). Interpreter FAQ. Retrieved March 14, 2015, from www.languageline.com/company/careers/interpreter-careers/faq/#LL2.

Launer, J. (1978). Taking medical histories through interpreters: Practice in a Nigerian outpatient department. *British Medical Journal*, 2, 934.

Leanza, Y. (2005). Roles of community interpreters in pediatrics as seen by interpreters, physicians and researchers. *Interpreting*, 7, 167–192.

Leanza, Y. (2008). Community interpreter's power: The hazards of a disturbing attribute. *Journal of Medical Anthropology*, 31, 211–220.

Leanza, Y., Boivin, I., & Rosenberg, E. (2010). Interruptions and resistance: A comparison of medical consultations with family and trained interpreters. *Social Science & Medicine*, 70, 1888–1895.

Leanza, Y., Boivin, I., & Rosenberg, E. (2013). The patient's Lifeworld: Building meaningful clinical encounters between patients, physicians and interpreters. *Communication & Medicine*, 10, 13–25.

LeCompte, M. D., & Goetz, J. P. (1982). Problems of reliability and validity in ethnographic research. *Review of Educational Research*, 52, 31–60.

Lee, J. (2009). Interpreting inexplicit language during courtroom examination. *Applied Linguistics*, 30, 93–114.

Lee, K. C., Winickoff, J. P., Kim, M. K., Campbell, E. G., Betancourt, J. R., Park, E. R., … Weissman, J. S. (2006). Resident physicians' use of professional and nonprofessional interpreters: A national survey. *Journal of the American Medical Association*, 296, 1050–1053.

Lee, L. J., Batal, H. A., Maselli, J. H., & Kutner, J. S. (2002). Effect of Spanish interpretation method on patient satisfaction in an urban walk-in clinic. *Journal of General Internal Medicine*, 17, 641–645.

Lee, R. G., & Llewellyn-Jones, P. (2011). *Re-visiting "role": Arguing for a multi-dimensional analysis of interpreter behaviour*. Paper presented at Supporting Deaf People 2011: An online conference from Direct Learn. http://clok.uclan.ac.uk/5031/1/Lee%20and%20 L-J%202011.pdf.

Lee, W. S., Wang, J., Chung, J., & Hertel, E. (1995). A sociohistorical approach to intercultural communication. *Howard Journal of Communications*, 6, 262–291.

Lehna, C. (2005). Interpreter services in pediatric nursing. *Pediatric Nursing*, 31, 292–296.

Levine, C. (2006). Use of children as interpreters. *Journal of the American Medical Association*, 296, 2802.

Lindholm, M., Hargraves, J. L., Ferguson, W. J., & Reed, G. (2012). Professional language interpretation and inpatient length of stay and readmission rates. *Journal of General Internal Medicine*, 27, 1294–1299.

Linell, P. (1997). Interpreting as communication. In Y. Gambier, D. Gile, & C. Taylor (Eds.), *Conference interpreting: Current trends in research; Proceedings of the International Conference on Interpreting: What do We Know and How? (Turku, August 25–27, 1994)* (pp. 49–67). Amsterdam, The Netherlands: John Benjamins.

Lion, K. C., Brown, J. C., Ebel, B. E., Klein, E. J., Strelitz, B., Gutman, C. K., . . . Mangione-Smith, R. (in press). Effect of telephone vs video interpretation on parent comprehension, communication, and utilization in the pediatric emergency department: A randomized clinical trial. *JAMA Pediatrics*.

Lion, K. C., Rafton, S. A., Shafii, J., Brownstein, D., Michel, E., Tolman, M., & Ebel, B. E. (2013). Association between language, serious adverse events, and length of stay among hospitalized children. *Hospital Pediatrics*, 3, 219–225.

Lion, K. C., Thompson, D. A., Cowden, J. D., Michel, E., Rafton, S. A., Hamdy, R. F., . . . Ebel, B. E. (2013). Clinical Spanish use and language proficiency testing among pediatric residents. *Academic Medicine*, 88, 1478–1484.

Llewellyn-Jones, P., & Lee, R. (2013). Getting to the core of role: Defining interpreters' role-space. *International Journal of Interpreter Education*, 5, 54–72.

Lo, M. C., & Bahar, R. (2013). Resisting the colonization of the lifeworld? Immigrant patients' experiences with co-ethnic healthcare workers. *Social Science & Medicine*, 87, 68–76.

Locatis, C., Williamson, D., Gould-Kabler, C., Zone-Smith, L., Detzler, I., Roberson, J., . . . Ackerman, M. (2010). Comparing in-person, video, and telephonic medical interpretation. *Journal of General Internal Medicine*, 25, 345–350.

Lu, D. (2001). Cultural features in speech acts: A Sino-American comparison. *Language Culture and Curriculum*, 14, 214–223.

Lubrano di Ciccone, B., Brown, R. F., Gueguen, J. A., Bylund, C. L., & Kissane, D. W. (2010). Interviewing patients using interpreters in an oncology setting: Initial evaluation of a communication skills module. *Annals of Oncology*, 21, 27–32.

Ma, G. X. (1999). Between two worlds: The use of traditional and Western health services by Chinese immigrants. *Journal of Community Health*, 24, 421–437.

MacPhail, S. L. (2014, July 2). Expanding interpreter role to include advocacy and care coordination improves efficiency and leads to high patient and provider satisfaction. Retrieved March 14, 2015, from https://innovations.ahrq.gov/profiles/expanding-interpreter-role-include-advocacy-and-care-coordination-improves-efficiency-and.

MacFarlane, A., Dzebisova, Z., Karapish, D., Kovacevic, B., Ogbebor, F., & Okonkwo, E. (2009). Arranging and negotiating the use of informal interpreters in general practice consultations: Experiences of refugees and asylum seekers in the west of Ireland. *Social Science & Medicine*, 69, 210–214.

Maclean, A. (2009). *Autonomy, informed consent and medical law: A relational challenge.* Cambridge, UK: Cambridge University Press.

McLaughlin, M., Nam, Y., May, W., Baezconde-Garbanati, L., Georgiou, P., & Ahn, Z. (2013). Technology-based medical interpretation for cross-language communication: In person, telephone, and videoconference interpretation and their comparative impact on Limited English Proficiency (LEP) patient and doctor. In P. L. P. Rau (Ed.), *Cross-cultural design: Cultural differences in everyday life* (Vol. 8024, pp. 137–146). New York: Springer.

McClean, K. L., & Card, S. E. (2004). Informed consent skills in internal medicine residency: How are residents taught, and what do they learn? *Academic Medicine, 79,* 128–133.

McDowell, I. (2006). *Measuring health: A guide to rating scales and questionnaires* (3rd ed.). Oxford, UK: Oxford University Press.

McKee, M. M., & Paasche-Orlow, M. K. (2012). Health literacy and the disenfranchised: The importance of collaboration between limited English proficiency and health literacy researchers. *Journal of Health Communication, 17,* 7–12.

Manson, A. (1988). Language concordance as a determinant of patient compliance and emergency room use in patients with asthma. *Medical Care, 26,* 1119–1128.

Marcos, L. R. (1979). Effects of interpreters on the evaluation of psychopathology in non-English-speaking patients. *American Journal of Psychiatry, 136,* 171–174.

Martin, L. T., Schonlau, M., Haas, A., Derose, K. P., Rosenfeld, L., Buka, S. L., & Rudd, R. (2011). Patient activation and advocacy: Which literacy skills matter most? *Journal of Health Communication, 16(sup3),* 177–190.

Mason, I., & Ren, W. (2012). Power in face-to-face interpreting events. *Translation and Interpreting Studies, 7,* 234–253.

Maul, L., Regenstein, M., Andres, E., Wright, R., & Wynia, M. K. (2012). Using a risk assessment approach to determine which factors influence whether partially bilingual physicians rely on their non-English language skills or call an interpreter. *Joint Commission Journal on Quality & Patient Safety, 38,* 328–336.

Mays, N., & Pope, C. (1995). Qualitative research: Observational methods in health care settings. *British Medical Journal, 311,* 182–184.

Mazor, S. S., Hampers, L. C., Chande, V. T., & Krug, S. E. (2002). Teaching Spanish to pediatric emergency physicians: Effects on patient satisfaction. *Archives of Pediatrics & Adolescent Medicine, 156,* 693–695.

Meeuwesen, L. (2012). Language barriers in migrant health care: A blind spot. *Patient Education and Counseling, 86,* 135–136.

Meeuwesen, L., Tromp, F., Schouten, B. C., & Harmsen, J. A. M. (2007). Cultural differences in managing information during medical interaction: How does the physician get a clue? *Patient Education and Counseling, 67,* 183–190.

Meeuwesen, L., Twilt, S., ten Thije, J. D., & Harmsen, H. (2010). "Ne diyor?" (What does she say?): Informal interpreting in general practice. *Patient Education and Counseling, 81,* 198–203.

Meeuwesen, L., van den Brink-Muinen, A., & Hofstede, G. (2009). Can dimensions of national culture predict cross-national differences in medical communication? *Patient Education and Counseling, 75,* 58–66.

Meischke, H., Chavez, D., Bradley, S., Rea, T., & Eisenberg, M. (2010). Emergency communications with limited-English-proficiency populations. *Prehospital Emergency Care, 14,* 265–271.

Mendoza, A. d. (1548). *Ordenanzas y copilación de leyes.* Mexico: Juan Pablos.

Messias, D. K. H., McDowell, L., & Estrada, R. D. (2009). Language interpreting as social justice work: Perspectives of formal and informal healthcare interpreters. *Advances in Nursing Science, 32,* 128–143.

Metzger, M. (1999). *Sign language interpreting: Deconstructing the myth of neutrality.* Washington, DC: Gallaudet University Press.

Meyer, B., Bührig, K., Kliche, O., & Pawlack, B. (2010). Nurses as interpreters? Aspects of interpreter training for bilingual medical employees. In B. Meyer & B. Apfelbaum (Eds.), *Multilingualism at work: From policies to practices in public, medical and business settings* (pp. 163–184). Amsterdam, The Netherlands: John Benjamins.

Mezulis, A. H., Abramson, L. Y., Hyde, J. S., & Hankin, B. L. (2004). Is there a universal positivity bias in attributions? A meta-analytic review of individual, developmental, and cultural differences in the self-serving attributional bias. *Psychological Bulletin, 130,* 711–747.

Mikkelson, H. (2003). Telephone interpreting: Boon or bane? In L. P. González (Ed.), *Speaking in tongues: Language across contexts and users* (pp. 251–269). Valencia, Spain: Universidad de València.

Miller, K., & Zook, E. G. (1997). Care partners for persons with AIDS: Implications for health communication. *Journal of Applied Communication Research, 25,* 57–74.

Miller, K. E., Martell, Z. L., Pazdirek, L., Caruth, M., & Lopez, D. (2005). The role of interpreters in psychotherapy with refugees: An exploratory study. *American Journal of Orthopsychiatry, 75,* 27–39.

Miller, W. L., & Crabtree, B. F. (1999). Depth interviewing. In B. F. Crabtree & W. L. Miller (Eds.), *Doing qualitative research* (2nd ed., pp. 89–107). Thousand Oaks, CA: Sage.

Miyaji, N. T. (1993). The power of compassion: Truth-telling among American doctors in the care of dying patients. *Social Science & Medicine, 36,* 249–264.

Montgomery, B. M. (1993). Relationship maintenance versus relationship change: A dialectical dilemma. *Journal of Social and Personal Relationships, 10(2),* 205–223.

Moreno, G., Tarn, D. M., & Morales, L. S. (2009). Impact of interpreters on the receipt of new prescription medication information among Spanish-speaking Latinos. *Medical Care, 47,* 1201–1208.

Moreno, M. R., Otero-Sabogal, R., & Newman, J. (2007). Assessing dual-role staff-interpreter linguistic competency in an integrated healthcare system. *Journal of General Internal Medicine, 22,* S331–335.

Morgan, D. L. (1988). *Focus groups as qualitative research.* Newbury Park, CA: Sage.

Morgan, L. (1998). Making the connection: Healthcare interpreters bridge the language gap. *Nurseweek (California Statewide Edition),* 11, 9.

Morris, R. (1995). The moral dilemmas of court interpreting. *The Translator, 1,* 25–46.

Morse, J. M., Bottorff, J., Anderson, G., O'Brien, B., & Solberg, S. (2006). Beyond empathy: Expanding expressions of caring. *Journal of Advanced Nursing, 53,* 75–87.

Moskowitz, M. L. (2001). *The haunting fetus: Abortion, sexuality, and the spirit world in Taiwan.* Honolulu, HI: University of Hawai'i Press.

Mueller, M.-R., Roussos, S., Hill, L., Salas, N., Villarreal, V., Baird, N., & Hovell, M. (2011). Medical interpreting by bilingual staff whose primary role is not interpreting: Contingencies influencing communication for dual-role interpreters. In J. J. Kronenfeld (Ed.), *Access to care and factors that impact access, patients as partners in care and changing roles of health providers* (pp. 77–91). Bingley, UK: Emerald.

Muller, J. H., & Desmond, B. (1992). Ethical dilemmas in a cross-cultural context: A Chinese example. *Western Journal of Medicine, 157,* 323–327.

Nápoles, A. M., Santoyo-Olsson, J., Karliner, L. S., O'Brien, H., Gregorich, S. E., & Pérez-Stable, E. J. (2010). Clinician ratings of interpreter mediated visits in underserved primary care settings with ad hoc, in-person professional, and video conferencing modes. *Journal of Health Care for the Poor and Underserved, 21,* 301–317.

National Council on Interpreting in Health Care. (2004). A national code of ethics for interpreters in health care. Retrieved March 14, 2015, from www.rwjf.org/content/dam/farm/toolkits/toolkits/2004/rwjf26946.

National Council on Interpreting in Health Care. (2005). National standards of practices for interpreters in health care. Retrieved November 5, 2015, from www.ncihc.org/assets/media/ncihc%20national%20standards%20of%20practice.pdf.

National Network of Libraries of Medicine. (2013). Health literacy. Retrieved March 14, 2015, from http://nnlm.gov/outreach/consumer/hlthlit.html.

Newman, I., & Benz, C. R. (1998). *Qualitative-quantitative research methodology: Exploring the interactive continuum*. Carbondale, IL: Southern Illinois University Press.

Ngo-Metzger, Q., Sorkin, D. H., Phillips, R. S., Greenfield, S., Massagli, M. P., Clarridge, B., & Kaplan, S. H. (2007). Providing high-quality care for limited English proficient patients: The importance of language concordance and interpreter use. *Journal of General Internal Medicine*, 22, S324–330.

Nicodemus, B., Swabey, L., & Witter-Merithew, A. (2011). Establishing presence and role transparency in healthcare interpreting: A pedagogical approach for developing effective practice. *Rivista di Psicolinguistica Applicata*, 11, 69–83.

Niska, H. (2007). From helpers to professionals: Training of community interpreters in Sweden. In C. Wadensjö, B. E. Dimitrova, & A.-L. Nilsson (Eds.), *The critical link 4: Professionalisation of interpreting in the community* (pp. 297–310). Amsterdam, The Netherlands: John Benjamins.

Nordentoft, K., & Fredsted, E. (1998). On semantic and pragmatic ambiguity. *Journal of Pragmatics*, 30(5), 527–541.

Norris, W. M., Wenrich, M. D., Nielsen, E. L., Treece, P. D., Jackson, J. C., & Curtis, J. R. (2005). Communication about end-of-life care between language-discordant patients and clinicians: Insights from medical interpreters. *Journal of Palliative Medicine*, 8, 1016–1024.

Nugus, P., Greenfield, D., Travaglia, J., Westbrook, J., & Braithwaite, J. (2010). How and where clinicians exercise power: Interprofessional relations in health care. *Social Science & Medicine*, 71, 898–909.

O'Leary, S. C. B., Federico, S., & Hampers, L. C. (2003). The truth about language barriers: One residency program's experience. *Pediatrics*, 111, e569–573.

Ono, N., Kiuchi, T., & Ishikawa, H. (2013). Development and pilot testing of a novel education method for training medical interpreters. *Patient Education and Counseling*, 93, 604–611.

Osborn, C. Y., Cavanaugh, K., Wallston, K. A., Kripalani, S., Elasy, T. A., Rothman, R. L., & White, R. O. (2011). Health literacy explains racial disparities in diabetes medication adherence. *Journal of Health Communication*, 16, 268–278.

Pantilat, S. (2008). Ethics fast fact: Autonomy vs. beneficence. Retrieved March 14, 2015, from http://missinglink.ucsf.edu/lm/ethics/Content%20Pages/fast_fact_auton_bene.htm.

Papic, O., Malak, Z., & Rosenberg, E. (2012). Survey of family physicians' perspectives on management of immigrant patients: Attitudes, barriers, strategies, and training needs. *Patient Education and Counseling*, 86, 205–209.

Parsons, S. K., Saiki-Craighill, S., Mayer, D. K., Sullivan, A. M., Jeruss, S., Terrin, N., … Block, S. (2007). Telling children and adolescents about their cancer diagnosis: Cross-cultural comparisons between pediatric oncologists in the US and Japan. *Psycho-Oncology*, 16, 60–68.

Parsons, T. (1951). *The social system*. Glencoe, IL: The Free Press.

Pearson, S. D., & Raeke, L. H. (2000). Patients' trust in physicians: Many theories, few measures, and little data. *Journal of General Internal Medicine*, 15, 509–513.

Penn, C., & Watermeyer, J. (2012). When asides become central: Small talk and big talk in interpreted health interactions. *Patient Education and Counseling*, 88, 391–398.

Peter, E., Lunardi, V. L., & Macfarlane, A. (2004). Nursing resistance as ethical action: Literature review. *Journal of Advanced Nursing*, 46, 403–416.

Pham, K., Thornton, J. D., Engelberg, R. A., Jackson, J. C., & Curtis, J. R. (2008). Alterations during medical interpretation of ICU family conferences that interfere with or enhance communication. *Chest*, 134, 109–116.

Phelan, M. (2012). Medical interpreting and the law in the European Union. *European Journal of Health Law*, 19, 333–353.

Phelan, M., & Parkman, S. (1995). How to do it: Work with an interpreter. *British Medical Journal*, 311, 555–557.

Phillips, C. (2013). Remote telephone interpretation in medical consultations with refugees: Meta-communications about care, survival and selfhood. *Journal of Refugee Studies*, 26, 505–523.

Pitaloka, D. (2014). *The (passive) violence of harmony and balance: Lived experienced of Javanese women with type 2 diabetes.* (Ph.D.), University of Oklahoma. Retrieved September 16, 2015, from http://hdl.handle.net/11244/10430.

Plunkett, B. A., Kohli, P., & Milad, M. P. (2002). The importance of physician gender in the selection of an obstetrician or a gynecologist. *American Journal of Obstetrics & Gynecology*, 186, 926–928.

Pöchhacker, F. (1999). "Getting organized": The evolution of community interpreting. *Interpreting*, 4, 125–140.

Pöchhacker, F. (2007a). Critical linking up: Kinship and convergence in interpreting studies. In C. Wadensjö, B. E. Dimitrova, & A.-L. Nilsson (Eds.), *The critical link 4: Professionalisation of interpreting in the community* (pp. 11–23). Amsterdam, The Netherlands: John Benjamins.

Pöchhacker, F. (2007b). Giving access – or not: A developing-country perspective on healthcare interpreting. In F. Pöchhacker, A.-L. Jakobson, & I. M. Mees (Eds.), *Interpreting studies and beyond* (pp. 121–137). Frederiksberg, Denmark: Samfundslitteratur.

Pöchhacker, F. (2013). *Introducing interpreting studies.* New York: Routledge.

Pöchhacker, F., & Kadric, M. (1999). The hospital cleaner as healthcare interpreter: A case study. *Translator*, 5, 161–178.

Pöchhacker, F., & Shlesinger, M. (2002). Introduction. In F. Pöchhacker & M. Shlesinger (Eds.), *The interpreting studies reader* (pp. 1–12). New York: Routledge.

Pöchhacker, F., & Shlesinger, M. (2005). Introduction: Discourse-based research on healthcare interpreting. *Interpreting*, 7, 157–165.

Politi, M. C., & Street, R. L. (2011). The importance of communication in collaborative decision making: Facilitating shared mind and the management of uncertainty. *Journal of Evaluation in Clinical Practice*, 17, 579–584.

Preloran, H. M., Browner, C. H., & Lieber, E. (2005). Impact of interpreters' approach on Latinas' use of amniocentesis. *Health Education & Behavior*, 32, 599–612.

Price, E. L., Perez-Stable, E. J., Nickleach, D., Lopez, M., & Karliner, L. S. (2012). Interpreter perspectives of in-person, telephonic, and videoconferencing medical interpretation in clinical encounters. *Patient Education and Counseling*, 87, 226–232.

Price, J. (1975). Foreign language interpreting in psychiatric practice. *Australian and New Zealand Journal of Psychiatry*, 9, 263–267.

Prince, D., & Nelson, M. (1995). Teaching Spanish to emergency medicine residents. *Academic Emergency Medicine*, 2, 32–37.

Pullon, S. (2008). Competence, respect and trust: Key features of successful interprofessional nurse-doctor relationships. *Journal of Interprofessional Care*, 22, 133–147.

Putsch, R. W., III. (1985). Cross-cultural communication: The special case of interpreters in health care. *Journal of the American Medical Association*, 254, 3344–3348.

Quill, T. E., & Brody, H. (1996). Physician recommendations and patient autonomy: Finding a balance between physician power and patient choice. *Annals of Internal Medicine*, 125, 763–769.

Ramirez, D., Engel, K. G., & Tang, T. S. (2008). Language interpreter utilization in the emergency department setting: A clinical review. *Journal of Health Care for the Poor and Underserved*, 19, 352–362.

Raven, B. H. (1993). The bases of power: Origins and recent developments. *Journal of Social Issues*, 49, 227–251.

Rawls, A. W. (1987). The interaction order sui generis: Goffman's contribution to social theory. *Sociological Theory*, 5, 136–149.

Raymond, C. W. (2014). Conveying information in the interpreter-mediated medical visit: The case of epistemic brokering. *Patient Education and Counseling*, 97, 38–46.

Rees, C. E., & Bath, P. A. (2000). Meeting the information needs of adult daughters of women with early breast cancer: Patients and health care professionals as information providers. *Cancer Nursing*, 23, 71–79.

The Registry of Interpreters for the Deaf. (2013). About RID Overview. Retrieved March 14, 2015, from www.rid.org/about-rid/.

Renée, M. (2013). The death of healthcare interpreting in The Netherlands. Retrieved March 14, 2015, from http://aiic.net/page/6612.

Reynolds, J. F., & Orellana, M. F. (2009). New immigrant youth interpreting in White public space. *American Anthropologist*, 111, 211–223.

Richie, J. (1964). Using an interpreter effectively. *Nursing Outlook*, 12, 27–29.

Ricoeur, P. (1976). *Interpretation theory: Discourse and the surplus of meaning*. Fort Worth, TX: Texas Christian University Press.

Ricoeur, P. (1981). *Hermeneutics and the human sciences: Essays on language, action and interpretation* (J. B. Thompson, Trans. J. B. Thompson Ed.). Cambridge University Press.

Rivadeneyra, R., Elderkin-Thompson, V., Silver, R. C., & Waitzkin, H. (2000). Patient centeredness in medical encounters requiring an interpreter. *American Journal of Medicine*, 108, 470–474.

Roat, C. E. (1996). *Bridging the gap: A basic training for medical interpreters*. Seattle, WA: Cross Cultural Health Care Program.

Roat, C. E. (2006). Certification of healthcare interpreters in the United States. Retrieved March 14, 2015, from www.calendow.org/uploadedFiles/certification_of_health_care_interpretors.pdf.

Roat, C. E., Kinderman, A., & Fernandez, A. (2011). Interpreting in palliative care. Retrieved March 14, 2015, from www.chcf.org/publications/2011/11/interpreting-palliative-care-curriculum.

Roat, C. E., Putsch, R. W., III, & Lucero, C. (1997). *Bridging the gap over the phone: A basic training for telephone interpreters serving medical settings*. Seattle, WA: Cross Cultural Health Care Program.

Robb, N., & Greenhalgh, T. (2006). "You have to cover up the words of the doctor": The mediation of trust in interpreted consultations in primary care. *Journal of Health Organization & Management*, 20, 434–455.

Roberts, R. P. (1997). Community interpreting today and tomorrow. In S. E. Carr, R. P. Roberts, A. Dufour, & D. Steyn (Eds.), *The critical link: Interpreters in the community* (pp. 7–26). Amsterdam, The Netherlands: John Benjamins.

Robinson, T. M., Alexander, S. C., Hays, M., Jeffreys, A. S., Olsen, M. K., Rodriguez, K. L., ... Tulsky, J. A. (2008). Patient–oncologist communication in advanced cancer: Predictors of patient perception of prognosis. *Supportive Care in Cancer*, 16, 1049–1057.

Rodin, J., & Janis, I. L. (1979). The social power of health-care practitioners as agents of change. *Journal of Social Issues*, 35(1), 60–81.

Rogg, L., Aasland, O. G., Graugaard, P. K., & Loge, J. H. (2010). Direct communication, the unquestionable ideal? Oncologists' accounts of communication of bleak prognoses. *Psycho-Oncology*, 19, 1221–1228.

Rose, D. E., Tisnado, D. M., Malin, J. L., Tao, M. L., Maggard, M. A., Adams, J., ... Kahn, K. L. (2010). Use of interpreters by physicians treating limited English proficient women with breast cancer: Results from the provider survey of the Los Angeles Women's Health Study. *Health Services Research*, 45, 172–194.

Rosenberg, E., Leanza, Y., & Seller, R. (2007). Doctor-patient communication in primary care with an interpreter: Physician perceptions of professional and family interpreters. *Patient Education and Counseling*, 67, 286–292.

Rosenberg, E., Richard, C., Lussier, M.-T., & Shuldiner, T. (2011). The content of talk about health conditions and medications during appointments involving interpreters. *Family Practice*, 28, 317–322.

Rosenberg, E., Seller, R., & Leanza, Y. (2008). Through interpreters' eyes: Comparing roles of professional and family interpreters. *Patient Education and Counseling*, 70, 87–93.

Roter, D. L., Geller, G., Bernhardt, B. A., Larson, S. M., & Doksum, T. (1999). Effects of obstetrician gender on communication and patient satisfaction. *Obstetrics and Gynecology*, 93, 635–641.

Rothman, D. J. (2001). The origins and consequences of patient autonomy: A 25-year retrospective. *Health Care Analysis*, 9, 255–264.

Roy, C. B. (2000). *Interpreting as a discourse process*. New York: Oxford University Press.

Ryan, R. M., & Deci, E. L. (2011). A self-determination theory perspective on social, institutional, cultural, and economic supports for autonomy and their importance for well-being. In V. I. Chirkov, R. M. Ryan, & K. M. Sheldon (Eds.), *Human autonomy in cross-cultural context* (Vol. 1, pp. 45–64). New York: Springer.

Sarver, J., & Baker, D. W. (2000). Effect of language barriers on follow-up appointments after an emergency department visit. *Journal of General Internal Medicine*, 15, 256–264.

Schattner, P., Shmerling, A., & Murphy, B. (1993). Focus groups: A useful research method in general practice. *Medical Journal of Australia*, 158, 622–625.

Schenker, Y., Fernandez, A., Kerr, K., O'Riordan, D., & Pantilat, S. Z. (2012). Interpretation for discussions about end-of-life issues: Results from a national survey of health care interpreters. *Journal of Palliative Medicine*, 15, 1019–1026.

Schenker, Y., Pérez-Stable, E. J., Nickleach, D., & Karliner, L. S. (2011). Patterns of interpreter use for hospitalized patients with limited English proficiency. *Journal of General Internal Medicine*, 26, 712–717.

Schenker, Y., Smith, A. K., Arnold, R. M., & Fernandez, A. (2012). "Her husband doesn't speak much English": Conducting a family meeting with an interpreter. *Journal of Palliative Medicine*, 15, 494–498.

Schenker, Y., Wang, F., Selig, S. J., Ng, R., & Fernandez, A. (2007). The impact of language barriers on documentation of informed consent at a hospital with on-site interpreter services. *Journal of General Internal Medicine*, 22, 294–299.

Scheper-Hughes, N. (1992). *Death without weeping: The violence of everyday life in Brazil.* Berkeley, CA: University of California Press.

Schmidt, S. J. (1984). The fiction is that reality exists: A constructivist model of reality, fiction, and literature. *Poetics Today*, 5, 253–274.

Scholl, J. C. (2007). The use of humor to promote patient-centered care. *Journal of Applied Communication Research*, 35, 156–176.

Scholl, J. C., & Ragan, S. L. (2003). The use of humor in promoting positive provider–patient interactions in a hospital rehabilitation unit. *Health Communication*, 15, 319–330.

Schouten, B. C., & Meeuwesen, L. (2006). Cultural differences in medical communication: A review of the literature. *Patient Education and Counseling*, 64, 21–34.

Schouten, B. C., Meeuwesen, L., & Harmsen, H. A. M. (2009). GPs' interactional styles in consultations with Dutch and ethnic minority patients. *Journal of Immigrant and Minority Health*, 11, 468–475.

Schouten, B. C., Meeuwesen, L., Tromp, F., & Harmsen, H. A. M. (2007). Cultural diversity in patient participation: The influence of patients' characteristics and doctors' communicative behaviour. *Patient Education and Counseling*, 67, 214–223.

Schouten, B. C., & Schinkel, S. (2014). Turkish migrant GP patients' expression of emotional cues and concerns in encounters with and without informal interpreters. *Patient Education and Counseling*, 97: 23–29.

Seale, C., Rivas, C., Al-Sarraj, H., Webb, S., & Kelly, M. (2013). Moral mediation in interpreted health care consultations. *Social Science & Medicine*, 98, 141–148.

Seale, C., Rivas, C., & Kelly, M. (2013). The challenge of communication in interpreted consultations in diabetes care: A mixed methods study. *British Journal of General Practice*, 63, e125–e133.

Searight, H. R., & Armock, J. A. (2013). Foreign language interpreters in mental health: A literature review and research agenda. *North American Journal of Psychology*, 15, 17–38.

Searle, J. R. (1979). *Expression and meaning: Studies in the theory of speech acts.* Cambridge, UK: Cambridge University Press.

Seeleman, C., Essink-Bot, M.-L., Selleger, V., & Bonke, B. (2012). Authors' response to letter from Bond et al. – The role of ad-hoc interpreters in teaching communication skills with ethnic minorities. *Medical Teacher*, 34, 81–82.

Sentell, T., & Braun, K. L. (2012). Low health literacy, limited English proficiency, and health status in Asians, Latinos, and other racial/ethnic groups in California. *Journal of Health Communication*, 17, 82–99.

Shaw, S. J., Huebner, C., Armin, J., Orzech, K., & Vivian, J. (2009). The role of culture in health literacy and chronic disease screening and management. *Journal of Immigrant and Minority Health*, 11, 460–467.

Simon, M. A., Ragas, D. M., Nonzee, N. J., Phisuthikul, A. M., Luu, T. H., & Dong, X. (2013). Perceptions of patient-provider communication in breast and cervical cancer-related care: A qualitative study of low-income English- and Spanish-speaking women. *Journal of Community Health*, 38, 707–715.

Simpson, K. R., & Lyndon, A. (2009). Clinical disagreements during labor and birth: How does real life compare to best practice? *MCN: The American Journal of Maternal/Child Nursing*, 34, 31–39.

Singy, P., & Guex, P. (2005). The interpreter's role with immigrant patients: Contrasted points of view. *Communication & Medicine*, 2, 45–51.

Sleptsova, M., Hofer, G., Morina, N., & Langewitz, W. (2014). The role of the health care interpreter in a clinical setting: A narrative review. *Journal of Community Health Nursing*, 31, 167–184.

Smith, J., Swartz, L., Kilian, S., & Chiliza, B. (2013). Mediating words, mediating worlds: Interpreting as hidden care work in a South African psychiatric institution. *Transcultural Psychiatry*, 50, 493–514.

Solomon, M. Z. (1997). From what's neutral to what's meaningful: Reflections on a study of medical interpreters. *The Journal of Clinical Ethics*, 8, 88–93.

Splevins, K. A., Cohen, K., Joseph, S., Murray, C., & Bowley, J. (2010). Vicarious post-traumatic growth among interpreters. *Qualitative Health Research*, 20, 1705–1716.

Stewart, D., & Shamdasani, P. (1990). *Focus groups: Theory and practice*. Newbury Park, CA: Sage.

Street, R. L., Jr. (2013). How clinician–patient communication contributes to health improvement: Modeling pathways from talk to outcome. *Patient Education and Counseling*, 92, 286–291.

Su, D., Li, L., & Pagán, J. A. (2008). Acculturation and the use of complementary and alternative medicine. *Social Science & Medicine*, 66, 439–453.

Sudore, R. L., Landefeld, C. S., Pérez-Stable, E. J., Bibbins-Domingo, K., Williams, B. A., & Schillinger, D. (2009). Unraveling the relationship between literacy, language proficiency, and patient–physician communication. *Patient Education and Counseling*, 75, 398–402.

Tam, N. T., Huy, N. T., Thoa, L. T. B., Long, N. P., Trang, N. T. H., Hirayama, K., & Karbwang, J. (2015). Participants' understanding of informed consent in clinical trials over three decades: Systematic review and meta-analysis. *Bulletin of the World Health Organization*, 93, 186–198H.

Tang, A. S., Kruger, J. F., Quan, J., & Fernandez, A. (2014). From admission to discharge: Patterns of interpreter use among resident physicians caring for hospitalized patients with limited English proficiency. *Journal of Health Care for the Poor and Underserved*, 25, 1784–1798.

Tang, J. (2008). Professionalization. In W. A. Darity, Jr. (Ed.), *International encyclopedia of the social sciences* (2nd ed., Vol. 6, pp. 515–517). New York: Macmillan.

Tannen, D., & Wallat, C. (1987). Interactive frames and knowledge schemas in interaction: Examples from a medical examination/interview. *Social Psychology Quarterly*, 50(2), 205–216.

Taylor, K. M. (1988). "Telling bad news": Physicians and the disclosure of undesirable information. *Sociology of Health & Illness*, 10, 109–132.

Thomas, P., Shabbir, M., & Yasmeen, S. (2010). Language, culture, and mental health. *Arab Journal of Psychiatry*, 21, 102–111.

Thompson, D. A., Hernandez, R. G., Cowden, J. D., Sisson, S. D., & Moon, M. (2013). Caring for patients with limited English proficiency: Are residents prepared to use medical interpreters? *Academic Medicine*, 88, 1485–1492.

Thomson, M. D., & Hoffman-Goetz, L. (2009). Defining and measuring acculturation: A systematic review of public health studies with Hispanic populations in the United States. *Social Science & Medicine*, 69, 983–991.

Thornton, J. D., Pham, K., Engelberg, R. A., Jackson, J. C., & Curtis, J. R. (2009). Families with limited English proficiency receive less information and support in interpreted intensive care unit family conferences. *Critical Care Medicine*, 37, 89–95.

Tocher, T. M., & Larson, E. B. (1996). Interpreter use and the impact of the process and outcome of care in type II diabetes. *Journal of General Internal Medicine, 11,* 150.

Tocher, T. M., & Larson, E. B. (1998). Quality of diabetes care for non-English-speaking patients: A comparative study. *Western Journal of Medicine, 168,* 504–511.

Tocher, T. M., & Larson, E. B. (1999). Do physicians spend more time with non-English-speaking patients? *Journal of General Internal Medicine, 14,* 303–309.

Todres, L., Galvin, K., & Dahlberg, K. (2007). Lifeworld-led healthcare: Revisiting a humanising philosophy that integrates emerging trends. *Medicine, Health Care and Philosophy, 10,* 53–63.

Tracy, K. (2013). *Everyday talk: Building and reflecting identities* (2nd ed.). New York: Guilford.

Treviño, A. J. (Ed.). (2001). *Talcott Parsons today: His theory and legacy in contemporary sociology.* Cumnor Hill, Oxford: Rowman & Littlefield.

Tribe, R., & Lane, P. (2009). Working with interpreters across language and culture in mental health. *Journal of Mental Health, 18,* 233–241.

Tribe, R., & Tunariu, A. (2009). Mind your language: Working with interpreters in healthcare settings and therapeutic encounters. *Sexual and Relationship Therapy, 24,* 74–84.

Ulrich, L. P. (2001). *The patient self-determination act: Meeting the challenges in patient care.* Washington, DC: Georgetown University Press.

The United Nations. (1948). The Universal Declaration of Human Rights. Retrieved March 14, 2015, from www.un.org/en/documents/udhr/.

Valdés, G. (2003). *Expanding definitions of giftedness: The case of young interpreters from immigrant communities.* Mahwah, NJ: Erlbaum.

VanderWielen, L. M., Enurah, A. S., Rho, H. Y., Nagarkatti-Gude, D. R., Michelsen-King, P., Crossman, S. H., & Vanderbilt, A. A. (2014). Medical interpreters: Improvements to address access, equity, and quality of care for limited-English-proficient patients. *Academic Medicine, 89,* 1324–1327.

Venuti, L. (2008). *The translator's invisibility: A history of translation* (2nd ed.). New York: Routledge.

Wade, C., Chao, M. T., & Kronenberg, F. (2007). Medical pluralism of Chinese women living in the United States. *Journal of Immigrant and Minority Health, 9,* 255–267.

Wadensjö, C. (1998). *Interpreting as interaction.* London: Longman.

Waitzkin, H. (1991). *The politics of medical encounters: How patients and doctors deal with social problems.* New Haven, CT: Yale University Press.

Wallbrecht, J., Hodes-Villamar, L., Weiss, S. J., & Ernst, A. A. (2014). No difference in emergency department length of stay for patients with limited proficiency in English. *Southern Medical Journal, 107,* 1–5.

Wallin, A.-M., & Ahlstrom, G. (2006). Cross-cultural interview studies using interpreters: Systematic literature review. *Journal of Advanced Nursing, 55,* 723–735.

Washington Courts. (1989). Rule 11.2: Code of conduct for court interpreters. Retrieved March 14, 2015, from www.courts.wa.gov/court_rules/?fa=court_rules.rulesPDF&ruleId=gagr11.2&pdf=1.

Watermeyer, J. (2011). "She will hear me": How a flexible interpreting style enables patients to manage the inclusion of interpreters in mediated pharmacy interactions. *Health Communication, 26,* 71–81.

Weaver, C., & Sklar, D. (1980). Diagnostic dilemmas and cultural diversity in emergency rooms. *The Western Journal of Medicine, 133,* 356–366.

Weisman, C. S., & Teitelbaum, M. A. (1985). Physician gender and the physician–patient relationship: Recent evidence and relevant questions. *Social Science & Medicine, 20,* 1119–1127.

Weissman, J. S., Betancourt, J., Campbell, E. G., Park, E. R., Kim, M., Clarridge, B., … Maina, A. W. (2005). Resident physicians' preparedness to provide cross-cultural care. *Journal of the American Medical Association*, 294, 1058–1067.

Wells, R. E., & Kaptchuk, T. J. (2012). To tell the truth, the whole truth, may do patients harm: The problem of the nocebo effect for informed consent. *American Journal of Bioethics*, 12, 22–29.

Westermeyer, J. (1985). Psychiatric diagnosis across cultural boundaries. *American Journal of Psychiatry*, 142, 798–805.

Westermeyer, J. (1990). Working with an interpreter in psychiatric assessment and treatment. *Journal of Nervous and Mental Disease*, 178, 745–749.

Westmyer, S. A., DiCioccio, R. L., & Rubin, R. B. (1998). Appropriateness and effectiveness of communication channels in competent interpersonal communication. *Journal of Communication*, 48(3), 27–48.

Whatley, M., & Batalova, J. (2013). Limited English proficient population of the United States. Retrieved February 8, 2015, from www.migrationpolicy.org/article/limited-english-proficient-population-united-states.

White, K., & Laws, M. (2009). Role exchange in medical interpretation. *Journal of Immigrant and Minority Health*, 11, 482–493.

Wierzbicka, A. (1985). Different cultures, different languages, different speech acts: Polish vs. English. *Journal of Pragmatics*, 9, 145–178.

Williams, G., Teixeira, P., Carraça, E., & Resnicow, K. (2011). Physical wellness, health care, and personal autonomy. In V. I. Chirkov, R. M. Ryan, & K. M. Sheldon (Eds.), *Human autonomy in cross-cultural context* (Vol. 1, pp. 133–162). New York: Springer.

Woloshin, S., Schwartz, L. M., Katz, S. J., & Welch, H. G. (1997). Is language a barrier to the use of preventive services? *Journal of General Internal Medicine*, 12, 472–477.

Wong, W. W., Gabriel, A., Maxwell, G. P., & Gupta, S. C. (2012). Bleeding risks of herbal, homeopathic, and dietary supplements: A hidden nightmare for plastic surgeons? *Aesthetic Surgery Journal*, 32, 332–346.

Wros, P. (2009). Giving voice: Incorporating the wisdom of Hispanic RNs into practice. *Journal of Cultural Diversity*, 16, 151–157.

Yang, C.-F., & Gray, B. (2008). Bilingual medical students as interpreters: What are the benefits and risks? *New Zealand Medical Journal*, 121, 15–28.

Yawman, D., McIntosh, S., Fernandez, D., Auinger, P., Allan, M., & Weitzman, M. (2006). The use of Spanish by medical students and residents at one university hospital. *Academic Medicine*, 81, 468–473.

Youdelman, M. K. (2008). The medical tongue: US laws and policies on language access. *Health Affairs*, 27, 424–433.

Yum, J. O. (1988). The impact of Confucianism on interpersonal relationships and communication patterns in East Asia. *Communication Monographs*, 55, 374–388.

Zimányi, K. (2013). Somebody has to be in charge of a session: On the control of communication in interpreter-mediated mental health encounters. *Translation and Interpreting Studies*, 8, 94–111.

INDEX